FINANCIAL ANALYSIS
with Microsoft® Excel

4e

Timothy R. Mayes
Metropolitan State College of Denver

•

Todd M. Shank
University of Portland

THOMSON
✴™
SOUTH-WESTERN

Australia · Brazil · Canada · Mexico · Singapore · Spain · United Kingdom · United States

THOMSON

SOUTH-WESTERN

Financial Analysis with Microsoft Excel, 4th Edition
Timothy R. Mayes and Todd M. Shank

VP/Editorial Director:
Jack W. Calhoun

VP/Editor-in-Chief:
Alex von Rosenberg

Executive Editor:
Michael Reynolds

Sr. Developmental Editor:
Trish Taylor

Marketing Manager:
Jason Krall

Content Project Manager:
Robert Dreas

Manager of Technology, Editorial:
Vicky True

Sr. Technology Project Editor:
Matt McKinney

Marketing Communications Manager:
Jim Overly

Sr. Print Buyer:
Sandee Milewski

Production House:
International Typesetting and Composition

Printer:
Thomson/West
Eagan, Minnesota

Art Director:
Bethany Casey

Internal Designer:
Timothy R. Mayes

Cover Designer:
Paul Neff Design

Cover Images:
©Photodisc, Inc.

Library of Congress Control Number:
2006906378

For more information about our products, contact us at:

Thomson Learning Academic Resource Center

1-800-423-0563

Thomson Higher Education
5191 Natorp Boulevard
Mason, OH 45040
USA

For Scott, Alejandra, and Ana Sophia

Contents

CHAPTER 2   *The Basic Financial Statements*   *45*

CHAPTER 12

Risk, Capital Budgeting, and Diversification **375**

Preface

Electronic spreadsheets have been available for microcomputers since the introduction of VisiCalc® for the Apple I in June 1979. The first version of Lotus 1-2-3® in 1982 convinced businesses that the IBM PC was a truly useful productivity-enhancing tool. Today, any student who leaves business school without at least basic spreadsheet skills is truly at a disadvantage. Much as earlier generations had to be adept at using a slide rule or financial calculator, today's manager needs to be proficient in the use of a spreadsheet. International competition means that companies must be as efficient as possible. No longer can the manager count on having a large staff of "number crunchers" at her disposal.

Microsoft first introduced Excel in 1985 for the Apple Macintosh and showed the world that spreadsheets could be both powerful and easy to use, not to mention fun. Excel 2.0 was introduced to the PC world in 1987 for Microsoft Windows version 1.0, where it enjoyed something of a cult following. With the introduction of version 3.0 of Windows, sales of Excel exploded so that today it is the leading spreadsheet on the market. As of this writing, Excel 2003 (also known as Excel version 11) is the current version. While the book has been written with this version in mind, it can be used just as well with older versions.

Purpose of the Book

Anyone who has been exposed to Lotus 1-2-3, Quattro Pro, or any of the multitude of other available spreadsheets will find it easy to adapt to Excel. The differences between Excel and the other spreadsheets are great enough however, that I feel it is necessary to have a book dedicated solely to the art of financial analysis with Excel. Furthermore, Excel is by far the dominant spreadsheet program in the market today.

Students with no prior experience with spreadsheets will find that using Excel is very intuitive, especially if they have used other Windows applications. For these students, *Financial Analysis with Microsoft Excel,* 4th Ed. will provide a thorough introduction to the use of spreadsheets from basic screen navigation skills to building fairly complex financial models. I have found that even students with good spreadsheet skills have learned a great deal more about using Excel than they expected.

Finally, I feel strongly that the trend in textbooks of providing pre-built spreadsheet templates for students to use should be reversed. I believe that students can gain valuable insights and a deeper understanding of financial analysis by actually building their own spreadsheets. Programming requires the student to actually confront many issues that might otherwise be swept under the carpet. It continually amazes me how thankful students are when they are actually forced to think rather than just to "plug and go." For this reason the book concentrates on spreadsheet-building skills (though all of the templates are included for instructors) so that students will be encouraged to think and truly understand the problems on which they are working.

Target Audience

Financial Analysis with Microsoft Excel is aimed at a wide variety of students and practitioners of finance. The topics covered generally follow those in an introductory financial management course for undergraduates or first-year MBA students. Because of the emphasis on spreadsheet-building skills, the book is also appropriate as a reference for case-oriented courses in which the spreadsheet is used extensively. I have been using the book in my Financial Modeling course since 1995, and students consistently say that it is the most useful course they have taken. A sizable number of my former students have landed jobs in large part due to their superior spreadsheet skills.

I have tried to make the book complete enough that it may also be used for self-paced learning, and, if my e-mail is any guide, many have sucessfully taken this route. I assume however, that the reader has some familiarity with the basic concepts of accounting and statistics. Instructors will find that their students can use this book on their own time to learn Excel, thereby minimizing the amount of class time required for teaching the rudiments of spreadsheets. Practitioners will find that the book will help them transfer skills from other spreadsheets to Excel and, at the same time, update their knowledge of corporate finance.

A Note to Students

As I have noted, this book is designed to help you learn finance and understand spreadsheets at the same time. Learning finance alone can be a daunting task, but I hope that learning to use Excel at the same time will make your job easier and more fun. However, you will likely find that learning is more difficult if you do not work the examples presented in each chapter. I encourage you to work along with, rather than just read, the book as each example is discussed. Make sure that you save your work often, and keep a current backup.

Organization of the Book

Financial Analysis with Microsoft Excel, 4th Ed. is organized along the lines of an introductory financial management textbook. The book can stand alone or be used as an adjunct to a regular text, but it is not "just a spreadsheet book." In most cases topics are covered at the same depth as the material in conventional textbooks; in many cases the topics are covered in greater depth. For this reason, I believe that *Financial Analysis with Microsoft Excel,* 4th Ed. can be used as a comprehensive primary text. The book is organized as follows:

- Chapter 1: Spreadsheet Basics
- Chapter 2: The Basic Financial Statements
- Chapter 3: The Cash Budget
- Chapter 4: Financial Statement Analysis Tools
- Chapter 5: Financial Forecasting
- Chapter 6: Break-Even and Leverage Analysis
- Chapter 7: The Time Value of Money

- Chapter 8: Common Stock Valuation
- Chapter 9: Bond Valuation
- Chapter 10: The Cost of Capital
- Chapter 11: Capital Budgeting
- Chapter 12: Risk, Capital Budgeting, and Diversification
- Chapter 13: Writing User-Defined Functions with VBA

Extensive use of built-in functions, charts, and other tools throughout the book encourages a much deeper exploration of the models presented than do more traditional methods. Questions such as, "What would happen if . . ." are easily answered with the tools and techniques taught in this book.

Outstanding Features

The most outstanding feature of *Financial Analysis with Microsoft Excel,* 4th Ed. is its use of Excel as a learning tool rather than just a fancy calculator. Students using the book will be able to demonstrate to themselves how and why things are the way they are. Once a student creates a worksheet, they understand how it works and the assumptions behind the calculations. Thus, unlike the traditional "template" approach, the student gains a deeper understanding of the material. In addition, the book greatly facilitates the professor's use of spreadsheets in their courses.

This text takes a self-teaching approach used by many other "how-to" spreadsheet books, but it provides opportunities for much more in-depth experimentation than the competition. For example, scenario analysis is an often recommended technique, but it is rarely demonstrated in any depth. The book uses the tools that are built into Excel to greatly simplify computation-intensive techniques, eliminating the boredom of tedious calculation. Other examples include regression analysis, linear programming, and Monte Carlo simulation. The book encourages students to actually use the tools that they have learned about in their statistics and management science classes.

Pedagogical Features

Financial Analysis with Microsoft Excel, 4th Ed. begins by teaching the basics of Excel. Then, the text uses Excel to build the basic financial statements that students encounter in all levels of financial management courses. This coverage then acts as a "springboard" into more advanced material such as performance evaluation, forecasting, valuation, and capital budgeting. Each chapter builds upon the techniques learned in prior chapters so that the student becomes familiar with Excel and finance at the same time. This type of approach facilitates the professor's incorporation of Excel into a financial management course since it reduces, or eliminates, the necessity of teaching spreadsheet usage in class. It also helps students to see how this vital "tool" is used to solve the financial problems faced by practitioners.

The chapters are organized so that a problem is introduced, solved by traditional methods, and then solved using Excel. I believe that this approach relieves much of the quantitative complexity while enhancing student understanding through repetition and experimentation. This approach also generates interest in the subject matter that a traditional lecture cannot (especially for nonfinance business majors who are required to take a course in financial management). Once they are familiar with Excel, my students typically enjoy using it and spend more time with the subject than they otherwise would. In addition, since charts are used extensively (and are created by the student), the material may be better retained.

A list of learning objectives precedes each chapter, and a summary of the major Excel functions discussed in the chapter is included at the end. In addition, each chapter contains homework problems, and many include Internet Exercises that introduce students to sources of information on the Internet.

Supplements

The Instructor's Manual and other resources, available online, contain the following:

(These materials are available to registered instructors at the product support Web Site, http://thomsonedu.com/finance/mayes).

- The completed worksheets with solutions to all problems covered in the text. Having this material on the Instructor's Resource CD-ROM and on the product Web Site http://thomsonedu.com/finance/mayes allows the instructor to easily create transparencies or give live demonstrations via computer projections in class without having to build the spreadsheets from scratch.

- Additional Excel spreadsheet problems for each chapter that relate directly to the concepts covered in that chapter. Each problem requires the student to build a worksheet to solve a common financial management problem. Often the problems require solutions in a graphical format.

- Complete solutions to the in-text homework problems and those in the Instructor's Manual and on the product Web Site, along with clarifying notes on techniques used.

- An Excel add-in program that contains some functions that simplify complex calculations such as the two-stage common stock valuation model and the payback period, among others. Also included is an add-in program for performing Monte Carlo simulations discussed extensively in Chapter 12. These programs will also appear on the product Web Site at http://thomsonedu.com/finance/mayes.

- Downloadable movies that demonstrate how to use some of the major features of Excel. I hope that these movies will help students to understand Excel better.

Typography Conventions

The main text of this book is set in the 10-point Times New Roman True Type font. Text or numbers that students are expected to enter are set in the 10-point Courier New True Type font.

The names of built-in functions are set in small caps and boldfaced. Function inputs can be either required or optional. Required inputs are set in small caps and are italicized and boldfaced. Optional inputs are set in small-caps and are italicized. As an example, consider the **Pv** function (introduced in Chapter 7):

$$\textbf{Pv}(\textbf{\textit{Rate, Nper, Pmt, Fv,}} \textit{Type})$$

In this function, **Pv** is the name of the function, *Rate, Nper, Pmt,* and *Fv* are the required arguments, and *Type* is optional. In equations and the text, equation variables (which are distinct from function input arguments) are italicized. As an example, consider the *PV* equation:

$$PV = \frac{FV_N}{(1 + i)^N}$$

I hope that these conventions will help to avoid confusion due to similar terms being used in different contexts.

Changes from the Third Edition

The overall organization of the book remains similar, but there have been many small changes throughout the book. There are three major changes that have been made: (1) I have updated the text to cover Excel 2003 which is different in small, but important, ways from Excel 2002. (2) I have divided the valuation chapter into two chapters (8 and 9). (3) I have added a completely new chapter on programming user-defined functions in VBA. I don't expect that most instructors will teach this chapter, but I do hope that students will find it useful. Finally, I have also attempted to fix the errors that were present in the previous edition. All of the chapters have been updated and corrected, but the more important changes include:

Chapter 1—Updated for Excel 2003 and added a section with some rules for good spreadsheet modeling technique.

Chapter 5—Added a discussion of how to use iteration (circular references) to automatically eliminate the discretionary financing needed from the pro forma balance sheet. This is an important, but underused, modeling technique.

Chapter 7—Added a section on the present value of graduated annuites, both regular and due. Also added a user-defined function to do this calculation.

Chapter 8—This chapter previously covered both stock and bond valuation. It now only covers stocks, which allowed me to add several additional valuation models. I have added coverage of the earnings model (present value of growth opportunities), the free cash flow model, and the relative value models (P/E, etc).

Chapter 9—This chapter used to be a part of the valuation chapter, but now is devoted to fixed-income securities. I have added extensive coverage of Malkiel's bond-pricing theorems, duration, and convexity.

Chapter 13—This entirely new chapter covers the basics of writing user-defined functions for Excel. It provides instructions for accessing and using the VBA editor. It covers enough information on the VBA language and programming technique to enable students to write their own functions. I hope that they will use this as a starting point for learning more about VBA and programming in general. In my opinion, programming is an excellent way to gain a better understanding of mathematical formulas.

A Note on the Internet

I have tried to incorporate Internet Exercises in those chapters where the use of the Internet is applicable. In many cases the necessary data simply is not available to the public or very difficult to obtain online (e.g., cash budgeting), so some chapters do not have Internet Exercises. For those chapters that do, I have tried to describe the steps necessary to obtain the data—primarily from either MSN Investor or Yahoo! Finance. It should be noted that Web sites change frequently, and these instructions and URLs may change in the future. I chose MSN Investor and Yahoo! Finance because I believe that these sites are the least likely to undergo severe changes and/or disappear completely. In many cases there are alternative sites for similar data, and a list of these is available at http://clem.mscd.edu/~mayest/Links/FinancialLinks.htm. (This URL is case sensitive.) All Excel spreadsheets for student and instructor use (as referenced in the book) are available at the product support Web Site http://thomsonedu.com/finance/mayes.

Acknowledgments

All books are collaborative projects with input from more than just the listed authors. That is true in this case as well. I wish to thank those colleagues and students who have reviewed and tested the book to this point. Any remaining errors are my sole responsibility, and they may be reported to me by e-mail.

For this edition, I would like to thank Amy Burnett for her help editing the first five chapters and for updating the Instructor's Manual. She also had good ideas for supplements. My colleagues at Metro State have also been helpful. Juan Dempere, Su-Jane Chen, and Tzu-man Huang were very kind to review chapters or sections of chapters. Tom Arnold of the University of Richmond was very generous in offering ideas for improvements in this edition. Two students, Edson Holland and Theresa Lewingdon, were also helpful in catching errors in the previous edition.

Many people provided invaluable help on the first and second editions of this text, and their assistance is still appreciated. Professional colleagues include Ezra Byler, Anthony Crawford, Charles Haley, David Hua, Stuart Michelson, Mohammad Robbani, Gary McClure, and John Settle. In addition, several of my now former students at Metropolitan State College of Denver were helpful. Most especially, Peter Ormsbee, Marjo Turkki, Kevin Hatch, Ron LeClere, and Christine Schouten. In particular, I would like to thank Nancy Jay of Mercer University–Atlanta for her scrupulous editing of the chapters and homework problems in each of the three previous editions.

Finally, I would like to express my sincere gratitude to the team at Thomson South-Western. Executive Editor Michael Reynolds has been a big supporter of this book since its earliest days. Trish Taylor, my developmental editor and friend, deserves special thanks for always pushing me to go beyond my self-imposed limits. The book is much better because of the support of Mike and Trish. Additionally, Bob Dreas has been outstanding as the content project manager, and is a joy to work with. I would be remiss if I didn't also acknowledge the important contributions of Mike Roche and Jason Krall. To anybody I have forgotten, I heartily apologize.

I encourage you to send your comments and suggestions, however minor they may seem to you, to mayest@mscd.edu.

Timothy R. Mayes
June 2006

CHAPTER 1

Spreadsheet Basics

After studying this chapter, you should be able to:

1. *Explain the basic purpose of a spreadsheet program.*
2. *Identify the various components of the Excel screen.*
3. *Navigate the Excel worksheet (entering, correcting, and moving data within the worksheet).*
4. *Explain the purpose and usage of Excel's built-in functions and macro functions.*
5. *Create graphics and know how to print and save files in Excel.*

The term "spreadsheet" covers a wide variety of elements useful for quantitative analysis of all kinds. Essentially, a spreadsheet is a simple tool consisting of a matrix of cells that can store numbers, text, or formulas. The spreadsheet's power comes from its ability to recalculate results as you change the contents of other cells. No longer does the user need to do these calculations by hand or on a calculator. Instead, with a properly constructed spreadsheet, changing a single number (say, a sales forecast) can result in literally thousands of automatic changes in the model. The freedom and productivity enhancement provided by modern spreadsheets presents an unparalleled opportunity for learning financial analysis.

Spreadsheet Uses

Spreadsheets today contain built-in analytical capabilities previously unavailable in a single package. Users often had to learn a variety of specialized software packages to do any relatively complex analysis. With the newest versions of Microsoft Excel, users can perform tasks ranging from the routine maintenance of financial statements to multivariate regression analysis to Monte Carlo simulations of various hedging strategies.

It is literally impossible to enumerate all of the possible applications for spreadsheets. You should keep in mind that spreadsheets are useful not only for financial analysis, but for any type of quantitative analysis whether your specialty is in marketing, management, engineering, statistics, or economics. For that matter, a spreadsheet can also prove valuable for personal uses. With Excel it is a fairly simple matter to build a spreadsheet to monitor your investment portfolio, plan for retirement, experiment with various mortgage options when buying a house, create and maintain a mailing list, etc. The possibilities are quite literally endless. The more comfortable you become with the spreadsheet, the more uses you will find. Using a spreadsheet can help you find solutions that you never would have imagined on your own. Above all, feel free to experiment and try new things as you gain more experience working with spreadsheet programs, particularly Excel.

Starting Microsoft Excel

Excel 2003 Icon

In Windows, you start programs like Excel by double-clicking on the program's icon. The location of the Excel icon will depend on the organization of your system. You may have the Excel icon (at left) on the desktop. Otherwise, you can start Excel by clicking the Windows start button and then choosing Microsoft Excel from the All Programs menu.

For easier access, you may wish to create a Desktop or Taskbar shortcut. To do this, right-click on the Excel icon in the All Programs menu and either choose Create Shortcut or drag the icon to the Desktop or Taskbar. Remember that a shortcut is not the program itself, so you can safely delete the shortcut if you later decide that you don't need it.

Parts of the Excel Screen

FIGURE 1-1
MICROSOFT EXCEL 2003

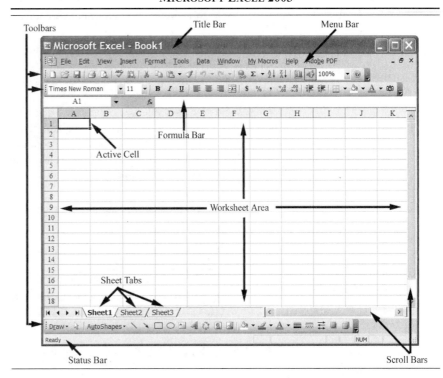

In Figure 1-1, note the labeled parts of the Excel screen. We will examine most of these parts separately. Please refer to Figure 1-1 as you read through each of the sections that follow.

The Menu Bar

FIGURE 1-2
THE EXCEL 2003 MAIN MENUS

The main menu bar in Excel provides access to nine menus, each of which leads to further choices. There are two ways to select a menu: click on the menu of choice with the mouse, or use the Alt key in combination with the underlined letter in the menu name. For example, to choose the File menu, you could either click on the word "File" or press Alt+F on the keyboard. Either method will lead to the File menu dropping down, allowing you to make another choice.

In Windows, menus are persistent, meaning that they stay visible on the screen until you either make a selection or cancel the menu by pressing the Esc key. While the menu is visible, you may use either the arrow keys or the mouse to select a function.

At times, some menu selections are displayed in a light gray font color (grayed out) instead of black. These options are not available for selection at the time that the menu is selected. For example, if you have not cut or copied a cell, the Paste option, from the Edit menu has nothing to paste, so it is grayed out. Only the menu options displayed in a black font color may be selected.

Refer to Appendix A for a short description of each menu selection.

The Toolbars

FIGURE 1-3
MOST COMMON EXCEL 2003 TOOLBARS

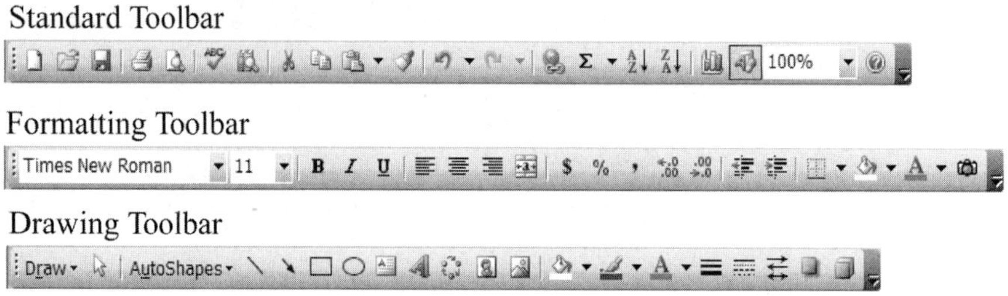

Standard Toolbar

Formatting Toolbar

Drawing Toolbar

Immediately below the menu bar, Excel displays a series of shortcut buttons on Toolbars. The exact buttons, and their order, may be different on different machines. The buttons provide a quick way to carry out certain commands without wading through menus and dialog boxes. To add, delete, or rearrange buttons, choose View Toolbars Customize from the menus. You can learn what function each button performs by simply placing the mouse pointer over a button on a Toolbar.

After a few seconds, a message will appear that informs you of the button's function. This message is called a ToolTip. ToolTips are used frequently by Excel to help you to identify the function of various items on the screen.

Note that you can move a Toolbar, or make it float over the worksheet, by clicking on a blank area of the Toolbar and dragging it to the new location. Dropping it over the worksheet area will leave it floating. The Toolbar will stay wherever you drop it, even after exiting and restarting Excel.

The Formula Bar

FIGURE 1-4
THE EXCEL 2003 FORMULA BAR

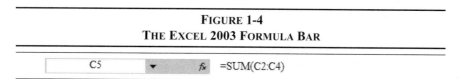

As you work more and more in Excel to create financial models, you will find that the formula bar is one its most useful features. The formula bar displays information about the currently selected cell, referred to as the active cell. The left part of the formula bar indicates the name or address of the selected cell (C5 in this case). The right part of the formula bar displays the contents of the selected cell. If the cell contains a formula, the formula bar displays the formula, and the cell displays the result of the formula. If text or numbers have been entered, then the text or numbers are displayed.

The f_x button on the formula bar is used to show the Insert Function dialog box. This dialog box helps you to find and enter functions without having to memorize them. See page 23 for more information.

The Worksheet Area

The worksheet area is where the real work of the spreadsheet is done. The worksheet is a matrix (256 columns and 65,536 rows) of cells, each of which can contain text, numbers, formulas, or graphics. Each cell is referred to by a column letter and a row number. Column letters (A,B,C,...,IV) are listed at the top of each column, and row numbers (1,2,3,...,65536) are listed to the left of each row. The cell in the upper left corner of the worksheet is therefore referred to as cell A1, the cell immediately below A1 is referred to as cell A2, the cell to the right of A1 is cell B1, and so on. This naming convention is common to all spreadsheet programs. You will become comfortable with it once you have gained some experience working in Excel.

The active cell (the one into which any input may be placed) can be identified by a solid black border around the cell. Note that the active cell is not always visible on the screen, but it is always named in the leftmost portion of formula bar.

The Sheet Tabs

FIGURE 1-5
THE SHEET TABS

Excel worksheets are stored in a format that allows you to combine multiple worksheets into one file known as a workbook. This allows several related worksheets to be contained in one file. The sheet tabs, near the bottom of the screen, enable you to move easily from one sheet to another in a workbook. You may rename, copy, or delete any existing sheet or insert a new sheet by clicking a tab with your right mouse button and making a choice from the resulting menu. You can easily change the order of the sheet tabs by left-clicking a tab and dragging it to a new position.

It is easy to do any of these operations on multiple worksheets at once, except renaming. Simply click the first sheet and then Ctrl+click each of the others. (You can select a contiguous group of sheets: select the first one and then Shift+click the last.) Now, right-click one of the selected sheets and select the appropriate option from the pop-up menu. When sheets are grouped, anything you do to one sheet gets done to all. This feature is useful if, for example, you need to enter identical data into multiple sheets or need to perform identical formatting on several sheets. To ungroup the sheets, either click on any non-grouped sheet or right-click a sheet tab and choose Ungroup Sheets from the pop-up menu. Another feature in Excel 2003 allows you to choose a color for each tab by right-clicking the tab and choosing a Tab Color from the pop-up menu.

The VCR-style buttons to the left of the sheet tabs are the sheet tab control buttons; they allow you to scroll through the list of sheet tabs. Right-clicking on any of the VCR-style buttons will display a pop-up menu that allows you to quickly jump to any sheet tab in the workbook. This is an especially helpful tool when you have too many tabs for them all to be shown.

The Status Bar

The status bar contains information regarding the current state of Excel, as well as certain messages. For example, most of the time the only message is "Ready," indicating that Excel is waiting for input.

FIGURE 1-6
THE STATUS BAR

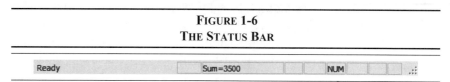

At other times, Excel may add "Calculate" to the status bar to indicate that it needs to recalculate the worksheet because of changes. You can also direct Excel to do certain calculations on the status bar. For example, in Figure 1-6 Excel is showing the sum of the cells that are highlighted in the worksheet. By right-clicking on this area of the status bar you can also get Excel to calculate the average, count, minimum, or maximum of any highlighted cells. This is useful if you need a quick calculation, but it doesn't need to be in the worksheet. The right side of the status bar shows if the Num Lock or Scroll Lock keys are on.

Navigating the Worksheet

There are two principal methods for moving around within the worksheet area: the arrow keys and the mouse. Generally speaking, for small distances the arrow keys provide an easy method of changing the active cell, but moving to more distant cells is usually easier with the mouse.

Most keyboards have a separate keypad containing arrows pointing up, down, left, and right. If your keyboard does not, then you can use the numeric keypad if the Num Lock function is off (you will see the word "NUM" in the status bar if Num Lock is on). To use the arrow keys, simply press the appropriate key once for each cell that you wish to move across. For example, assuming that the current cell is A1 and you wish to move to cell D1, simply press the Right arrow key three times. To move from D1 to D5 press the Down arrow key four times. You can also use the Tab key to move one cell to the right.

The mouse is even easier to use. While the mouse pointer is over the worksheet area it will be in the shape of a fat cross. To change the active cell, move the mouse pointer over the destination cell and click the left button. To move to a cell that is not currently displayed on the screen, click on the scroll bars until the cell is visible and then click on it. For example, if the active cell is A1 and you wish to make A100 the active cell, merely click on the arrow at the bottom of the scroll bar on the right-hand part of the screen until A100 is visible. Move the mouse pointer over cell A100 and click with the left button. Each click on the scroll bar moves the worksheet up or down one page. If you wish to move up, click above the thumb. If you wish to move down, click beneath the thumb. The thumb is the small button that moves up and down the scroll bar to indicate your position in the worksheet. To move more quickly, you can drag the thumb to the desired position.

If you know the name or address of the cell to which you wish to move (for large worksheets, remembering the cell address isn't easy, but you can use named ranges), use the Go To command. The Go To command will change the active cell to whatever cell you indicate. The Go To dialog box can be used by choosing the Edit menu and then the Go To command, by pressing the F5 function key, or by pressing the Ctrl+G key combination. To move to cell A50, simply press F5, type: A50 in the Reference box, and then press Enter. You will notice that cell A50 is now highlighted and visible on the screen. You can also use Go To to find certain special cells (e.g., the last cell that has data in it) by pressing the Special . . . button in the Go To dialog box.

Selecting a Range of Cells

Many times you will need to select more than one cell at a time. For example, you may wish to apply a particular number format to a whole range of cells, or you might wish to clear a whole range. Since it would be cumbersome to do this one cell at a time, especially for a large range, Excel allows you to simultaneously select a whole range and perform various functions on all of the cells at once. The easiest way to select a contiguous range of cells is to use the mouse. Simply point to the cell in the upper left corner of the range, click and hold down the left button, and drag the mouse until the entire range is highlighted. As you drag the mouse, watch the left side of the formula bar. Excel will inform you of the number of selected rows and columns.

You can also use the keyboard to select a range. First change the active cell to the upper left corner of the range to be selected, press and hold down the Shift key, and use the arrow keys to highlight the entire range. Note that if you release the Shift key while pressing an arrow key you will lose the highlight. A very useful keyboard shortcut is the Shift+Ctrl+Arrow (any arrow key will work) combination. This is used to select all of the cells from the active cell up to, but not including, the first blank cell. For example, if you have 100 numbers in a column and need to apply a format, just select the first cell and then press Shift+Ctrl+Down arrow to select them all. This is faster and more accurate than using the mouse.

Many times it is also useful to select a discontiguous range (i.e., two or more unconnected ranges) of cells. To do this, simply select the first range as usual, and then hold down the Ctrl key as you select the other ranges.

The ability to select cells in Excel is crucial because Excel, like most other Windows applications, works in the "select, then act" mode. (In the old days, users of DOS programs were familiar with the "act, then select" method of operation.) In Excel, you first select the cells that you wish to act on and then you choose the operation (e.g., Edit Copy) that you want to perform. This would seem to be a minor point, but it is actually a big productivity improvement. In the "select, then act" method, the cells stay selected after the operation has been performed, thereby allowing another operation on those cells without reselecting them.

Using Named Ranges

A named range is a cell, or group of cells, for which you have supplied a name. Range names can be useful in several different ways, but locating a range on a big worksheet is probably the most common use. To name a range of cells, start by selecting the range. For example, select A1:C5 and then choose Insert Name Define from the menus. In the edit box at the top of the Define Name dialog box, enter a name, say MyRange (note that a range name cannot contain spaces or most special characters). Now, click the Add button and the range is named. Figure 1-7 shows how the dialog box should look. Note that at the bottom, the Refers To edit box shows the address to which the name refers.[1]

---

1. Notice that the name is actually defined as a formula. This is important for some of the more advanced uses of named ranges. For example, you can use a name to define constants, or create a reference to a range that grows as data is added.

FIGURE 1-7
THE DEFINE NAME DIALOG BOX

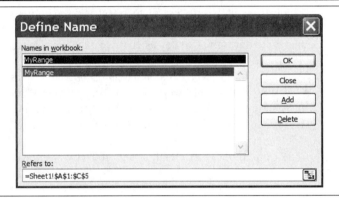

Once the range is named, you can select it using the Go To command. The name will appear in the list on the Go To dialog box. An even faster method is to use the Name Box on the left side of the formula bar. Simply drop the list and choose the named range that you wish to select.

Named ranges can also be used in formulas in place of cell addresses, and they can be used in the ChartSeries function for charts. As useful as they can be at times, there is no requirement to use them.

Entering Text and Numbers

Each cell in an Excel worksheet can be thought of as a miniature word processor. Text can be entered directly into the cell and then formatted in a variety of ways. To enter a text string, first select the cell where you want the text to appear and then begin typing. It is that simple.

Excel is smart enough to know the difference between numbers and text, so there are no extra steps for entering numbers. Let's try the following example of entering numbers and text into the worksheet.

Move the cell pointer to cell A1 (using the arrow keys, mouse, or the Go To command) and type: Microsoft Corporation Sales. In cell A2 enter: (Millions of Dollars). Select cell A3 and type: 2000 to 2005. Note that the entry in cell A3 will be treated as text by Excel because of the spaces and letters included. In cells A4 to F4 we now want to enter the years. In A4 type: 2005, in B4

AutoFill Handle

type: 2004; now select A4:B4 and move the mouse pointer over the lower right corner of the selection. The mouse pointer will now change to a skinny cross, indicating that you can use the AutoFill feature.[2] Click and drag the mouse to the right to fill in the remaining years. Notice that the most recent data is typically entered at the left, and the most distant data at the right. This convention allows us to easily recognize and concentrate on what is usually the most important data.

We have now set up the headings for our first worksheet. Now let's add Microsoft's sales (in millions of dollars) for the years 2000 to 2005 into cells A5 to F5 as shown in Exhibit 1-1.[3]

EXHIBIT 1-1
THE FIRST WORKSHEET

	A	B	C	D	E	F
1	Microsoft Corporation Sales					
2	(Millions of Dollars)					
3	2000 to 2005					
4	2005	2004	2003	2002	2001	2000
5	39788	36835	32187	28365	25296	22956

Formatting and Alignment Options

The worksheet in Exhibit 1-1 isn't very attractive. Notice that the text is displayed at the left side of the cells, while the numbers are at the right. By default this is the way that Excel aligns text and numbers. However, we can easily change the way that these entries are displayed through the use of the formatting and alignment options.

Before continuing, we should define a few typographical terms. A "typeface" is a particular style of drawing letters and numbers. For example, the main text of this book is set in the Times New Roman typeface. However, the text that you are expected to enter into a worksheet is displayed in the Courier New typeface.

---

2. The AutoFill feature can be used to fill in any series that Excel can recognize. For example, type: January in one cell and February in an adjacent cell. Select both cells and drag the AutoFill handle to automatically and completely fill in a series of month names. You can also define your own series by using the Custom Lists tab in the Options dialog box (**T**ools **O**ptions **C**ustom Lists).

3. All of the data for Microsoft in this chapter was obtained from the Microsoft Corp. Web site at http://www.microsoft.com/msft/download/financialhistoryFY.xls.

Typeface also refers to whether the text is drawn in **bold**, *italics*, or perhaps ***bold italics***.

The term "type size" refers to the size of the typeface. When typewriters were commonly used, type size was defined in characters per inch (cpi). This convention was somewhat confusing because the larger the cpi number, the smaller was the text. Today, with computers we normally refer to the type size in "points." Each point represents an increment of 1/72nd of an inch, so there are 72 points to the inch. A typeface printed at a 12-point size is larger than the same typeface printed at a size of 10 points.

Generally, we refer to the typeface and type size combination as a font. So when we say "change the font to 12-point bold Times New Roman," it is understood that we are referring to a particular typeface (Times New Roman, bolded) and type size (12 point).

For text entries, the term "format" refers to the typeface and type size and cell alignment used to display the text. Let's change the font of the text that was entered to Times New Roman, 12-point, bold. First, select the range from A1 to A3 by clicking on A1 and dragging to A3. Now select the Format menu and choose Cells. A dialog box allows you to change the various attributes of the cells. Click on the tab labeled "Font" so that the font choices are displayed. We want to select Times New Roman from the font list, bold from the style list, and 12 from the size list. Notice that there is a preview of this font displayed in the lower right corner of the dialog box, so you can see how the chosen font will look on the worksheet. Since none of these changes actually take effect until you validate them by clicking the OK button, you can experiment until the text in the sample window looks right. Click on the OK button or press the Enter key to make the change take effect. You can also make all of these changes with the Formatting Toolbar.

We can just as easily change the font for numbers. Suppose that we want to change the years in cells A4:F4 to 12-point italic Times New Roman. First select the range A4:F4 by clicking on A4 and dragging the mouse until the highlight extends to F4. Choose Format Cells (the font dialog box should be displayed since that was the last change that was made) and select the attributes. Click on the OK button and the change will be made. Note that this change could also have been made at the same time as the text was changed, or you could now choose Edit Repeat Font from the menus. In many cases the Edit menu will contain a choice that allows you to repeat or undo the last action. In addition, the F4 key, or Ctrl+Y, will repeat the last action.

Our worksheet is now beginning to take on a better look, but it still isn't quite right. We are used to seeing the titles of tables nicely centered over the table, but our title is way over at the left. We can remedy this by using Excel's alignment options. Excel provides for seven different horizontal alignments within a cell. We can have the text (or numbers) aligned with the left or right sides of the cell or centered within the cell boundaries. Excel also allows centering text across a range of cells.

Let's change the alignment of the year numbers first. Highlight cells A4:F4 and select Format Cells from the menu. Click on the Alignment tab to display the alignment choices. Horizontal alignment refers to the left and right alignment, vertical refers to the up and down alignment, and orientation refers to the way that the font is rotated. For now, we simply want to change the horizontal alignment to centered. Choose "Center" from the horizontal choices and click on the OK button. Notice that the numbers are all centered within their respective cells.

Next, we want to center the table title across the whole range of numbers that we have entered. To do this, we must select the entire range across which we want to center our titles. Highlight cells A1:F3 and select Format Cells from the menu. You will again be presented with the alignment dialog box, from which you should select "Center across selection." Click on the OK button and notice that the titles are indeed centered across the columns A to F. Note that there is also a button on the Formatting Toolbar that will "Merge and Center" the selected cells. This button will have the appearance of doing the same thing as "Center across selection," but it doesn't. In addition to centering the text, it also merges all of the selected cells into one big cell. Using this button may create alignment problems if you later decide to insert additional columns into the worksheet. Generally speaking, it is better not to use the Merge and Center button.

Formatting Numbers

Aside from changing the typeface and type size, when dealing with numbers we can also change their appearance by adding commas and dollar signs, and by altering the number of decimal places displayed. Furthermore, we can make the numbers appear different depending on whether they are positive or negative. For example, we might want negative numbers to be red in color and displayed in parentheses rather than using the negative sign. You can experiment with designing your own number formats, but for now we will stick to the more common pre-defined formats.

Microsoft is a large company, and its sales have ranged from nearly $23 billion to almost $40 billion over the 2000 to 2005 time period. Numbers this large, even when expressed in millions of dollars, become difficult to read unless they are written with commas separating every third digit. Let's format our sales numbers so that they are easier to read.

Select the range of sales numbers (A5:F5), choose F**o**rmat C**e**lls from the menus, and then click on the Number tab. You are presented with the Number Format dialog box, which contains a list of formatting categories. For now, select Number from the category list. This will give you the option to choose the number of decimal places displayed, choose whether or not to use a 1000 separator, and select the format of negative numbers. We want to display the sales numbers with commas separating every third digit and two decimal places, so change the decimal places to 2 and check the box to add a 1000 separator.[4] Click on the OK button and notice that the numbers are now displayed in this more readable format.

At this point, we have made several formatting changes to the Microsoft Sales worksheet. Your worksheet should look like the one in Exhibit 1-2. All of this formatting may seem tedious at the moment, but it will quickly become easy as you become more familiar with the menus. Furthermore, the payoff in readability will be worth far more than the few seconds spent in formatting the worksheet.

EXHIBIT 1-2
ORIGINAL WORKSHEET REFORMATTED

	A	B	C	D	E	F
1	Microsoft Corporation Sales					
2	(Millions of Dollars)					
3	2000 to 2005					
4	2005	2004	2003	2002	2001	2000
5	39,788.00	36,835.00	32,187.00	28,365.00	25,296.00	22,956.00

Adding Borders and Shading

Text formatting is not the only design element that is available in Excel. We can also enliven worksheets by placing borders around cells and shading them. In your worksheet, select A4:F4 (the years). From the menus, choose F**o**rmat C**e**lls and then select the Border tab from the dialog box. There are 13 different line styles that can

---

4. Note that in the United States a comma is used as a 1000 separator. In many other countries a decimal point is used instead. Excel determines which to use based on the settings in the Windows Control Panel's regional and language settings utility.

be applied, and you can change the color of the lines. Click on the thick solid line (fifth down on the right side) and then click on both of the top and bottom lines in the sample view. Click the OK button to see the change.

Next, with A4:F4 still selected, we will add shading. As before, choose Format Cells from the menus, but this time select the Patterns tab. This tab allows you to set the background color and pattern of the cells. Click on the lightest gray color and then press the OK button. Now, to make the text more readable, make it bold. Your worksheet should now look like the one in Exhibit 1-3.

EXHIBIT 1-3
THE WORKSHEET WITH BORDERS AND SHADING

	A	B	C	D	E	F
1	Microsoft Corporation Sales					
2	(Millions of Dollars)					
3	2000 to 2005					
4	*2005*	*2004*	*2003*	*2002*	*2001*	*2000*
5	39,788.00	36,835.00	32,187.00	28,365.00	25,296.00	22,956.00

Entering Formulas

So far, we haven't done anything that couldn't just as easily be done in any word processing application. The real power of spreadsheets becomes obvious when formulas are used. Formulas will enable us to convert the data that we have entered into useful information.

At the moment, our sample worksheet contains only sales data for Microsoft. Suppose, however, that we are interested in performing a simple analysis of the profitability of Microsoft over the 2000 to 2005 time period. In this case we would also need to see the net income for each of the years under study. Let's make some modifications to the worksheet to make it more useful.

Add the data from Table 1-1 to the sample worksheet in cells A6:F6, immediately below the sales data, and apply the same format. Now, we have a couple of problems. The title of our worksheet, in cell A1, is no longer accurate. We are now putting together a profitability analysis, so we should change the title to reflect this change of focus. Select cell A1 (even though the title is centered across A1:F1, Excel still keeps the data in A1) by clicking on it. Notice that the text appears in the right-hand side of the formula bar. To edit the title, click on the formula bar just to the right of the word "Sales." Backspace over the word "Sales" and then type: `Profitability Analysis` and press Enter to accept the change.

TABLE 1-1
MICROSOFT NET INCOME 2000 TO 2005

Year	Net Income
2005	12,254.00
2004	8,168.00
2003	7,531.00
2002	5,355.00
2001	7,346.40
2000	9,421.00

Our only remaining problem is that the data in the table are not clearly identified. Ideally, we would like to have the data labeled in the column just to the left of the first data point. But, there is no column to the left of the data! There are several ways to overcome this problem. The easiest is to simply tell Excel to insert a column to the left of column A. To accomplish this, select column A entirely by clicking on the column header where it has an "A." Notice that the whole column is highlighted (we can do this with rows as well). Now, from the menus, choose Insert Columns. The new column is magically inserted, and all of our data have been moved one column to the right. In cell A5 type: `Sales`, and in A6 type: `Net Income`.

If you are following the examples exactly, the words "Net Income" probably do not fit exactly into A6. Instead, part of the text is cut off so as not to overflow onto the data in B6. We can easily remedy this by changing the width of column A. Again select column A, and then choose Format Column Width... which will cause a dialog box to be displayed. In the edit box type: `20` and press the Enter key. Column A should now be wide enough to hold the text that we have added and will add later.

We can now proceed with our profitability analysis. Because of the dramatic growth in sales over the years, it isn't immediately clear from the data whether Microsoft's profitability has improved or not, even though net income has increased over this time. In this type of situation, it is generally preferable to look at net income as a percentage of sales (net profit margin) instead of dollar net income. Thankfully, we do not have to type in more data to do this. Instead, we can let Excel calculate these percentages for us. All we need to do is to enter the formulas.

Formulas in Excel are based upon cell addresses. To add two cells together, we simply tell Excel to take the contents of the first cell and add it to the contents of the second. The result of the formula will be placed in the cell in which the formula is entered. In our problem, we need to find net income as a percentage of sales. We will do this first for 2005.

Before entering our first formula, we should insert a label identifying the data. In cell A7 type: Net Profit Margin. Change the active cell to B7, where we want to place the result of the calculation. The problem that we want to solve is to take the number in cell B6 and divide it by the number in B5. In Excel, division is represented by the forward slash (/), so in B7 type: =B6/B5. *The equals sign must precede all formulas in Excel*, otherwise it will treat the formula as text and will not calculate the result. Press the Enter key to make Excel calculate the formula (you should get 0.3080 as the result).

In this example, we typed the formula directly into the cell because the small size of our worksheet made it easy to know what cells we wanted to use in the formula. In many instances, this is not the case. In more complicated worksheets it is usually easier to use the "pointer mode" to enter formulas. In pointer mode, we use the mouse to point to the cells that we want included, and Excel inserts them into the formula. Move to C7, and we will enter the formula using the pointer mode. First, type: = which places Excel into edit mode. Now, instead of typing C6, click on C6 with the mouse. Notice that C6 appears in the formula bar to the right of the equals sign. Press the forward slash key to indicate division and then click on C5. In the formula bar you should see the formula "=C6/C5." Press the Enter key to calculate the result of the formula (you should get 0.2217 as the result).

Let's change the format of these cells so that they are easier to read. In this case, it would be nice to see them in percentage format with two decimal places. First, highlight cells B7:C7. Choose Format Cells and click on the Number tab. From the Category list, click on Percentage and then set the Decimal places to 2. Press the Enter key or click the OK button. You could also apply this format by using the Percent Style button on the Formatting Toolbar. To get two decimal places, you need to click the Increase Decimal button on the same Toolbar. Figure 1-8 shows these and other formatting icons.

FIGURE 1-8
NUMBER FORMATTING ICONS

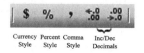

Currency   Percent Comma   Inc/Dec
Style   Style   Style   Decimals

Copying and Moving Formulas

We have now calculated the net profit margin for 2005 and 2004, but that still leaves four years for which we need to enter formulas. Repeatedly typing essentially the same formula can get tedious. Fortunately, we can simply copy the formula, and Excel will update the cell addresses to maintain the same relative relationships. For example, we know that for 2003 the formula should read "=D6/D5." If we copy the formula from C7 to D7, Excel will change the formula from "=C6/C5" to "=D6/D5" automatically.

This works because Excel treats all cell references as relative. When you typed the formula in cell B7 (=B6/B5) Excel read that as "take the contents of the cell that is one row above the current cell and divide that by the contents of the cell that is two rows above the current cell." When copying formulas, Excel maintains the same relative cell relationships so that the formulas are updated. When we copy to the left or right, Excel updates the columns in the formulas. When we copy up or down, Excel changes the rows.

To change this behavior, we could use *absolute references* instead. An absolute reference always refers to the same cell, no matter where you copy it. To create an absolute reference, type dollar signs before the column letter and row number. For example, $B$6 will always refer to cell B6. The $ tells Excel not to change the reference. We can also create *mixed references*. In a mixed reference only the column or row remains constant, not both. For example, $B6 is a mixed reference (column absolute, row relative). If the formula is copied down, it will change to $B7, but if it is copied across it will still be $B6. On the other hand, B$6 (column relative, row absolute) will still be B$6 if copied down, but will change to C$6 if copied across. We will make heavy use of absolute and mixed references in later chapters. Note that you can use the F4 key to cycle through every possible reference type. Simply enter a cell address and repeatedly press F4 until you get the type of reference you need (e.g., $B$6, B$6, $B6, B6).

EXHIBIT 1-4
A PROFITABILITY ANALYSIS FOR MICROSOFT

	A	B	C	D	E	F	G
1		Microsoft Corporation Profitability Analysis					
2		(Millions of Dollars)					
3		2000 to 2005					
4		2005	2004	2003	2002	2001	2000
5	Sales	39,788.00	36,835.00	32,187.00	28,365.00	25,296.00	22,956.00
6	Net Income	12,254.00	8,168.00	7,531.00	5,355.00	7,346.40	9,421.00
7	Net Profit Margin	30.80%	22.17%	23.40%	18.88%	29.04%	41.04%

Rather than retyping the formula for our other cells, let's simply copy from C7. First, select C7 and then choose **E**dit **C**opy from the menus. Now highlight cells D7:G7 and choose **E**dit **P**aste from the menus. At this point, your worksheet should closely resemble the one in Exhibit 1-4.

We can see from Exhibit 1-4 that Microsoft's net profit margin decreased markedly over the 2001 to 2004 period before finally recovering in 2005. The declining profit margins in 2001 to 2004 are roughly aligned with the economic recession and the beginning of the bear market in 2000, and the 2000 net profit margin was probably higher than usual due to the Y2K problem and the technology boom. Still, the margins are quite high compared to most other company's margins.

In addition to copying formulas (which maintains the relative cell references), we can also move them. Moving a formula to a different cell has no effect on the cell references. For example, we could move the formula in B7 (=B6/B5) to B8. To do this, select B7 and then choose **E**dit **C**ut from the menus. Next, select B8 and choose **E**dit **P**aste from the menus. Notice that the result in B8 is exactly the same as before. Furthermore, the formula is unchanged.

Formulas (or anything else) may also be moved with the mouse. Simply select the cells containing the data that you want to move, position the mouse pointer at the edge of the cell so that it changes to an arrow, and then click the left mouse button and drag the cell to its new location. Now move the formula back to B7. Highlight B8 and drag it back to B7. Or, select B8 and choose **E**dit **C**ut, and select B7 and choose **E**dit **P**aste. The worksheet should again resemble the one in Exhibit 1-4.

Mathematical Operators

Aside from division, which we have already seen, there are four additional primary mathematical operations: addition, subtraction, multiplication, and exponentiation. All of these operations are available in Excel and can be used as easily as division. Table 1-2 summarizes the five basic operations and the result that you should get from entering the example formula into cell B8.

TABLE 1-2
MATHEMATICAL OPERATIONS

Operation	Key	Example	Result in B8
Addition	+	=B5+B6	52,042
Subtraction	–	=B5–B6	27,534
Multiplication	*	=B5*B7	12,254
Division	/	=B6/B7	39,788
Exponentiation	^	=15^2	225

Parentheses and the Order of Operations

Using the mathematical operators provided by Excel is straightforward in most instances. However, there are times when it gets a bit complicated. For example, let's calculate the rates of growth of Microsoft's sales and net income. To calculate the growth rates we will usually want the compound annual growth rate (geometric mean growth rate) rather than the arithmetic average growth rate. The general equation for the geometric mean growth rate is:

$$\overline{G} = \sqrt[(N-1)]{\frac{X_N}{X_0}} - 1 = \left(\frac{X_N}{X_0}\right)^{\frac{1}{(N-1)}} - 1 \qquad (1\text{-}1)$$

where $\overline{G}$ is the geometric mean, N is the count of the numbers in the series, X_0 is the first number in the series (2000 sales in our example), and X_N is the last number in the series (2005 sales).

Translating this equation into Excel is not as simple as it may at first appear. To do this correctly requires knowledge of operator precedence. In other words, Excel doesn't necessarily evaluate formulas from left to right. Instead, it performs some operations before others. Exponentiation is usually performed first. Multiplication and division are usually performed next, but they are considered equal in precedence so any multiplication and division are evaluated from left to right. Finally, addition and subtraction are evaluated, and they are also considered equal in precedence to each other.

We can modify the order of operations by using parentheses. Operations enclosed in parentheses are always evaluated first. As a simple example, how would you evaluate the following expression?

$$X = 2 + 4/3$$

Is X equal to 2 or 3.33? Algebraically, X is equal to 3.33 because the division should be performed before the addition (as Excel would do). If the answer we were seeking was 2, we could rewrite the expression using parentheses to clarify:

$$X = (2 + 4)/3$$

The parentheses clearly indicate that the addition should be performed first, so the answer is 2. When in doubt, always use parentheses, because using them unnecessarily will not cause any problems.

To calculate the compound annual growth rate of sales, move to cell A8 and type: `Sales Growth`. Now, enter the following into B8: `=(B5/G5)^(1/5)-1`. Pressing the Enter key will reveal that the growth rate of sales for the five-year period was 11.63% per year (you may have to reformat the cell to display as a percentage with two decimal places). To determine the average growth rate of net income, type: `Net Income Growth` into A9, and then copy the formula from B8 to B9. You should find that the compound annual rate of growth of net income has been 5.40% per year and that the formula in B9 is: `=(B6/G6)^(1/5)-1`.

Using Excel's Built-In Functions

We could build some pretty impressive worksheets with the techniques that we have examined so far. But why should we have to build all of our formulas from scratch, especially when some of them can be quite complex and therefore error prone? Excel comes with hundreds of built-in functions, and more than 50 of them are financial functions. These functions are ready to go; all they need is for you to supply cell references as inputs. We will be demonstrating the use of many of these functions throughout the book, but for now let's redo our growth rate calculations using the built-in functions.

Since we want to know the compound annual *rate of growth*, we can use Excel's built-in **GEOMEAN** function.[5] To use this function, the syntax is:

$$=\textbf{GEOMEAN}(\textit{Number1}, \textit{Number2},...)$$

The **GEOMEAN** function takes up to 30 cell addresses (or ranges) separated by commas. As is usual in Excel, we can also supply a range of cells rather than specifying the cells individually. Remember, we want to find the geometric mean *rate of growth* of sales, not the geometric mean of the dollar amount of sales. Since the **GEOMEAN** function simply calculates the N*th* root of the product of the inputs, we need to redefine our inputs (we used the dollar amount of sales in our custom-built formula). Let's add a row of percentage changes in sales to our worksheet.

Move to A10 and enter the label: `% Change in Sales`, then select B10 and enter the formula: `=B5/C5-1`. The result in B10 should be 0.0802, indicating that sales grew by 8.02% from 2004 to 2005. Now copy the formula from B10 to each cell in the C10:F10 range. Note that we don't copy the formula into G10. That would cause an error, because H10 doesn't contain any data (try it, and you will see #DIV/0! in G10, meaning that your formula tried to divide by zero).

Now, to calculate the compound annual rate of sales growth, we need to enter the **GEOMEAN** function into B11: `=geomean(B10:F10)`. Since our data points are in one contiguous range, we chose to specify the range rather than each individual cell. Let's also supply a label so that when we come back later, we can recall what this cell represents. Move to A11 and enter: `Sales Growth`.

Have you noticed any problems with the result of the **GEOMEAN** function? The result was 11.40%, rather than the 11.63% that we got when using our custom formula. Either our custom formula is incorrect, or we have misused the **GEOMEAN** function. Actually, this type of error is common and easily overlooked. What has happened is that when using the **GEOMEAN** function, we didn't fully understand what goes on behind the scenes. Remember that **GEOMEAN** simply takes the N*th* root of the product of the numbers. When multiplying numbers that are less than

---

5. We could calculate the arithmetic mean using the **AVERAGE** function, but this would ignore the compounding and overstate the true average growth rate. This function is defined as =**AVERAGE**(*Number1*, *Number2*,...).

one, the result is even smaller—not larger, as is the case with numbers greater than one. What we should have done is calculated the geometric mean of the relative changes (i.e., one plus the percentage change).

To correct the error, replace the formula in B10 with: =B5/C5 and copy it to the other cells. Now replace the formula in B11 with: =geomean(B10:F10)-1. The result is 11.63%, exactly the same as our previous result. To avoid errors like this one, you absolutely must understand what the built-in formula is doing. *Never blindly accept results just because Excel has calculated them for you.* There is an old saying in computer science: "garbage in, garbage out."

At this point, your worksheet should closely resemble the one pictured in Exhibit 1-5.

EXHIBIT 1-5
ANALYSIS OF MICROSOFT'S GROWTH RATES

	A	B	C	D	E	F	G
1		Microsoft Corporation Profitability Analysis					
2		(Millions of Dollars)					
3		2000 to 2005					
4		*2005*	*2004*	*2003*	*2002*	*2001*	*2000*
5	Sales	39,788.00	36,835.00	32,187.00	28,365.00	25,296.00	22,956.00
6	Net Income	12,254.00	8,168.00	7,531.00	5,355.00	7,346.40	9,421.00
7	Net Profit Margin	30.80%	22.17%	23.40%	18.88%	29.04%	41.04%
8	Sales Growth	11.63%					
9	Net Income Growth	5.40%					
10	% Change in Sales	1.0802	1.1444	1.1347	1.1213	1.1019	
11	Sales Growth	11.63%					

Using the Insert Function Dialog Box

With the hundreds of built-in functions that are available in Excel, it can be difficult to remember the name of the one you want to use, the order of the arguments, and so forth. To help you with this problem, Excel provides the Insert Function dialog box, a series of dialog boxes that guide you through the process of selecting and entering a built-in formula.

fx

Let's use Insert Function to insert the **GEOMEAN** function into B11. First, Select cell B11 and then clear the current formula by choosing Edit Clear All from the menus (or, press the Delete key on the keyboard). Find the Insert Function button (pictured at left) on the Formula Bar. Click this button to bring up the first Insert Function dialog box.

In the first dialog box, click on Statistical in the "select a category" list. The "Select a function" list will now contain all of the built-in statistical functions. Scroll down this list and click on **GEOMEAN**. Notice that there is a definition of the function at the bottom of the dialog box. Click on the OK button to change to the next dialog box, which is pictured in Figure 1-9.[6]

FIGURE 1-9
THE EXCEL 2003 FUNCTION ARGUMENTS DIALOG BOX

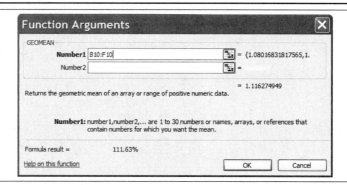

In the second dialog box you will see prompts and definitions for each of the inputs to the selected function. In this case, we want to click and drag the mouse over the B10:F10 range. This range will appear in the "Number 1" edit box. Click on the OK button to have the function entered. Notice that the result is 1.1163, not the 0.1163 that we expected. We need to subtract 1 from the result of the function, so click in the Formula Bar and type: −1 after the **GEOMEAN** function and then press Enter. The formula in B11 should be: =Geomean(B10:F10)−1.

Insert Function is an easy way to discover new functions and to use familiar ones. Using it will make Excel much easier for you to learn.

Using Function Macros

There are times when you need to calculate a complex function and Excel doesn't have a built-in function that will do the job. In this case you can either type the formula into a cell (which can be very tedious) or use a function macro. A *function macro* is similar to a built-in function, except that it was created by somebody other

---

6. Note that this dialog box is frequently in the way of your work. You may click and drag any portion of the dialog box to move it out of the way.

than the Excel development team at Microsoft. You can purchase macro functions, download them from the Internet, or create your own. Writing function macros in Excel's macro language (Visual Basic for Applications, see Chapter 13) is beyond the scope of this chapter, but several functions have been included in the Famefncs.xla file that can be found on the official Web site for this book. Download the file and save it to your hard drive in an easy-to-remember location. These functions will be used occasionally throughout the book.

Before using the function, you must open Famefncs.xla. This file is a special type of Excel file known as an add-in. An add-in can be opened just like any other Excel file, or it can be set to open automatically every time you start Excel. To make the functions in this file available at all times, go to Tools Add-Ins. This will open the Add-Ins dialog box as pictured in Figure 1-10.

FIGURE 1-10
THE ADD-INS DIALOG BOX

Click the Browse button, navigate to the directory where you saved the file, and choose Famefncs.xla. It will be added to the Add-Ins dialog box as shown above, and the functions in the file will now be available to use in all of your worksheets.

Using a function macro is almost exactly the same as using a built-in function. The only difference is that the file containing the functions must be opened in order for the functions to be known to Excel. You can even use the Insert Function dialog box with macro functions (select the User Defined function category).

As an example of the use of function macros, we have created a macro to calculate the geometric mean rate of growth of sales from the dollar amounts. The macro is defined as:[7]

FAME_GEOMEAN(SALES)

FAME_GEOMEAN is the name of the function, and **SALES** is the required range of cells that contain the sales figures. The function automatically calculates the formula given in equation (1-1).

Now, in your original worksheet, select cell B12 and then bring up the Insert Function dialog box. From the "select a category" list, choose User Defined to display a list of the functions that were supplied with this book. In the "Select a function" list, select the macro named **FAME_GEOMEAN** and then click the OK button. In the edit box for Dollar Values, enter: `B5:G5` which is the range that contains Microsoft's sales. Click on the OK button and see that the answer is exactly the same as before. The function in B12 is: `=FAME_Geomean(B5:G5)`.

Creating Graphics

In our simple profitability analysis, it is obvious that Microsoft's profit margins have been increasing in the last three years. Many times, you will build much more complicated worksheets where the key trends are not so easy to spot; especially for others, who didn't build the worksheet. You may also find that you need to give a presentation, perhaps to a group of investors to convince them to invest in your firm. In cases such as these, tables full of numbers may actually obscure your point. People (and students too!) tend to get a glazed look in their eyes when examining tables of numbers. The solution to this problem is to present a chart of the numbers to illustrate your point. Fortunately, high-quality graphics are a snap with Excel.

There are two ways that charts can be created in Excel: in separate chart sheets, or embedded in the worksheet. We will cover each of these methods in turn.

---

7. This function was written specifically to calculate a compound average growth rate from dollar values. It does not duplicate Excel's **GEOMEAN** function, so do not use it as a substitute for that function.

Creating Charts in a Chart Sheet

Before the advent of graphical user interfaces (GUIs), worksheets and graphics were separate entities. The original Lotus 1-2-3 actually used a separate program to create charts of worksheet data. Today, charts are usually created within the main program. In Excel, we can create a stand-alone chart, separate from the worksheet by selecting the data and inserting a new chart sheet. Excel will then help you to create the chart with the Chart Wizard. Let's try creating a graph of Sales versus Net Income for Microsoft.

First select the data in the A5:G6 range and then right-click the tab for the current worksheet (which is probably labeled "Sheet 1"). From the menu that appears, choose Insert. You will now be presented with a list of different file types from which to select. Since we want to create a chart, select Chart from the list and press Enter or click OK.

The Chart Wizard will guide you through the process of creating the chart. The first dialog box asks you to choose the type of chart. In this case, a column chart probably best suits the data, so choose the Column type by double-clicking on it. The second dialog box asks for your data range; if you have selected A5:G6 the range will already be in the edit box. Note that the example of the chart shows that the X-axis is labeled with the numbers 1 through 6. Since it would be better to have the years on the X-axis, we need to specify the location of the X-axis labels. Click the Series tab, pictured in Figure 1-11, and enter the range into the edit box labeled "Category (X) axis labels." Note that you have to be very specific if you choose to type in the date range. You must type the range in the form: =Sheet1!B4:G4.[8] Alternatively, you can simply click in the edit box and then select the range using the mouse. You'll see that the axis is now correctly labeled.

---

8. Simply typing B4:G4 will not work. Excel will interpret this as the label for the first data point. Therefore, you must include the name of the worksheet in the range.

FIGURE 1-11
THE SOURCE DATA DIALOG BOX OF THE CHART WIZARD

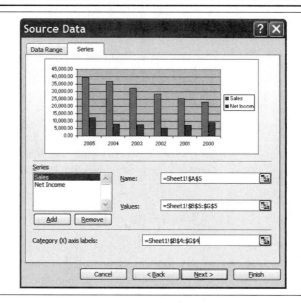

Click the Next button, and you are asked to enter a chart title and titles for the axes. For the chart title enter: Microsoft Sales vs. Net Income. For the X-axis enter: Years. For the Y-axis enter: Millions of Dollars.

Click the Finish button, and Excel will open a new chart sheet with a chart resembling that in Exhibit 1-6.

EXHIBIT 1-6
A STAND-ALONE CHART

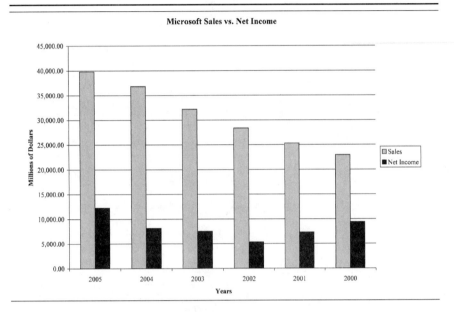

Microsoft Sales vs. Net Income

Creating Embedded Charts

You may want to create a chart that will be saved and displayed within the worksheet itself. Such a chart is referred to as an "embedded chart" because it appears within the worksheet. Unlike a stand-alone chart sheet, embedded charts can be displayed and printed on the same page as the worksheet data. Furthermore, embedded charts don't require any extra steps to display them. Once created, embedded charts are always opened and closed along with the worksheet automatically. If necessary, embedded charts can be saved and printed separately from the worksheet.

To create an embedded chart, first switch to Sheet 1. Now select the data as before, click on the Chart Wizard button (on the Toolbar; see icon in margin), and follow the prompts exactly as you did to create the stand-alone chart. The chart will appear in the middle of your worksheet. To resize the chart, click and drag any of the selection boxes on its perimeter. To move the chart, click on a blank area inside the chart and drag it to wherever you want it to be. Your worksheet should now resemble the one in Exhibit 1-7, except for some minor formatting changes.

Note that you can change your embedded chart into a stand-alone chart sheet, and vice versa. There is no need to invoke the Chart Wizard. Just right-click in the chart and choose <u>L</u>ocation from the shortcut menu. You can even move your chart to a different worksheet in this way.

EXHIBIT 1-7
A WORKSHEET WITH AN EMBEDDED CHART

	A	B	C	D	E	F	G
1		Microsoft Corporation Profitability Analysis					
2		(Millions of Dollars)					
3		2000 to 2005					
4		*2005*	*2004*	*2003*	*2002*	*2001*	*2000*
5	Sales	39,788.00	36,835.00	32,187.00	28,365.00	25,296.00	22,956.00
6	Net Income	12,254.00	8,168.00	7,531.00	5,355.00	7,346.40	9,421.00
7	Net Profit Margin	30.80%	22.17%	23.40%	18.88%	29.04%	41.04%
8	Sales Growth	11.63%					
9	Net Income Growth	5.40%					
10	% Change in Sales	1.0802	1.1444	1.1347	1.1213	1.1019	
11	Sales Growth	11.63%					
12							
13							
14							
15							
16							
17							
18							
19							
20							
21							

Microsoft Sales vs. Net Income

Formatting Charts

We have now created a basic chart of Sales versus Net Income, but it probably isn't quite what you expected. First of all, we normally expect that the most recent data in a chart is at the right side and the oldest at the left. Because we have created our worksheet data in the opposite direction, our chart is backward, and a quick glance might suggest that sales and profits have been declining.

In Excel, every element of a chart is treated as a separate "object." This means that each element can be selected and edited separately from the other elements. In addition, these chart objects are somewhat intelligent. They "know" what actions can be performed on them and will present a menu of these actions if you click on them with the right mouse button. The major objects in any chart include each data series, the plot area, the gridlines, the axes, the axis titles, the chart title, and any other text strings entered into the chart. To select an object, all you need to do is to click on it with the left mouse button. Once the object is selected, it will be redisplayed with small squares (selection boxes) surrounding it. With this knowledge, let's edit our chart.

First, we want to turn the x-axis around so that the data are presented in the order that we normally expect. Click on the x-axis (or axis labels) with the right mouse button to cause the shortcut menu to appear. You will know that the x-axis is selected when you see a small square at both ends of the axis. The shortcut menu will be different depending on which graphic object you click on, so it is important to click directly on the x-axis or the labels.

Once the menu appears, choose Format Axis and then click on the Scale tab. From the resulting dialog box, select "Categories in reverse order" and press Enter. Notice that the x-axis has reversed, but the y-axis is now on the right side of the chart. That doesn't look right, so go back to the Scale tab and click on "Value (Y) axis crosses at maximum category." We could have checked both of these boxes at the same time.

If you did not add the titles in the Chart Wizard, adding a title and axis labels to our chart simply requires a menu choice and a little typing. To add a chart title, select Chart Chart Options from the menus and then enter the titles in the appropriate edit boxes. You can also access the Chart Options dialog box by right-clicking in a blank area of the chart and choosing Chart Options from the shortcut menu. You can now edit the titles directly in the chart by selecting them, or you can return to the Chart Options dialog box.

Suppose, for example, that we wanted to change the title so that it mentions the years that are covered by the data. Simply click on the title in the chart to select it, then click at the end of the title. You could begin typing immediately, but we want to put the new text on a second line. Press Enter to begin a new line, then type: 2000 to 2005 and press the Esc key or click anywhere else on the chart.

Next, let's move the legend to the bottom of the chart to see if it looks better there. Click on the legend with the right mouse button, and choose Format Legend from the shortcut menu. Now, select the Placement tab and select Bottom from the choices. Press the Enter key to return to the chart. Now the plot area of the chart looks squashed. To fix this, click in the plot area to select it and drag the selection boxes until the plot area is the proper size.

To return to editing the worksheet, click anywhere in the worksheet. Your worksheet should now resemble the one in Exhibit 1-8.

EXHIBIT 1-8
WORKSHEET WITH REFORMATTED CHART

	A	B	C	D	E	F	G
1		Microsoft Corporation Profitability Analysis					
2		(Millions of Dollars)					
3		2000 to 2005					
4		*2005*	*2004*	*2003*	*2002*	*2001*	*2000*
5	Sales	39,788.00	36,835.00	32,187.00	28,365.00	25,296.00	22,956.00
6	Net Income	12,254.00	8,168.00	7,531.00	5,355.00	7,346.40	9,421.00
7	Net Profit Margin	30.80%	22.17%	23.40%	18.88%	29.04%	41.04%
8	Sales Growth	11.63%					
9	Net Income Growth	5.40%					
10	% Change in Sales	1.0802	1.1444	1.1347	1.1213	1.1019	
11	Sales Growth	11.63%					
12							
13							
14							
15							
16							
17							
18							
19							
20							
21							

Changing the Chart Type

Excel offers many different types of charts, everything from the bar chart that we have created to three-dimensional bar charts and radar plots. Some of these chart types are very sophisticated, even allowing you to rotate them to see a different view of the data.[9] Despite these potential complexities, changing the chart type is very straightforward.

Let's assume that we would prefer to see the data in our chart presented as two lines, rather than as columns. To make this change, right-click on a blank area around the outside edge of the chart and choose Chart **T**ype from the menu. Select a type of

9. You can learn about the types of charts that Excel can create, complete with examples, at http://office.microsoft.com/en-us/assistance/HP052623191033.aspx.

line chart, and click on the OK button. The chart is now displayed as a line chart. You can even change the individual data series chart type. For example, you might want to see Sales as a column chart and Net Income as a line on the same chart. Give it a try. Simply right-click on the Net Income data series and change the chart type to a line. To try other types of charts, be sure to select the Custom tab of the Chart Wizard.

You can also change other formatting in the chart very easily. For example, to change the color of the bars for Sales, simply right-click on one of the data points and choose F̲ormat Data Series. On the Patterns tab you can choose a different color, and it will be applied to each of the bars for that data series. You can also change the border around the bars and add a shadow for a three-dimensional effect.

Printing

Many times, a worksheet displayed on-screen accomplishes all that you need. At other times, there is no escaping the need for a hard copy. Excel makes printing a worksheet both easy and flexible. For small worksheets, all that need be done is to choose F̲ile P̲rint from the menus and let Excel take care of the details. Larger printing tasks are only slightly more complex.

Suppose that our profitability analysis of Microsoft needs to be printed so that it can be distributed at a meeting. As a first step, we need to decide if we want to print the entire worksheet, or only a portion of it. In this case, let's assume that we wish to print the whole worksheet, except that we want to print the graph on a separate page so that it can more easily be converted to an overhead transparency.

Because we wish to print the numbers and chart separately, we need to tell Excel the range of cells that we want printed. Select the range A1:G11 and then choose F̲ile Prin̲t Area S̲et Print Area from the menus. Notice that a light gray dashed line now surrounds the range that we have selected for printing. Before actually printing a worksheet, it is good practice to preview the output to make sure that it looks exactly like you want it to look. This will save both time and paper. From the F̲ile menu, select Print Prev̲iew. Excel will now display, on the screen, a likeness of the actual printed page.

If you have followed the examples to this point, you might, depending on the kind of printer you are using and the font size, notice that our worksheet is too wide to fit on one page. Since we would ideally like to fit the whole worksheet on one page, we have some adjustments to make. Essentially we have two options: either change the page orientation to print sideways (i.e., landscape mode) or have Excel reduce the printout to fit on one page. Each of these methods is equally viable, but let's go for the reduction to one page.

From the Print Preview mode, we can press the Setup button to change various options for printing. Clicking on Setup brings up the Page Setup dialog box. This dialog box may also be reached from outside of Print Preview by choosing Page Setup from the File menu. There are many options available in this dialog box, but the Scaling options are what we want now. Click on the Page tab and then select Fit to: __ pages wide by __ tall, and enter a 1 in both boxes. We also don't want the gridlines to print. Click on the Sheet tab and make sure that the Cell Gridlines option is deselected (no check mark in the box.) Press the Enter key to return to Print Preview. Before actually printing the worksheet, it is a good idea to zoom in and check more closely that it looks the way we want it to look. To zoom in, simply click on the page. Your view will now be enlarged for closer inspection.

At this point, everything should be ready for printing, so click on the "Print..." button. Excel now returns to the normal view and presents you with the Print dialog box. Because we want to print the whole range that we have selected, make sure your printer is ready (turned on, has paper, etc.) and click on the OK button. Your page should look nearly identical to the on-screen version.

To print the chart on a separate page, we first need to click on it so that it is selected. Now, to print the chart, simply select File Print and then from the Print dialog box, click on the OK button. Presto! The chart prints out on its own page. Of course, you can use Print Preview and Page Setup for charts, just as we did for the worksheet.

What if you wanted to print the chart on the same page as the worksheet? Simple; just select the entire range that you want to print, including the chart. Now repeat the steps from above, and the worksheet and chart will print on the same page. An easier alternative is to select the range to print, choose File Print, and make sure that Selection is selected in the Print What section of the Print dialog box. Now, click on the OK button.

Saving and Opening Files

Now that we have created a worksheet, you should save it so that it will be available at a later time. To save this file, choose **F**ile Save **A**s… from the menus. This will cause a dialog box to be displayed that allows you to supply a name for the file and the location where you would like it stored.

After saving a file, you can open it at any time by choosing **F**ile **O**pen… from the menus. This will cause a dialog box to be displayed, from which you may select the file. Once a file has been named and saved the first time, you may save further changes by choosing **F**ile **S**ave.

Note that you can change the default directory that Excel will open first. Go to **T**ools **O**ptions and select the General tab. Enter the full path to the directory in the **D**efault file location edit box. Instead of typing the path, you may find it easier to open the directory in Windows Explorer and the copy the path from the address bar. Now, return to the dialog box and press Ctrl+v to paste it in the edit box.

Saving Worksheets for the Internet

In addition to saving worksheets in Excel's native file format, you can also save files as a Web page for the Internet in HTML format. Even better, the HTML file can be reopened and edited in Excel 2003 without losing any formatting. To save a file in HTML format, choose **F**ile Save as Web Pa**g**e. In the dialog box, you simply give the page a name and select the location. Click the OK button, and you've created a Web version of your worksheet. Note that the dialog box also allows you to enter a title for the page by clicking the **C**hange Title button. This title will appear in your browser's title bar when the page is displayed.

Finally, you can also post the worksheet directly to your Web site by clicking the **P**ublish button. On the Publish as Web Page dialog box, enter the address of your Web server (or FTP site) in the File **n**ame edit box. You can also add nearly complete functionality to your page by checking the box labeled "**A**dd interactivity with:".

Using Excel with Other Applications

Suppose that you are writing a report on the profitability of Microsoft for the past six years. Chances are good that you are writing the report in one of the major word processing programs. Your word processor probably allows for the creation of tables that can display all of the information that you have created in Excel, but it lacks the computational sophistication and graphics power of Excel. Similarly, Excel lacks the text processing power that you need to write the report. Fortunately, it is very easy to harness the strengths of both programs and combine the results.

While some word processors will read Excel files directly from your disk, this is not usually the easiest way to incorporate spreadsheets into your word processing files. Instead, it is usually easiest to use some variant of copy and paste, just like we've used within Excel itself. Every time you copy data from Excel, it goes to the clipboard. The contents of the clipboard are available to any other application that is used to access them. All you need to do is copy the data from within Excel, switch to the other application, and then choose **E**dit **P**aste from its menus.

Simply pasting the Excel data into a word processor usually results in the word processor reading the data and creating a table. While this may be all that you need, many times it would be more convenient if you could still edit the data in its native environment. In other words, it would be nice if you could still take advantage of Excel's built-in functions and recalculation ability. You can. Instead of using **E**dit **P**aste, use **E**dit Paste **S**pecial.

The Paste Special command allows much more freedom in how the data is stored inside the word processor. For example, if you choose to paste the data as an "Microsoft Excel Worksheet Object," you will be able to edit the data from within the word processor by simply double-clicking on it. The menus and toolbars of your word processor will change to those of Excel, and you can edit the data exactly as if you were in Excel. This process is known as Object Linking and Embedding (OLE).

Alternatively, you can link the data to your worksheet so that when you make changes in Excel, they are automatically reflected in your word processor. Finally, you can paste a non-editable picture of your data into your document. Either of these last two methods will consume less memory than embedding the worksheet with the OLE technique.

Quitting Excel

To exit from Excel, you can either select **F**ile E**x**it from the menus or double-click on the system menu box in the upper left corner of the Excel window. Note that if you attempt to exit Excel without saving your work, Excel will warn you and ask if you would like to save the file.

Creating Good Spreadsheet Models

A spreadsheet model (specifically a financial model in this book) is simply a spreadsheet that is designed to solve a particular problem. A properly designed model requires a good deal of thought even before the first formula is written. It should be functional, flexible, easy to use, and nice looking. While we cannot tell you what font you should use, we can provide several rules that are common to good spreadsheet design.

1. Create an area specifically for the variables (inputs) in the model. The input area should be separate from the calculation area whenever possible. If there are a lot of variables, then the input area should be on a separate worksheet. This will make it easy to change the assumptions behind the model.

2. Do not enter a number directly into a formula, unless it will never change. Numbers that may be changed should be entered into the input area, or calculated if possible. This will help to minimize errors in the model, and it greatly simplifies the changing of assumptions. It is much better to change a number in one cell than to have to remember to change it in five formulas.

3. Your model should be well organized and nicely formatted. This will not only help you to minimize errors but also make the model easier for others to understand. A haphazardly created model may return the correct answers, but it will be difficult to understand. Even if nobody else will ever see your spreadsheet, you will probably have to look it over in the future. The effort that you expend in designing the model will be paid back many times over in future time savings.

4. If your formulas are long or use complex logic, make sure to document them. A simple explanatory cell comment (**I**nsert Co**m**ment) or a textbox describing the logic of the model can save

enormous effort when debugging formulas. Writing your own function macros in Visual Basic for Applications (VBA; see Chapter 13) can help to simplify your model, particularly if the formula is needed in several places.

5. Always test your model thoroughly before declaring it finished. While your model may produce correct answers for your expected input values, it may not work properly in every conceivable case. It is important to change your inputs several times and verify the output. Make sure to use some numbers that don't seem realistic to see what happens. This will often uncover errors in formula logic. Your formulas should be written so that they can handle anything that you may throw at them. **IF** statements are quite useful in this regard.

Keep these five rules in mind when building your models, and you will be much more productive—and less likely to create flawed models.

Summary

In this chapter we have discussed the basics of Microsoft Excel. You should have gained a basic understanding of such topics as entering text and numbers, entering formulas, formatting, graphics, and printing. We also discussed some important considerations for designing spreadsheet models.

In the chapters ahead, we will cover many of these topics in more depth. We will, at the same time, introduce you to financial analysis and how Excel can make this analysis easier and more productive. Along the way, we hope to help you develop the reasoning, critical thinking, and quantitative skills that are so necessary in the field of finance today.

FUNCTIONS INTRODUCED IN THIS CHAPTER

Purpose	Function	Page
Calculate the geometric mean	**GEOMEAN**(*NUMBER1*, *NUMBER2*,...)	22
Calculate the arithmetic mean	**AVERAGE**(*NUMBER1*, *NUMBER2*,...)	22
An alternate way to calculate the geometric mean using dollar values	**FAME_GEOMEAN**(*SALES*)	26

Problems

1. Suppose that at the beginning of January 2000, you purchased shares in Advanced Micro Devices, Inc. (NYSE: AMD). It is now five years later, and you decide to evaluate your holdings to see if you have done well with this investment. The table below shows the market prices of AMD.

AMD Stock Prices	
Date	Price
2000	13.81
2001	15.86
2002	6.46
2003	14.90
2004	22.02
2005	30.60

   a. Enter the data, as shown, into a worksheet and format the table as shown.

   b. Create a formula to calculate your rate of return for each year. Format the results as percentages with two decimal places.

   c. Calculate the total return for the entire holding period. What is the compound average annual rate of return?

   d. Create a line chart showing the stock price from January 2000 to January 2005. Make sure to title the chart and label the axes.

   e. Experiment with the formatting possibilities of the chart. For example, you might try changing the line to a three-dimensional line and filling the plot area with a marble background.

2. In your position as research assistant to a portfolio manager, you need to analyze the profitability of the companies in the portfolio. Using the data for Exxon Mobil Corporation below:

Fiscal Year	2005	2004	2003	2002	2001
Total Revenue	370,998	291,252	237,054	200,949	208,715
Net Income	36,130	25,330	21,510	11,460	15,320

a. Calculate the net profit margin for each year.

b. Calculate the average annual growth rates for revenue and net income using the **GEOMEAN** function. Is net income growing more slowly or faster than total revenue? Is this a positive for your investment in the company?

c. Calculate the average annual growth rate of total revenue using the **AVERAGE** function. Is this result more or less accurate than your result in the previous question? Why?

d. Create a column chart of total revenue and net income. Be sure to change the chart so that the x-axis labels contain the year numbers, and format the axis so that 2005 is on the far right side of the axis.

3. Repeat Problem 2 using the data below for the 3M Company. However, this time you should create a copy of your worksheet to use as a template. Replace the data for Exxon Mobil with that of 3M.

Fiscal Year	2005	2004	2003	2002	2001
Total Revenue	21,167	20,011	18,232	16,332	16,054
Net Income	3,199	2,990	2.403	1,974	1,430

a. Do you think that 3M can maintain the current growth rates of sales and net income over the long run? Why or why not?

b. Which company was more profitable in 2005? Which was more profitable if you take a longer view? Would this affect your desire to invest in one company over the other?

4. Using the data for Cullen/Frost Bankers (NYSE: CFR) presented below:

Fiscal Year	2005	2004	2003	2002	2001
Sales	$740.20	$618.70	$584.30	$590.60	$653.90
EBIT	362.90	271.20	247.70	255.90	281.10
Net Income	165.40	141.30	130.50	117.00	80.90
Dividends/Share	1.17	1.04	0.94	0.88	0.84
Basic EPS	3.15	2.74	2.54	2.29	1.51
Diluted EPS	3.07	2.66	2.48	2.23	1.51
Total Assets	11,741.40	9,952.80	9,672.10	9,552.30	8,369.60
Long-term Debt	415.40	377.70	255.80	248.10	250.80
Total Liabilities	10,759.20	9,130.40	8,902.10	8,848.50	7,774.70
Common Equity	982.20	822.40	770.00	703.80	594.90
Oper. Cash Flow	132.40	128.80	202.40	272.20	97.60
Free Cash Flow	39.50	52.50	140.60	186.60	31.80

a. Calculate the ratio of the latest year to the previous year data for each of the above items for Cullen/Frost Bankers (CFR is the ticker symbol). For example: for year 2005, the ratio for sales is $740.2/$618.7 = 1.1964.

b. From your calculations in part A, calculate each year's rate of growth. Using the example in part A, the ratio is 1.1964, so the percentage growth in sales for 2005 is 1.1964 − 1 or 19.64%.

c. Calculate the average growth rate (using the AVERAGE function) of each of the above items using the results you calculated in part B. These averages are arithmetic averages.

d. Use the GEOMEAN function to estimate the compound annual growth rate (CAGR) for each of the above items using the results you calculate in part A. Be sure to subtract 1 from the result of the GEOMEAN function to arrive at a percent change. These averages are geometric averages.

e. Compare the results from part C (arithmetic averages using the **AVERAGE** function) to those for part D (geometric averages using the **GEOMEAN** function) for each item. Is it true that the arithmetic average growth rate is always greater than or equal to the geometric average (CAGR)?

f. Contrast the results for the geometric averages to those for the arithmetic average for the variables listed below. What do you observe about the differences in the two growth estimates for Sales and Diluted EPS? What do you observe about the differences in the two estimates for Net Cash from Operating Activities and Free Cash Flows? Hint: Look at the results from part B (the individual yearly growth rates) for each variable to draw some conclusions about the variation between the arithmetic and geometric averages.

   1. Sales

   2. EBIT

   3. Diluted EPS

   4. Operating cash flow

   5. Free cash flow

Internet Exercise

1. Choose your own company and repeat the analysis from Problem 3. You can get the data from MoneyCentral Investor at http://moneycentral.msn.com/investor/home.asp. To retrieve the data for your company, go to the Stocks area and enter the ticker symbol. Now choose Financial Results and then Statements from the menu on the left side of the screen. Display the annual income statement, and copy the sales and net income data. Now enter the data into your template.

CHAPTER 2

The Basic Financial Statements

After studying this chapter, you should be able to:

1. *Explain the purpose and understand the format of the firm's three basic financial statements: the income statement, the balance sheet, and the statement of cash flows.*

2. *Construct each of these statements in Excel with data for any company.*

3. *Link worksheets together so that formulas in one worksheet can reference data in another.*

4. *Use Excel's Outline tool to selectively display or hide parts of a financial statement.*

Much of financial analysis takes as its starting point the basic financial statements of the firm. It is therefore crucial that the analyst have a strong fundamental understanding of these statements. There are three basic financial statements:

1. The *income statement* summarizes the results of the firm's operations over a period of time. The income statement tells us the total revenues and expenses for the time period, and also contains several different measures of the accounting profits earned by the firm. Typically, income statements are prepared for different time periods, usually monthly, quarterly, and annually.

2. The *balance sheet* describes the assets, liabilities, and equity of the firm at a specific point in time. Assets are the (tangible or intangible) things that a firm owns. Liabilities are the firm's debts. Equity is the difference between what the firm owns and what it owes to others. Because the balance sheet is specific to a point in time, it is much like a photograph. What it shows was true when the snapshot was taken, but it is not necessarily true when it is viewed.

3. The *statement of cash flows* outlines the sources of the firm's cash inflows and shows where the cash outflows went. Activities that bring cash into the firm are referred to as *sources* of cash, while those that take cash out of the firm are referred to as *uses* of cash.

In this chapter we will build each of these three statements for Elvis Products International, a small producer of Elvis memorabilia. Each financial statement will be created in its own worksheet in the workbook, and we will create links between the sheets as necessary. Before beginning, open a new workbook.

The Income Statement

The income statement is a fairly simple document that begins by listing a firm's revenues (perhaps by sources or in total) followed by all of the firm's expenses. The result of the income statement is the net income for the period. Net income represents the accounting profit left over after all expenses have been paid from the revenue for the period.

Building an Income Statement in Excel

Exhibit 2-1 presents the income statement for Elvis Products International (EPI) for the year ending December 31, 2007. We will build this income statement first, and then use it as a base for creating the 2006 income statement.

EXHIBIT 2-1
EPI'S INCOME STATEMENT FOR 2007 AND 2006

	A	B	C
1	Elvis Products International		
2	Income Statement		
3	For the Year Ended Dec. 31, 2007		
4		*2007*	*2006*
5	Sales	3,850,000	3,432,000
6	Cost of Goods Sold	3,250,000	2,864,000
7	*Gross Profit*	*600,000*	*568,000*
8	Selling and G&A Expenses	330,300	240,000
9	Fixed Expenses	100,000	100,000
10	Depreciation Expense	20,000	18,900
11	*EBIT*	*149,700*	*209,100*
12	Interest Expense	76,000	62,500
13	*Earnings Before Taxes*	*73,700*	*146,600*
14	Taxes	29,480	58,640
15	*Net Income*	*44,220*	*87,960*
16			
17	Notes:		
18	Tax Rate	40%	

Principle 1:
Make Excel do as much of the work as possible. Whenever possible, a formula should be used rather than entering numbers. In the long run this will minimize errors.

Principle 2:
Format the worksheet so that it is easy to understand. Borders, shading, and font choices are more than just decorations. Properly chosen, they can make important numbers stand out and get the attention they deserve.

While we are building the income statement, we want to keep a couple of general principles in mind. Principle 1 says that we want to make Excel do as much of the work as possible. Any time a value can be calculated, we should use Excel to do so. The reasoning behind this principle is that we want to avoid mistakes and increase productivity. A little thought before beginning the design of a worksheet can help to minimize data entry errors and increase productivity by reducing the amount of data that needs to be entered. Principle 2 says that we should format the worksheet in such a way as to make it easy to comprehend. There are many times that you will be creating a worksheet for others to use, or for your own use at a later date. Properly organizing the cells and judicious use of color and fonts can make the worksheet easier to use and modify.[1] Worksheets that are disorganized and sloppily formatted do not engender faith in their results.

---

1. We would like to emphasize the word "judicious." Some people overuse fonts and end up producing documents with a definite ransom-note appearance. Do yourself, and others, a favor by limiting your use of fonts to one or two per document.

It is usually helpful when working with multiple worksheets in a workbook for each sheet to be given a name other than the default. With the right mouse button, click on the sheet tab labeled "Sheet1." From the menu choose Rename and then enter: Income Statement when prompted for the new name of the sheet. This step is important because when we later begin referencing data on this sheet, the references will require the name of the sheet in addition to the cell reference. Note, however, that you can always rename the sheet later, and any formulas referencing it will automatically be updated.[2]

We will begin building the income statement with the titles in A1:A3. Remember, if the need arises, we can always insert new rows or columns into the worksheet at a later time. In A1 type: Elvis Products International; in A2: Income Statement; in A3: For the Year Ended Dec. 31, 2007. The first line of the title identifies the company, the second identifies the type of statement, and the third identifies the time period that the statement covers. Now center the titles by selecting A1:C3, choose Format Cells, select the Alignment tab, and then select "Center Across Selection" under Horizontal. Note that Excel provides an icon on the formatting toolbar that is titled "Merge and Center" and accomplishes a similar alignment. However, in addition to centering the titles over the selected columns, it also merges the cells into one. This creates a problem if we later decide to insert a new column. In general, you should never use the Merge and Center icon.

How to proceed from this point is largely a matter of preference. We could move line by line through the income statement, entering a label followed by the value. An alternative is to enter all of the labels and then all of the numbers. The second method seems preferable at this point so that we may concentrate on the numbers. The labels are going to be stored in column A, and the numbers will be in column B. It is good practice to enter a label indicating the end of the period above the data, so move to B4 and type: 2007.

Beginning in A5, enter the labels exactly as they appear in Exhibit 2-1. Once you have entered the labels, you are likely to find that some of these labels are too long to fit in only one cell. To remedy this problem, we need to change the width of column A. There are several ways to accomplish this in Excel. The slowest method is to select the whole column (click on the column header), choose Format Column Width, and

---

2. This is always true for references within the same workbook. However, suppose that we have two workbooks called X and Y. If X contains a reference to a cell in Y, it will be updated automatically as long as both workbooks are open. If X is closed when the sheet name is changed in Y, then you will see a #REF! error the next time you open X and will have to manually change the reference.

enter: 30 in the column width edit box. If you are using some font other than 12-point Times New Roman, you will have to experiment with different numbers to find the appropriate width for the column. Instead of entering a specific number for the column width, we can also let Excel determine the appropriate width. Select column A, and choose Format Column Autofit Selection, and Excel will automatically make the column wide enough to accommodate the longest text in the column.

As usual, there is an alternative for mouse users. If you slowly move the mouse pointer over the column headers, you will notice that the pointer changes its shape (to that pictured at left) as it passes over the boundary between columns. Press the left mouse button while the pointer is over this boundary, and drag until the column is wide enough to accommodate the text. You can also double-click on the column boundary, and Excel will set the column width to the best fit for the data. Each of these techniques can also be used to change the height of a row.

When entering data for large companies, it is often preferable to display the numbers in thousands or millions of dollars, rather than the full amount. For EPI, we will enter the numbers in full precision and later apply a custom number format. Move to B5 and enter: 3,850,000.[3] Keeping principle 2 in mind, we would like the numbers to be displayed with commas and no decimal places. Since each cell can maintain a number format, regardless of whether it contains any numbers, we will preformat the cells that we are going to use. Select cells B5:C15, choose Format Cells from the menus, click on the Number tab, and click the Number category. Now set the number of decimal places to 0 and make sure to click on Use 1000 Separator. When we enter numbers into these cells, they will automatically take on the format that we want.

Move to B6 and type: 3,250,000 for Cost of Goods Sold. This is the total cost of the products sold to customers, including inventory shrinkage and write-downs for damaged or outdated products. Notice that, as promised, the number in B6 appears with commas.

Gross profit is the amount that is left over after paying for the goods that were sold. To calculate gross profit, we subtract cost of goods sold from sales. Again, we want Excel to make all of the calculations, so in B7 type: =B5-B6. Selling, General and Administrative (SG&A) Expense is an input, so enter: 330,300 in B8. Fixed

3. There is no need for you to type the commas. We are showing them here for clarity. However, Excel will accept the numbers with commas if you wish to type them in.

expenses (rent, salaries, etc.) for the period are an input, so enter: 100,000 in B9. Depreciation is also an input in this case, so in B10 enter: 20,000.

Earnings Before Interest and Taxes (EBIT) is gross profit less all remaining expenses other than interest and taxes. Any of several formulas could be used for this calculation; for example, the obvious formula for EBIT in B11 is: =B7-B8-B9-B10. However, obvious formulas aren't always the best. We could simplify this equation somewhat by making use of the **SUM** function. The new formula would be: =B7-Sum(B8:B10). **SUM** is a built-in Excel function that returns the summation of the arguments. **SUM** is defined as:

$$\text{SUM}(\textbf{\textit{NUMBER1}}, \text{NUMBER2}, \ldots)$$

where **NUMBER1** is the first number (or cell address), NUMBER2 is the second, and so on. Excel will also accept ranges of numbers in place of any individual number. There are two advantages of using the **SUM** function in this case: (1) It is faster and more compact; and (2) the range will automatically expand if we insert a new row. The second advantage is the most important. If we add another category of expense by adding another row above row 9, for example, our formula would automatically incorporate the new row by changing to: B7 – Sum (B8:B11). If we used the original formula, we would have to remember to change it after adding the new row.

SUM is one of the more commonly used built-in functions, so common that Microsoft has included the AutoSum button (pictured at left) on the toolbar to automate the summation of rows or columns of numbers. To use the AutoSum button, simply select the cell where you want the formula to be placed and then click the button. Excel will make an intelligent guess about which cells you want included, and it is usually correct. If it guesses wrong, merely select the range that you wish to include, and Excel will make the change. Note that the AutoSum button does not work when you are already in edit mode.

The AutoSum button has proved so popular that its functionality has been improved. If you click the little arrow to the right of the AutoSum button, it will drop down a list of alternative functions. Now you can more quickly use the **AVERAGE**, **COUNT**, **MAX**, or **MIN** functions just by choosing a function from the menu.

In B12 enter: 76,000 for the interest expense. Next, we will calculate Earnings Before Taxes with the formula: =B11-B12 in cell B13. EPI pays taxes at the rate of 40% on taxable income, so in B18 type: 40%. We will calculate the dollar amount of taxes in B14 with: =B13*$B18. Note that this lets us easily change the tax rate without having to edit formulas. Finally, *Net Income* is the profit earned by the firm after all revenues and expenses have been taken into account. To calculate net income, enter: =B13-B14 in cell B15.

As you can see, EPI's net income for the fiscal year 2007 was $44,220. However, for analysis purposes, we normally are not overly concerned with net income. Net income does not accurately represent the funds that a firm has available to spend. In the calculation of net income, we include depreciation expense (and/or other non-cash expenses such as depletion or amortization), which ostensibly accounts for the decline in the value of the long-term assets of the firm. Since nobody actually wrote a check for the depreciation expense, it should be added back to the net income number to give a better, though not complete, picture of the cash flow for the period. Cash flow is the number one concern for financial analysts.

To create EPI's income statement for 2006 doesn't take nearly as much work. First, select B4:B15 and copy the cells using **E**dit **C**opy or the Copy button on the Toolbar. Select C4 and choose **E**dit **P**aste. Don't forget to change C4 to: 2006. Now you have an exact copy of the 2007 income statement. Enter the numbers from Table 2-1 into the appropriate cells.

TABLE 2-1
EPI'S 2006 INCOME AND EXPENSES

Category	Value
Sales	3,432,000
Cost of Goods Sold	2,864,000
SG&A Expenses	240,000
Depreciation Expense	18,900
Interest Expense	62,500

Notice that you only had to enter the new numbers. The formulas are updated and recalculated automatically. So instead of entering 11 cells of formulas or numbers, you only had to enter six numbers and no formulas at all. Your worksheet should now resemble the one in Exhibit 2-1.

The layout of the income statement that we have seen is the one normally used by analysts outside the firm. Those inside the firm will have more information and may find that Excel's Outline display will make the worksheet easier to understand and maintain. To learn about outlining, see page 66.

The Balance Sheet

The balance sheet is usually depicted in two sections: the assets section at the top or left side, and the liabilities and owner's equity section at the bottom or right side. It is important to realize that the balance sheet must balance (thus the name). That is, total assets must equal the sum of total liabilities and total owner's equity. Each of these sections is usually further divided into subsections.

On the asset side, there are two subsections. The *current assets* section describes the value of the firm's short-term assets. "Short-term", in this case, is defined as one year or the time it takes for the asset to go through one cash flow cycle (i.e., from purchase to sale to collection). Typical current assets are cash, accounts receivable, and inventories. *Fixed assets* are those assets with lives longer than one year. Examples of fixed assets include vehicles, property, buildings, and so on.

Like assets, liabilities can be subdivided into two sections. *Current liabilities* are those liabilities that are expected to be retired within one year. Examples are items such as accounts payable, wages payable, and so forth. *Long-term liabilities* are those that will not be paid off within the current year. Generally, long-term liabilities are made up of various types of bonds, bank loans, etc.

Owner's equity represents the difference between the value of the total assets and liabilities of the firm. This part of the balance sheet is subdivided into contributed capital and retained earnings. *Contributed capital* is the investment made by the common and preferred stockholders of the firm. *Retained earnings* is the accumulation of the undistributed profits of the firm.

Building a Balance Sheet in Excel

The process of building a balance sheet in Excel is very similar to building the income statement. We will build EPI's 2007 and 2006 balance sheets, as shown in Exhibit 2-2, for an example.

We will keep EPI's balance sheets in the same workbook, but on a different worksheet, as the income statement. Keeping related data in the same workbook allows for easy referencing. Using separate worksheets allows us to keep the worksheets uncluttered and makes it easier to design worksheets. Click on the "Sheet2" tab with the right mouse button, and select Rename... from the menu. Type: Balance Sheet as the new name for this worksheet.

Enter the labels from Exhibit 2-2 into the blank worksheet. Notice that many of the labels in the balance sheet are indented. There are two ways to accomplish this effect. The method that we usually use, and are using here, is first to type the text into the cell and then to click the "Increase Indent" button on the formatting toolbar (pictured at left).

The alternative is to insert the indented labels into column B instead of column A. This way, by controlling the width of column A, we can control the depth of the indentation. The labels in column A will simply overlap into column B as long as there is no text in the cell to the right.

EXHIBIT 2-2
EPI'S BALANCE SHEET

	A	B	C
1	Elvis Products International		
2	Balance Sheet		
3	As of Dec. 31, 2007		
4	*Assets*	*2007*	*2006*
5	Cash and Equivalents	52,000	57,600
6	Accounts Receivable	402,000	351,200
7	Inventory	836,000	715,200
8	*Total Current Assets*	*1,290,000*	*1,124,000*
9	Plant & Equipment	527,000	491,000
10	Accumulated Depreciation	166,200	146,200
11	*Net Fixed Assets*	*360,800*	*344,800*
12	*Total Assets*	*1,650,800*	*1,468,800*
13	*Liabilities and Owner's Equity*		
14	Accounts Payable	175,200	145,600
15	Short-term Notes Payable	225,000	200,000
16	Other Current Liabilities	140,000	136,000
17	*Total Current Liabilities*	*540,200*	*481,600*
18	Long-term Debt	424,612	323,432
19	*Total Liabilities*	*964,812*	*805,032*
20	Common Stock	460,000	460,000
21	Retained Earnings	225,988	203,768
22	*Total Shareholder's Equity*	*685,988*	*663,768*
23	**Total Liabilities and Owner's Equity**	**1,650,800**	**1,468,800**

In EPI's balance sheet, nearly everything is a direct input, so we won't discuss every cell. The italicized entries are formulas that we will discuss for 2007. The formulas for the 2006 balance sheet can be copied from the 2007 balance sheet. As with the income statement, you should enter the numbers as shown and apply the same number format.

In the assets section, the first formula is for total current assets in B8. This is simply the sum of all of the current asset accounts, so the formula is: =SUM(B5:B7). Next, we calculate EPI's net fixed assets. This is equal to plant and equipment less accumulated depreciation, so in B11 enter: =B9-B10. Finally, calculate total assets by adding the current assets and net fixed assets with the formula: =B8+B11.

The liabilities and owner's equity section is similar. We will calculate several subtotals and then a grand total in B23. Total current liabilities in B17 are calculated with: =SUM(B14:B16). Total liabilities are calculated with the formula: =B17+B18 in B19. Total shareholder's equity is calculated in B22 with: =B20+B21. And, finally, we calculate the total liabilities and owner's equity in B23 with: =B19+B22. Copy these formulas into the appropriate cells in column C to create the 2006 balance sheet.

To achieve the underlining and shading effects pictured in the exhibits, select the cells, then choose Format Cells from the menus, and then click on the Border tab. To set the type of border, first click on the line type on the right side of the dialog, and then click on the location of the line in the Border area of the dialog. If you want to shade the selection, click on the Patterns tab and then select the color and pattern for the shading. It is usually best to make the text in a shaded cell bold so that it can be clearly seen. Before continuing, make sure that your worksheet looks like the one in Exhibit 2-2.

Improving Readability: Custom Number Formats

When the dollar amounts on a financial statement are very large, they can be a little confusing and hard to read. To make the numbers easier to read, we can display them in thousands of dollars using a custom number format. For example, EPI's sales for 2007 were 3,850,000. We can apply a custom number format that will display this amount as 3,850.00. This is commonly done in annual reports, or any other report that lists large dollar amounts.

Return to the Income Statement worksheet and select B5:C15. To create the custom number format, choose Format Cells from the menus. On the Number tab, choose the Custom category. This will allow us to define our own number format. First we choose a predefined number format; here we will choose the "#,##0.00" format from the list. If we add a comma after the format, Excel will display the numbers as if they have been divided by 1,000. Two commas would display the numbers as if they had been divided by 1,000,000, and so on. In the Type edit box, add a single comma after the chosen format so that it looks like "#,##0.00,". Note that Excel will show a sample of what your formatted numbers will look like. The numbers that you have entered will appear to have been divided by 1,000, but this affects only the appearance of the numbers. It is usually better to enter the full number and let Excel format it to look like you wish. The manner in which Excel displays numbers will not affect any calculations. Regardless of the format, Excel always stores numbers with full precision. The format merely changes what we see on the screen, not what is kept in memory. To see the full number, select the cell and look in the formula bar.

Before continuing, edit cell A3 so that it says: For the Year Ended Dec. 31, 2007 ($ in 000's). This will allow anyone looking at your worksheet to instantly understand that the numbers are displayed in thousands. Your income statement should now look like the one in Exhibit 2-3.

EXHIBIT 2-3
THE INCOME STATEMENT WITH A CUSTOM NUMBER FORMAT

	A	B	C
1	Elvis Products International		
2	Income Statement		
3	For the Year Ended Dec. 31, 2007 ($ in 000's)		
4		2007	2006
5	Sales	3,850.00	3,432.00
6	Cost of Goods Sold	3,250.00	2,864.00
7	Gross Profit	600.00	568.00
8	Selling and G&A Expenses	330.30	240.00
9	Fixed Expenses	100.00	100.00
10	Depreciation Expense	20.00	18.90
11	EBIT	149.70	209.10
12	Interest Expense	76.00	62.50
13	Earnings Before Taxes	73.70	146.60
14	Taxes	29.48	58.64
15	Net Income	44.22	87.96
16			
17	Notes:		
18	Tax Rate	40%	

Since the income statement has been reformatted, it only makes sense to use the same number format on the balance sheet. Switch to the Balance Sheet worksheet and select cells B5:C23 (see Exhibit 2-2, page 53). Now, choose Format Cells and go to the Custom category. Select the format that you just created from the list (it should be at the bottom of the list). Finally, change the title in A3 so that it indicates that the dollar amounts are shown in thousands. Your balance sheet should now look like the one in Exhibit 2-4.

EXHIBIT 2-4
THE BALANCE SHEET WITH A CUSTOM NUMBER FORMAT

	A	B	C
1	Elvis Products International		
2	Balance Sheet		
3	As of Dec. 31, 2007		
4	*Assets*	*2007*	*2006*
5	Cash and Equivalents	52.00	57.60
6	Accounts Receivable	402.00	351.20
7	Inventory	836.00	715.20
8	*Total Current Assets*	*1,290.00*	*1,124.00*
9	Plant & Equipment	527.00	491.00
10	Accumulated Depreciation	166.20	146.20
11	*Net Fixed Assets*	*360.80*	*344.80*
12	**Total Assets**	**1,650.80**	**1,468.80**
13	**Liabilities and Owner's Equity**		
14	Accounts Payable	175.20	145.60
15	Short-term Notes Payable	225.00	200.00
16	Other Current Liabilities	140.00	136.00
17	*Total Current Liabilities*	*540.20*	*481.60*
18	Long-term Debt	424.61	323.43
19	*Total Liabilities*	*964.81*	*805.03*
20	Common Stock	460.00	460.00
21	Retained Earnings	225.99	203.77
22	*Total Shareholder's Equity*	*685.99*	*663.77*
23	**Total Liabilities and Owner's Equity**	**1,650.80**	**1,468.80**

Creating your own number formats in Excel is easy, if you understand a few key points. The number format code is a series of wildcard characters. Both the # sign and 0 work as a stand-in for any number. The difference between them is how leading and trailing zeros to the right of the decimal point are handled. The # sign will not display leading or trailing zeros, while 0 will. Generally, use # signs to the left of the decimal point, and 0 to the right. For example, to display 1542.2 with a thousands separator and two decimal places, we might use a format code of "#,###.00" and see 1,542.20. If we left off the last 0 in the code, the result would be 1,542.2 (notice that the trailing zero is missing). If some of your numbers will be less than zero, then using "#,##0.00" would be better because it would preserve the zero to the left of the decimal point.

Custom formats can do many other tricks. We can add color, have different formats for positive and negative numbers, and add text. To learn more about creating custom formats, search for "Number format codes" in the online help.

Common-Size Financial Statements

A widely used technique among financial analysts is to examine *common-size financial statements*, which display the data not as dollar amounts, but as percentages. These statements provide the analyst with two key benefits:

1. They allow for easy comparisons between firms of different sizes.

2. They can aid in spotting important trends that otherwise might not be obvious when looking at dollar amounts.

As we'll see, common-size financial statement are easy to create, and they make it simple to glean important insights that are not immediately obvious when looking at dollar amounts.

Creating Common-Size Income Statements

A common-size income statement is one that shows all of the data as a percentage of the firm's total revenues. Before beginning, remember that we want to make full use of Excel's capabilities to be as productive as possible. Instead of creating a new, blank worksheet and retyping all of the labels, we will make a copy of the Income Statement worksheet. Right-click on the sheet tab and choose **M**ove or Copy... from the shortcut menu. To create a copy, be sure to click on "**C**reate a copy" at the bottom of the dialog box. Note that the copy can be placed anywhere in the current workbook, in a new workbook, or any other open workbook. Place it before the Balance Sheet workbook. Right-click on the sheet tab, and rename the worksheet to: Common-size Income Statement.

We now have a perfect copy of the income statement that we can convert into a common-size income statement. The formulas that we use will reference data from the Income Statement worksheet, so it is helpful to understand how these references are created. In order for Excel to know where to get the data, it has to be told the location and name of the file, the name of the worksheet, and the cell address. For example, a reference to a cell in another workbook would look like the following:

$$=C:\backslash[Filename.xls]Sheet1!A1$$

Notice that the path to the file is listed first, then the name of the file is in brackets. This allows Excel to find the file on your computer. The file name is followed by the name of the worksheet, then an exclamation point, and then the cell address. If the path, file name, or worksheet name contain spaces, then everything after the equals sign and before the exclamation point will be enclosed in single quotes. Fortunately, you won't have to type all of this. Instead, just type an equals sign and then switch to the appropriate worksheet and click on the cell you want to reference. Excel will fill in all of the details. If the data in the original worksheet changes, then the data will be automatically updated in the worksheet with the reference.

We can now create the common-size income statement with only two simple changes. First, in B5 type: = and then switch to the Income Statement worksheet. Now click on B5 and type: / and then click on B5 again. Finally, press the Enter key and your formula will be: `='Income Statement'!B5/'Income Statement'!B$5`.[4] Now, change the number format (F**o**rmat C**e**lls) to a Percentage format with 2 decimal places. You should now see that the result is 100.00%.

---

4. Note that we are using a mixed reference (see page 18) in the denominator. That is because we always want our denominator to refer to Sales, in row 5. We aren't using an absolute reference because we are going to copy the formula to column C, and we want to refer to the correct years' Sales.

FIGURE 2-1
THE PASTE SPECIAL DIALOG BOX

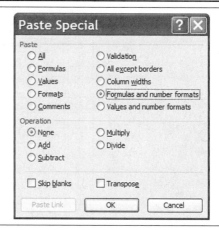

At this point, we want to copy this formula to every other cell in the worksheet. However, if we do a normal copy and paste, our underline formatting will be destroyed. To get around this problem, copy the cell and then select all of the other cells (B6:C15 and C5). Now, instead of pasting, choose Edit Paste Special. As shown in Figure 2-1, this will allow us to choose exactly what and how to paste the data. In the list of options, choose "Formulas and number formats."

You have now created a common-size income statement with a minimum number of steps. It should resemble the one shown in Exhibit 2-5. You can easily see why this is a useful tool for analysts. By looking at row 8, you can instantly see that Selling and G&A expenses have risen quite sharply in 2007 relative to sales. Also, looking at row 15 instantly shows that the firm's net profit margin (see page 124) has decreased by half.

EXHIBIT 2-5
EPI's COMMON-SIZE INCOME STATEMENTS

	A	B	C
1	Elvis Products International		
2	Common-size Income Statement		
3	For the Year Ended Dec. 31, 2007		
4		2007	2006
5	Sales	100.00%	100.00%
6	Cost of Goods Sold	84.42%	83.45%
7	*Gross Profit*	*15.58%*	*16.55%*
8	Selling and G&A Expenses	8.58%	6.99%
9	Fixed Expenses	2.60%	2.91%
10	Depreciation Expense	0.52%	0.55%
11	*EBIT*	*3.89%*	*6.09%*
12	Interest Expense	1.97%	1.82%
13	*Earnings Before Taxes*	*1.91%*	*4.27%*
14	Taxes	0.77%	1.71%
15	*Net Income*	*1.15%*	*2.56%*
16			
17	Notes:		
18	Tax Rate	40%	

Creating a Common-Size Balance Sheet

You can create a common-size balance sheet just as we did for the income statement. The only difference is that the balance sheet entries are displayed as a percentage of the firm's total assets instead of total revenues.

To create the common-size balance sheets for EPI, proceed in the same manner as for the common-size income statements. Create a copy of the existing Balance Sheet worksheet, and rename the sheet to Common-size Balance Sheet. In B5 enter: ='Balance Sheet'!B5/'Balance Sheet'!B$12. Now, copy and then use Edit Paste Special as we did before. Your common-size balance sheet should look like the one in Exhibit 2-6.

EXHIBIT 2-6
EPI'S COMMON-SIZE BALANCE SHEET

	A	B	C
1	**Elvis Products International**		
2	**Common-size Balance Sheet**		
3	**As of Dec. 31, 2007**		
4	*Assets*	*2007*	*2006*
5	Cash and Equivalents	3.15%	3.92%
6	Accounts Receivable	24.35%	23.91%
7	Inventory	50.64%	48.69%
8	*Total Current Assets*	*78.14%*	*76.53%*
9	Plant & Equipment	31.92%	33.43%
10	Accumulated Depreciation	10.07%	9.95%
11	*Net Fixed Assets*	*21.86%*	*23.47%*
12	**Total Assets**	**100.00%**	**100.00%**
13	**Liabilities and Owner's Equity**		
14	Accounts Payable	10.61%	9.91%
15	Short-term Notes Payable	13.63%	13.62%
16	Other Current Liabilities	8.48%	9.26%
17	*Total Current Liabilities*	*32.72%*	*32.79%*
18	Long-term Debt	25.72%	22.02%
19	*Total Liabilities*	*58.45%*	*54.81%*
20	Common Stock	27.87%	31.32%
21	Retained Earnings	13.69%	13.87%
22	*Total Shareholder's Equity*	*41.55%*	*45.19%*
23	**Total Liabilities and Owner's Equity**	**100.00%**	**100.00%**

Building a Statement of Cash Flows[5]

A firm participates in essentially two kinds of financial transactions: those that increase the cash balance (cash inflows, or *sources* of funds) and those that decrease the cash balance (cash outflows, or *uses* of funds).

---

5. Prior to the November 1987 release of FASB standard 95, this statement was known as the Statement of Changes in Financial Position. The Sources and Uses of Funds statement, as it was also known, contained the same information but was organized differently.

61

One way that a financial analyst can determine how well a firm's management is performing is to examine how they are managing the shareholders' money. The accounting profession has developed a useful tool for this type of analysis. The tool is known as the *Statement of Cash Flows*. The statement of cash flows summarizes the causes of changes in the firm's cash balance. Changes in the cash balance can be determined as shown in Table 2-2.

TABLE 2-2
DETERMINING THE CHANGE IN THE CASH BALANCE

	Beginning Cash Balance
+	Cash inflows (sources)
−	Cash outflows (uses)
=	Ending Cash Balance

The statement of cash flows is organized into three sections according to how the cash flows were generated. The first section is "Cash Flows from Operations," which describes the cash flows generated by the firm in the ordinary course of conducting its business. The next section, "Cash Flows from Investing," describes cash flows due to the firm altering its mix of fixed assets. The final section, "Cash Flows from Financing," describes the cash flows that are generated in the course of financing the firm.

The most obvious source of operating cash flow is sales and other revenues. Similarly, the most obvious uses of cash are the firm's expenses. However, we already have this information on the income statement and don't need to repeat it in the statement of cash flows. Therefore, instead of putting nearly the entire income statement into the Cash Flows from Operations section, we will enter only net income, which is a summary of the entire income statement. In addition, we will add back the depreciation expense (and other non-cash charges) since, in reality, there was no cash outflow associated with depreciation. The rest of the entries on the statement of cash flows will be *changes* in balance sheet items, though a few will be left out for reasons we will discuss below.

Unlike the income statement and balance sheet, which are mostly exercises in data entry, the statement of cash flows is primarily composed of formulas. Since these formulas reference many different cells in the workbook, it is generally easiest to use Excel's pointer mode when entering them. To begin, rename "Sheet3" to: `Statement of Cash Flows` and enter the labels as shown in Exhibit 2-7. Next, apply our custom number format to the cells in B5:C20.

EXHIBIT 2-7
STATEMENT OF CASH FLOWS FOR EPI

	A	B	C
1	Elvis Products International		
2	Statement of Cash Flows		
3	For the Year Ended Dec. 31, 2007 ($ in 000's)		
4	**Cash Flows from Operations**		
5	Net Income	44.22	
6	Depreciation Expense	20.00	
7	Change in Accounts Receivable	-50.80	
8	Change in Inventories	-120.80	
9	Change in Accounts Payable	29.60	
10	Change in Other Current Liabilities	4.00	
11	**Total Cash Flows from Operations**		-73.78
12	**Cash Flows from Investing**		
13	Change in Plant & Equipment	-36.00	
14	**Total Cash Flows from Investing**		-36.00
15	**Cash Flows from Financing**		
16	Change in Short-term Notes Payable	25.00	
17	Change in Long-term Debt	101.18	
18	Change in Common Stock	0.00	
19	Cash Dividends Paid to Shareholders	-22.00	
20	**Total Cash Flows from Financing**		104.18
21	**Net Change in Cash Balance**		-5.60

The first two items under Cash Flows from Operations are Net Income and Depreciation Expense. As previously mentioned, these are unique items because they are the only ones on the statement of cash flows that come from the income statement and are also the only items that are not represented as changes from a previous period.[6] Also realize that Net Income summarizes every other item on the income statement. Therefore, if we were to include Sales, for example, we would be double counting. To enter the net income first type an = in B5 and then (before pressing the Enter key) click on the sheet tab for the Income Statement. Excel will change to the worksheet containing the income statement. Now click on C15 and press Enter. At this point, Excel will switch back to the Statement of Cash Flows worksheet and your formula in B5 should read: =`'Income Statement'!C15`. This formula directs Excel to put the value from cell C15 on the Income Statement worksheet into B5. If we should change some values in the income statement, any change in net income will automatically be reflected in the statement of cash flows.

---

6. Actually, we could calculate depreciation expense as the change in accumulated depreciation.

We can actually make referencing other sheets slightly easier if we display two or more sheets on the screen at once. We will use this technique to complete the statement of cash flows.

First, switch to the Income Statement sheet and then choose **W**indow **N**ew Window from the menus. This will open a second copy of the workbook. Now choose **W**indow **A**rrange and then H**o**rizontal. You should now see two identical copies of the workbook. In one of the copies, click on the sheet tab for the Statement of Cash Flows. In B6, type: = and then click anywhere on the other workbook. Now scroll down so that cell C10 is visible, click on it, and press the Enter key. The formula in B6 of the Statement of Cash Flows should read: `='Income Statement'!C10`, and the value should be 20,000. Notice that the custom format we applied to the income statement is not carried over. Therefore we need to apply the same format to the cells that we will be using. Select B5:C20 and then F**o**rmat C**e**lls, and apply the same custom format. Alternatively, you can click on any cell in the Income Statement worksheet and then click the Format Painter icon on the formatting toolbar (pictured at left) to copy the format. Now, select B5:C20 on the Statement of Cash Flows worksheet to paste the format. Regardless of the method you use, the value in B6 will show 20.00.

The rest of the statement of cash flows can be completed in a similar manner. Since we are done with the income statement, we now want to display the balance sheet in that workbook. Click on the sheet tab labeled Balance Sheet. You should now have both the Statement of Cash Flows sheet and the Balance Sheet displayed.

At this point, we must be careful with respect to the signs of the numbers entered into the statement of cash flows. In general, when an asset account increases it represents a cash outflow (i.e., a *use* of funds). An asset account which decreases represents a cash inflow (i.e., a *source* of funds). Liability and equity accounts are exactly the opposite. We represent uses of funds as negative numbers and sources of funds as positive numbers on the statement of cash flows.

Table 2-3 shows how to always get the sign correct. As an example, EPI's accounts receivable balance increased from $351,200 in 2006 to $402,000 in 2007. Because the firm invested in accounts receivable by making more loans to customers, it represents a use of funds and should be indicated with a negative sign on the statement of cash flows. On the other hand, the accounts payable balance increased and, because it is a liability, represents a source of funds. It will have a positive sign on the statement of cash flows.

TABLE 2-3
SIGNS OF CASH FLOWS FOR THE STATEMENT OF CASH FLOWS

Type of Account	Direction of Change		Order of Subtraction
	Increase	Decrease	
Asset	–	+	Older – Newer
Liability or Equity	+	–	Newer – Older

The formula for the change in accounts receivable in B7 should be: =`'Balance Sheet'!C6-'Balance Sheet'!B6`. We can get the change in inventories by simply copying this formula down to B8. Note that for these asset accounts, the direction of the subtraction is 2006 value – 2007 value. For liability and equity accounts the direction of the subtraction is reversed. This will ensure that the sign is always correct.

The formula to calculate the change in accounts payable in B9 is: =`'Balance Sheet'!B14-'Balance Sheet'!C14`. In B10, to get the change in other current liabilities, we use the formula: =`'Balance Sheet'!B16-'Balance Sheet'!C16`. Now we calculate the total cash flows from operations in C11 with: =`SUM(B5:B10)`. Note that we have skipped over the short-term notes payable. That is because notes payable is not an operating current liability. Generally, any interest-bearing liability is included in the Cash Flows from Financing section.

Cash flows from investing are those cash flows generated from investments (or dis-investments) in long-term assets. In the case of EPI, that means plant and equipment. This change can be calculated in B13 by the formula: =`'Balance Sheet'!C9-'Balance Sheet'!B9`. For consistency, we will calculate the total cash flows from investing in C14 with: =`B13`.

For the final section, our first item is the change in notes payable. This account increased from $200,000 in 2006 to $225,000 in 2007, representing a cash inflow of $25,000. In B16 enter the formula: =`'Balance Sheet'!B15-'Balance Sheet'!C15`. Next, we can calculate the change in long-term debt with the formula: =`'Balance Sheet'!B18-'Balance Sheet'!C18`. Even though common stock didn't change during the year, it is a good idea to include it anyway. In B18, enter: =`'Balance Sheet'!B20-'Balance Sheet'!C20`.

Cash dividends paid to shareholders in 2007 were $22,000 (dividends paid are always a use of funds). This is calculated with the formula:

$$\text{Dividends Paid} = \text{Net Income} - \text{Change in Retained Earnings}$$

so in B19 enter the formula: =-('Income Statement'!B15-('Balance Sheet'!B21-'Balance Sheet'!C21)). Note that the parentheses are important in this case, and that the result should be –22,000 (dividends paid are always a use of funds). Again, we can total the cash flows from financing in C20 with: =SUM(B16:B19).

Finally, in C20 we calculate the net change in the cash balance by adding up the subtotals, so the formula is: =SUM(C11:C19). Note that this should exactly equal the actual change in the cash balance from 2006 to 2007, otherwise you have made an error. The most common errors are likely to be either a wrong sign or an omitted item.

Since you no longer need the second copy of the worksheet, you may close either copy by clicking the Close button in the upper-right corner of the window. Note that choosing **File Close** will also work, but it will close both copies. Make sure that your worksheet resembles that pictured in Exhibit 2-7 on page 63.

Using Excel's Outliner

Most people were first introduced to outlining as a tool to help organize a paper by considering the major ideas first and progressively moving to the details. Excel's outliner works similarly, except that it is not really a tool for organizing ideas, but a tool to show or hide whatever level of detail is appropriate in a spreadsheet.

Excel can automatically build an outline based on the formulas that you have entered. It looks for cells that summarize information in other cells and considers those to be top level. For example, consider the statement of cash flows that we created in Exhibit 2-7. Once the outline is applied to this sheet, we can collapse it so that it appears like the screen fragment in Exhibit 2-8.

EXHIBIT 2-8
STATEMENT OF CASH FLOWS WITH ONLY LEVEL 1 DISPLAYED

Click here to show levels 1 and 2

Click here to show level 1 only →

Click any of these buttons to expand just part of the outline →

		A	B	C
	1	Elvis Products International		
	2	Statement of Cash Flows		
	3	For the Year Ended Dec. 31, 2007 ($ in 000's)		
+	11	Total Cash Flows from Operations		-73.78
+	14	Total Cash Flows from Investing		-36.00
+	20	Total Cash Flows from Financing		104.18
	21	Net Change in Cash Balance		-5.60

To create the outline, open the file containing your financial statements (**F**ile **O**pen...) if necessary. Excel is sometimes smart enough to apply an outline automatically (**D**ata **G**roup and Outline **A**uto Outline), but we will do it manually to get exactly the result that we want. Select A4:C10 and then press Shift+Alt+Right Arrow (or **D**ata **G**roup and Outline **G**roup). In this case we want to group by rows, so just press Enter. You will see an outline symbol appear at the left of the selected cells. If you click on the symbol, the outline will collapse so that it shows only the summary cell. Clicking the outline symbol again will restore the display. To create the other parts of the outline, select A12:C13 and A15:C19 and repeat the above steps for each range. If you make a mistake, or decide that you don't like the outline feature, you can clear the outline by choosing **D**ata **G**roup and Outline **C**lear Outline from the menus.

Outlining is especially useful for presentations to people who don't need to see all of the details. It frees you from creating a separate summary worksheet. We could create an outline of an income statement. Suppose that the income statement worksheet that we use inside the firm contains a breakdown of sales by product, several categories of cost of goods sold, and so on. When we need to provide the income statement to those outside the firm, we may not wish to provide all of that detail. Instead, simply print a copy from the outline with the appropriate level of detail. Note that if you print an outlined worksheet, only the levels displayed on-screen will print. However, if you copy an outlined worksheet, all of the details will be copied and can be pasted elsewhere.

Summary

In this chapter we discussed the three primary financial statements: the income statement, the balance sheet, and the statement of cash flows. You should have a basic understanding of the purpose of each of these statements and know how to build them in Excel.

We demonstrated how worksheets can be linked so that formulas in one worksheet can reference data on another sheet. Custom number formatting was introduced, and we saw how the outliner can be a useful tool for selectively displaying or hiding data.

Make sure that you have saved a copy of the EPI workbook, because we will be making use of this data in future chapters.

FUNCTIONS INTRODUCED IN THIS CHAPTER

Purpose	Function	Page
Total numbers or a range of numbers	SUM(*NUMBER1*,*NUMBER2*, . . .)	50

Problems

1. Using the data presented below:

	A	B	C
1	**Spacely's Space Sprockets**		
2	**Income Statements**		
3	**For the Years 2006 and 2007**		
4		*2007*	*2006*
5	Sales	$2,900,000	$2,350,000
6	Cost of Goods	2,030,000	1,645,000
7	**Gross Profit**	**870,000**	**705,000**
8	Depreciation	62,000	58,000
9	Selling & Admin. Expense	425,000	390,000
10	Lease Expense	65,000	65,000
11	**Net Operating Income**	**318,000**	**192,000**
12	Interest Expense	112,000	68,000
13	**Earnings Before Taxes**	**206,000**	**124,000**
14	Taxes	72,100	43,400
15	**Net Income**	**$133,900**	**$80,600**
16			
17	Notes:		
18	Tax Rate	35.00%	35.00%
19	Shares	38,000	30,000
20	Earnings per Share	$3.52	$2.69

	A	B	C
1	**Spacely's Space Sprockets**		
2	**Balance Sheet**		
3	**For the Year Ended December 31, 2007**		
4		*2007*	*2006*
5	*Assets*		
6	Cash	$52,000	$41,000
7	Marketable Securities	25,000	21,000
8	Accounts Receivable	420,000	372,000
9	Inventory	515,000	420,000
10	*Total Current Assets*	1,012,000	854,000
11	Gross Fixed Assets	2,680,000	2,170,000
12	Accumulated Depreciation	547,000	485,000
13	*Net Plant & Equipment*	2,133,000	1,685,000
14	*Total Assets*	$3,145,000	$2,539,000
15			
16	*Liabilities & Owner's Equity*		
17	Accounts Payable	$505,000	$310,000
18	Accrued Expenses	35,000	30,000
19	*Total Current Liabilities*	540,000	340,000
20	Long-term Debt	1,168,100	1,061,000
21	*Total Liabilities*	1,708,100	1,401,000
22	Common Stock ($2 par)	76,000	60,000
23	Additional Paid-in-Capital	691,000	542,000
24	Retained Earnings	669,900	536,000
25	*Total Owner's Equity*	1,436,900	1,138,000
26	*Total Liab. & Owner's Equity*	$3,145,000	$2,539,000

a. Recreate the income statement and balance sheet using formulas wherever possible. Each statement should be on a separate worksheet. Try to duplicate the formatting exactly.

b. On another worksheet, create a statement of cash flows for 2007. Do not enter any numbers directly on this worksheet. All formulas should be linked directly to the source on previous worksheets.

c. Using Excel's outlining feature, create an outline on the statement of cash flows that, when collapsed, shows only the subtotals for each section.

d. Suppose that sales were $3,200,000 in 2007 rather than $2,900,000. What is the 2007 net income and retained earnings?

e. Undo the changes from part D, and change the tax rate to 40%. What is the 2007 net income and retained earnings?

2. Using the data from the previous problem:

a. Create a common-size income statement for 2006 and 2007. This statement should be created on a separate worksheet with all formulas linked directly to the income statement.

b. Create a common-size balance sheet for 2006 and 2007. This statement should be created on a separate worksheet with all formulas linked directly to the balance sheet.

3. Download the file named "Chapter 2 Problem 3.xls" from the text support Web site (http://www.thomsonedu.com/finance/mayes).

a. Fill in the blanks on the financial statements for Boovins Baked Goods with formulas. Some of the formulas will require links to other worksheets in the workbook.

b. Create a common-size income statement and balance sheet using your answers from part A. Using the techniques you have learned in this chapter, you should be able to do these statements in less than one minute each with formatting that is identical to that in the original worksheets.

Internet Exercise

1. EdgarScan is a service of the ABAS Technology Group of PricewaterhouseCoopers, which provides free access to all filings made by public companies in the United States. The site can be accessed at http://edgarscan.pwcglobal.com/servlets/edgarscan. EdgarScan makes it easy to download financial statements directly into Excel with just a click of a button. Using your Internet browser, go to the EdgarScan Web site and enter a ticker symbol or company name into the appropriate box. Click the Search button to see a list of the filings that are available. In the list, click on the most recent Form 10K.

   a. On the page that appears, click on the link for the Excel Spreadsheet for the Income Statement. This will either open Excel with the data loaded, or it will save an Excel file to your disk.

   b. Repeat part A for the Balance Sheet.

   c. Now, repeat Problems 1 and 2 using the data for your chosen company.

CHAPTER 3

The Cash Budget

After studying this chapter, you should be able to:

1. *Explain the purpose of the cash budget and how it differs from an income statement.*

2. *Calculate a firm's expected total cash collections and disbursements for a particular month.*

3. *Calculate a firm's expected ending cash balance and short-term borrowing needs.*

4. *Demonstrate how Excel can be used to determine the optimal timing of major cash expenditures.*

5. *Use the Scenario Manager to evaluate different assumptions in a model.*

6. *Use the various tools that Excel provides to find and fix errors in formulas.*

Of all the topics covered in this book, perhaps no other task benefits so much from the use of spreadsheets as the cash budget. As we'll see, the cash budget can be a complex document with many interrelated entries. Manually updating a cash budget, especially for a large firm, is not a chore for which one volunteers. However, once the initial cash budget is set up in a spreadsheet, updating and playing "what if" becomes very easy.

A *cash budget* is simply a listing of the firm's anticipated cash inflows and outflows over a specified period. Unlike a pro forma income statement (discussed in Chapter 5), the cash budget includes only actual cash flows. For example, depreciation expense does not appear on the cash budget, but principal payments on debt obligations (which are not on the income statement) do. Because of its emphasis on cash income and expenditures, the cash budget is particularly useful for planning short-term borrowing and the timing of expenditures. As with all budgets, another important benefit of the cash budget comes from reconciling actual after-the-fact cash flows with those from the forecast.

We'll see that a cash budget is composed of three parts:

1. The worksheet area;
2. A listing of each of the cash inflows (collections) and outflows (disbursements);
3. Calculation of the ending cash balance and borrowing needs.

We are simplifying things somewhat. In reality, many of the given variables in this chapter would come from other budgets. For example, a firm would usually have at least a sales budget from which our sales forecasts are taken, a salary budget, a capital expenditure budget, and so on. All of these different budgets would be created before the cash budget, and they require a great deal of thought and research. The cash budget worksheet would then pull values in from those other budgeting worksheets.

Throughout the chapter, we will create a complete cash budget for June to September 2008 Bithlo Barbecues, a small manufacturer of barbecue grills. The financial staff of the firm has compiled the following set of assumptions and forecasts to be used in the cash budgeting process:

1. Actual and expected sales through October are as given in Table 3-1.
2. 40% of sales are for cash. Of the remaining sales, 75% are collected in the following month and 25% are collected two months after the sale.
3. Inventory purchases are equal to 50% of the following month's sales (e.g., June purchases are 50% of expected July sales). 60% of purchases are paid for in the month following the purchase, and the remainder are paid in the following month.
4. Wages are forecasted to be equal to 20% of expected sales.
5. Leasing expense for the property, plant, and equipment is $10,000 per month.

6. Interest payments of $30,000 on long-term debt are due in June and September.

7. A $50,000 dividend will be paid to common shareholders in June.

8. Tax prepayments of $25,000 will be paid in June and September.

9. A $200,000 capital improvement is scheduled to be paid in July, but management is flexible on the scheduling of this outlay.

10. Bithlo Barbecues must keep a minimum cash balance of $15,000 by agreement with its bank. Its cash balance at the end of May was $20,000.

TABLE 3-1

BITHLO BARBECUES ACTUAL AND EXPECTED SALES FOR 2008*

Month	Sales
April	291,000
May	365,000
June	387,000
July	329,000
August	238,000
September	145,000
October	92,000

*April and May sales are actual.

The Worksheet Area

The worksheet area is not necessarily a part of the cash budget. However, it is useful because it summarizes some of the most important calculations in the budget. This section includes a breakdown of expected sales, accounts receivable collections, and payments for materials (inventory) purchases.

Open a new workbook and rename Sheet1 to Cash Budget. Like any other financial statement, we begin the cash budget with the titles. In A1 enter: Bithlo Barbecues; in A2 type: Cash Budget; and in A3 enter: For the Period

75

June to September 2008. Center these titles across columns A:I. Next, enter the names of the months from Table 3-1 in C4:I4 using the AutoFill feature (see page 11).

The starting point for a cash budget is the sales forecast. Many of the other forecasts in the cash budget are driven (at least indirectly) by this forecast. The sales forecast has been provided for us by Bithlo's marketing department in Table 3-1. In A5 enter the label Sales, and then copy the expected sales to C5:I5 in your worksheet.

Note that sales have a strong seasonal component. In this case, barbecuing is mostly a summer phenomenon, and we expect that sales will peak in June before falling dramatically in the fall and winter months. Such seasonality is important in many types of business; for example, retail sales in the fourth quarter may be 30% or more of annual sales.[1] Seasonal patterns must be included in your sales forecast if your cash budget is to be accurate.

Collections

For most firms, at least a portion of sales are made on credit. It is therefore important that the firm know how quickly it can expect to collect on those sales. In the case of Bithlo Barbecues, experience has shown that in the past about 40% of its sales are cash and 60% are on credit. Of the 60% of sales made on credit, about 75% will be collected during the month following the sale, and the remaining 25% will be collected two months after the sale. In other words, 45% (= 0.60 x 0.75) of total sales in any month will be collected during the following month, and 15% (= 0.60 x 0.25) will be collected within two months.[2]

Our goal is to determine the total collections in each month. In A6 type: Collections:, and then in A7 enter the label: Cash. This will indicate the cash sales for the month. In A8 enter: First Month to indicate collections from the sales made in the previous month. In A9 enter: Second Month to indicate collections on sales made two months previously. Since our estimates of the collection percentages may change, it is important that they not be entered directly into formulas. Instead, enter these percentages in B7:B9.

---

1. As an example, Target Corp. reported that fourth-quarter revenues were about 32.50% of full-year sales in both 2003 and 2004.

2. For simplicity, we assume that 100% of sales will be collected. Most firms would include an allowance for "bad debts."

Since the budget is for June to September we will begin our estimates of collections in E7. (Note that April and May sales are included here only because we need to reference sales from the two previous months to determine the collections from credit sales.) To calculate the cash collections for June we multiply the expected June sales by the percentage of cash sales, so enter: =E5* $B7 into E7. To calculate collections from cash sales for the other months, simply copy this formula to F7:H7.

Collections on credit sales can be calculated similarly. In E8, we will calculate June collections from May sales with the formula: =D5* $B8. Copy this formula to F8:H8. Finally, collections from sales two months ago, in E9, can be calculated with the formula: =C5* $B9. After copying this formula to F9:H9, calculate the total collections in row 10 for each month by using the SUM function. Check your numbers against those in Exhibit 3-1 and format your worksheet to match. This is a good time to save your workbook.

EXHIBIT 3-1
CALCULATING COLLECTIONS IN THE WORKSHEET AREA

	A	B	C	D	E	F	G	H	I
1					Bithlo Barbeques				
2					Cash Budget				
3					For the Period June to September 2008				
4			April	May	June	July	August	September	October
5	Sales		291,000	365,000	387,000	329,000	238,000	145,000	92,000
6	Collections:								
7	Cash	40%			154,800	131,600	95,200	58,000	
8	First Month	45%			164,250	174,150	148,050	107,100	
9	Second Month	15%			43,650	54,750	58,050	49,350	
10	Total Collections				362,700	360,500	301,300	214,450	
11	Purchases	50%	182,500	193,500	164,500	119,000	72,500	46,000	
12	Payments:								
13	First Month	60%			116,100	98,700	71,400	43,500	
14	Second Month	40%			73,000	77,400	65,800	47,600	
15	Total Payments				189,100	176,100	137,200	91,100	

Purchases and Payments

In this section of the worksheet area, we calculate the payments that are made for inventory purchases. Bithlo Barbecues purchases inventory (equal to 50% of sales) the month before the sale is made. For example, June inventory purchases will be 50% of expected July sales. However, it does not pay for the inventory immediately. Instead, 60% of the purchase price is paid in the following month, and the other 40% is paid two months after the purchase.

We first need to calculate the amount of inventory purchased in each month. As noted, this is 50% of the following month's sales. So in A11 type: `Purchases` and in B11 enter: `50%`. We will calculate April purchases in C11 with the formula: `=$B11*D5`. Copying this formula to D11:H11 completes the calculation of purchases.

Credit purchases are not cash outflows, so we need to calculate the actual cash payments for inventory in each month. This is very similar to the way we calculated total cash collections. First, enter labels. In A12 type: `Payments:`. In A13 and A14 enter: `First Month` and `Second Month` respectively, and enter: `Total Payments` in A15. Now enter `60%` in B13 and `40%` in B14. In June Bithlo Barbecues will pay for 60% of purchases made in May. So the formula in E13 is: `=$B13*D11`. Copy this to F13:H13 to complete the first month's payments. To calculate the June payment for April purchases in E14, use the formula: `=$B14*C11`. Copy this to F14:H14 and then calculate the total payments for each month in row 15.

At this point your worksheet should look like the one in Exhibit 3-1. Check your numbers carefully to make sure that they agree with those in the exhibit. To clarify the logic of these formulas, examine Exhibit 3-2, which is the same as Exhibit 3-1 except it has arrows drawn in to show the references for June.

EXHIBIT 3-2
THE WORKSHEET AREA OF A CASH BUDGET

	A	B	C	D	E	F	G	H	I
1	Bithlo Barbeques								
2	Cash Budget								
3	For the Period June to September 2008								
4			April	May	June	July	August	September	October
5	Sales		291,000	365,000	387,000	329,000	238,000	145,000	92,000
6	Collections:								
7	Cash	40%			154,800	131,600	95,200	58,000	
8	First Month	45%			164,250	174,150	148,050	107,100	
9	Second Month	45%			43,650	54,750	58,050	49,350	
10	Total Collections				362,700	360,500	301,300	214,450	
11	Purchases	50%	182,500	193,500	164,500	119,000	72,500	46,000	
12	Payments:								
13	First Month	60%			116,100	98,700	71,400	43,500	
14	Second Month	40%			73,000	77,400	65,800	47,600	
15	Total Payments				189,100	176,100	137,200	91,100	

Collections and Disbursements

This section of the cash budget is the easiest to set up in a spreadsheet because there are no complex relationships between the cells as there are in the worksheet area. The collections and disbursements area is very much like a cash-based income statement (i.e., there are no non-cash expenses). We simply list the cash inflows and outflows that are expected for each month.

We will begin by summarizing the cash collections for each month. Enter the label: Collections in A17. In E17:H17 the formulas simply reference the total collections that were calculated in E10:H10. So, for example, the formula in E17 is: =E10. Copy this formula to F17:H17.

In A18, enter the label: Less Disbursements:. The first cash outflow that we will enter is the inventory payment, which was calculated in the worksheet area. Enter Inventory Payments as the label in A19 and the formula in E19 as: =E15. Wages are assumed to be equal to 20% of sales. In A20 add the label: Wages and in B20 type: 20%, which will be used to calculate the expected monthly wage expense. The formula to calculate wages in E20 is: =$B20*E5. Now copy these formulas to F19:H20. By now, you should be able to finish this section by entering the remaining labels and numbers as pictured in Exhibit 3-3.

EXHIBIT 3-3
COLLECTIONS AND DISBURSEMENTS

	A	B	C	D	E	F	G	H
17	Collections				362,700	360,500	301,300	214,450
18	*Less Disbursements:*							
19	Inventory Payments				189,100	176,100	137,200	91,100
20	Wages	20%			77,400	65,800	47,600	29,000
21	Lease Payment				10,000	10,000	10,000	10,000
22	Interest				30,000	0	0	30,000
23	Dividend (Common)				50,000	0	0	0
24	Taxes				25,000	0	0	25,000
25	Capital Outlays				0	200,000	0	0
26	**Total Disbursements**				**381,500**	**451,900**	**194,800**	**185,100**

There are a couple of points to note about this portion of the cash budget. First, we have assumed that the only cash inflows are from selling the firm's products. In other cases, however, it is possible that the firm might plan to sell some assets or bonds or stock. Any of these actions would bring cash into the firm and should be included under collections.

Second, we have included dividends, which do not appear on the income statement. The reason they are on the cash budget is that dividends represent a very real cash expenditure for the firm. They don't appear on the income statement because dividends are paid from after-tax dollars. In other problems, there may be other similar outlays, such as a principal payment to be made on a loan. Remember, the cash budget is not an income statement. For the cash budget, we do not use accrual accounting; we include all cash inflows and outflows when they are expected to occur, whether they will be on the income statement or not.

Finally, Bithlo Barbecues has scheduled capital outlays of $200,000 in July. Even though they are paying the full cost in July, it is unlikely that they would be allowed to expense this entire amount during 2008. Instead, the income statement would reflect the depreciation of these assets over a longer period of time. Regardless of tax laws or accounting conventions, it is important to include all expected cash inflows and outflows on the cash budget.

Calculating the Ending Cash Balance

This last section of the cash budget calculates the expected ending cash balance at the end of each month. This is the most important part of the cash budget because it helps the manager understand the firm's short-term borrowing requirements. Knowing the borrowing requirements in advance allows managers to arrange for financing when they need it and provides the time necessary to evaluate possible alternatives. Managers can also use this information to determine the best timing for major expenditures.

Table 3-2 shows the series of calculations necessary to determine the firm's ending cash balance. Essentially, this is the same procedure we saw in Table 2-2 on page 62. In the next section we will add a few steps to this calculation, but the basic procedure is always as outlined in Table 3-2.

We have already made most of the calculations necessary to complete the cash budget. Before we finish this last section, however, we need to add another detail. The management of Bithlo Barbecues has decided that they would like to keep a minimum cash balance of $15,000 to meet any unexpected expenses. If the

TABLE 3-2
CALCULATING THE ENDING CASH BALANCE

	Beginning Cash Balance
+	Total Collections
−	Total Disbursements
=	Unadjusted Cash Balance
+	Current Borrowing
=	Ending Cash Balance

projected cash balance falls below this amount, they will need to borrow to bring the balance back to this minimum. In A32 enter the label: Notes:. We will use cells below A32 to indicate important assumptions about our cash budget. The first of these is the minimum cash balance requirement. In A33 enter the label: Minimum Acceptable Cash and in B33 enter: 15,000.

In cells A27:A31 enter the labels as shown in Exhibit 3-4. (Notice that this is exactly the same as was outlined in Table 3-2.) We start with the unadjusted cash balance in May. Enter: 20,000 into D29. In D30 enter: 0 because the firm had no short-term borrowing needs in May. The ending cash balance for the month is simply the unadjusted cash balance plus current borrowing, so the formula in D31 is: =sum(D29:D30). This formula will be the same for each month, so copy it across to E31:H31.

EXHIBIT 3-4
ENDING CASH BALANCE CALCULATION

	A	B	C	D	E	F	G	H
27	Beginning Cash Balance				20,000	15,000	15,000	121,500
28	Collections - Disbursements				(18,800)	(91,400)	106,500	29,350
29	Unadjusted Cash Balance			20,000	1,200	(76,400)	121,500	150,850
30	Current Borrowing			0	13,800	91,400	0	0
31	**Ending Cash Balance**			**20,000**	**15,000**	**15,000**	**121,500**	**150,850**
32	Notes:							
33	Minimum Acceptable Cash	15,000						

The beginning cash balance for any month is the same as the ending cash balance from the previous month. Therefore, we can simply reference the previous month's ending cash balance calculation. In E27 enter the formula: =D31 and copy this across to F27:H27. At this point, your beginning cash balance for each month, except June, will be 0 because we have not yet entered any formulas in E28:H30.

Since we have already calculated the total collections and total disbursements, there is no need to have separate rows for those calculations in this section. Instead, we will calculate the net collections for June in E28 with the formula: =E17-E26. Copy this formula to F28:H28. For June, the result is −$18,800, which indicates that the firm expects to spend more than it will collect. In other words, the cash balance is expected to decline by $18,800 in June. This decline will be reflected in the unadjusted cash balance.

The unadjusted cash balance is what the cash balance would be if the firm did not have any short-term borrowing during the month. We simply add the beginning cash balance and the net collections for the month. The formula in E29 is: =Sum(E27:E28). The result is $1,200, which is less than the firm's minimum acceptable cash balance of $15,000. Therefore, Bithlo Barbecues will need to borrow $13,800 to bring the balance up to this minimum.

How did we determine that the firm needs to borrow $13,800? It is probably obvious to you, even without giving it much thought. However, you need to think it through carefully to create a formula which will work under all circumstances. We could use the following equation:

$$\text{Current Borrowing} = \text{Minimum Cash} - \text{Unadjusted Cash} \qquad \text{(3-1)}$$

In this case we find that Bithlo Barbecues needs to borrow:

$$\$13,800 = \$15,000 - \$1,200$$

Equation 3-1 works in this case, but it is not appropriate in all circumstances. Suppose, for example, that the unadjusted cash balance had been $20,000. This would suggest that the firm needs to borrow −$5,000, which is absurd.[3] In a case such as this, we would like to see current borrowing at 0.

---

3. Unless, of course, you assume that negative borrowing is the same as investing. But we will consider investing excess funds in the next section.

The calculation that we need can be stated as follows: "**If** the unadjusted cash balance is less than the minimum, **then** we borrow an amount equal to minimum cash – unadjusted cash. **Otherwise**, current borrowing is zero." With the formulas that we have used so far, this type of calculation is impossible. However, Excel has a built-in function that can handle situations where the result depends on some condition—the **IF** statement.

The **IF** statement returns one of two values, depending on whether a statement is true or false:

$$\textbf{IF } (\textbf{\textit{LOGICAL\_TEST}}, \textbf{\textit{VALUE\_IF\_TRUE}}, \textit{VALUE\_IF\_FALSE})$$

LOGICAL_TEST is any statement which can be evaluated as being either true or false, and ***VALUE_IF_TRUE*** and *VALUE_IF_FALSE* are the return values which depend on whether ***LOGICAL_TEST*** was true or false. If you are familiar with computer programming, you will recognize this as the equivalent of the If–Then–Else construct that is supported by most programming languages.

The formula to calculate the firm's borrowing needs for June, in E30, is: `=IF(E29<$B33,$B33-E29,0)`. Since the unadjusted cash balance is only $1,200, the result should indicate the need to borrow $13,800 as we found earlier. Copy this formula to F30:H30 to complete the calculation of current borrowing. Notice that, because of large positive net collections, the firm does not need to borrow funds in August or September.

We have already entered formulas for the ending cash balance in each month. You should now check your numbers and formatting against those in Exhibit 3-5.

EXHIBIT 3-5
A COMPLETED SIMPLE CASH BUDGET

	A	B	C	D	E	F	G	H
1	Bithlo Barbeques							
2	Cash Budget							
3	For the Period June to September 2008							
4			April	May	June	July	August	September
5	Sales		291,000	365,000	387,000	329,000	238,000	145,000
6	Collections:							
7	Cash	40%			154,800	131,600	95,200	58,000
8	First Month	45%			164,250	174,150	148,050	107,100
9	Second Month	15%			43,650	54,750	58,050	49,350
10	Total Collections				362,700	360,500	301,300	214,450
11	Purchases	50%	182,500	193,500	164,500	119,000	72,500	46,000
12	Payments:							
13	First Month	60%			116,100	98,700	71,400	43,500
14	Second Month	40%			73,000	77,400	65,800	47,600
15	Total Payments				189,100	176,100	137,200	91,100
17	Collections				362,700	360,500	301,300	214,450
18	Less Disbursements:							
19	Inventory Payments				189,100	176,100	137,200	91,100
20	Wages	20%			77,400	65,800	47,600	29,000
21	Lease Payment				10,000	10,000	10,000	10,000
22	Interest				30,000	0	0	30,000
23	Dividend (Common)				50,000	0	0	0
24	Taxes				25,000	0	0	25,000
25	Capital Outlays				0	200,000	0	0
26	Total Disbursements				381,500	451,900	194,800	185,100
27	Beginning Cash Balance				20,000	15,000	15,000	121,500
28	Collections - Disbursements				(18,800)	(91,400)	106,500	29,350
29	Unadjusted Cash Balance			20,000	1,200	(76,400)	121,500	150,850
30	Current Borrowing			0	13,800	91,400	0	0
31	Ending Cash Balance			20,000	15,000	15,000	121,500	150,850
32	Notes:							
33	Minimum Acceptable Cash	15,000						

At this point the managers of Bithlo Barbecues know that they will need to arrange to borrow $13,800 before June, and $91,400 before July. It is also obvious that they will have enough cash to pay off these borrowings in August, but we will postpone the repayment of loans until later in this chapter.

Using the Cash Budget for Timing Large Expenditures

Besides being useful for planning the firm's short-term borrowing needs, the cash budget can be useful in timing collections and expenditures. For example, suppose that the firm is concerned about the amount of borrowing that will be necessary in June and July. What we want to do is to see what happens if we make certain changes in our assumptions.

One way that the company may be able to reduce the borrowing needs is to try to speed up collections on sales and to slow down the payments for inventory purchases (they will effectively be borrowing from suppliers instead of the bank). Suppose that the firm is able to collect 50% of sales during the following month, thereby reducing collections in the second month to 10%. Furthermore, assume that they can slow down their payments for inventory purchases to 50% in the first month after the purchase instead of the current 60%.

Change B8 to 50%, B9 to 10%, B13 to 50%, and B14 to 50%. You will see that borrowing will fall in June to $9,000 from $13,800. Borrowing in July will rise to $93,200 from $91,400. Therefore, the total amount of borrowing will decrease from the original $105,800 to $102,200. This has two benefits: it reduces the interest cost of borrowing (which we will consider in the next section), and it shifts that interest expense to a later point in time. Of course, there may also be an opportunity cost in the form of lost discounts due to paying suppliers later, and customers may go to competitors who offer better credit terms. Before moving on, make sure to change the percentages back to their original values.

As another example, consider Bithlo Barbecues' $200,000 expenditure currently planned for July 2008. This expenditure is the primary cause of the borrowing need in July. Indeed, without this $200,000 outlay, the firm wouldn't need to borrow in July.

Assuming that there is some flexibility in scheduling this outlay, in which month should the expenditure be made? The answer, of course, depends on a number of factors, but we might decide to make the decision based on minimizing borrowing needs. That is, schedule the project such that the firm's short-term borrowing needs are minimized. This might be especially important if the firm expected borrowing needs in excess of its line of credit in a given month.

You can experiment a bit by changing the month in which the capital expenditure is made. First, however, it would be helpful to know the total expected borrowing for the four-month period. In I30, enter the formula: =Sum(E30:H30) to calculate total borrowing. Now, by moving the capital expenditure to different months, you should be able to verify the numbers in Table 3-3.

TABLE 3-3
OPTIMAL SCHEDULING FOR A CAPITAL EXPENDITURE

Month of Outlay	Total Four-Month Borrowing
June	$ 213,800
July	105,200
August	13,800
September	13,800

Obviously, by this criteria, the best time to schedule the outlay would be in either August or September. Before continuing, be sure to move the $200,000 outlay back to July.

The Scenario Manager

In the previous section, we performed what has come to be called a "what-if" analysis. That is, we changed the timing of the large capital expenditure to see what would happen to the total amount of borrowing for the period. The problem with doing it "by hand" as we did is that you lose the original results of your analysis after it is done. Also, every person who looks at your spreadsheet will need to perform that same analysis. Excel provides a better way—the Scenario Manager. This tool allows us to store several scenarios (alternative input variables) in the spreadsheet and display them at will. Figure 3-1 shows the Scenario Manager dialog box before any scenarios have been created.

FIGURE 3-1
SCENARIO MANAGER DIALOG BOX WITH NO SCENARIOS DEFINED

To access this tool, choose **T**ools Sc**e**narios from the menu. When the dialog box is showing, we can begin to create our four scenarios. To begin, click the **A**dd button. In the next dialog box enter: Expenditure in June for the Scenario **n**ame. The Changing cells are those cells that will be different under each scenario. In this case, they will be the capital outlay for each month, so enter: E25:H25 and click the OK button. You will now be prompted to enter values for each of the changing cells for this scenario. Since our first scenario calls for the expenditure to be made in June, enter 200000 in the first box and 0 in each of the others. The Scenario Values dialog box should look like that in Figure 3-2. Now click the **A**dd button to create the next scenario. Repeat these steps until you have four scenarios with the expenditure occurring in different months.

FIGURE 3-2
SCENARIO VALUES DIALOG BOX FOR JUNE EXPENDITURE

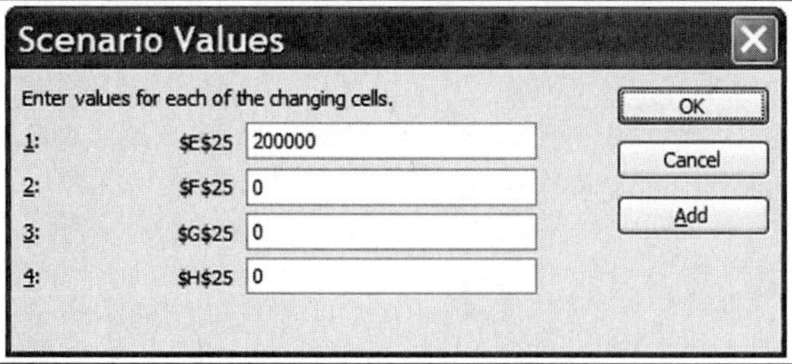

Note that the Scenario Values dialog box prompts you for values using the cell addresses as labels. That can be confusing, especially if the cells are not visible on the screen. One way to make this situation better is to use defined names for the cells, as we discussed in Chapter 1 (page 9). First, close the Scenario Manager and then click on cell E25 and choose **I**nsert **N**ame **D**efine from the menus. Now, type: June in the edit box and click on the **A**dd button. Now name the other cells similarly. Return to the Scenario Manager and select the "Expenditures in June" scenario. Click on the **E**dit button, then the OK button on the Edit Scenario dialog, and your Scenario Values dialog box should look like the one in Figure 3-3.

FIGURE 3-3
SCENARIO VALUES DIALOG BOX WITH DEFINED NAMES

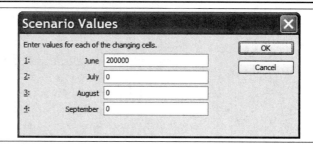

Many of the other tools supplied with Excel work with range names in a similar way. This is a useful trick to remember since it can simplify entering data. As we will see shortly, using range names will also improve the Scenario Summary sheets.

After creating your scenarios, the Scenario Manager dialog box will look like the one in Figure 3-4.

FIGURE 3-4
SCENARIO MANAGER DIALOG BOX WITH FOUR SCENARIOS

To display a particular scenario, simply select it from the list and click the Show button. Excel will alter the contents of your changing cells to reflect the values that you entered. Of course, the entire worksheet will be recalculated, and you can see the results under the selected scenario. Note that to be able to scroll around and see the entire worksheet, you must click the Close button on the Scenario Manager dialog box. Take a look at the results of each scenario, but remember to reset the scenario to "Expenditure in July" (our default case) before continuing. If you forget to reset to the default scenario, Excel will always display the last chosen scenario. This can cause confusion when you later open your workbook.

Being able to change quickly between scenarios is quite helpful, but the real advantage of the Scenario Manager is its ability to summarize the results of all of your scenarios. In this case, we would like to compare the total borrowing that results under each scenario to determine the best time for the expenditure. Recall that we added a formula in I30 to calculate the total borrowing for the period. Before continuing, define a name for this cell such as "Total_Borrowing." (Recall that we use the underscore in place of a space, because spaces are not allowed in range names.)

Return to the Scenario Manager and click on the Summary button. You will be asked to enter Result cells. A result cell is a cell (or a range of cells) that shows the end result of each scenario. In this case, we are interested in total borrowing, so enter: I30 as the **R**esult cell and click the OK button. Excel will now create a new worksheet that summarizes your scenario results. For our scenarios, the results are in Exhibit 3-6. Note that these results are exactly the same as those in Table 3-3.

EXHIBIT 3-6
SCENARIO SUMMARY

	A	B	C	D	E	F	G	H
1								
2		Scenario Summary						
3				Current Values:	Expenditure in June	Expenditure in July	Expenditure in August	Expenditure in September
4		Changing Cells:						
5			June	0	200,000	0	0	0
6			July	200,000	0	200,000	0	0
7			August	0	0	0	200,000	0
8			September	0	0	0	0	200,000
9		Result Cells:						
10			Total_Borrowing	105,200	213,800	105,200	13,800	13,800
11		Notes: Current Values column represents values of changing cells at						
12		time Scenario Summary Report was created. Changing cells for each						
13		scenario are highlighted in gray.						

Notice that the values in column D are whatever values were active when the scenario summary was created. In most cases that will just be a repeat of one of the existing scenarios. In this example, the numbers in columns D and F are identical, so column D can be safely deleted.

Adding Interest and Investment of Excess Cash

In the previous section you created a basic cash budget for Bithlo Barbecues. In this section we will refine the calculation of the ending cash balance by considering two additional factors. First, we will add interest payments on borrowed funds; then we will consider the investment of excess cash.

Before beginning let's create a copy of the previous cash budget in the same workbook. Right-click the sheet tab labeled "Cash Budget" and select **M**ove or Copy from the menu. On the dialog box make sure to check the box labeled **C**reate a Copy, and select "(move to end)" from the list. The copied sheet will now be named Cash Budget (2). Right-click the sheet tab and rename the new sheet: Complex Cash Budget.

Next, we will need to make a few additions to the notes at the bottom of the worksheet. We will now assume that Bithlo Barbecues will invest any cash in excess of $40,000. In A34 add the label: Maximum Acceptable Cash and in B34 enter: 40,000. Furthermore, the firm will have to pay interest on its short-term borrowings and will earn interest on invested funds. In A35 type: Borrowing Rate (Annual) and in B35 enter: 8%. In A36 add the label: Lending Rate (Annual) and enter: 6% in B36.

Since we are working with monthly time periods, we need to convert these annual rates into monthly rates of interest. So, in C35 and C36 enter the label: Monthly. We will convert the annual rate to a monthly rate by dividing by 12. In D35 enter the formula: =B35/12, and copy this to D36.[4] You should see that the monthly borrowing rate is 0.67% and the monthly lending rate is 0.50%.

We are now ready to expand the cash budget to include investing and the interest expense and income. Before entering any new formulas, we need to insert a few new rows. Select row 23 (the dividend on common stock) and then choose **I**nsert **R**ows from the menu. This will insert a row above the selection. In A23 enter the label: Short-Term Interest Expense (Inc.). Next, select row 32 (the ending cash balance), insert a row, and enter: Current Investing into A32. Finally, select rows 34 and 35 and choose **I**nsert **R**ows from the menu. This will insert two rows above the selection. In A34 type: Cumulative Borrowing (Investing) and in A35 type: Cumulative Interest Expense (Inc.). We need to calculate the cumulative amount that is borrowed/invested so that we can calculate the monthly short-term interest expense/income.

We will start by entering the formulas to calculate the cumulative amount of borrowing (investing) in D34. Positive amounts will represent borrowing while negative numbers will represent investing. To calculate the *cumulative* amount, we need to add the previous period's cumulative amount to current borrowing and subtract current investing. For May, in D34, the formula is: =C34+D31-D32, and the result should be 0. Copy this formula to E34:H34. Note that at this point the result for each month should be equal to the cumulative current borrowing.

Short-term interest expense (income) can now be calculated by multiplying the cumulative amount of borrowing (investing) from the previous month by the appropriate interest rate. So, in E23 we will use an **IF** statement to determine which rate to use. If the cumulative amount of borrowing (investing) is positive, we will

---

4. Entering the 12 into the denominator might seem to violate our prohibition on entering numbers into formulas. However, there will always be 12 months in a year, so this number will never change.

multiply it by the borrowing rate. Otherwise, use the lending rate. The formula for June, E23, is: =IF(D34>0,D34*$D$39,D34*$D$40). In June, since the firm has not had previous borrowing or lending, the result should be 0. Copy this across to F23:H23. At this point, the last section of your worksheet should resemble the fragment in Exhibit 3-7.

EXHIBIT 3-7
THE WORKSHEET WITH INTEREST CALCULATIONS

	A	B	C	D	E	F	G	H
17	Collections				362,700	360,500	301,300	214,450
18	*Less Disbursements:*							
19	Inventory Payments				189,100	176,100	137,200	91,100
20	Wages	20%			77,400	65,800	47,600	29,000
21	Lease Payment				10,000	10,000	10,000	10,000
22	Interest				30,000	0	0	30,000
23	Short-term Interest Expense (Inc.)				0	92	702	702
24	Dividend (Common)				50,000	0	0	0
25	Taxes				25,000	0	0	25,000
26	Capital Outlays				0	200,000	0	0
27	**Total Disbursements**				381,500	451,992	195,502	185,802
28	Beginning Cash Balance				20,000	15,000	15,000	120,798
29	Collections - Disbursements				(18,800)	(91,492)	105,798	28,648
30	Unadjusted Cash Balance			20,000	1,200	(76,492)	120,798	149,446
31	Current Borrowing			0	13,800	91,492	0	0
32	Current Investing							
33	**Ending Cash Balance**			20,000	15,000	15,000	120,798	149,446
34	Cumulative Borrowing (Investing)			0	13,800	105,292	105,292	105,292
35	Cumulative Interest Expense (Inc.)							
36	Notes:							
37	Minimum Acceptable Cash	15,000						
38	Maximum Acceptable Cash	40,000						
39	Borrowing Rate (Annual)	8%	Monthly	0.67%				
40	Lending Rate (Annual)	6%	Monthly	0.50%				

We can now calculate the cumulative interest expense (income) in E35. To do this we simply add the previous month's interest expense (income) to the current month's interest expense (income). For June, the formula is: =D35+E23. This formula should be copied across to F35:H35. The only purpose of this row is to help evaluate the results of a scenario that we will examine later.

Calculating Current Borrowing

Determining the amount of current borrowing and current investing is the most complex part of this cash budget. We have already calculated current borrowing, but since we are now considering investments and interest, the formula will need to be changed. For current borrowing, the logic can be explained this way: "If the unadjusted cash balance is less than the minimum acceptable cash, then borrow enough to bring the balance to the minimum. However, if the firm has some investments, reduce the amount of borrowing by the amount of the investments (or total borrowing needs, whichever is less). If the unadjusted cash balance is greater than the minimum and the firm has previous borrowing, then use the cash above the minimum to reduce the outstanding borrowing." Writing a formula to implement this logic is complex, and it should be built in small pieces. After each piece, verify the result and then add on the next piece.

Writing this formula requires the use of nested **If** statements. That is, we embed a second **If** statement within the first. In pseudocode this is:

If Unadjusted Cash < Minimum Cash then {Firm needs to raise funds}
   If Cumulative Borrowing (Investing) < 0 then {Firm has investments it can sell}
      Current Borrowing = Minimum Cash + Cumulative Borrowing (Investing) – Unadjusted Cash
   Else Current Borrowing = Minimum Cash – Unadjusted Cash {Must Borrow it all}
Else {Firm doesn't need to raise funds}
   If Cumulative Borrowing (Investing) > 0 then {Use excess funds to reduce previous borrowings}
      Current Borrowing = –Minimum(Cumulative Borrowing (Investing), Unadjusted Cash – Minimum
Cash)
   Else Current Borrowing = 0
End If

The formula to calculate current borrowing in June, E31, is:
`=IF(E30<$B$37,IF(D34<0,MAX($B$37+D34-E30,0),$B$37-E30),IF(D34>0,-MIN(D34,E30-$B$37),0))`. Type this formula carefully, and then copy it to F31:H31. Note that we have also used the built-in **Max** and **Min** functions. **Max** returns the largest and **Min** returns the smallest of the supplied arguments. These functions are defined as:

$$\textbf{Max}(\textit{Number1, Number2, ...})$$

$$\textbf{Min}(\textit{Number1, Number2, ...})$$

In these functions, **Number1**, **Number2**, etc. are the set of up to 30 arguments. In this formula, the **Max** function is required to be sure that we don't end up with negative borrowing if the investments are more than sufficient to cover cash needs (i.e., we don't want to sell all of the investments if we don't need to). The **Min** function is used when the firm has excess cash and has some outstanding loans to pay off. It finds the minimum of either (1) the cumulative amount of borrowing outstanding, or (2) the difference between the unadjusted cash balance and the minimum acceptable cash balance. Note that we had to use the negative result of the **Min** function in order to get the correct result.

Using the Formula Auditing Tools to Avoid Errors

Sometimes the logic you need to solve a problem can get a bit complicated, as above. It is important to carefully think it through and build your formulas one small piece at a time. In this way, we can slowly build up a large, complex formula that always works. That's exactly how the above formula was created. However, no matter how careful you are in building a complex formula there is always the possibility of errors creeping in. Fortunately, there are several ways to identify these errors before they become serious problems (i.e., cost you or your company real money).

One of the best ways to avoid errors is to thoroughly test your formulas. The easiest way to do this is to change some numbers that the formula depends on and make sure that you are still getting correct answers. For example, we might temporarily change our ending cash balance in May. Then, carefully work through the ending cash balance calculations to make sure they are working correctly.

Debugging Formulas

Finding errors in the first version of a complex formula is almost guaranteed. Fortunately, Excel provides several tools to help find and correct the cause. In the following subsections we will take a short detour from our example to discuss these tools.

Using the F9 Function Key

In previous versions (before 2002), one of Excel's most useful and probably least-known tools was the F9 function key. This is still available and very valuable. Normally, pressing F9 causes a worksheet to recalculate, but when you use it in the formula bar it shows the contents of a cell address or the result of a calculation. For example, select E31 and highlight the first condition in the **If** statement as shown in Figure 3-5.

FIGURE 3-5
USING THE F9 KEY IN THE FORMULA BAR

Before pressing F9

✗ ✓ *ƒₓ* =IF(E30<$B$37,IF(D34<0,$B$37+D34-E30,$B$37-E30),IF(D34>0,-MIN(D34,E30-$B$37),0))

After pressing F9, we see that the expression is true

✗ ✓ *ƒₓ* =IF(TRUE,IF(D34<0,$B$37+D34-E30,$B$37-E30),IF(D34>0,-MIN(D34,E30-$B$37),0))

When you press F9, Excel evaluates the expression "E30<$B$37" and then reports that the result is true (E30 is, in fact, less than B37). Note that we also could have highlighted just the "E30" part of this expression and, after pressing F9, Excel would show that the value in E30 is equal to 1,200. Now, applying the same technique to the other part of the expression would show that B37 is equal to 15,000. At this point, the first part of the formula would show as "1200<15000" which is obviously true. This technique is very useful for checking parts of an equation to make sure they are accurate.

One caveat to this trick is that if you now press Enter to return to the worksheet, your equation will be changed to include the results instead of reverting to the cell addresses. It is crucial to press the Esc key rather than Enter in order to avoid locking in the changes you've made.

Color-Coded Cell Addresses

Another member of the error-checking toolkit is the use of color coding in formulas. When you create or edit a formula, Excel colors the cell addresses and highlights each of those cells in that same color. This allows you to easily see which cells are being used. If you notice that you've used an incorrect cell or range, you can grab the colored outline and expand, contract, or move it to another location. This will change the appropriate cell or range of cells in your formula.

Automatic Error Checking

For the last several versions, Excel has had the Formula Auditing toolbar; but it was greatly improved in Excel 2002. To see this toolbar go to **V**iew **T**oolbars and click on Formula Auditing.[5]

FIGURE 3-6
THE FORMULA AUDITING TOOLBAR

---

5. If the Formula Auditing toolbar is not on this menu, you'll need to choose **C**ustomize at the bottom of the menu. On the Toolbars tab, click the checkbox next to Formula Auditing. It's a good idea to look at some of the other toolbars to see what else you might find useful.

The first icon on the Formula Auditing toolbar is for error checking. Excel will examine your worksheet for common types of errors and will walk you through them. However, unless you have turned off background error checking (go to **T**ools **O**ptions Error Checking tab), Excel performs this error checking automatically. If background error checking is on, a green triangle will appear in the upper-left corner of the cell along with a Smart Tag that explains the error and offers a solution. Errors in logic cannot, of course, be detected; but many other types of errors can be.

Be aware that in some cases Excel will think you've made an error when you have not. Don't automatically accept the proposed fix. If this happens repeatedly, you can tell Excel to stop checking for that type of error, or turn off background error checking completely.

Tracing Precedent and Dependent Cells

The next five icons in the Formula Auditing toolbar are for tracing precedent or dependent cells. A precedent cell is one upon which a formula depends, while a dependent cell is one that depends on the result of the formula in the active cell. If the active cell contains a formula, clicking the Trace Precedents icon will display arrows from the precedent cells. The arrows in Exhibit 3-2 (page 78) were created in this way. The Trace Dependents icon works the same way, except that the arrows point to dependent cells.

The Watch Window

When working on a large worksheet, it is common to find yourself changing a value in one location and jumping to another to check the result. The Watch Window in Excel 2003 is a powerful tool which helps to speed up formula debugging by letting you watch a distant cell without having to scroll to it. To activate this tool, click on the next-to-last icon on the Formula Auditing toolbar or go to **T**ools Formula A**u**diting Show **W**atch Window.

Once the Watch Window is displayed, you can choose one or more cells to watch by clicking the Add Watch button and choosing the cell. In Figure 3-7 we have selected E31. With this window displayed, you can scroll to any part of the worksheet, change a cell value, and see what happens to E31. Note that if you close the Watch Window (or even save and close the workbook), the watch cells are not cleared. That allows you to open it again to continue watching the cell.

FIGURE 3-7
THE WATCH WINDOW

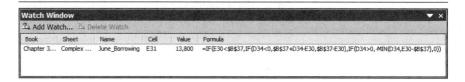

The Evaluate Formula Tool

Finally, perhaps the best feature for formula debugging is the Evaluate Formula tool. This tool lets you step through a formula piece by piece as Excel evaluates it. It works much like the F9 function key, except that it will step through the entire formula one step at a time. To activate this tool, click on the last icon on the Formula Auditing toolbar or go to **T**ools Formula A**u**diting Evaluate **F**ormula.

Figure 3-8 shows the Evaluate Formula dialog box with the formula in E31 ready to be evaluated. Note that E30 is underlined, indicating that it will be evaluated first. Simply click the **E**valuate button and "E30" will be replaced with "1200." Now, $B$37 will be underlined and ready to be evaluated. You can continue to click the **E**valuate button to work through the entire formula.

FIGURE 3-8
THE EVALUATE FORMULA TOOL

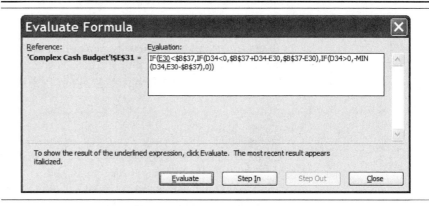

An additional feature is the Step **I**n function. For those expressions that themselves are the result of a formula, you can "step in" to the previous formula and evaluate it. For example, D34 is actually the result of the formula =C34+D31−D32. When D34 is underlined, clicking the Step **I**n button will allow you to evaluate this formula and then return to evaluating the rest of the original formula.

One of the most difficult tasks in the process of building a spreadsheet model is making sure that it works correctly under all conditions. Making use of the tips and tools discussed here can make the job much simpler. Let's now return to our cash budgeting example.

Calculating Current Investing

If Bithlo Barbecues has cash in excess of the maximum ($40,000 in this case), the cash should be invested in short-term securities. This is the essential idea behind the current investing item. Note that since we have added the Current Investing line, we must adjust our ending cash balance formula to take investing into account. The correct formula, in D33, is: =SUM(D30:D31)−D32. That is, our ending cash balance is now going to be the Unadjusted Cash Balance plus the Current Borrowing minus Current Investing. (Investing is a cash outflow, so it must be subtracted.) Copy this formula to E33:H33.

The current borrowing formula was constructed so that the firm will first sell any existing short-term investments before borrowing. Therefore, if the sum of the unadjusted cash balance and current borrowing is less than the minimum required cash, the firm needs to sell some investments. Otherwise, if the unadjusted cash balance plus current borrowing is greater than the maximum acceptable cash, the firm must invest the excess.

To implement this logic, we will again use nested **IF** statements. We also need to use the **AND** statement, which allows us to evaluate several conditions and then returns true only if all of the arguments are true. The **AND** statement is defined as follows:

$$\text{AND}(\textbf{\textit{LOGICAL1}}, \textit{LOGICAL2},\ldots)$$

In this function, **_LOGICAL1_**, _LOGICAL2_, etc. are up to 30 arguments, each of which can be evaluated as true or false. We will use this statement to determine if both of the following conditions are true: (1) unadjusted cash + current borrowing is less than the minimum cash, and (2) cumulative borrowing (investing) is negative (meaning that the firm has investments).

The formula to calculate the amount of current investing, in E32, is: =IF(AND(E30+E31<$B$37,D34<0),E30+E31-$B$37, IF(E30+E31>$B$38,E30+E31-$B$38,0)). Enter this formula and copy it across to F32:H32. Now copy the formula to D32 as well. Again, this is a complex formula, but it can be broken down into more understandable components:

If Unadjusted Cash + Borrowing < Minimum Cash **and** Cumulative Borrowing (Investing) < 0 then
   Current Investing = Unadjusted Cash + Borrowing – Minimum Cash
Else
  If Unadjusted Cash + Borrowing > Maximum Cash then
    Current Investing = Unadjusted Cash + Borrowing – Maximum Cash
  Else
    Current Investing = 0
End.

At this point, this portion of your cash budget should resemble that in Exhibit 3-8.

Working Through the Example

To understand the complex cash budget, you must work through it line by line. In this section, we will do just that. Follow along in Exhibit 3-8.

June (column E): The unadjusted cash balance in June is projected to be only $1,200. Since this is less than the $15,000 minimum, the firm needs to raise funds. In this case it has no investments to sell, so it must borrow $13,800 to bring the ending cash balance to $15,000.

July (column F): The firm is projecting that it will be overdrawn by $76,492. Again, it has no investments to sell and must borrow an additional $91,492. Note that its cumulative borrowing is now $105,292.

EXHIBIT 3-8
CALCULATING THE CASH BALANCE WITH BORROWING AND INVESTING

	A	B	C	D	E	F	G	H
28	Beginning Cash Balance				20,000	15,000	15,000	15,506
29	Collections - Disbursements				(18,800)	(91,492)	105,798	29,350
30	Unadjusted Cash Balance			20,000	1,200	(76,492)	120,798	44,856
31	Current Borrowing			0	13,800	91,492	(105,292)	0
32	Current Investing			0	0	0	0	4,856
33	**Ending Cash Balance**			**20,000**	**15,000**	**15,000**	**15,506**	**40,000**
34	Cumulative Borrowing (Investing)			0	13,800	105,292	0	(4,856)
35	Cumulative Interest Expense (Inc.)				0	92	794	794
36	Notes:							
37	Minimum Acceptable Cash	15,000						
38	Maximum Acceptable Cash	40,000						
39	Borrowing Rate (Annual)	8%	Monthly	0.67%				
40	Lending Rate (Annual)	6%	Monthly	0.50%				

August (column G): The firm is projecting an unadjusted cash balance of $120,798, well in excess of the maximum allowable cash. Before investing the excess, however, it needs to pay off the $105,292 of existing short-term debt. In this case, the firm can pay off the entire balance and still remain above the minimum cash requirement. However, after paying down the loans, its cash balance is not high enough to cause investment of excess funds.

September (column H): The firm is projecting that the unadjusted cash balance will be $44,856. In this case, there is no borrowing balance, so the $4,856 in excess of the maximum allowable cash can be invested, and the ending cash balance will be $40,000. Note that the Cumulative Borrowing (Investing) in H34 is negative, indicating that the funds represent investments.

In any complex worksheet such as this one, it is important that you work through the calculations by hand to check the results. Never accept the output until you are sure that it is absolutely correct. With this in mind, let's change the maximum acceptable cash in B38 to $15,000 and work through this alternative scenario. First, make sure that this portion of your worksheet is the same as that in Exhibit 3-9.

EXHIBIT 3-9
CASH BALANCE AFTER CHANGING MAXIMUM CASH TO $15,000

	A	B	C	D	E	F	G	H
28	Beginning Cash Balance				15,000	15,000	15,000	15,000
29	Collections - Disbursements				(18,775)	(91,492)	105,798	29,353
30	Unadjusted Cash Balance			20,000	(3,775)	(76,492)	120,798	44,353
31	Current Borrowing			0	13,775	91,492	(105,267)	0
32	Current Investing			5,000	(5,000)	0	531	29,353
33	**Ending Cash Balance**			**15,000**	**15,000**	**15,000**	**15,000**	**15,000**
34	Cumulative Borrowing (Investing)			(5,000)	13,775	105,267	(531)	(29,884)
35	Cumulative Interest Expense (Inc.)				(25)	67	769	766
36	Notes:							
37	Minimum Acceptable Cash	15,000						
38	Maximum Acceptable Cash	15,000						
39	Borrowing Rate (Annual)	8%	Monthly	0.67%				
40	Lending Rate (Annual)	6%	Monthly	0.50%				

May (column D): The unadjusted cash balance is greater than the minimum cash, so the firm does not need to borrow. In fact, it has $5,000 more than the maximum allowable cash that can be invested. The ending cash balance is $15,000.

June (column E): The firm is projecting the unadjusted cash balance to be −$3,775, but it does not borrow $18,775 (=$15,000 − [−$3,775]) because it has $5,000 in investments from May that reduce the borrowing need to only $13,775. Current Investing, therefore, is −$5,000.

July (column F): The unadjusted cash balance is projected to be −$76,492, and there are no investments that can be sold. Therefore, the firm must borrow $91,492. The cumulative borrowing is now $105,267.

August (column G): The firm is expected to have a large surplus of funds that can be used to pay off the entire loan balance. Furthermore, it will have $531 in excess of the maximum allowable cash which is available to invest. **September** (column H): The unadjusted cash balance is expected to be $44,353 which is $29,353 in excess of the maximum. This amount can be invested.

You are encouraged to experiment by changing values throughout the cash budget to see what happens. In particular, changing the projected sales and/or the payment schedule can be very enlightening. For example, suppose that Bithlo Barbecues' management decides to slow down payments for inventory purchases. Specifically, assume that it decides to pay only 40% in the month after the purchase, and 60% two months after the purchase. You should find that this is not as good an idea as it sounds. Table 3-4 shows Cumulative Borrowing (Investing) before and after the change, assuming that the maximum cash is still $15,000. Note that the firm would end up borrowing a little more under this scenario, and the total interest paid would be higher.

TABLE 3-4
CUMULATIVE BORROWING (INVESTING)

Month	Before	After
May	(5,000)	(5,000)
June	13,775	11,575
July	105,267	108,852
August	(531)	12,178
September	(29,984)	(7,791)
Cumulative Interest Expense Through September	766	859

Summary

In this chapter we have seen that the cash budget is simply a listing of the firm's expected *cash* inflows and outflows over a period of time. Cash budgets are useful in determining the firm's short-term borrowing and investing needs, as well as scheduling transactions. The cash budget is composed of three sections: (1) the worksheet area; (2) collections and disbursements; and (3) the ending cash balance. We also saw how Excel's Scenario Manager tool can greatly simplify "what-if" analysis and display a table of the results.

One of the most important lessons in this chapter is that complex spreadsheets should be built up from simpler spreadsheets. In other words, start by building a simple version of the worksheet that covers the basics, and then gradually add the complex details. In this chapter, we started with a very simple cash budget, then added borrowing, interest on borrowing, and finally investing and the interest on invested funds. This method will make building the worksheet much easier, and it will be less likely to contain errors. If you do find errors, we have covered some of the tools that Excel provides to help you find and fix them quickly. The Watch Window and Evaluate Formula tools are especially helpful in this regard.

FUNCTIONS INTRODUCED IN THIS CHAPTER

Purpose	Function	Page
Returns a value based on a logical test	IF(*LOGICAL_TEST, VALUE_IF_TRUE, VALUE_IF_FALSE*)	83
Determines the minimum of a list of arguments	MIN(*NUMBER1, NUMBER2,...*)	93
Returns true only if all arguments are true	AND(*LOGICAL1, LOGICAL2,...*)	98

Problems

1. Littleton Electronics' ending cash balance as of January 31, 2008 (the end of its fiscal year 2007) was $25,000. Its expected cash collections and payments for the next six months are given in the following table.

Month	Collections	Payments
February	$15,000	$18,000
March	17,500	19,700
April	21,300	24,200
May	26,000	25,900
June	32,000	26,700
July	37,500	28,400

    a. Calculate the firm's expected ending cash balance for each month.

    b. Assuming that the firm must maintain an ending cash balance of at least $20,000, how much must they borrow during each month?

    c. If the firm must pay 8% annual interest on its short-term borrowing, how does this affect your ending cash balance calculations?

    d. Finally, how would your ending cash balance change if the firm uses any cash in excess of the minimum to pay off its short-term borrowing in each month?

2. Loblaw Manufacturing has asked you to create a cash budget in order to determine its borrowing needs over August to December period. You have gathered the following information.

Month	Sales	Other Payments
August	160,000	80,000
September	110,000	65,000
October	95,000	60,000
November	84,000	45,000
December	76,000	48,000
January 2009	90,000	

June and July sales were $125,000 and $140,000, respectively. The firm collects 30% of its sales during the month, 60% the following month, and 10% two months after the sale. Each month it purchases inventory equal to 65% of the next month's expected sales. The company pays for 40% of its inventory purchases in the same month, and 60% in the following month. However, the firm's suppliers give it a 2% discount if it pays during the same month as the purchase. A minimum cash balance of $30,000 must be maintained each month, and the firm pays 9% annually for short-term borrowing from its bank.

a. Create a cash budget for August to December 2008. The cash budget should account for short-term borrowing and payback of outstanding loans.

b. Bob Loblaw, the president, is considering stretching out the firm's inventory payments. He believes that it may be less expensive to borrow from suppliers than from the bank. He has asked you to use the Scenario Manager to see what the total interest cost for this time period would be if the company paid for 0%, 10%, 30%, or 40% of its inventory purchases in the same month. The balance would be paid in the following month. Create a scenario summary and describe whether or not the results support Bob's beliefs.

3. Huggins and Griffin Financial Planners have forecasted revenues for the first six months of 2008, as shown in the following table.

Month	Revenue
November 2007	$48,000
December	45,000
January 2008	25,000
February	27,000
March	30,000
April	38,000
May	40,000
June	45,000

The firm collects 60% of its sales immediately, 39% one month after the sale, and 1% are written off as bad debts two months after the sale. The firm assumes that wages and benefits paid to clerical personnel will be $7,000 per month while commissions to sales associates average 25% of collectable sales. Each of the two partners is paid $5,000 per month or 20% of net sales, whichever is greater. Commissions and partner salaries are paid one month after the revenue is earned. Rent expense for their office space is $2,500 per month, and lease expense for office equipment is $800/Utilities average $175 per month, except in May and June when they average only $100. The ending cash balance in December 2007 was $12,000.

a. Create a cash budget for January to June 2008, and determine the firm's ending cash balance in each month assuming that the partners wish to maintain a minimum cash balance of $8,000.

b. Huggins and Griffin are thinking of obtaining a line of credit from their bank. Based on their expectations for the first six months of the year, what is the minimum amount that would be necessary? Round your answer to the next highest $1,000 and ignore interest charges on short-term debt. (Hint: Look up the ROUNDUP function in the online help.)

c. Create three scenarios (best case, base case, and worst case) assuming that sales are 10% better than expected, exactly as expected, or 10% worse than expected. What is the maximum that the firm would need to borrow to maintain its minimum cash balance in all three cases? Use the Scenario Manager and create a summary of your results. Would this change your answer in part B?

4. You have recently been hired to improve the financial condition of Idaho Springs Hardware, a small chain of three hardware stores in the mountain communities of Colorado. On your first day the owner, Chuck Vitaska, told you that the biggest problem facing the firm has been periodic unexpected cash shortages that have made it necessary for him to delay wage payments to his employees. Having recently received a degree in finance, you immediately realize that your first priority is to develop a cash budget and to arrange for a short-term borrowing agreement with the firm's bank. After looking at the firm's past financial records, you developed a sales forecast for the remainder of the year, as presented in the following table.

Month	Sales
June 2008	$62,000
July	73,000
August	76,000
September	70,000
October	59,000
November	47,000
December	41,000

In addition to the seasonality of sales, you have observed several other patterns. Individuals account for about 40% of the firm's sales, and they pay in cash. The other 60% of sales are to contractors with credit accounts, and due to the credit policy, they have up to 60 days to pay. As a result, about 20% of sales to contractors are paid one month after the sale, and the other 80% is paid two months after the sale. Each month the firm purchases inventory equal to about 45% of the following month's sales. About 30% of this inventory is paid for in the month of delivery, while the remaining 70% is paid one month later.

Each month the company pays its hourly employees a total of $9,000, including benefits. Its salaried employees are paid $12,000, also including benefits. In the past the company has had to borrow to build its stores and for the initial inventories. This debt has resulted in monthly interest payments of $4,000 and monthly principal payments of $221. On average, maintenance at the stores is expected to cost about $700 per month—except in the October to December period, when snow removal costs will add about $200 per month. Sales taxes are 7% of quarterly sales and must be paid in June, September, and December. Other taxes are also paid during those months and are expected to be about 4% of quarterly sales in each of those months. The owner wishes to maintain a cash balance of at least $12,000 to limit the risk of cash shortages. The cash balance at the end of May is expected to be $15,000 (before any borrowing or investing).

a. Create a simple cash budget for Idaho Springs Hardware for June to December. Note that your records indicate that sales in April and May were $51,000 and $57,000, respectively. January 2009 sales are expected to be $36,000. What would the ending cash balances be if the firm does not borrow to maintain its $12,000 minimum?

b. Now assume that the firm can borrow from the bank at a rate of 9% per annum to maintain its liquidity and meet its required minimum cash balance. In addition, if the firm has funds in excess of the minimum, it will use the excess to pay off any previous balance.

c. While negotiating a line of credit, the bank's cash management department offered to sweep any cash in excess of the minimum into a money market fund that will return an average of 4% per year after expenses. If you accept this offer, how will it affect the firm's ending cash balances and need to borrow in each month? Note that the firm must have paid off all short-term loans before any excess cash can be invested, and invested funds will be used instead of borrowing when needed.

d. After completing your cash budget, you begin to think of ways to further reduce the firm's borrowing needs. One idea that comes to mind is changing the firm's credit policy with contractors because they always seem to pay at the last minute. Three scenarios come to mind: (1) In the best case, contractors are required to pay for 100% of their purchases during the month after the sale. You believe that this would cause a 5% decline in sales. (2) In the base case, everything remains as already outlined. (3) In the worst case, contractors would be required to pay for 100% of their purchases during the month after the sale, and you believe that this would cause a 20% drop in sales. You decide to use the Scenario Manager to evaluate these scenarios. To summarize the impact of the change, you will examine the impact on the firm's maximum borrowing needs, and cumulative net interest cost (after accounting for investment earnings). In your opinion, should the firm change its credit policy?

CHAPTER 4

Financial Statement Analysis Tools

After studying this chapter, you should be able to:

1. *Describe what financial ratios are and who uses them.*

2. *Define the five major categories of ratios (liquidity, efficiency, leverage, coverage, and profitability).*

3. *Calculate the common ratios for any firm by using income statement and balance sheet data.*

4. *Use financial ratios to assess a firm's past performance, identify its current problems, and suggest strategies for dealing with these problems.*

5. *Calculate the economic profit earned by a firm.*

In previous chapters we have seen how the firm's basic financial statements are constructed. In this chapter we will see how financial analysts can use the information contained in the income statement and balance sheet for various purposes.

You can use several tools to evaluate a company, but some of the most valuable are financial ratios. Ratios are an analyst's microscope; they allow us get a better view of the firm's financial health than does just looking at the raw financial statements. Ratios are useful both to internal and external analysts of the firm. For internal purposes, ratios can be useful in planning for the future, setting goals, and evaluating the performance of managers. External analysts use ratios to decide whether to grant credit, to monitor financial performance, to forecast financial performance, and to decide whether to invest in the company.

We will look at many different ratios, but you should be aware that these are, of necessity, only a sampling of the ratios that might be useful. Furthermore, different analysts may calculate ratios slightly differently, so you will need to know exactly how the ratios are calculated in a given situation. The keys to understanding ratio analysis are experience and an analytical mind.

We will divide our discussion of the ratios into five categories based on the information provided:

1. *Liquidity ratios* describe the ability of a firm to meets its current obligations.

2. *Efficiency ratios* describe how well the firm is using its investment in various types of assets to produce sales. They may also be called asset management ratios.

3. *Leverage ratios* reveal the degree to which debt has been used to finance the firm's asset purchases. These ratios are also known as debt management ratios.

4. *Coverage ratios* are similar to liquidity ratios in that they describe the ability of a firm to pay certain expenses.

5. *Profitability ratios* provide indications of how profitable a firm has been over a period of time.

Before we begin the discussion of individual financial ratios, open your Elvis Products International workbook from Chapter 2 and add a new worksheet named "Ratios."

Liquidity Ratios

The term "liquidity" refers to the speed with which an asset can be converted into cash without large discounts to its value. Some assets, such as accounts receivable, can easily be converted to cash with only small discounts. Other assets, such as buildings, can be converted into cash very quickly only if large price concessions are given. We therefore say that accounts receivable are more liquid than buildings.

All other things being equal, a firm with more liquid assets will be more able to meet its maturing obligations (i.e., its bills) than a firm with fewer liquid assets. As you might imagine, creditors are particularly concerned with a firm's ability to pay its bills. To assess this ability, it is common to use the current ratio and/or the quick ratio.

The Current Ratio

Generally, a firm's current assets are converted to cash (e.g., collecting on accounts receivables or selling its inventories), and this cash is used to retire its current liabilities. Therefore, it is logical to assess the firm's ability to pay its bills by comparing the size of its current assets to the size of its current liabilities. The current ratio does exactly this. It is defined as:

$$\text{Current Ratio} = \frac{\text{Current Assets}}{\text{Current Liabilities}} \tag{4-1}$$

Obviously, the higher the current ratio, the higher the likelihood that a firm will be able to pay its bills. So, from the creditor's point of view, higher is better. However, from a shareholder's point of view this is not always the case. Current assets usually have a lower expected return than do fixed assets, so the shareholders would like to see that only the minimum amount of the company's capital is invested in current assets. Of course, too little investment in current assets could be disastrous for both creditors and owners of the firm.

We can calculate the current ratio for 2007 for EPI by looking at the balance sheet (Exhibit 2-2, page 53). In this case, we have:

$$\text{Current Ratio} = \frac{1290.00}{540.20} = 2.39 \text{ times}$$

meaning that EPI has 2.39 times as many current assets as current liabilities. We will determine later whether this is sufficient or not.

Exhibit 4-1 shows the beginnings of our "Ratios" worksheet. Enter the labels as shown.

EXHIBIT 4-1

RATIO WORKSHEET FOR EPI[1]

	A	B	C	D
1	Elvis Products International			
2	Ratio Analysis for 2006 and 2007			
3	Ratio		2007	2006
4	Liquidity Ratios			
5	Current Ratio		2.39x	2.33x

We can calculate the current ratio for 2007 in C5 with the formula: `='Balance Sheet'!B8/'Balance Sheet'!B17`. After formatting to show two decimal places, you will see that the current ratio is 2.39. Copy the formula to D5.

Notice that we have applied a custom number format (see page 54 to refresh your memory) to the result in C5. In this case, the custom format is `0.00"x"`. Any text that you include in quotes will be shown along with the number. However, the presence of the text in the display does not affect the fact that it is still a number and may be used for calculations. As an experiment, in C6 enter the formula: `=C5*2`. The result will be 4.78, just as if we hadn't applied the custom format. Now, in C7 type: `2.39x` and then copy the formula from C6 to C8. You will get a #VALUE error because the value in C7 is a text string, not a number. This is one of the great advantages to custom number formatting: we can have both text and numbers in a cell and still use the number for calculations. Delete C6:C8 so that we can use the cells in the next section.

The Quick Ratio

Inventories are often the least liquid of the firm's current assets.[2] For this reason, many believe that a better measure of liquidity can be obtained by excluding inventories. The result is known as the quick ratio (sometimes called the acid-test ratio), and is calculated as:

$$\text{Quick Ratio} = \frac{\text{Current Assets} - \text{Inventories}}{\text{Current Liabilities}} \tag{4-2}$$

For EPI in 2007, the quick ratio is:

---

1. We are reserving column B for use later in the chapter.
2. That is why you so often see 50% off sales when firms are going out of business.

$$\text{Quick Ratio} = \frac{1290.00 - 836.00}{540.20} = 0.84 \text{ times}$$

Notice that the quick ratio will always be less than the current ratio. This is by design. However, a quick ratio that is too low relative to the current ratio may indicate that inventories are higher than they should be.

We can calculate EPI's 2007 quick ratio in C6 with the formula: `=('Balance Sheet'!B8-'Balance Sheet'!B7)/'Balance Sheet'!B17`. Copying this formula to D6 reveals that the 2006 quick ratio was 0.85. Be sure to remember to enter a label in column A for all of the ratios.

Efficiency Ratios

Efficiency ratios, as the name implies, provide information about how well the company is using its assets to generate sales. For example, if two firms have the same level of sales, but one firm has a lower investment in inventories, we would say that the firm with lower inventories is more efficient with respect to its inventory investment.

There are many different types of efficiency ratios that could be defined. However, we will illustrate five of the most common.

Inventory Turnover Ratio

The inventory turnover ratio measures the number of dollars of sales that are generated per dollar of inventory. It also tells us the number of times that a firm replaces its inventories during a year. It is calculated as:

$$\text{Inventory Turnover Ratio} = \frac{\text{Cost of Goods Sold}}{\text{Inventory}} \tag{4-3}$$

Note that it is also common to use sales in the numerator. Since the only difference between sales and cost of goods sold is a markup, this causes no problems. In addition, you will frequently see the average level of inventories throughout the year in the denominator. Whenever using ratios, you need to be aware of the method of calculation to be sure that you are comparing "apples to apples."

For 2007, EPI's inventory turnover ratio was:

$$\text{Inventory Turnover Ratio} = \frac{3,250.00}{836.00} = 3.89 \text{ times}$$

meaning that EPI replaced its inventories about 3.89 times during the year. Alternatively, we could say that EPI generated $3.89 in sales for each dollar invested in inventories.

To calculate the inventory turnover ratio for EPI, enter the formula: =`'Income Statement'!B6/'Balance Sheet'!B7` into C8 and copy this formula to D8. Notice that this ratio has deteriorated somewhat from 4 times in 2006 to 3.89 times in 2007. Generally, high inventory turnover is considered to be good because it means that storage costs are low, but if it is too high the firm may be risking inventory outages and the loss of customers.

Accounts Receivable Turnover Ratio

Businesses grant credit to customers for one main reason: to increase sales. It is important, therefore, to know how well the firm is managing its accounts receivable. The accounts receivable turnover ratio (and the average collection period, below) provides us with this information. It is calculated by:

$$\text{Accounts Receivable Turnover Ratio} = \frac{\text{Credit Sales}}{\text{Accounts Receivable}} \qquad \text{(4-4)}$$

For EPI, the 2007 accounts receivable turnover ratio is (assuming that all sales are credit sales):

$$\text{Accounts Receivable Turnover Ratio} = \frac{3,850.00}{402.00} = 9.58 \text{ times}$$

So each dollar invested in accounts receivable generated $9.58 in sales. In cell C9 of your worksheet, enter: =`'Income Statement'!B5/'Balance Sheet'!B6`. The result is 9.58, which is the same as we found above. Copy this formula to D9 to get the 2006 accounts receivable turnover.

Whether or not 9.58 is a good accounts receivable turnover ratio is difficult to know at this point. We can say that higher is generally better, but too high might indicate that the firm is denying credit to creditworthy customers (thereby losing sales). If the ratio is too low, it would suggest that the firm is having difficulty collecting on its sales. We would have to see if the growth rate in accounts receivable exceeds the growth rate in sales to determine whether the firm is having difficulty in this area.

Average Collection Period

The average collection period (also known as days sales outstanding) tells us how many days, on average, it takes to collect on a credit sale.

$$\text{Average Collection Period} = \frac{\text{Accounts Receivable}}{\text{Annual Credit Sales}/360} \qquad (4\text{-}5)$$

Note that the denominator is simply credit sales per day.[3] In 2007, it took EPI an average of 37.59 days to collect on their credit sales:

$$\text{Average Collection Period} = \frac{402.00}{3{,}850.00/360} = 37.59 \text{ days}$$

We can calculate the 2007 average collection period in C10 with the formula: `='Balance Sheet'!B6/('Income Statement'!B5/360)`. Copy this to D10 to find that in 2006 the average collection period was 36.84, days, which was slightly better than in 2007.

Note that this ratio actually provides us with the same information as the accounts receivable turnover ratio. In fact, it can easily be demonstrated by simple algebraic manipulation:

$$\text{Accounts Receivable Turnover Ratio} = \frac{360}{\text{Average Collection Period}}$$

or alternatively:

$$\text{Average Collection Period} = \frac{360}{\text{Accounts Receivable Turnover Ratio}}$$

Since the average collection period is (in a sense) the inverse of the accounts receivable turnover ratio, it should be apparent that the inverse criteria apply to judging this ratio. In other words, lower is usually better, but too low may indicate lost sales.

---

3. The use of a 360-day year dates back to the days before computers. It was derived by assuming that there are 12 months, each with 30 days (known as a "Banker's Year"). You may also use 365 days; the difference is irrelevant as long as you are consistent.

Fixed Asset Turnover Ratio

The fixed asset turnover ratio describes the dollar amount of sales that are generated by each dollar invested in fixed assets. It is given by:

$$\text{Fixed Asset Turnover} = \frac{\text{Sales}}{\text{Net Fixed Assets}} \qquad (4\text{-}6)$$

For EPI, the 2007 fixed asset turnover is:

$$\text{Fixed Asset Turnover} = \frac{3,850.00}{360.80} = 10.67 \text{ times}$$

So, EPI generated $10.67 in revenue for each dollar invested in fixed assets. In your "Ratios" worksheet, entering: =`'Income Statement'!B5/'Balance Sheet'!B11` into C11 will confirm that the fixed asset turnover was 10.67 times in 2007. Again, copy this formula to D11 to get the 2006 ratio.

Total Asset Turnover Ratio

Like the other ratios discussed in this section, the total asset turnover ratio describes how efficiently the firm is using all of its assets to generate sales. In this case, we look at the firm's total asset investment:

$$\text{Total Asset Turnover} = \frac{\text{Sales}}{\text{Total Assets}} \qquad (4\text{-}7)$$

In 2007, EPI generated $2.33 in sales for each dollar invested in total assets:

$$\text{Total Asset Turnover} = \frac{3,850.00}{1,650.80} = 2.33 \text{ times}$$

This ratio can be calculated in C12 on your worksheet with: =`'Income Statement'!B5/'Balance Sheet'!B12`. After copying this formula to D12, you should see that the 2006 value was 2.34, essentially the same as 2007.

We can interpret the asset turnover ratios as follows: higher is better. However, you should be aware that some industries will naturally have lower turnover ratios than others. For example, a consulting business will almost surely have a very low investment in fixed assets, and therefore a high fixed asset turnover ratio. On the other hand, an electric utility will have a large investment in fixed assets and a low fixed asset turnover ratio. This does not mean, necessarily, that the utility company is more poorly managed than the consulting firm. Rather, each is simply responding to the demands of their very different industries.

At this point your worksheet should resemble the one in Exhibit 4-2. Notice that we have applied the custom format, discussed above, to most of these ratios. In C10 and D10, however, we used the custom format 0.00" days" because the average collection period is measured in days.

EXHIBIT 4-2
EPI'S FINANCIAL RATIOS

	A	B	C	D
1	Elvis Products International			
2	Ratio Analysis for 2006 and 2007			
3	Ratio		2007	2006
4	Liquidity Ratios			
5	Current Ratio		2.39x	2.33x
6	Quick Ratio		0.84x	0.85x
7	Efficiency Ratios			
8	Inventory Turnover		3.89x	4.00x
9	A/R Turnover		9.58x	9.77x
10	Average Collection Period		37.59 "days"	36.84 "days"
11	Fixed Asset Turnover		10.67x	9.95x
12	Total Asset Turnover		2.33x	2.34x

Leverage Ratios

In physics, leverage refers to a multiplication of force. Using a lever and fulcrum, you can press down on one end of a lever with a given force, and get a larger force at the other end. The amount of leverage depends on the length of the lever and the position of the fulcrum. In finance, leverage refers to a multiplication of changes in profitability measures. For example, a 10% increase in sales might lead to a 20% increase in net income.[4] The amount of leverage depends on the amount of debt that a firm uses to finance its operations, so a firm that uses a lot of debt is said to be "highly leveraged."

Leverage ratios describe the degree to which the firm uses debt in its capital structure. This is important information for creditors and investors in the firm.

---

4. As we will see in Chapter 6, this would mean that the degree of combined leverage is 2.

Creditors might be concerned that a firm has too much debt and will therefore have difficulty in repaying loans. Investors might be concerned because a large amount of debt can lead to a large amount of volatility in the firm's earnings. However, most firms use some debt. This is because the tax deductibility of interest can increase the wealth of the firm's shareholders. We will examine several ratios that help to determine the amount of debt that a firm is using. How much is too much depends on the nature of the business.

The Total Debt Ratio

The total debt ratio measures the total amount of debt (long-term and short-term) that the firm uses to finance its assets:

$$\text{Total Debt Ratio} = \frac{\text{Total Debt}}{\text{Total Assets}} = \frac{\text{Total Assets} - \text{Total Equity}}{\text{Total Assets}} \quad \text{(4-8)}$$

Calculating the total debt ratio for EPI, we find that debt financing makes up about 58.45% of the firm's capital structure:

$$\text{Total Debt Ratio} = \frac{964.81}{1,650.80} = 58.45\%$$

The formula to calculate the total debt ratio in C14 is: =`'Balance Sheet'!B19/'Balance Sheet'!B12`. The result for 2007 is 58.45%, which is higher than the 54.81% in 2006.

The Long-Term Debt Ratio

Many analysts believe that it is more useful to focus on just the long-term debt (LTD) instead of total debt. The long-term debt ratio is the same as the total debt ratio, except that the numerator includes only long-term debt:

$$\text{Long-Term Debt Ratio} = \frac{\text{Long-Term Debt}}{\text{Total Assets}} \quad \text{(4-9)}$$

EPI's long-term debt ratio is:

$$\text{Long-Term Debt Ratio} = \frac{424.61}{1,650.80} = 25.72\%$$

In C15, the formula to calculate the long-term debt ratio for 2007 is: =`'Balance Sheet'!B18/'Balance Sheet'!B12`. Copying this formula to D15 reveals that in 2006 the ratio was only 22.02%. Obviously, EPI has increased its long-term debt at a faster rate than it has added assets.

The Long-Term Debt to Total Capitalization Ratio

Similar to the previous two ratios, the long-term debt to total capitalization ratio tells us the percentage of long-term sources of capital that is provided by long-term debt (LTD). It is calculated by:

$$\text{LTD to Total Capitalization} = \frac{\text{LTD}}{\text{LTD + Preferred Equity + Common Equity}} \quad \text{(4-10)}$$

For EPI, we have:

$$\text{LTD to Total Capitalization} = \frac{424.61}{424.61 + 685.99} = 38.23\%$$

Since EPI has no preferred equity, its total capitalization consists of long-term debt and common equity. Note that common equity is the total of common stock and retained earnings. We can calculate this ratio in C16 of the worksheet with: =`'Balance Sheet'!B18/('Balance Sheet'!B18+'Balance Sheet'!B20+'Balance Sheet'!B21)`. In 2006 this ratio was only 32.76%.

The Debt to Equity Ratio

The debt to equity ratio provides exactly the same information as the total debt ratio, but in a slightly different form that some analysts prefer:

$$\text{Debt to Equity} = \frac{\text{Total Debt}}{\text{Total Equity}} \quad \text{(4-11)}$$

For EPI, the debt to equity ratio is:

$$\text{Debt to Equity} = \frac{964.81}{685.99} = 1.41 \text{ times}$$

In C17, this is calculated as: =`'Balance Sheet'!B19/'Balance Sheet'!B22`. Copy this to D17 to find that the debt to equity ratio in 2006 was 1.21 times.

To see that the total debt ratio and the debt to equity ratio provide the same information, realize that:

$$\frac{\text{Total Debt}}{\text{Total Equity}} = \frac{\text{Total Debt}}{\text{Total Assets}} \times \frac{\text{Total Assets}}{\text{Total Equity}} \qquad (4\text{-}12)$$

but from rearranging equation (4-8) we know that:

$$\frac{\text{Total Assets}}{\text{Total Equity}} = \frac{1}{1 - \text{Total Debt Ratio}} \qquad (4\text{-}13)$$

so, by substitution we have:

$$\frac{\text{Total Debt}}{\text{Total Equity}} = \frac{\text{Total Debt}}{\text{Total Assets}} \times \frac{1}{1 - \dfrac{\text{Total Debt}}{\text{Total Assets}}} \qquad (4\text{-}14)$$

We can convert the total debt ratio into the debt to equity ratio without any additional information (the result is not exact due to rounding):

$$\frac{\text{Total Debt}}{\text{Total Equity}} = 0.5845 \times \frac{1}{1 - 0.5845} = 1.41$$

The Long-Term Debt to Equity Ratio

Once again, many analysts prefer to focus on the amount of long-term debt that a firm carries. For this reason, many analysts like to use the long-term debt to total equity ratio:

$$\text{Long-Term Debt to Equity} = \frac{\text{LTD}}{\text{Preferred Equity} + \text{Common Equity}} \qquad (4\text{-}15)$$

EPI's long-term debt to equity ratio is:

$$\text{Long-Term Debt to Equity} = \frac{424.61}{685.99} = 61.90\%$$

The formula to calculate EPI's 2007 long-term debt to equity ratio in C18 is: ='Balance Sheet'!B18/'Balance Sheet'!B22. After copying this formula to E16, note that the ratio was only 48.73% in 2006.

At this point, your worksheet should look like the one in Exhibit 4-3.

EXHIBIT 4-3
EPI'S FINANCIAL RATIOS WITH THE LEVERAGE RATIOS

	A	B	C	D
1	Elvis Products International			
2	Ratio Analysis for 2006 and 2007			
3	Ratio		2007	2006
4	Liquidity Ratios			
5	Current Ratio		2.39x	2.33x
6	Quick Ratio		0.84x	0.85x
7	Efficiency Ratios			
8	Inventory Turnover		3.89x	4.00x
9	A/R Turnover		9.58x	9.77x
10	Average Collection Period		37.59 days	36.84 days
11	Fixed Asset Turnover		10.67x	9.95x
12	Total Asset Turnover		2.33x	2.34x
13	Leverage Ratios			
14	Total Debt Ratio		58.45%	54.81%
15	Long-term Debt Ratio		25.72%	22.02%
16	LTD to Total Capitalization		38.23%	32.76%
17	Debt to Equity		1.41x	1.21x
18	LTD to Equity		61.90%	48.73%

Coverage Ratios

The coverage ratios are similar to liquidity ratios in that they describe the quantity of funds available to "cover" certain expenses. We will examine two very similar ratios that describe the firm's ability to meet its interest payment obligations. In both cases, higher ratios are desirable to a degree. However, if they are too high, it may indicate that the firm is underutilizing its debt capacity, and therefore not maximizing shareholder wealth.

The Times Interest Earned Ratio

The times interest earned ratio measures the ability of the firm to pay its interest obligations by comparing earnings before interest and taxes (EBIT) to interest expense:

$$\text{Times Interest Earned} = \frac{\text{EBIT}}{\text{Interest Expense}} \tag{4-16}$$

For EPI in 2007 the times interest earned ratio is:

$$\text{Times Interest Earned} = \frac{149.70}{76.00} = 1.97 \text{ times}$$

In your worksheet, the times interest earned ratio can be calculated in C20 with the formula: `='Income Statement'!B11/'Income Statement'!B12`. Copy the formula to D20 and notice that this ratio has declined rather precipitously from 3.35 in 2006.

The Cash Coverage Ratio

EBIT does not really reflect the cash that is available to pay the firm's interest expense. That is because a non-cash expense (depreciation) has been subtracted in the calculation of EBIT. To correct for this deficiency, some analysts like to use the cash coverage ratio instead of times interest earned. The cash coverage ratio is calculated as:

$$\text{Cash Coverage Ratio} = \frac{\text{EBIT} + \text{Non-Cash Expenses}}{\text{Interest Expense}} \qquad \text{(4-17)}$$

The calculation for EPI in 2007 is:

$$\text{Cash Coverage Ratio} = \frac{149.70 + 20.00}{76.00} = 2.23 \text{ times}$$

Note that the cash coverage ratio will always be higher than the times interest earned ratio. The difference depends on the amount of depreciation expense, and therefore the amount and age of fixed assets.

The cash coverage ratio can be calculated in cell C21 of your "Ratios" worksheet with: `=('Income Statement'!B11+'Income Statement'!B10)/'Income Statement'!B12`. In 2006, the ratio was 3.65.

Profitability Ratios

Investors, and therefore managers, are particularly interested in the profitability of the firms that they own. As we'll see, there are many ways to measure profits. Profitability ratios provide an easy way to compare profits to earlier periods or to other firms. Furthermore, by simultaneously examining the first three profitability ratios, an analyst can discover categories of expenses that may be out of line.

Profitability ratios are the easiest of all of the ratios to analyze. Without exception, high ratios are preferred. However, the definition of "high" depends on the industry in which the firm operates. Generally, firms in mature industries with lots of competition will have lower profitability measures than will firms in younger industries with less competition. For example, grocery stores will have lower profit margins than computer software companies will. In the grocery business, a net profit margin of 3% would be considered quite high, but the same margin would be abysmal in the software business.

The Gross Profit Margin

The gross profit margin measures the gross profit relative to sales. It indicates the amount of funds available to pay the firm's expenses other than its cost of sales. The gross profit margin is calculated by:

$$\text{Gross Profit Margin} = \frac{\text{Gross Profit}}{\text{Sales}} \qquad \textbf{(4-18)}$$

In 2007, EPI's gross profit margin was:

$$\text{Gross Profit Margin} = \frac{600.00}{3,850.00} = 15.58\%$$

which means that cost of goods sold consumed about 84.42% ($= 1 - 0.1558$) of sales revenue. We can calculate this ratio in C23 with: `='Income Statement'!B7/'Income Statement'!B5`. After copying this formula to D23, you will see that the gross profit margin has declined from 16.55% in 2006.

The Operating Profit Margin

Moving down the income statement, we can calculate the profits that remain after the firm has paid all of its usual (non-financial) expenses.

The operating profit margin is calculated as:

$$\text{Operating Profit Margin} = \frac{\text{Net Operating Income}}{\text{Sales}} \qquad (4\text{-}19)$$

For EPI in 2007, the operating profit margin is:

$$\text{Operating Profit Margin} = \frac{149.70}{3,850.00} = 3.89\%$$

The operating profit margin can be calculated in C24 with the formula: =`'Income Statement'!B11/'Income Statement'!B5`. Note that this is significantly lower than the 6.09% from 2006, indicating that EPI seems to be having problems controlling its operating costs.

The Net Profit Margin

The net profit margin relates net income to sales. Since net income is profit after all expenses, the net profit margin tells us the percentage of sales that remains for the shareholders of the firm:

$$\text{Net Profit Margin} = \frac{\text{Net Income}}{\text{Sales}} \qquad (4\text{-}20)$$

The net profit margin for EPI in 2007 is:

$$\text{Net Profit Margin} = \frac{44.22}{3,850.00} = 1.15\%$$

which can be calculated on your worksheet in C25 with: =`'Income Statement'!B15/'Income Statement'!B5`. This is lower than the 2.56% in 2006. If you take a look at the common-size income statement (Exhibit 2-5, page 60), you can see that profitability has declined because cost of goods sold, SG&A expense, and interest expense have risen more quickly than sales.

Taken together, the three profit margin ratios that we have examined show a company that may be losing control over its costs. Of course, high expenses mean lower returns, and we'll see this confirmed by the next three profitability ratios.

Return on Total Assets

The total assets of a firm are the investment that the shareholders have made. Much like you might be interested in the returns generated by your investments, analysts are often interested in the return that a firm is able to get from its investments. The return on total assets is:

$$\text{Return on Total Assets} = \frac{\text{Net Income}}{\text{Total Assets}} \qquad (4\text{-}21)$$

In 2007, EPI earned about 2.68% on its assets:

$$\text{Return on Total Assets} = \frac{44.22}{1650.80} = 2.68\%$$

For 2007, we can calculate the return on total assets in cell C26 with the formula: `='Income Statement'!B15/'Balance Sheet'!B12`. Notice that this is more than 50% lower than the 5.99% recorded in 2006. EPI's total assets obviously increased in 2007 at a faster rate than did its net income (which actually declined).

Return on Equity

While total assets represent the total investment in the firm, the owners' investment (common stock and retained earnings) usually represent only a portion of this amount (some is debt). For this reason it is useful to calculate the rate of return on the shareholder's invested funds. We can calculate the return on (total) equity as:

$$\text{Return on Equity} = \frac{\text{Net Income}}{\text{Total Equity}} \qquad (4\text{-}22)$$

Note that if a firm uses no debt, then its return on equity will be the same as its return on assets. The more debt a firm uses, the higher its return on equity will be relative to its return on assets.

In 2007, EPI's return on equity was:

$$\text{Return on Equity} = \frac{44.22}{685.99} = 6.45\%$$

which can be calculated in C27 with: `='Income Statement'!B15/ 'Balance Sheet'!B22`. Again, copying this formula to D27 reveals that this ratio has declined from 13.25% in 2006.

Return on Common Equity

For firms that have issued preferred stock in addition to common stock, it is often helpful to determine the rate of return on just the common stockholders' investment:

$$\text{Return on Common Equity} = \frac{\text{Net Income Available to Common}}{\text{Common Equity}} \quad (4\text{-}23)$$

Net income available to common is net income less preferred dividends. In the case of EPI, this ratio is the same as the return on equity because the firm has no preferred shareholders:

$$\text{Return on Common Equity} = \frac{44.22 - 0}{685.99} = 6.45\%$$

For EPI, the worksheet formula for the return on common equity is exactly the same as for the return on equity.

The Du Pont Analysis

The return on equity (ROE) is important to both managers and investors. The effectiveness of managers is often measured by changes in ROE over time. Therefore, it is important that they understand what they can do to improve the firm's ROE, and that requires knowledge of what causes changes in ROE over time. For example, we can see that EPI's return on equity dropped precipitously from 2006 to 2007. As you might imagine, both investors and managers are probably trying to figure out why this happened. The Du Pont system is one way to look at this problem.

The Du Pont system is a way to break down the ROE into its components. Let's first take another look at the return on assets (ROA):

$$\text{ROA} = \frac{\text{Net Income}}{\text{Total Assets}} = \frac{\text{Net Income}}{\text{Sales}} \times \frac{\text{Sales}}{\text{Total Assets}} \quad (4\text{-}24)$$

So, the ROA shows the combined effects of profitability (as measured by the net profit margin) and the efficiency of asset usage (the total asset turnover). Therefore, the ROA could be improved by increasing profitability through expense reductions, or by increasing sales relative to total assets.

As mentioned earlier, the amount of leverage a firm uses is the linkage between the ROA and ROE. Specifically:

$$\text{ROE} = \frac{\text{Net Income}}{\text{Equity}} = \frac{\text{Net Income}}{\text{Total Assets}} \times \frac{\text{Total Assets}}{\text{Equity}} \qquad \textbf{(4-25)}$$

Note that the second term in (4-25) is sometimes called the "equity multiplier" and from (4-13), we know it is equal to:

$$\frac{\text{Total Assets}}{\text{Total Equity}} = \frac{1}{1 - \text{Total Debt Ratio}} = \frac{1}{1 - \dfrac{\text{Total Debt}}{\text{Total Assets}}} \qquad \textbf{(4-26)}$$

Substituting (4-26) into (4-25) and rearranging, we have:

$$\text{ROE} = \frac{\text{Net Income}}{\text{Total Assets}} \div \left(1 - \frac{\text{Total Debt}}{\text{Total Assets}} \right) \qquad \textbf{(4-27)}$$

We can now see that the ROE is a function of the firm's ROA and the total debt ratio. If two firms have the same ROA, the one using more debt will have a higher ROE.

We can make one more substitution to completely break down the ROE into its components. Since the first term in (4-27) is the ROA, we can replace it with (4-24):

$$\text{ROE} = \frac{\dfrac{\text{Net Income}}{\text{Sales}} \times \dfrac{\text{Sales}}{\text{Total Assets}}}{1 - \dfrac{\text{Total Debt}}{\text{Total Assets}}} \qquad \textbf{(4-28)}$$

Or, to simplify it somewhat:

$$\text{ROE} = \frac{\text{Net Profit Margin} \times \text{Total Asset Turnover}}{1 - \text{Total Debt Ratio}} \qquad \textbf{(4-29)}$$

To prove this to yourself, in A30 enter the label: `Du Pont ROE`. Now, in C30 enter the formula: `=(C25*C12)/(1-C14)`. The result will be 6.45%, as we found earlier. Note that if a firm uses no debt, then the denominator of equation (4-29) will be 1, and the ROE will be the same as the ROA.

Analysis of EPI's Profitability Ratios

Obviously, EPI's profitability has slipped rather dramatically in the past year. The sources of these declines can be seen most clearly if we look at all of EPI's ratios. At this point your worksheet should resemble the one in Exhibit 4-4.

The gross profit margin in 2007 is lower than in 2006, but not significantly (at least compared to the declines in the other ratios). The operating profit margin, however, is significantly lower in 2007 than in 2006. This indicates potential problems in controlling the firm's operating expenses, particularly selling, general, and administrative expenses. The other profitability ratios are lower than in 2006, partly because of the "trickle-down" effect of the increase in operating expenses. However, they are also lower because EPI has taken on a lot of extra debt in 2007, resulting in interest expense increasing faster than sales. This can be confirmed by examining EPI's common-size income statement (Exhibit 2-5, page 60).

Finally, the Du Pont analysis of the firm's ROE has shown us that it could be improved by any of the following: (1) increasing the net profit margin; (2) increasing the total asset turnover; or (3) increasing the amount of debt relative to equity. Our ratio analysis has shown that operating expenses have grown considerably, leading to the decline in the net profit margin. Reducing these expenses should be the primary objective of management. Since the total asset turnover ratio is near the industry average, as we'll soon see, it may be difficult to increase this ratio. However, the firm's inventory turnover ratio is considerably below the industry average, and inventory control may provide one method of improving the total asset turnover. An increase in debt is not called for, since the firm already has somewhat more debt than the industry average.

EXHIBIT 4-4
COMPLETED RATIO WORKSHEET FOR EPI

	A	B	C	D
1	Elvis Products International			
2	Ratio Analysis for 2006 and 2007			
3	Ratio		2007	2006
4	Liquidity Ratios			
5	Current Ratio		2.39x	2.33x
6	Quick Ratio		0.84x	0.85x
7	Efficiency Ratios			
8	Inventory Turnover		3.89x	4.00x
9	A/R Turnover		9.58x	9.77x
10	Average Collection Period		37.59 days	36.84 days
11	Fixed Asset Turnover		10.67x	9.95x
12	Total Asset Turnover		2.33x	2.34x
13	Leverage Ratios			
14	Total Debt Ratio		58.45%	54.81%
15	Long-term Debt Ratio		25.72%	22.02%
16	LTD to Total Capitalization		38.23%	32.76%
17	Debt to Equity		1.41x	1.21x
18	LTD to Equity		61.90%	48.73%
19	Coverage Ratios			
20	Times Interest Earned		1.97x	3.35x
21	Cash Coverage Ratio		2.23x	3.65x
22	Profitability Ratios			
23	Gross Profit Margin		15.58%	16.55%
24	Operating Profit Margin		3.89%	6.09%
25	Net Profit Margin		1.15%	2.56%
26	Return on Total Assets		2.68%	5.99%
27	Return on Equity		6.45%	13.25%
28	Return on Common Equity		6.45%	13.25%
29				
30	Du Pont ROE		6.45%	13.25%

Financial Distress Prediction

The last thing any investor wants is to invest in a firm that is nearing a bankruptcy filing or about to suffer through a period of severe financial distress. Starting in the late 1960s and continuing today, scholars and credit analysts have spent considerable time and effort trying to develop models that could identify such companies in advance. The best-known of these models was created by Professor Edward Altman in 1968.[5] We will discuss Altman's original model and a later one developed for privately held companies.

The Original Z-Score Model

The Z-score model was developed using a statistical technique known as Multiple Discriminant Analysis. This technique allows an analyst to place a company into one of two (or more) groups depending on the score. If the score is below the cutoff point, it is placed into group 1 (soon to be bankrupt); otherwise, it is placed into group 2. In fact, Altman also identified a third group that fell into a so-called "gray zone." These companies could go either way, but should definitely be considered greater credit risks than those in group 2. Generally, the lower the Z-score, the higher the risk of financial distress or bankruptcy.

The original Z-score model for publicly traded companies is:

$$Z = 1.2X_1 + 1.4X_2 + 3.3X_3 + 0.6X_4 + X_5 \qquad (4\text{-}30)$$

where the variables are the following financial ratios:

X_1 = net working capital/total assets

X_2 = retained earnings/total assets

X_3 = EBIT/total assets

X_4 = market value of all equity/book value of total liabilities

X_5 = sales/total assets

Altman reports that this model is 80–90% accurate if we use a cutoff point of 2.675. That is, a firm with a Z-score below 2.675 can reasonably be expected to experience severe financial distress, and possibly bankruptcy, within the next year.

---

5. See E. Altman, "Financial Ratios, Discriminant Analysis and the Prediction of Corporate Bankruptcy," *Journal of Finance*, September 1968. The models discussed in this section are from an updated version of this paper written in July 2000: E. Altman, "Predicting Financial Distress of Companies: Revisiting the Z-Score and ZETA Models." This paper may be obtained from http://www.defaultrisk.com/pp_score_14.htm.

The predictive ability of the model is even better if we use a cutoff point of 1.81. There are, therefore, three ranges of Z-scores:

Z < 1.81	Bankruptcy predicted within one year
1.81 < Z < 2.675	Financial distress, possible bankruptcy
Z > 2.675	No financial distress predicted

We can easily apply this model to EPI in the Ratios worksheet. However, first note that we haven't supplied information regarding the market value of EPI's common stock. In A31 enter the label: `Market Value of Equity` and in C31 enter: `884,400`. The market value of the equity is found by multiplying the share price by the number of shares outstanding. Next, enter: `Z-Score` into A32, and in C32 enter the formula: `=1.2*('Balance Sheet'!B8-'Balance Sheet'!C17)/'Balance Sheet'!B12+1.4*('Balance Sheet'!B21/'Balance Sheet'!B12)+3.3*('Income Statement'!B11/'Balance Sheet'!B12)+0.6*(C31/'Balance Sheet'!B19)+('Income Statement'!B5/'Balance Sheet'!B12)`. If you've entered the equation correctly, you will find that EPI's Z-score in 2007 is 3.92, which is safely above 2.675, so bankruptcy isn't predicted.

The Z-Score Model for Private Firms

Because variable X_4 in equation (4-30) requires knowledge of the firm's market capitalization (including both common and preferred equity), we cannot easily use the model for privately held firms. Estimates of the market value of these firms can be made, but the result is necessarily very uncertain. Alternatively, we could substitute the book value of equity for its market value, but that wouldn't be correct. Most publicly traded firms trade for several times their book value, so such a substitution would seem to call for a new coefficient for X_4. In fact, all of the coefficients in the model changed when Altman reestimated it for privately held firms.

The new model for privately held firms is:

$$Z' = 0.717X_1 + 0.847X_2 + 3.107X_3 + 0.420X_4 + 0.998X_5 \tag{4-31}$$

where all of the variables are defined as before, except that X_4 uses the book value of equity instead of market value. Altman reports that this model is only slightly

131

less accurate than the one for publicly traded firms when we use the new cutoff points shown below.

$$Z' < 1.21 \qquad \text{Bankruptcy predicted within one year}$$

$$1.23 < Z' < 2.90 \qquad \text{Financial distress, possible bankruptcy}$$

$$Z' > 2.90 \qquad \text{No financial distress predicted}$$

If we treat EPI as a privately held firm, its Z-score for 2007 is 3.35, and for 2006 it is 3.55. These scores show that EPI is not likely to file for bankruptcy anytime soon.

Using Financial Ratios

Calculating financial ratios is a pointless exercise unless you understand how to use them. One overriding rule of ratio analysis is this: *A single ratio provides very little information, and may be misleading.* You should never draw conclusions from a single ratio. Instead, several ratios should support any conclusions that you make.

With that precaution in mind, there are several ways that ratios can be used to draw important conclusions.

Trend Analysis

Trend analysis involves the examination of ratios over time. Trends, or lack of trends, can help managers gauge their progress toward a goal. Furthermore, trends can highlight areas in need of attention. While we don't really have enough information on Elvis Products International to perform a trend analysis, it is obvious that many of its ratios are moving in the wrong direction.

For example, all of EPI's profitability ratios have declined in 2007 relative to 2006, some rather dramatically. Management should immediately try to isolate the problem areas. For example, the gross profit margin has declined only slightly, indicating that increasing materials costs are not a major problem (though a price increase may be called for). The operating profit margin has fallen by about 36%, and since we can't blame increasing costs of goods sold, we must conclude that operating costs have increased at a more rapid rate than revenues. This increase in operating costs has led, to a large degree, to the decline in the other profitability ratios.

One potential problem area for trend analysis is seasonality. We must be careful to compare similar time periods. For example, many firms generate most of their sales during the holidays in the fourth quarter of the year. For this reason they may begin building inventories in the third quarter when sales are low. In this situation, comparing the third-quarter inventory turnover ratio to the fourth-quarter inventory turnover would be misleading.

Comparing to Industry Averages

Aside from trend analysis, one of the most beneficial uses of financial ratios is to compare similar firms within a single industry. Most often this is done by comparing to the industry average ratios, which are published by organizations such as Robert Morris Associates and Standard & Poor's. These industry averages provide a standard of comparison so that we can determine how well a firm is performing relative to its peers.

As an example of the use of industry averages, consider Exhibit 4-5 (page 134), which shows EPI's financial ratios and the industry averages for 2007. You can enter the industry averages from Exhibit 4-5 into your worksheet starting in B3 with the label: Industry 2007. To get the text to wrap, as we have done, choose Format Cells... and then the Alignment tab. Click on "Wrap Text" so that there is an X in the box. To enter the numbers, first select B5:B28, and notice that B5 will not be darkened. Type: 2.70 into B5 and then press the Enter key. Notice that the active cell will change to B6 as soon as the Enter key is pressed. This may be a more efficient method of entering a lot of numbers because your fingers never have to leave the number keypad. This technique is especially helpful when entering numbers into multiple columns and discontiguous cells.

It should be obvious that EPI is not being managed as well as the average firm in the industry. From the liquidity ratios we can see that EPI is less able to meet its short-term obligations than the average firm, though they are probably not in imminent danger of missing payments. The efficiency ratios show us that EPI is not managing its assets as well as would be expected, especially their inventories. It is also obvious that EPI is using substantially more debt than its peers. The coverage ratios indicate that EPI has less cash to pay its interest expense than the industry average. This is due to its carrying more than average debt. Finally, all of these problems have led to sub-par profitability measures that seem to be getting worse, rather than better.

It is important to note that industry averages may not be appropriate in all cases. In many cases it is probably more accurate to define the "industry" as the target

EXHIBIT 4-5

EPI's RATIOS VS. INDUSTRY AVERAGES

	A	B	C	D
1	Elvis Products International			
2	Ratio Analysis for 2006 and 2007			
3	Ratio	Industry 2007	2007	2006
4	Liquidity Ratios			
5	Current Ratio	2.70x	2.39x	2.33x
6	Quick Ratio	1.00x	0.84x	0.85x
7	Efficiency Ratios			
8	Inventory Turnover	7.00x	3.89x	4.00x
9	A/R Turnover	10.70x	9.58x	9.77x
10	Average Collection Period	33.64 days	37.59 days	36.84 days
11	Fixed Asset Turnover	11.20x	10.67x	9.95x
12	Total Asset Turnover	2.60x	2.33x	2.34x
13	Leverage Ratios			
14	Total Debt Ratio	50.00%	58.45%	54.81%
15	Long-term Debt Ratio	20.00%	25.72%	22.02%
16	LTD to Total Capitalization	28.57%	38.23%	32.76%
17	Debt to Equity	1.00x	1.41x	1.21x
18	LTD to Equity	40.00%	61.90%	48.73%
19	Coverage Ratios			
20	Times Interest Earned	2.50x	1.97x	3.35x
21	Cash Coverage Ratio	2.80x	2.23x	3.65x
22	Profitability Ratios			
23	Gross Profit Margin	17.50%	15.58%	16.55%
24	Operating Profit Margin	6.25%	3.89%	6.09%
25	Net Profit Margin	3.50%	1.15%	2.56%
26	Return on Total Assets	9.10%	2.68%	5.99%
27	Return on Equity	18.20%	6.45%	13.25%
28	Return on Common Equity	18.20%	6.45%	13.25%

company's most closely related competitors. This group is probably far smaller (maybe only three to five companies) than the entire industry as defined by the four-digit SIC code. The new six-digit NAICS codes will improve, but not eliminate, this situation.[6]

---

6. North American Industry Classification System. This system was created by the U.S. Census Bureau and its Canadian and Mexican counterparts in 1997 and is slowly replacing the SIC codes. See http://www.census.gov/epcd/www/naics.html for more information.

Company Goals and Debt Covenants

Financial ratios are often the basis of company goal setting. For example, a CEO might decide that one goal of the firm should be to earn at least 15% on equity (ROE = 15%). Obviously, whether or not this goal is achieved can be determined by calculating the return on equity. Further, by using trend analysis managers can gauge progress toward meeting goals, and they can determine whether goals are realistic or not.

Another use of financial ratios can be found in covenants loan to contracts. When companies borrow money, the lenders (bondholders, banks, or other lenders) place restrictions on the company, very often tied to the values of certain ratios. For example, the lender may require that the borrowing firm maintain a current ratio of at least 2.0. Or, it may require that the firm's total debt ratio not exceed 40%. Whatever the restriction, it is important that the firm monitor its ratios for compliance, or the loan may be due immediately.

Automating Ratio Analysis

Ratio analysis is a very subjective endeavor. Different analysts are likely to render somewhat different judgements on a firm. Nonetheless, you can have Excel do a rudimentary analysis for you. Actually, the analysis could be made quite sophisticated if you are willing to put in the effort. The technique that we will illustrate is analogous to creating an expert system, though we wouldn't call it a true expert system at this point.

An *expert system* is a computer program that can diagnose problems or provide an analysis by using the same techniques as an expert in the field. For example, a medical doctor might use an expert system to diagnose a patient's illness. The doctor would tell the system about the symptoms, and the expert system would consult its list of rules to generate a likely diagnosis.

Building a true ratio analysis expert system in Excel would be very time-consuming, and there are better tools available. However, we can build a very simple system using only a few functions. Our system will analyze each ratio separately and will determine only whether a ratio is either "Good," "Ok," or "Bad." To be really useful, the system would need to consider the interrelationships between the ratios, the industry that the company is in, and so forth. We leave it to you to improve the system.

As a first step in developing our expert system, we need to specify the rules that will be used to categorize the ratios. In most cases, we have seen that the higher the ratio the better. Therefore, we would like to see that the ratio is higher in 2007 than in 2006, and that the 2007 ratio is greater than the industry average.

We can use Excel's built-in **IF** statement to implement our automatic analysis. Recall that the **IF** statement returns one of two values, depending on whether a statement is true or false:

$$\textbf{IF}(\textbf{\textit{LOGICAL\_TEST}}, \textbf{\textit{VALUE\_IF\_TRUE}}, \textit{VALUE\_IF\_FALSE})$$

Where **_LOGICAL_TEST_** is any statement that can be evaluated as true or false, and **_VALUE_IF_TRUE_** and _VALUE_IF_FALSE_ are the return values that depend on whether **_LOGICAL_TEST_** was true or false.

We actually want to make two tests to determine whether a ratio is "Good," "Ok," or "Bad." First, we will test to see if the 2007 ratio is greater than the 2006 ratio. To do this, we divide the 2007 value by the 2006 value. If the result is greater than one, then the 2007 ratio is greater than the 2006 ratio. Using only this test, our formula for the current ratio would be: `=IF(C5/D5>=1,"Good","Bad")` in E3. In this case the result should be "Good" since the 2007 value is greater than the 2006 value. If you copy this formula to E6, the result will be "Bad" since the 2007 quick ratio is lower than the 2006 quick ratio.

We can also modify this formula to take account of the industry average. If the 2007 ratio is greater than the 2006 ratio **and** the 2007 ratio is greater than the industry average, then the ratio is "Good". To accomplish this, we need to use the **AND** function. This function will return true only if all arguments are true:

AND(*LOGICAL1*, *LOGICAL2*,...)

In this function *LOGICAL1* and *LOGICAL2* are the two required arguments that can each be evaluated to be either true or false. You can have up to 29 arguments, but only two are required. The modified function in E5 is now: `=IF(And(C5/D5>=1,C5/B5>=1),"Good","Bad")`. Now, the ratio will be judged as "Good" only if both conditions are true. Note that they are not for the current ratio.

One final improvement can be made by adding "Ok" to the possible outcomes. We will say that the ratio is "Ok" if the 2007 value is greater than the 2006 value, **or** the 2007 value is greater than the industry average. We can accomplish this by nesting a second **IF** statement inside the first in place of "Bad." For the second **IF** statement, we need to use Excel's **OR** function:

OR(*LOGICAL1*, *LOGICAL2*,...)

This function is identical to the **AND** function, except that it returns true if any of its arguments are true. The final form of our equation is: `=IF(AND(C5/D5>=1,C5/B5>=1),"Good",IF(OR(C5/D5>=1,C5/B5>=1),"Ok", "Bad"))`. For the current ratio, this will evaluate to "Ok." You can now evaluate all of EPI's ratios by copying this formula to E6:E28.

One more change is necessary. Recall that for leverage ratios, lower is generally better. Therefore, change all of the ">=" to "<=" in E14:E18. You also need to make the same change in E10 for the average collection period. Your worksheet should now resemble that in Exhibit 4-6 on page 138.

You should see that nearly all of EPI's ratios are judged to be "Bad." This is exactly what our previous analysis has determined, except that Excel has done it automatically. Many changes could be made to improve on this simple ratio analyzer, but we will leave that job as an exercise for you.

EXHIBIT 4-6
EPI'S RATIOS WITH AUTOMATIC ANALYSIS

	A	B	C	D	E
1	Elvis Products International				
2	Ratio Analysis for 2006 and 2007				
3	Ratio	Industry 2007	2007	2006	Analysis
4	Liquidity Ratios				
5	Current Ratio	2.70x	2.39x	2.33x	Ok
6	Quick Ratio	1.00x	0.84x	0.85x	Bad
7	Efficiency Ratios				
8	Inventory Turnover	7.00x	3.89x	4.00x	Bad
9	A/R Turnover	10.70x	9.58x	9.77x	Bad
10	Average Collection Period	33.64 days	37.59 days	36.84 days	Bad
11	Fixed Asset Turnover	11.20x	10.67x	9.95x	Ok
12	Total Asset Turnover	2.60x	2.33x	2.34x	Bad
13	Leverage Ratios				
14	Total Debt Ratio	50.00%	58.45%	54.81%	Bad
15	Long-term Debt Ratio	20.00%	25.72%	22.02%	Bad
16	LTD to Total Capitalization	28.57%	38.23%	32.76%	Bad
17	Debt to Equity	1.00x	1.41x	1.21x	Bad
18	LTD to Equity	40.00%	61.90%	48.73%	Bad
19	Coverage Ratios				
20	Times Interest Earned	2.50x	1.97x	3.35x	Bad
21	Cash Coverage Ratio	2.80x	2.23x	3.65x	Bad
22	Profitability Ratios				
23	Gross Profit Margin	17.50%	15.58%	16.55%	Bad
24	Operating Profit Margin	6.25%	3.89%	6.09%	Bad
25	Net Profit Margin	3.50%	1.15%	2.56%	Bad
26	Return on Total Assets	9.10%	2.68%	5.99%	Bad
27	Return on Equity	18.20%	6.45%	13.25%	Bad
28	Return on Common Equity	18.20%	6.45%	13.25%	Bad

Economic Profit Measures of Performance

Economic profit is the profit earned in excess of the firm's costs, including its implicit opportunity costs (primarily its cost of capital). Accounting profit (net income), however, measures profit as revenues minus all of the firm's explicit costs. It takes into account a firm's cost of debt capital (interest expense), but it ignores the implicit cost of the firm's equity capital. The concept of economic profit is an old one, but it has been revived in the past few years by consulting firms promising to improve the financial performance and executive compensation practices of their clients.[7] Many large firms have switched to various measures of economic profit—some with good results and some not. In any case, the method has generated a lot of interest, and we will include a short discussion of measuring economic profit in this section.

The basic idea behind economic profit measures is that the firm cannot increase shareholder wealth unless it makes a profit in excess of its cost of capital.[8] Because we will be taking account of the cost of capital explicitly, we cannot use the normal accounting measures of profit directly. The adjustments to the financial statements vary depending on the firm and who is doing the calculations. At the moment, there is no completely accepted standard. With this in mind, we will present a simplified economic profit calculation.

Mathematically, economic profit is:

$$\text{Economic Profit} = \text{NOPAT} - \text{After-tax cost of operating capital} \qquad \text{(4-32)}$$

where NOPAT is net operating profit after taxes. The after-tax cost of operating capital is the dollar cost of all interest-bearing debt instruments (i.e., bonds and notes payable) plus the dollar cost of preferred and common equity. Generally, the firm's after-tax cost of capital (a percentage amount) is calculated and then multiplied by the amount of operating capital to obtain the dollar cost.

To calculate the economic profit, we must first calculate NOPAT, total operating capital, and the firm's cost of capital. For our purposes in this chapter, the cost of capital will be given (see Chapter 10 for the calculations). NOPAT is the after-tax operating profit of the firm:

$$\text{NOPAT} = \text{EBIT}(1 - \text{tax rate}) \qquad \text{(4-33)}$$

Note that the NOPAT calculation does not include interest expense, because it will be explicitly accounted for when we subtract the cost of all capital.

---

7. The leader in this effort is the consulting firm Stern Stewart and Company, which refers to economic profit by the copyrighted name Economic Value Added (EVA).

8. Economic profit is also measured by net present value (NPV), which is introduced in Chapter 11. The primary difference is that in this chapter we are trying to calculate the actual economic profit that was earned over some previous time period (usually the previous year). NPV measures the expected economic profit of a future investment.

Total operating capital is the sum of non-interest-bearing current assets and net fixed assets, less non-interest-bearing current liabilities. We ignore interest-bearing current assets because they are not operating assets, and we ignore interest-bearing current liabilities (e.g., notes payable) because the cost of these liabilities is included in the cost of capital.

We will demonstrate the calculation of economic profit using the Elvis Products International data for 2006 and 2007. Make sure that the workbook containing EPI's financial statements is open, and insert a new worksheet for our economic profit calculations. Set up your new worksheet as shown in Exhibit 4-7 and rename the sheet "Economic Profit."

EXHIBIT 4-7
ECONOMIC PROFIT CALCULATION FOR EPI

	A	B	C
1	Elvis Products International		
2	Economic Profit Calculations		
3		2007	2006
4	Tax Rate	40%	40%
5	NOPAT		
6	Total Operating Capital		
7	After-tax Cost of Capital	13%	13%
8	Dollar Cost of Capital		
9	Economic Profit		

Note that we are assuming that the firm's cost of capital is 13%, and the tax rate should be pulled from the income statement with the formula: `='Income Statement'!$B18`. All of the other numbers must be calculated as discussed above.

Recall that NOPAT is simply EBIT times 1 minus the tax rate, so in B5 enter the formula: `='Income Statement'!B11*(1-B4)`. You should see that EPI has generated an operating profit of $89,820 in 2007. Copy this formula to C5 to get the NOPAT for 2006.

The next step is to calculate the amount of operating capital. Since EPI has no short-term investments, we merely add current assets to net fixed assets and then subtract current liabilities less notes payable. In B6 enter the formula: `='Balance Sheet'!B8+'Balance Sheet'!B11-('Balance Sheet'!B17-'Balance Sheet'!B15)`. Your result should show that total operating capital for 2007 was $1,335,600. Copy the formula to C6.

To calculate the dollar cost of capital in B8, enter the formula: =B7*B6, and copy this to C8. Recall that economic profit is simply NOPAT minus the dollar cost of capital, so we can calculate the economic profit in B9 with the formula: =B5-B8. You should find that EPI earned an economic profit of −$83,808 in 2007. Copy this formula to C9 and you will see that EPI's economic profit in 2006 was −$28,876.

This example shows how misleading accounting measures of profit (particularly net income) can be. In this case, EPI reported positive profits in both 2006 and 2007, but it was actually decreasing shareholder wealth over the past two years. This result essentially confirms the results from our ratio analysis. EPI's management has not been doing a good job, at least over this period. Your economic profit worksheet should now look like the one in Exhibit 4-8.

EXHIBIT 4-8
EPI'S COMPLETED ECONOMIC PROFIT WORKSHEET

	A	B	C
1	Elvis Products International		
2	Economic Profit Calculations		
3		2007	2006
4	Tax Rate	40%	40%
5	NOPAT	89,820	125,460
6	Total Operating Capital	1,335,600	1,187,200
7	After-tax Cost of Capital	13%	13%
8	Dollar Cost of Capital	173,628	154,336
9	Economic Profit	(83,808)	(28,876)

Summary

In this chapter we have seen how various financial ratios can be used to evaluate the financial health of a company, and therefore the performance of the managers of the firm. You have also seen how Excel can make the calculation of ratios quicker and easier than doing it by hand. We looked at five categories of ratios: *Liquidity ratios* measure the ability of a firm to pays its bills; *efficiency ratios* measure how well the firm is making use of its assets to generate sales; *leverage ratios* describe how much debt the firm is using to finance its assets; *coverage ratios* tell how much cash the firm has available to pay specific expenses; and *profitability ratios* measure how profitable the firm has been over a period of time.

We have also seen how Excel can be programmed to do a rudimentary ratio analysis automatically, using only a few of the built-in logical functions. The following table provides a summary of the ratio formulas that were presented in this chapter. Finally, we looked at the concept of economic profit and saw how it can give a much clearer picture of a firm's financial health than traditional accounting profit measures can.

SUMMARY OF FINANCIAL RATIOS

Name of Ratio	Formula	Page
Liquidity Ratios		
Current Ratio	$\dfrac{\text{Current Assets}}{\text{Current Liabilities}}$	111
Quick Ratio	$\dfrac{\text{Current Assets} - \text{Inventories}}{\text{Current Liabilities}}$	112
Efficiency Ratios		
Inventory Turnover	$\dfrac{\text{Cost of Goods Sold}}{\text{Inventory}}$	113
Accounts Receivable Turnover	$\dfrac{\text{Credit Sales}}{\text{Accounts Receivable}}$	114
Average Collection Period	$\dfrac{\text{Accounts Receivable}}{\text{Annual Credit Sales}/360}$	115
Fixed Asset Turnover	$\dfrac{\text{Sales}}{\text{Net Fixed Assets}}$	116
Total Asset Turnover	$\dfrac{\text{Sales}}{\text{Total Assets}}$	116
Leverage Ratios		
Total Debt Ratio	$\dfrac{\text{Total Debt}}{\text{Total Assets}}$	118
Long-Term Debt Ratio	$\dfrac{\text{Long-Term Debt}}{\text{Total Assets}}$	118

SUMMARY OF FINANCIAL RATIOS (CONTINUED)

Name of Ratio	Formula	Page
LTD to Total Capitalization	$$\frac{\text{LTD}}{\text{LTD + Preferred Equity + Common Equity}}$$	119
Debt to Equity	$$\frac{\text{Total Debt}}{\text{Total Equity}}$$	119
LTD to Equity	$$\frac{\text{LTD}}{\text{Preferred Equity + Common Equity}}$$	120
Coverage Ratios		
Times Interest Earned	$$\frac{\text{EBIT}}{\text{Interest Expense}}$$	121
Cash Coverage Ratio	$$\frac{\text{EBIT + Non-Cash Expenses}}{\text{Interest Expense}}$$	122
Profitability Ratios		
Gross Profit Margin	$$\frac{\text{Gross Profit}}{\text{Sales}}$$	123
Operating Profit Margin	$$\frac{\text{Net Operating Income}}{\text{Sales}}$$	124
Net Profit Margin	$$\frac{\text{Net Income}}{\text{Sales}}$$	124
Return on Total Assets	$$\frac{\text{Net Income}}{\text{Total Assets}}$$	125
Return on Equity	$$\frac{\text{Net Income}}{\text{Total Equity}}$$	125
Return on Common Equity	$$\frac{\text{Net Income Available to Common}}{\text{Common Equity}}$$	126
Du Pont Analysis of ROE	$$\frac{\text{Net Profit Margin} \times \text{Total Asset Turnover}}{1 - \text{Total Debt Ratio}}$$	127

FUNCTIONS INTRODUCED IN THIS CHAPTER

Purpose	Function	Page
Returns a value dependent on test	**IF(LOGICAL_TEST, VALUE_IF_TRUE, VALUE_IF_FALSE)**	136
Returns true if all arguments are true	**AND(LOGICAL1, LOGICAL2,…)**	137
Returns true if one argument is true	**OR(LOGICAL1, LOGICAL2,…)**	137

Problems

1. Copy the Spacely's Space Sprockets financial statements from Problem 1 in Chapter 2 into a new workbook.

   a. Set up a ratio worksheet similar to the one in Exhibit 4-4, page 129, and calculate all of the ratios for Spacely's Space Sprockets.

   b. Identify at least two areas of potential concern using the ratios. Identify at least two areas that have shown improvement.

   c. In 2007 Spacely's Space Sprockets' ROE increased. Explain, in words, why this increase occurred using the Du Pont method as shown in equation (4-29).

   d. Spacely's Space Sprockets has shown an accounting profit in each of the past two years. Calculate their economic profit for these years and compare it to net income. Assume that Aspen's cost of capital is 11%.

   e. Using Altman's model for privately held firms, calculate the Z-score for Spacely's Space Sprockets. Does it appear that the firm is in imminent danger of bankruptcy?

2. A computer problem at DV Transcoding, Inc. has resulted in incomplete financial statements. Management of the company has asked you to see if you can fill in the missing data.

	A	B	C	D	E
1	DV Transcoding, Inc.			DV Transcoding, Inc.	
2	Income Statement			Balance Sheet	
3	For the Year Ended December 31, 2007			As of December 31, 2007	
4		2007			2007
5	Sales	Ratio		Assets	
6	Cost of Goods Sold	Ratio		Cash	500
7	*Gross Profit*	Formula		Accounts Receivable	Ratio
8	Operating Expenses	47,000		Inventories	45,500
9	*Earnings Before Interest and Taxes*	Formula		*Total Current Assets*	Formula
10	Interest Expense	Ratio		Gross Fixed Assets	126,000
11	*Earnings Before Taxes*	Formula		Accumulated Depreciation	Formula
12	Taxes	Formula		*Net Fixed Assets*	Ratio
13	*Net Income*	Ratio		**Total Assets**	150,000
14				**Liabilities and Owner's Equity**	
15	Notes: Tax Rate	30%		Accounts Payable	22,000
16				Short-term Bank Notes	Formula
17				*Total Current Liabilities*	Ratio
18				Long-term Debt	Ratio
19				Common Equity	Ratio
20				**Total Liabilities and Owner's Equity**	Formula

a. Recreate the financial statements as shown, then use formulas with the ratios given below to fill in the cells with the word "Ratio." Use the **ROUND** function to round each of these answers to the nearest $10.

Ratio	Value
Current Ratio	0.898550
Inventory Turnover	2.109890
A/R Turnover	10.000000
Fixed Asset Turnover	1.818180
LTD to Equity	0.395350
Times Interest Earned	2.786890
Net Profit Margin	0.047688
Return on Total Assets	0.050870
Return on Equity	0.131440

b. Complete the financial statements by using formulas that refer to existing data to fill in the remaining cells.

Internet Exercise

1. Choose your own company and repeat the analysis from Problem 1. You can get the data from MoneyCentral Investor at http://moneycentral.msn.com/investor/home.asp. To retrieve the data for your company, go to the Stocks area and enter the ticker symbol. Now choose Financial Results and then Statements from the menu on the left side of the screen. Display the annual income statement, select the entire data section, and copy. Now paste this data directly into a new worksheet. The data will be pasted in HTML format. In Excel 2003 a Smart Tag will appear that will allow you to either "Keep Source Formatting" or "Match Destination Formatting." Experiment to see which one you like best. Repeat these steps for the balance sheet.

(Note: At the time of this writing, MoneyCentral uses data from Hemscott, Inc. The data have been consolidated into consistent categories for easy comparison of different companies. (However, there may be some mistakes.) If you need error-free data, you should use a source such as Standard & Poor's Compustat or the SEC's Edgar database.)

CHAPTER 5

Financial Forecasting

After studying this chapter, you should be able to:

1. *Explain how the "percent of sales" method is used to develop pro forma financial statements and know how to construct such statements in Excel.*

2. *Use circular references to handle iterative calculations.*

3. *Use the* **TREND** *function for forecasting sales or any other trending variables.*

4. *Perform a regression analysis with Excel's built-in regression tools.*

Forecasting is an important activity for a wide variety of people in business. Nearly all of the decisions made by financial managers are made on the basis of forecasts of one kind or another. For example, in Chapter 3 we've seen how the cash budget can be used to forecast short-term borrowing and investing needs. Every item in the cash budget is itself a forecast. In this chapter we will examine several methods of forecasting. The first, the percent of sales method, is the simplest. We will also look at more advanced techniques, such as regression analysis.

The Percent of Sales Method

Forecasting financial statements is important for a number of reasons. Among these reasons are planning for the future and providing information to the company's investors. The simplest method of forecasting income statements and balance sheets is the percent of sales method. This method has the added advantage of requiring relatively little data to make a forecast.

The fundamental premise of the percent of sales method is that many (but not all) income statement and balance sheet items maintain a constant relationship to the level of sales. For example, if the cost of goods sold has averaged 65% of sales over the last several years, we would assume that this relationship would hold for the next year. If sales were expected to be $10 million next year, our cost of goods forecast would be $6.5 million (10 million $\times$ 0.65 $=$ 6.5 million). Of course, this method assumes that the forecasted level of sales is already known.

Forecasting the Income Statement

As an example of income statement forecasting, consider the Elvis Products International statements that you created in Chapter 2 (page 47, Exhibit 2-1). The income statement is recreated here in Exhibit 5-1. Recall that we have used a custom number format to display this data in thousands of dollars, but that the full-precision numbers are there. Open the workbook that you created in Chapter 2, and make a copy of the Income Statement worksheet. Rename the new worksheet to Pro Forma Income Statement.

The level of detail that you have in an income statement will affect how many items will fluctuate directly with sales. In general, we will proceed through the income statement line by line, asking the question, "Is it likely that this item will change directly with sales?" If the answer is yes, then we calculate the percentage of sales and multiply the result by the sales forecast for the next period. Otherwise, we will take one of two actions: Leave the item unchanged, or use other information to change the item.[1]

---

1. Realize that you may have important information regarding one or more of these items. For example, if you know that the lease for the company's headquarters building has a scheduled increase, then you should be sure to include this information in your forecast for fixed costs.

EXHIBIT 5-1
EPI'S INCOME STATEMENTS FOR 2006 AND 2007

	A	B	C
1	Elvis Products International		
2	Income Statement		
3	For the Year Ended Dec. 31, 2007 ($ in 000's)		
4		*2007*	*2006*
5	Sales	3,850.00	3,432.00
6	Cost of Goods Sold	3,250.00	2,864.00
7	*Gross Profit*	*600.00*	*568.00*
8	Selling and G&A Expenses	330.30	240.00
9	Fixed Expenses	100.00	100.00
10	Depreciation Expense	20.00	18.90
11	*EBIT*	*149.70*	*209.10*
12	Interest Expense	76.00	62.50
13	*Earnings Before Taxes*	*73.70*	*146.60*
14	Taxes	29.48	58.64
15	*Net Income*	*44.22*	*87.96*
16			
17	Notes:		
18	Tax Rate	40%	

For EPI, only one income statement item will clearly change with sales: the cost of goods sold. One other item, the selling, general, and administrative expense (SG&A), is a conglomeration of many things, some that will probably change with sales and some that won't. For our purposes we choose to believe that, on balance, SG&A will change along with sales.

Changes in the other items are not directly related to a change in sales. Depreciation expense, for example, depends on the amount and age of the firm's fixed assets. Interest expense is a function of the amount and maturity structure of debt in the firm's capital structure. These items may, and probably will, change; but we will need additional information. Taxes depend directly on the firm's taxable income, though this indirectly depends on the level of sales. All of the other items on the income statement are calculated.

Before getting started with the forecast, insert a column to the left of column B. Note that a Smart Tag will appear that will give you three choices: (1) Format Same As **L**eft; (2) Format Same As **R**ight; or (3) **C**lear Formatting. Choose the second option so that the number formats and column width will automatically be applied. So that we can experiment later if we choose, enter 40% for the tax rate in B18.

To generate our income statement forecast, we first determine the percentage of sales for each of the prior years for each item that changes. In this case, for 2007 we have:

$$\text{Cost of Goods Sold 2007 Percentage of Sales} \quad \frac{\$3,250,000}{3,850,000} = 0.8442 = 84.42\%$$

$$\text{SG\&A Expense 2007 Percentage of Sales} \quad \frac{\$330,300}{3,850,000} = 0.0858 = 8.58\%$$

The 2006 percentages (83.45% and 6.99%, respectively) can be found in exactly the same manner. We now calculate the average of these percentages and use this average as our estimate of the 2008 percentage of sales. The forecast is then found by multiplying these percentages by next year's sales forecast. Assuming that sales are forecasted to be $4,300,000, then for 2008 we have:

$$\text{Cost of Goods Sold 2008 Forecast} \quad \$4,300,000 \times 0.8393 = 3,609,108$$

$$\text{SG\&A Expense 2008 Forecast} \quad \$4,300,000 \times 0.0779 = 334,803$$

Exhibit 5-2 shows a completed forecast for the 2008 income statement. To create this forecast in your worksheet, in B4 enter: 2008.[2] Because the 2008 income statement will be calculated in exactly the same way as 2007, the easiest way to proceed is to copy E5:E15 into C5:C15. This will save you from having to enter formulas to calculate subtotals (e.g., EBIT) and will apply the cell borders.

First, in B5 enter the sales forecast: 4,300,000. Now, we can calculate the 2008 cost of goods forecast in B6 with the formula: =AVERAGE(C6/C$5,D6/D$5)*B$5. This formula calculates the average of the cost of goods as a percentage of sales for the last two years and then multiplies it by the sales forecast. The result should be as shown above. Now copy this formula to B8 to get the forecast for SG&A expense.

---

2. We have chosen to apply a custom format so that the number has an asterisk to indicate a footnote that informs the reader that these are forecasts. The custom format is ####"*".

EXHIBIT 5-2
PERCENT OF SALES FORECAST FOR 2008

	A	B	C	D
1	Elvis Products International			
2	Pro Forma Income Statement			
3	For the Year Ended Dec. 31, 2007			
4		*2008**	*2007*	*2006*
5	Sales	4,300.00	3,850.00	3,432.00
6	Cost of Goods Sold	3,609.11	3,250.00	2,864.00
7	*Gross Profit*	*690.89*	*600.00*	*568.00*
8	Selling and G&A Expenses	334.80	330.30	240.00
9	Fixed Expenses	100.00	100.00	100.00
10	Depreciation Expense	25.00	20.00	18.90
11	*EBIT*	*231.09*	*149.70*	*209.10*
12	Interest Expense	76.00	76.00	62.50
13	*Earnings Before Taxes*	*155.09*	*73.70*	*146.60*
14	Taxes	62.04	29.48	58.64
15	*Net Income*	*93.05*	*44.22*	*87.96*
16	* Forecast			
17				
18	Notes:			
19	Tax Rate	40%	40%	
20	Additional Depreciation	5.00		

Note that instead of performing the entire calculation in cells B6 and B8, we could have used a *helper column*. A helper column is used for doing intermediate calculations and is sometimes useful. In this case, we could have calculated the average percentage of sales for each item in, say, column K. We would then use these values to perform the final calculation in column B. For example, K8 might contain the formula: =AVERAGE(C6/C$5,D6/D$5). Then the formula in B6 would be: =K8*B$5. This technique would allow you to easily see the average percentages (as in a common-size income statement) that are being used to generate the forecast. While this might be helpful, it can be an inefficient use of the spreadsheet unless it is necessary.

Assume that we do not have any information regarding changes in fixed expenses, so copy the value from C9. However, we have been informed that the firm intends to invest $50,000 in fixed assets in 2008. This will cause depreciation expense to rise by $5,000. We need to document this assumption, so in A20 type: Additional Depreciation, and in B20 enter: 5000. We will come back to add a formula in B20 in the next section. The formula to calculate depreciation expense in B10 is:

=C10+B20. Since we don't yet know how the firm will finance these investments, leave the interest expense at the same level as 2007. To calculate the taxes, in B14, use the formula: =B19*B13. Your worksheet should now look like the one in Exhibit 5-2.

Forecasting Assets on the Balance Sheet

We can forecast the balance sheet in exactly the same way as the income statement, with some major exceptions. For those items that can be expected to vary directly with sales, our formulas will be similar to those we have already seen. We will explain how to handle the other items below.

Create the percent of sales balance sheet for 2008 by selecting column B and inserting a new column (Insert Columns). In B4 type the label: 2008. As before, apply a custom number format to display an asterisk after the number. Like we did with the income statement, we will move, line by line, through the balance sheet to determine which items will vary with sales.

The firm's cash balance is the first, and perhaps most difficult, item with which we need to work. Does the cash balance vary, in constant proportion, with sales? Your first response might be, "Of course it does. As the firm sells more goods, it accumulates cash." This line of reasoning neglects two important facts. The firm has other things to do with its cash aside from accumulating it, and, because cash is a low-return (perhaps zero or negative return when inflation is considered) asset, firms should seek to minimize the amount of their cash balance.[3] For these reasons, even though the cash balance will probably change, it probably will not change by the same percentage as sales. Therefore, we will simply use the cash balance from 2007 as our forecast, so enter: =C5 into cell B5.

The next two items, accounts receivable and inventory, are much easier. Both of these accounts are likely to fluctuate roughly in proportion to sales. Using the same methodology that we used for the pro forma income statement, we will find the average percentage of sales for the past two years and multiply that amount by our sales forecast for 2008. For the accounts receivable, the formula in B6 is: =AVERAGE(C6/'Income Statement'!B$5,D6/'Income Statement'!C$5)*'Pro Forma Income Statement'!$B$5. Instead of typing the references to the income statement, it is easier to insert them by

---

3. Within reason, of course. Firms need some amount of cash to operate, but the amount needed does not necessarily vary directly with the level of sales.

displaying both the income statement and balance sheet (choose **W**indow **N**ew Window from the menus) and selecting the appropriate cells with the mouse. Since we will use the same formula for Inventory, we can simply copy this formula down to B7. Total Current Assets in B8 is a calculated value, so we can copy the formula directly from cell C8.

In B9 we have the 2008 gross plant and equipment. This is the historical purchase price of the buildings and equipment that the firm owns. As noted earlier, the firm plans to make net new investments of $50,000 in 2008. We will document this assumption by entering `Net Additions to Plant and Equipment` in A28, and `50000` in B28. Now, the formula in B9 is: `=C9+B28`. Note that this increase is not necessarily due to the expected increase in sales. While gross fixed assets may rise or fall in any given year, most companies always operate with spare capacity so the changes are not, in the short run, directly related to sales.

We now need to calculate the additional depreciation. We will assume that the expected life of the new equipment is 10 years, and that it will be depreciated using the straight-line method to a salvage value of zero. In A29 enter the label: `Life of New Equipment in Years`, and in B29 enter `10`. In A30 enter: `New Depreciation (Straight Line)`, and in B30 enter the formula: `=B28/B29`. The additional depreciation expense will be $5,000. Now, return to the pro forma income statement, where we will enter a formula in B20: `='Pro Forma Balance Sheet'!B30`. This last step allows us to change the amount of the new investment and have the additional depreciation expense reflected on the pro forma income statement.

Now, return to the pro forma balance sheet. Accumulated depreciation will definitely increase in 2008, but not because of the forecasted change in sales. Instead, accumulated depreciation will increase by the amount of the depreciation expense for 2008. To determine the accumulated depreciation for 2008 we will add 2008's depreciation expense to 2007's accumulated depreciation. The formula is: `=C10+'Pro forma Income Statement'!B10`.

To complete the asset side of the balance sheet, we note that both net fixed assets and total assets are calculated values. We can simply copy the formulas from C11:C12 and paste them into B11:B12.

Forecasting Liabilities on the Balance Sheet

Once the assets are completed, the rest of the balance sheet is comparatively simple because we can mostly copy formulas already entered. Before continuing, however, we need to distinguish among the types of financing sources. We have already seen that the types of financing that a firm uses can be divided into three categories:

- Current liabilities

- Long-term liabilities

- Owner's equity

These categories are not sufficiently distinguished for our purposes here. Instead, we will divide the liabilities and equity of a firm into two categories:

- *Spontaneous sources of financing* — These are the sources of financing that arise during the ordinary course of doing business. An example is the firm's accounts payable. Once the credit account is established with a supplier, no additional work is required to obtain credit; it just happens spontaneously when the firm makes a purchase. Note that not all current liabilities are spontaneous sources of financing (e.g., short-term notes payable, long-term debt due in one year, etc.).

- *Discretionary sources of financing* — These are the financing sources that require a large effort on the part of the firm to obtain. In other words, the firm must make a conscious decision to obtain these funds. Furthermore, the firm's upper-level management will use its discretion to determine the appropriate type of financing. Examples of this type of financing include any type of bank loan, bonds, and common and preferred stock.

Generally speaking, spontaneous sources of financing can be expected to vary directly with sales. Changes in discretionary sources, on the other hand, will not have a direct relationship to changes in sales. We always leave discretionary sources of financing unchanged, for reasons that will soon become clear.

Returning now to our forecasting problem, the first item to consider is accounts payable. As noted above, accounts payable is a spontaneous source of financing and will, therefore, change directly with sales. To enter the formula, all that is necessary is to copy the formula from one of the other items that we have already completed.

Copy the contents of B6 (or B7, it doesn't matter which) and paste it into B14. The result should indicate a forecasted accounts payable of $189.05.

The next item to consider is the short-term notes payable. Since this is a discretionary source of financing, we will leave it unchanged from 2007. In reality, we might handle this item differently if we had more information. For example, if we knew that the notes would be retired before the end of 2008, we would change our forecast to zero. Alternatively, if the payments on the notes include both principal and interest, our forecast would be the 2007 amount less principal payments that we expect to make in 2008. Since we are leaving it unchanged, the formula in B15 is: =C15.

If we assume that the "other current liabilities" account represents primarily accrued expenses, then it is a spontaneous source of financing. We can, therefore, simply copy the formula from B14 and paste it into B16. The forecasted amount is $163.38.

Long-term debt, in B18, and common stock, in B20, are both discretionary sources of financing. We will leave these balances unchanged from 2007. In B18 the formula is: =C18 and in B20 the formula is: =C20.

The final item that we must consider is retained earnings. Recall that retained earnings is an accumulation account. That is, the balance in any year is the accumulated amount that has been added in previous years plus any new additions. The amount that will be added to retained earnings is given by

Change in Retained Earnings = Net Income − Dividends

where the dividends are those that are paid to both the common and preferred stockholders. The formula for retained earnings will require that we reference forecasted 2008 net income from the income statement, and the dividends from statement of cash flows (see Exhibit 2-7, page 63). Note that we are assuming the 2008 dividends will be the same as the 2007 dividends. We can reference these cells in exactly the same way as before, so the formula is: =C21+'pro Forma Income Statement'!B15+'Statement of Cash Flows'!B19. The results should show that we are forecasting retained earnings to be $297.04 in 2008.

At this point, you should go back and calculate the subtotals in B17, B19, and B22. Finally, we calculate the total liabilities and owner's equity in B23 with =B19+B22.

Discretionary Financing Needed

Sharp-eyed readers will notice that our pro forma balance sheet does not balance. While this appears to be a serious problem, it actually represents one of the purposes of the pro forma balance sheet. The difference between total assets and total liabilities and owner's equity is referred to as *discretionary financing needed* (DFN, also called additional funds needed or required new funds). In other words, this is the amount of discretionary financing that the firm thinks it will need to raise in the next year. Due to the amount of time and effort required to raise these funds, it is important that the firm be aware of its needs well in advance. The pro forma balance sheet fills this need. Frequently, the firm will find that it is forecasting a higher level of assets than liabilities and equity. In this case, the managers would need to arrange for more liabilities and/or equity to finance the level of assets needed to support the volume of sales expected. This is referred to as a *deficit* of discretionary funds. If the forecast shows that there will be a higher level of liabilities and equity than assets, the firm is said to have a *surplus* of discretionary funds. Remember that, in the end, the balance sheet must balance. The "plug figure" necessary to make this happen is the DFN.

We should add an extra line at the bottom of the pro forma balance sheet to calculate the discretionary financing needed. Type `Discretionary Financing Needed` in A25, and in B25 add the formula =B12-B23. This calculation tells us that EPI expects to need $38,119.50 (displayed as 38.12 with the custom number format) more in discretionary funds to support its forecasted level of assets. In this case, EPI is forecasting a deficit of discretionary funds. Apply the same custom format to this number as to the rest of the balance sheet.

To make clear that this amount is a deficit (note that the sign is the opposite of what might be expected), we can have Excel inform us whether we will have a surplus or deficit of discretionary funds. To do this requires that we make use of the **IF** statement. Realize that if the discretionary financing needed is a positive number, then we have a deficit; otherwise we have a surplus. So the formula in C25 is: `=IF(B25>=0,"Deficit","Surplus")`.[4] Your balance sheet should now resemble that in Exhibit 5-3.

---

4. You could also design a custom number format. One possible format is: `#,###.00," Deficit";#,###.00," Surplus"`. The benefit of this approach is that you don't need to use a separate cell and you don't need to enter a formula. Of course, this method may require that the column be wider in some instances.

EXHIBIT 5-3
EPI'S PRO FORMA BALANCE SHEET FOR 2008

	A	B	C	D
1	Elvis Products International			
2	Pro Forma Balance Sheet			
3	As of Dec. 31, 2007			
4	Assets	2008*	2007	2006
5	Cash and Equivalents	52.00	52.00	57.60
6	Accounts Receivable	444.51	402.00	351.20
7	Inventory	914.90	836.00	715.20
8	Total Current Assets	1,411.40	1,290.00	1,124.00
9	Plant & Equipment	577.00	527.00	491.00
10	Accumulated Depreciation	191.20	166.20	146.20
11	Net Fixed Assets	385.80	360.80	344.80
12	Total Assets	1,797.20	1,650.80	1,468.80
13	Liabilities and Owner's Equity			
14	Accounts Payable	189.05	175.20	145.60
15	Short-term Notes Payable	225.00	225.00	200.00
16	Other Current Liabilities	163.38	140.00	136.00
17	Total Current Liabilities	577.43	540.20	481.60
18	Long-term Debt	424.61	424.61	323.43
19	Total Liabilities	1,002.04	964.81	805.03
20	Common Stock	460.00	460.00	460.00
21	Retained Earnings	297.04	225.99	203.77
22	Total Shareholder's Equity	757.04	685.99	663.77
23	Total Liabilities and Owner's Equity	1,759.08	1,650.80	1,468.80
24	* Forecast			
25	Discretionary Financing Needed	38.12	Deficit	
26				
27	Notes:			
28	Net Addition to Plant & Equipment	50.00		
29	Life of New Equipment in Years	10		
30	New Depreciation (Straight Line)	5.00		

157

Using Iteration to Eliminate DFN

Circular errors result when a formula refers to itself, either directly or indirectly through another formula. A simple example would be if the formula in B18 was =B18. When Excel tries to calculate this, it cannot because the result depends on itself (it is self-referential). In most cases, this is undesirable even if the formula eventually converges to a solution. However, there are circumstances that are necessarily self-referential and cannot be solved in any other way. For example, if we wish to eliminate the DFN deficit the firm must raise that amount of money. Suppose that any discretionary funds will be raised with long-term debt. Simply adding $38.12 to the long-term debt in B18 will not quite solve the problem, because that will lead to other changes. Specifically, additional long-term debt will increase interest expense and result in lower net income. In turn, this will reduce retained earnings and still leave us with a (smaller) deficit of funding. We can repeat this cycle as many times as necessary until DFN is equal to zero (or within some allowable tolerance).

By default, Excel will not allow such calculations because the result may not converge. This would lead to an infinite loop of calculations that would tie up your computer in an endless series of calculations. However, if we know that the result will converge (as it will in this case) we can enable these kinds of self-referential, or iterative, calculations. To do so, go to Tools Options and then to the Calculation tab. In the middle of the dialog box is an option called Iteration. Check that option to enable iterative calculations. Note that we can set the maximum number of iterations as well as the convergence criteria. The default settings will cause the calculation to stop after 100 iterations, or if the change is 0.001 or less. Since we should need only a few iterations, leave these at their default settings.

Before we can eliminate the DFN, we need to make a few changes to the pro forma income statement and balance sheet. On the pro forma income statement, we need to add an interest rate. In A21 add the label: `Interest Rate` and then type `11.70%` into B21. This will allow us to calculate the total interest expense as the amount of debt changes. In B12 we will calculate the interest expense for 2008 with the formula: `=B21*('Pro Forma Balance Sheet'!B15+'Pro Forma Balance Sheet'!B18)`. Note that the interest expense is 11.70% of the sum of short-term notes payable and long-term debt. At this point, the value in B12 should be the same as before (76.00).

On the pro forma balance sheet, we need to add our self-referential formula. Our goal is to have the long-term debt (in B18) increase by the amount of the DFN (in B25). However, we can't just set the formula in B18 to =B25. If we did, then long-term debt would be 38.12, which would lead to a bigger DFN. This would cause the debt to grow and the DFN to shrink, which would then cause the debt to shrink and the DFN to grow. It will never converge and will bounce back and forth forever.

To solve this problem by hand, we would start with the current amount of long-term debt (424.61) and then add the DFN to that. This will increase long-term debt, increase interest expense, lower net income, and reduce retained earnings leading to a lower DFN. We now start over again by adding the new DFN amount to long-term debt, and the cycle will repeat. If we do this three or four times, DFN will get very close to zero. It may take 20 or 30 cycles for DFN to converge to exactly zero.[5]

Fortunately, we don't have to do this by hand. With the right formula for long-term debt, we can make the amount accumulate over many cycles. In B18 enter the formula: =B18+B25. This formula will take the current amount of long-term debt and add the DFN. This will lead to a chain of calculations that will lead to lower DFN. This amount will then be added to the long-term debt, and so on. Eventually, it will converge so that DFN equals zero and long-term debt is 465.61. Note also that interest expense is 80.80, net income is 90.17, and retained earnings is 294.16. The pro forma balance sheet should now look similar to the one in Exhibit 5-4, except that we have a couple of important modifications to make.

This whole process will occur very rapidly, and you may not even see the changes taking place. It will be instructive to step through the process one iteration at a time. To do this, go to Tools Options and then to the Calculation tab. Set the Maximum Iterations to 1 (the default is 100). Now, reenter the formula in B18 (you must do this to reset the calculation). You should see that long-term debt is now 0.00, and DFN is 465.61. To step through the calculation, simply press the F9 key. This will cause the workbook to recalculate one cycle of the iterative formula. Long-term debt will now be 465.61 and DFN will be −32.69. Press F9 again to repeat the calculation, and you will see how the numbers change. Keep pressing F9 until DFN goes to zero. Make sure to go back and reset the maximum number of iterations to 100 or more before continuing.

---

5. You are strongly urged to try doing this by hand. This exercise will greatly improve your understanding of the process.

EXHIBIT 5-4
THE PRO FORMA BALANCE SHEET AFTER ITERATION

	A	B	C	D
1	Elvis Products International			
2	Pro Forma Balance Sheet			
3	As of Dec. 31, 2007			
4	*Assets*	*2008**	*2007*	*2006*
5	Cash and Equivalents	52.00	52.00	57.60
6	Accounts Receivable	444.51	402.00	351.20
7	Inventory	914.90	836.00	715.20
8	*Total Current Assets*	*1,411.40*	*1,290.00*	*1,124.00*
9	Plant & Equipment	577.00	527.00	491.00
10	Accumulated Depreciation	191.20	166.20	146.20
11	*Net Fixed Assets*	*385.80*	*360.80*	*344.80*
12	*Total Assets*	*1,797.20*	*1,650.80*	*1,468.80*
13	*Liabilities and Owner's Equity*			
14	Accounts Payable	189.05	175.20	145.60
15	Short-term Notes Payable	225.00	225.00	200.00
16	Other Current Liabilities	163.38	140.00	136.00
17	*Total Current Liabilities*	*577.43*	*540.20*	*481.60*
18	Long-term Debt	465.61	424.61	323.43
19	*Total Liabilities*	*1,043.04*	*964.81*	*805.03*
20	Common Stock	460.00	460.00	460.00
21	Retained Earnings	294.16	225.99	203.77
22	*Total Shareholder's Equity*	*754.16*	*685.99*	*663.77*
23	*Total Liabilities and Owner's Equity*	*1,797.20*	*1,650.80*	*1,468.80*
24	* Forecast			
25	Discretionary Financing Needed	0.00	Balanced	
26	Total Accumulated DFN	41.00		
27				
28	Notes:			
29	Net Addition to Plant & Equipment	50.00		
30	Life of New Equipment	10		
31	New Depreciation (Straight Line)	5.00		
32	Iteration	1		

Let's now improve our iterative calculations a bit. It is very helpful to have the capability to enable or disable the iterative calculations. This can be done in the Calculation tab of the Options dialog box, but that is tedious. Instead, we can use a cell value (0 or 1), combined with **IF** statements, to do the job. In A31, enter: `Iteration` and in B31 enter: `0`. This will disable iteration, while a 1 will enable iteration. Now, in B18 change the formula for long-term debt so that it is: `=IF(B31=1,B18+B25,C18)`. If iteration is turned on (B31 = 1), then the formula will be the same as before. Otherwise, if iteration is off, then long-term debt will be the same as it was in 2007.

One final change is necessary. We would like to know exactly how much new financing is required. It should be clear that the original $38.12 is not the correct answer, because each time we iterate we add more long-term debt. So, we need a cell to calculate the accumulated DFN. Select row 26 and insert a row. Now, in A26 enter the label: `Total  Accumulated  DFN`, and in B26 enter the formula: `=IF(B32=1,B26+B25,B25)`. If iteration is on, this formula will keep track of the additions to DFN. Otherwise, it will be equal to the DFN without iteration. Experiment by changing B32 to 0 and back to 1 to see the effect of these changes.

This worksheet could be further refined in several ways. As one example, instead of raising all of the DFN using long-term debt, we could allocate some of it to new equity. In this case, we would use the long-term debt ratio to determine how much should be long-term debt. The balance would be allocated to equity. Note that additional equity would result in more dividends, which would complicate the situation a bit.

Note that using circular references should be a last resort. They should be used only when absolutely necessary, as in this case. If your calculation does not converge to a single value, then Excel will eventually stop trying to calculate it, and you will have wrong answers. Furthermore, this technique is quite calculation intensive and will cause recalculation of a large spreadsheet to slow to a crawl. If at all possible, you should try to find another method of solving the problem that doesn't involve circular references.

Other Forecasting Methods

The primary advantage of the percent of sales forecasting method is its simplicity. Many other more sophisticated forecasting techniques can be implemented in a spreadsheet program. In this section we will look at two particularly useful techniques.

Linear Trend Extrapolation

Suppose that you were asked to perform the percent of sales forecast for EPI. The first step in that analysis requires a sales forecast. Since EPI is a small company, nobody regularly makes such forecasts, and you will have to generate your own. Where do you start?

Your first idea might be to see if there has been a clear trend in sales over the past several years and to extrapolate that trend, if it exists, to 2008. To see if there has been a trend, you first gather data on sales for EPI for the past five years. Table 5-1 presents the data that you have gathered.

TABLE 5-1
EPI SALES FOR 2003 TO 2007

Year	Sales
2003	1,890,532
2004	2,098,490
2005	2,350,308
2006	3,432,000
2007	3,850,000

Add a new worksheet to your EPI workbook, and rename it "Trend Forecast" so that it can be easily identified. Enter the labels and data from Table 5-1 into your worksheet beginning in A1.

The easiest way to see if there has been a trend in sales is to create a chart that plots the sales data versus the years. Create this chart using the Chart Wizard by first selecting A1:B6. Make sure to select an XY chart and to enter the title as: EPI Sales for 2003 to 2007. Your worksheet should resemble that in Exhibit 5-5.

EXHIBIT 5-5
EPI TREND FORECAST WORKSHEET

	A	B	C	D	E	F	G	H
1	Year	Sales						
2	2003	1,890,532						
3	2004	2,098,490						
4	2005	2,350,308						
5	2006	3,432,000						
6	2007	3,850,000						
7								
8								
9								
10								

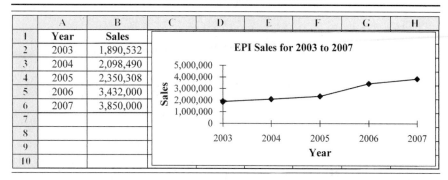

Examining the chart leads us to the conclusion that sales have definitely been increasing over the past five years, but not at a constant rate. There are several ways to generate a forecast from this data, even though the sales are not increasing at a constant rate.

One of these methods is to let Excel determine a linear trend. That is, let Excel fit a straight line to the data and extrapolate that line to 2008 (or beyond). The line that is generated is in the form:

$$Y = mX + b$$

which you should recognize as the same equation used in algebra courses to describe a straight line. In this equation, m is the slope and b is the intercept.

To determine the parameters for this line (m and b), Excel uses regression analysis which we will examine later. To generate a forecast based on the trend, we need to use the **TREND** function, which is defined as:

TREND(*KNOWN_Y'S*, *KNOWN_X'S*, *NEW_X'S*, *CONST*)

In the **TREND** function definition, *KNOWN_Y'S* is the range of the data that we wish to forecast (the dependent variable), and *KNOWN_X'S* is the optional range of data (the independent variable) that we want to use to determine the trend in the dependent variable. Since the **TREND** function is generally used to forecast a time-based trend, *KNOWN_X'S* will usually be a range of years, though it can be any set of consecutive numbers (e.g., 1, 2, 3,...). *NEW_X'S* is a continuation of the *KNOWN_X'S* for which we don't yet know the value of the dependent variable. *CONST* is a Boolean

(True/False) variable that tells Excel whether or not to include an intercept in its calculations (generally this should be set to true or omitted; both actions have the same result).

Using the **TREND** function is easier than it may at first seem. To generate a forecast for 2008, first enter 2008 into A7. This will provide us with the *NEW_X'S* value that we will use to forecast 2008 sales. Next, enter the **TREND** function as: =TREND(B$2:B$6,A$2:A$6,A7,TRUE) into B7. The result is a sales forecast of $4,300,000, which is the same sales forecast that we used in the percent of sales forecasting method for the financial statements.

We can extend our forecast to 2009 and 2010 quite easily. To do this, first enter 2009 into A8 and 2010 into A9. Now copy the formula from B7 to B8:B9. You should see that the forecasted sales for 2009 and 2010 are $4,825,244 and $5,350,489, respectively.

An interesting feature of charts in Excel is that we can tell Excel to add a trend line to the chart. Adding this line requires no more work than making a menu choice; we do not have to calculate the data ourselves. To add a trend line to our chart, select the plot line and click on it with the right mouse button. Click on Add Trendline… and then click on the OK button on the resulting dialog box to see the default linear trend line. You can also show trend lines that aren't linear. For example, if sales had been increasing at an accelerating rate, you might want to fit an exponential trend instead of a linear one. Excel also offers five other trend lines that it can calculate, including a moving average of user-determined length.

Excel can even do a forecast automatically in the chart! (Note that you will not get the actual numerical forecast using this method.) First, delete the trend line that we added by selecting it and then pressing the Delete key on your keyboard, or right-click the trend line and choose Clear from the shortcut menu. Now, select the original plot line again, and insert a linear trend line. Before clicking on the OK button, click on the Options tab. In the Forecast section, set Forward to 1 unit. After clicking on the OK button you will see a trend line that extends to 2008. We could also extend the forecast to 2009 or 2010 by setting Forward to 2 or 3. Note that we don't have to delete the trend line before showing the forecast. Instead, you could have right-clicked the existing trend line, chosen Format Trendline and the Options tab, and entered the forecast period as before.

Recall that we said Excel generates the equation for the trend line and uses this equation to make the forecast. We can have Excel show this equation on the chart by selecting the appropriate options. Right-click on the trend line and choose

Format Trendline from the short cut menu. Select the Options tab and then click on Display Equation on Chart. Click on the OK button, and you should see the equation appear on the chart.

The equation that Excel displays is:

$$y = 525245x - 1E+09$$

which is Excel's way of saying:

$$y = 525245x - 1,000,000,000$$

However, you should be suspicious of rounding problems any time you see scientific notation. In some cases the rounding isn't important, but in this case it is. We can fix the problem by right-clicking on the equation and choosing Format Data Labels from the shortcut menu. Now select the Number tab and apply another format. You should now see that the equation is actually:[6]

$$y = 525,244.60x - 1,050,391,157.00$$

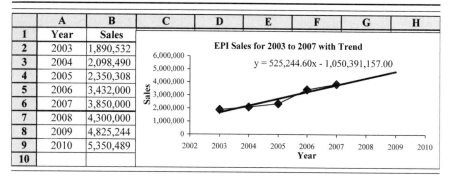

EXHIBIT 5-6
EPI TREND FORECAST WORKSHEET

	A	B	C	D	E	F	G	H
1	Year	Sales						
2	2003	1,890,532						
3	2004	2,098,490						
4	2005	2,350,308						
5	2006	3,432,000						
6	2007	3,850,000						
7	2008	4,300,000						
8	2009	4,825,244						
9	2010	5,350,489						
10								

We can see that this equation does indeed generate the forecast for 2008 by substituting 2008 for *x*. At this point, your worksheet should look like the one in Exhibit 5-6.

---

6. You could even apply the custom number format that we've used for the financial statements.

Regression Analysis

The term *"regression analysis"* (also known as ordinary least squares or OLS regression) is a sophisticated-sounding term for a rather simple concept: fitting the best line to a data set. As simple as it sounds, the mathematics behind regression analysis are beyond the scope of this book. However, Excel can easily handle quite complex regression models with minimal knowledge on your part. We will make use of Excel's regression tools without delving too deeply into the underlying mathematics.

As we've noted, regression analysis is a technique for fitting the best line to a data set: a very powerful tool for determining the relationship between variables and for forecasting. You could, for example, simply plot the data and draw in what appears to be the line that best fits the data, but there is no guarantee that the line you choose is actually the best line. In regression analysis, the best line is defined as the one that minimizes the sum of the squared errors. The errors are the difference between the actual data points and those predicted by the model.

In our previous example, we used regression analysis (disguised within the **TREND** function) to forecast EPI's level of sales for 2008. Aside from forecasting, the second major use of regression analysis is to understand the relationship between variables. In this section we will use Excel's regression tool to perform a regression analysis.[7]

Consider the following example, in which we will make use of regression analysis in order to get a better forecast of next year's cost of goods sold for EPI. Table 5-2 provides the historical data for sales and cost of goods sold.

TABLE 5-2
EPI'S HISTORICAL SALES AND COST OF GOODS

Year	Sales	Cost of Goods
2003	$ 1,890,532	$ 1,570,200
2001	2,098,490	1,695,694
2002	2,350,308	1,992,400
2003	3,432,000	2,864,000
2007	3,850,000	3,250,000

---

7. The regression tool is not a built-in function in the same sense as **TREND**. Instead, it is a part of the data analysis tools included with Excel. There is a regression function, **LINEST**. However, this function is more complex to use because it returns an array of values instead of a single value. Furthermore, the return values are not labeled. See the online help for more information.

Recall that we previously calculated the average percentage of sales for 2006 and 2007 and used that average to generate our forecast for 2008. Suppose, however, you are concerned that there may possibly be a more systematic relationship between sales and cost of goods sold. For example, it is entirely possible that as sales rise, cost of goods sold will rise at slower rate. This may be due to efficiencies in the production process, quantity discounts on materials, and so on. Alternatively, there may be another relationship, or none at all. Regression analysis can help us to gain a better understanding of the historical relationship and, hopefully, to generate better forecasts of the future cost of goods sold.

Before running the regression, let's create a chart of the data to help get a visual picture of the historical relationship. Enter the data from Table 5-2 into a new worksheet beginning in cell A1. Now select B2:C6 and create an XY (Scatter) chart of the data. To facilitate our visualization, change the scale on each axis as follows: Select the axis, right-click it, and choose Format Axis. Now, select the Scale tab and change the Minimum to 1,500,000, the Maximum to 4,500,000, and the Major unit to 1,000,000. This will ensure that the scale of each axis is the same, which makes it much easier to see the relationship between our two variables.

The chart in Figure 5-1 shows what appears to be a pretty consistent relationship. Furthermore, the slope of the line is something less than 45 degrees, so we know

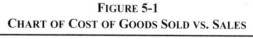

FIGURE 5-1
CHART OF COST OF GOODS SOLD VS. SALES

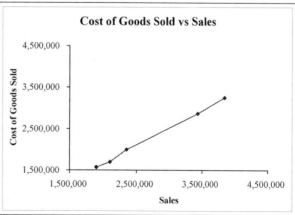

that a change in sales of $1 will lead to a change in cost of goods sold of less than $1. The problem is that we can't know the exact relationship from reading the chart. What we can do is to run a regression analysis on the data to find the exact slope and intercept of best-fitting line for this data.

Excel provides several functions to calculate the parameters of a regression equation. For example, the **TREND**, **LINEST**, and **FORECAST** functions all use linear regression to generate equation parameters or forecasts. There are also functions for nonlinear regression (e.g., **GROWTH AND LOGEST**). However, Excel also includes another method that we will cover here: the regression tool in the Data Analysis ToolPak.[8] This tool works very much like any statistical program that you may have used. It will ask for the data and then output a table of the regression results.

To run the regression tool, choose **T**ools **D**ata Analysis from the menus. Next, select Regression from the list of analysis tools that are available. Figure 5-2 shows the dialog box. (Note that the data are already filled in.)

FIGURE 5-2
THE REGRESSION TOOL

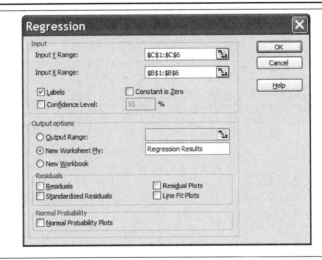

---

8. Note that the Data Analysis ToolPak is generally not a part of the default installation of Excel. To see if it is installed on your PC, look on the **T**ools menu. If you have an item called **D**ata Analysis, then it is installed. If not, go to **T**ools Add-**I**ns and see if you have an item called Analysis ToolPak. If so, make sure there is a check mark next to it. If not, you will need to insert your installation CD to install the Analysis ToolPak.

Before running the analysis, we need to determine the theoretical relationship between the variables of interest. In this case we are hypothesizing that the level of sales can be used to predict the cost of goods sold. Therefore we say that the cost of goods sold is dependent on sales. So the cost of goods sold is referred to as the dependent (Y) variable, and sales is the independent (X) variable.[9] Our mathematical model is:

$$\text{Cost of Goods Sold}_t = \alpha + \beta(\text{Sales}_t) + \tilde{e}_t \qquad \text{(5-1)}$$

where α is the intercept, β is the slope of the line, and e is the random error term in period t.

There are many options on this dialog box, but for our simple problem we are only concerned with four of them. First, we need to tell Excel where the dependent (Y) variable data are located. In the "Input **Y** Range" edit box, enter: `$C$1:$C$6` or merely select this range with the mouse. In the "Input **X** Range" edit box, enter: `$B$1:$B$6`. Since we have included the labels in our input ranges, we must make sure that a check mark is in the **L**abels box. Finally, we want to tell Excel to create a new worksheet within the current workbook for the output. Click on the box to the left of "New Worksheet **P**ly:" in the Output section, and type: `Regression Results` in the edit box to give a name to the new worksheet. After, you click the OK button, Excel will calculate the regression statistics and create a new worksheet named "Regression Results." We could also have Excel enter the output in the same worksheet by specifying the **O**utput Range. Note that you need to specify only the upper-left corner of the area where you want the output. (Beware that Excel has a minor bug. When you click on the radio button for the **O**utput Range, the cursor will return to the edit box for the Y range. Before selecting your output range, you must click in the proper edit box; otherwise, you will overwrite your Y range. This bug has existed in the past several versions of Excel.)

---

9. Many regression models have more than one independent variable. These models are known as multiple regressions, and Excel can handle them just as easily as our bivariate regression.

EXHIBIT 5-7
REGRESSION RESULTS

	A	B	C	D	E	F	G
1	SUMMARY OUTPUT						
2							
3	*Regression Statistics*						
4	Multiple R	99.91%					
5	R Square	99.83%					
6	Adjusted R Square	99.77%					
7	Standard Error	35,523.08					
8	Observations	5					
9							
10	ANOVA						
11		*df*	*SS*	*MS*	*F*	*Significance F*	
12	Regression	1	2.20596E+12	2.20596E+12	1748.14121	3.01101E-05	
13	Residual	3	3785666909	1261888970			
14	Total	4	2.20975E+12				
15							
16		*Coefficients*	*Standard Error*	*t Stat*	*P-value*	*Lower 95%*	*Upper 95%*
17	Intercept	(63,680.8247)	58,134.6760	(1.0954)	0.3534	(248,691.4831)	121,329.8337
18	Sales	0.8583	0.0205	41.8108	0.0000	0.7929	0.9236

Exhibit 5-7 shows the output of the regression tool (it has been reformatted to make it a bit easier to read). The output may appear to be complex if you are not familiar with regression analysis. However, we are primarily concerned with the output, which gives the parameters of the regression line.[10] In cells B17:B18 are the parameters of the regression equation. If we substitute these numbers into equation (5-1), we find:

$$\text{Cost of Goods Sold}_t = -63,680.82 + 0.8583(\text{Sales}_t) + \bar{e}_t.$$

The equation tells us that all other things being equal, each dollar increase in sales will lead to about an $0.86 increase in cost of goods sold.

Before we use this equation to make our forecast, let's evaluate it to make sure there is a statistically significant relationship between the variables. We will begin by looking at the R Square (R^2) in cell B5. The R^2 is the coefficient of determination and tells us the proportion of the total variation in the dependent variable that is explained by the independent variable. In this case, sales are able to explain nearly 100% of the variability in the cost of goods sold. That is a stronger relationship than you will normally find, but it indicates that this equation is likely to work very well, as long as we have a good forecast of next years' sales.

---

10. We are not trying to minimize the importance of this other output. On the contrary, it would be foolish to attempt to use regression methods for any important purpose without understanding the model completely. We are merely trying to illustrate how Excel can be used for this type of analysis as simply as possible.

Next, we look at the t-statistics for our regression coefficients (D18; normally we aren't too concerned with the significance of the intercept). Usually, we want to know whether a coefficient is statistically distinguishable from zero (i.e., "statistically significant"). Note that the magnitude of the coefficient is not the issue. If the coefficient for sales is significantly different from zero, then we know that sales is useful in predicting cost of goods sold. The t-statistic tells us how many standard deviations away from zero the coefficient is. Obviously, the higher this number, the more confidence we have that the coefficient is different from zero. In this case, the t-statistic is 41.81. A general rule of thumb is that, for large samples, a t-statistic greater than about 2.00 is significant at the 95% confidence level or more. Even though we don't have a large sample, we can be quite sure that the coefficient for sales is significant. Note that we can also use the p-value (E18) to determine the exact confidence level. Simply subtract the p-value from 1 to find the confidence level. Here, the p-value is 0.00003, so we are essentially 100% (actually, 99.997%) confident that our coefficient is significant.

We are very confident that the coefficient for sales is not zero, but we don't know for sure that the correct value is 0.8583. That number is simply the best point estimate given our set of sample data. Note that in F18:G18 we have numbers labeled "Lower 95%" and "Upper 95%." This gives us a range of values between which we can be 95% sure the true value of this coefficient lies. In other words, we can be 95% confident that the true change in cost of goods sold per dollar change in sales is between $0.7929 and $0.9236. Of course, there is a small chance (5%) that the true value lies outside of this range. As an aside, note that the 95% confidence range for the intercept contains 0. This indicates that we cannot statistically distinguish the intercept coefficient from zero (this is also confirmed by the rather high p-value for the intercept). However, since we are merely using this model for forecasting, the significance of the intercept is not important.

We are now quite confident that our model is useful for forecasting cost of goods sold.[11] To make a forecast for the 2008 cost of goods sold, we merely plug our 2008 sales forecast into the equation:

$$\text{Cost of Goods Sold}_{2008} = -63,680.82 + 0.8583(4,300,000) = 3,626,854.68$$

Recall that using the percent of sales method, our forecast for 2008 cost of goods sold was $3,609,107.56. Our regression result agrees fairly closely with this number, so either number is probably usable for a forecast. However, note that both

---

11. One issue we have ignored is that we are using quite a small sample with only five observations. This reduces our confidence somewhat. It would be preferable to use higher-frequency data such as quarterly sales and cost of goods sold.

of these methods depend critically on our sales forecast. Without a good forecast of sales, all of our other forecasts are questionable.

To generate this forecast yourself, return to your worksheet with the data from Table 5-2. In A7 enter: `2008` for the year and in B7 enter the sales forecast of: `4,300,000`. Now, calculate the forecast by using the regression output. The equation in C7 is: `='Regression Results'!B17+'Regression Results'!B18*B7`.

As we did with the **TREND** function, we can replicate this regression directly in the XY chart that was completed earlier. Simply right-click on one of the data points, and choose Add Trendline. Now, using the Options tab, place the equation on the chart and have the trend line extended to forecast one period ahead. Your worksheet should now look like the one in Exhibit 5-8. As you can see, our regression line nearly perfectly matches the chart of the original data; this confirms our analysis of the regression results.

EXHIBIT 5-8
COMPLETED REGRESSION WORKSHEET WITH FORECAST

	A	B	C	D	E	F
1		**Sales**	**Cost of Goods**			
2	2003	1,890,532	1,570,200			
3	2004	2,098,490	1,695,694			
4	2005	2,350,308	1,992,400			
5	2006	3,432,000	2,864,000			
6	2007	3,850,000	3,250,000			
7	2008*	4,300,000	3,626,855			
8						

Cost of Goods Sold vs Sales

$y = 0.8583x - 63{,}680.8247$

$R^2 = 0.9983$

(Chart: Cost of Goods Sold (y-axis, 1,500,000 to 4,500,000) vs Sales (x-axis, 1,500,000 to 4,500,000))

*Forecast

Summary

In this chapter we have examined three methods of forecasting financial statements and variables. We used the percent of sales technique to forecast the firm's income statement and balance sheet based upon an estimated level of sales. We used a time-trend technique to forecast sales as an input to the percent of sales method. Finally, we looked at regression analysis to help generate a better forecast of the cost of goods sold by using the relationship between that and sales over the past five years.

We have barely scratched the surface of forecasting methodologies. However, we hope that this chapter has stimulated an interest in this important subject. If so, be assured that Excel, either alone or through an add-in program, can be made to handle nearly all of your forecasting problems. Please remember that any forecast is almost assuredly wrong. We can only hope to get reasonably close to the actual future outcome. How close you get depends upon the quality of your model and the inputs to that model.

FUNCTIONS INTRODUCED IN THIS CHAPTER

Purpose	Function	Page
Forecast future outcomes based on a time trend	TREND(*KNOWN_Y'S*, *KNOWN_X'S*, *NEW_X'S*, *CONST*)	163

Problems

1. Using the data in the file P&G.xls (downloadable from the text support site at http://thomsonedu.com/finance/mayes) forecast the June 30, 2006, income statement and balance sheet for Procter & Gamble. Use the percent of sales method and the following assumptions: (1) Sales in FY 2006 will be $60,048; (2) The tax rate will be 30%; and (3) Each item that changes with sales will be the five-year average percentage of sales.

   a. What is the discretionary financing needed in 2006? Is this a surplus or deficit?

    b.   Assume that the DFN will be absorbed by long-term debt and common stock. Set up an iterative worksheet to eliminate it.

    c.   Create a chart of Cash vs. Sales and add a linear trend line. Does there appear to be a consistent trend in this relationship?

    d.   Use the regression tool to verify your results from part B. Is the trend statistically significant? Use at least three methods to show why or why not.

    e.   Use the Scenario Manager to set up three scenarios:
1) Best Case—Sales are 10% higher than expected.
2) Base Case—Sales are exactly as expected.
3) Worst Case—Sales are 10% less than expected.
What is the DFN under each scenario?

2.   Use the same data as in Problem 1.

    a.   Recalculate the percentage of sales income statement, but this time use the TREND function to forecast depreciation expense, other income, and interest expense.

    b.   Recalculate the percentage of sales balance sheet, but this time use the TREND function to forecast cash, property plant and equipment (gross), intangibles, and other non-current assets.

    c.   Do these new values appear to be more realistic than the original values? Does this technique make sense for each of these items? Might other income statement or balance sheet items be forecasted in this way?

3.   The file "Chapter 5 Problem 3.xls" (downloadable from the text support Web site) contains monthly total returns for General Electric (NYSE: GE) and the S&P 500 index (using AMEX: SPY as a proxy) from January 2001 to December 2005.

a. Create an XY (Scatter) plot of the returns, and set the scales on the axes so that they range from −20% to 20%. Describe, in words, the relationship between the returns of GE and the S&P 500. Estimate the slope of a regression equation of this data.

b. Add a linear trend line to the chart, and place the equation and R^2 on the chart. Does this equation confirm your guess from part a? How much of the variability in GE returns can be explained by variability in the broad market?

c. Using the Analysis ToolPak add-in, run a regression analysis on this data. Your dependent variable is the GE returns. Does this confirm the earlier results? Is the relationship between the two sets of returns statistically significant? Explain.

Internet Exercise

1. Since you are reading this after the end of Proctor & Gamble's fiscal year 2006, how do your forecasts from the previous problems compare to the actual FY 2006 results? Does it appear that more information would have helped to generate better forecasts? Insert Proctor & Gamble's actual sales for 2006 into your forecast. Does this improve your forecast of earnings?

2. Choose your own company and the repeat the analysis from Problem 1. You can get the data from MoneyCentral Investor at http://moneycentral.msn.com/investor/home.asp. To retrieve the data for your company, go to the Stocks area and enter the ticker symbol. Now choose Financial Results and then Statements from the menu on the left side of the screen. Display the annual income statement, select the entire data section, and copy. Now paste this data directly into a new worksheet. Repeat these steps for the balance sheets.

3. Choose your own company and repeat Problem 3. The data can be easily obtained from Yahoo! Finance (http://finance.yahoo.com). Enter a ticker symbol and get a stock price quote. On the left side of the page, click the link for "Historical Prices." Set the dates for

a five-year period, and the frequency to monthly. Click the link at the bottom of the page to load the data into Excel. Now, repeat the steps using the ticker symbol SPY (an exchange-traded fund that mimics the S&P 500). Now, combine the monthly closing prices on one worksheet and calculate the monthly percentage changes. You should now have the data necessary to answer the questions from Problem 3. Note that to improve your results, you can also get the dividends and calculate the monthly total returns.

CHAPTER 6

Break-Even and Leverage Analysis

After studying this chapter, you should be able to:

1. *Differentiate between fixed and variable costs.*

2. *Calculate operating and cash break-even points, and find the number of units that need to be sold to reach a target level of EBIT.*

3. *Define the terms "business risk" and "financial risk," and describe the origins of each of these risks.*

4. *Use Excel to calculate the DOL, DFL, and DCL and explain the significance of each of these risk measures.*

5. *Explain how the DOL, DFL, and DCL change as the firm's sales level changes.*

In this chapter we will consider the decisions that managers make regarding the cost structure of the firm. These decisions will, in turn, impact the decisions they make regarding methods of financing the firm's assets (i.e., its capital structure) and pricing the firm's products.

In general, we will assume that the firm faces two kinds of costs:

1. *Variable costs* are those costs that are expected to change at the same rate as the firm's sales. Variable costs are constant per unit, so as more units are sold, total variable costs will rise. Examples of variable costs include sales commissions, costs of raw materials, hourly wages, and so on.

2. *Fixed costs* are those costs that are constant, regardless of the quantity produced, over some relevant range of production. Total fixed cost per unit will decline as the number of units increases. Examples of fixed costs include rent, salaries, and depreciation.

Figure 6-1 illustrates these costs.[1]

FIGURE 6-1
TOTAL FIXED AND TOTAL VARIABLE COSTS

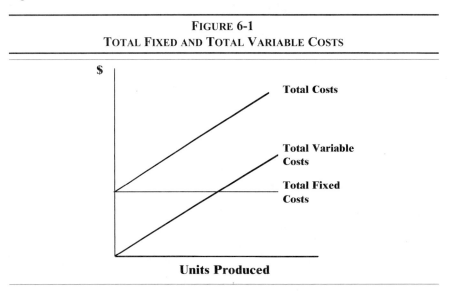

Break-Even Points

We can define the *break-even point* as the level of sales (either units or dollars) that causes profits (however measured) to equal zero. Most commonly, we define the break-even point as the unit sales required for earnings before interest and taxes (EBIT) to be equal to zero. This point is often referred to as the *operating break-even point*.

Define Q as the quantity sold, P as the price per unit, V as the variable cost per unit, and F as total fixed costs. With these definitions, we can say:

$$Q(P - V) - F = \text{EBIT} \qquad \text{(6-1)}$$

---

1. Most firms will also have some semi-variable costs that are fixed over a certain range of output, but will change if output rises above that level. For simplicity, we will assume that these costs are fixed.

If we set EBIT in equation (6-1) to zero, we can solve for the break-even quantity (Q^*):

$$Q^* = \frac{F}{P - V} \qquad \text{(6-2)}$$

Assume, for example, that a firm is selling widgets for $30 per unit while variable costs are $20 per unit and fixed costs total $100,000. In this situation, the firm must sell 10,000 units to break even:

$$Q^* = \frac{100,000}{30 - 20} = 10,000 \text{ units}$$

The quantity $P - V$ is often referred to as the *contribution margin* per unit, because this is the amount that each unit sold contributes to coverage of the firm's fixed costs. Using equation (6-1), you can verify that the firm will break even if it sells 10,000 widgets:

$$10,000(30 - 20) - 100,000 = 0$$

We can now calculate the firm's break-even point in dollars by simply multiplying Q^* by the price per unit:

$$\$BE = P \times Q^* \qquad \text{(6-3)}$$

In this example, the result shows that the firm must sell $300,000 worth of widgets to break even.

Note that we can substitute equation (6-2) into (6-3):

$$\$BE = P \times \frac{F}{(P - V)} = \frac{F}{(P - V)/P} = \frac{F}{CM\%} \qquad \text{(6-4)}$$

So, if we know the contribution margin as a percentage of the selling price ($CM\%$), we can easily calculate the break-even point in dollars. In the previous example, $CM\%$ is 33.33% so the break-even point in dollars must be:

$$\$BE = \frac{100,000}{0.3333} = \$300,000$$

which confirms our earlier result.

Calculating Break-Even Points in Excel

We can, of course, calculate break-even points in Excel. Consider the income statement for Spuds and Suds, a very popular sports bar that serves only one product: a plate of gourmet french fries and a pitcher of imported beer for $16 per serving. The income statement is presented in Exhibit 6-1.

EXHIBIT 6-1
INCOME STATEMENT FOR SPUDS AND SUDS

	A	B
1	Spuds and Suds	
2	Income Statement	
3	For the Year Ended Dec. 31, 2007	
4		2007
5	Sales	$ 2,500,000
6	Less: Variable Costs	1,500,000
7	Less: Fixed Costs	400,000
8	Earnings Before Interest and Taxes	600,000
9	Less: Interest Expense	100,000
10	Earnings Before Taxes	500,000
11	Taxes	200,000
12	Net Income	300,000
13		
14	Less: Preferred Dividends	100,000
15	Net Income Available to Common	200,000
16	Common Shares Outstanding	1,000,000
17	Earnings per Share	$ 0.20
18		
19	Assumptions	
20	Price per Unit	$ 16.00
21	Unit Sales	156,250
22	Variable Costs as a Percent of Sales	60%
23	Tax Rate	40%

Before calculating the break-even point, enter the labels into a new worksheet as shown in Exhibit 6-1. Since we will be expanding this example, it is important that you enter formulas where they are appropriate. Before doing any calculations, enter the numbers in B20:B23.

We will first calculate the dollar amount of sales (in B5) by multiplying the per unit price by the number of units sold: =B20*B21. Variable costs are always 60% of sales (as shown in B22), so the formula in B6 is: =B22*B5. Both Fixed Costs (in B7) and Interest Expense (in B9) are constants so they are simply entered directly. The simple subtraction and multiplication required to complete the income statement through B12 should be obvious.

In B14:B17 we have added information that is not immediately useful, but the figures will become central when we discuss operating and financial leverage. In cell B14 we have added preferred dividends, which will be subtracted from net income. The result (in B15) is net income available to the common shareholders. Preferred dividends are simply input into B14, and the formula in B15 is: =B12-B14. In B16, enter the number of common shares outstanding: 1,000,000. Earnings per share is then calculated as: =B15/B16 in cell B17.

Now we can calculate the break-even points. In cell A25 enter the label: Break-even Point (Units). Next, copy this label to A26, and change the word "Units" to Dollars. In B25, we can calculate the break-even point in units using equation (6-2). The formula is: =B7/(B20-B6/B21). Notice that we have to calculate the variable cost per unit by dividing total variable costs (B6) by the number of units sold (B21). You can see that Spuds and Suds must sell 62,500 units in order to break even and that they are well above this level. We can calculate the break-even point in dollars simply by multiplying the unit break-even point by the price per unit. In B26 enter the formula: =B25*B20. You will see that the result is $1,000,000.

Other Break-Even Points

Recall that we found the break-even point by setting EBIT, in equation (6-1), equal to zero. However, there is no reason that we can't set EBIT equal to any amount that we might desire. For example, if we define $EBIT_{Target}$ as the target level of EBIT, we find that the firm can earn the target EBIT amount by selling:

$$Q^*_{Target} = \frac{F + EBIT_{Target}}{P - V}$$

(6-5)

Consider that Spuds and Suds might want to know the number of units that they need to sell in order to have EBIT equal $800,000. Mathematically, we can see that:

$$Q^*_{800,000} = \frac{400,000 + 800,000}{16 - 9.60} = 187,500 \text{ units}$$

need to be sold to reach this target. You can verify that this number is correct by typing: 187,500 into B21 and checking the value in B8. To return the worksheet to its original values, enter: 156,250 into B21, or choose **E**dit **U**ndo Typing '187500' in B21.

We can do the same thing, with more flexibility, by modifying our worksheet. Select row 22 and insert a new row. In A22 enter the label: `Target EBIT` and in B22 enter: `800,000`. In A29 type: `Units to Meet EBIT Target` and then in B29 enter the formula: `=(B7+B22)/(B20-B6/B21)`. The result will be 187,500 units as before. However, we can now easily change the target EBIT and see the unit sales required to reach the goal. Your worksheet should now look like the one in Exhibit 6-2.

EXHIBIT 6-2
BREAK-EVEN POINTS

	A	B
1	**Spuds and Suds**	
2	**Income Statement**	
3	**For the Year Ended Dec. 31, 2007**	
4		**2007**
5	Sales	$ 2,500,000
6	Less: Variable Costs	1,500,000
7	Less: Fixed Costs	400,000
8	*Earnings Before Interest and Taxes*	*600,000*
9	Less: Interest Expense	100,000
10	*Earnings Before Taxes*	*500,000*
11	Taxes	200,000
12	*Net Income*	*300,000*
13		
14	Less: Preferred Dividends	100,000
15	*Net Income Available to Common*	*200,000*
16	Common Shares Outstanding	1,000,000
17	*Earnings per Share*	*$ 0.20*
18		
19	**Assumptions**	
20	Price per Unit	$ 16.00
21	Unit Sales	156,250
22	Target EBIT	$ 800,000
23	Variable Costs as a Percent of Sales	60%
24	Tax Rate	40%
25		
26	Operating Break-even Point (Units)	62,500
27	Operating Break-even Point (Dollars)	1,000,000
28		
29	Units to Meet EBIT Target	187,500

Recall from page 51 that we defined cash flow as net income plus non-cash expenses. We do this because the presence of non-cash expenses (principally depreciation) in the accounting numbers distort the actual cash flows. We can make a similar adjustment to our break-even calculations by setting $EBIT_{Target}$ equal to the negative of the depreciation expense. This results in a type of break-even that we refer to as the *cash break-even point*:

$$Q^*_{Cash} = \frac{F - Depreciation}{P - V} \qquad \text{(6-6)}$$

Note that the cash break-even point will always be lower than the operating break-even point because we don't have to cover the depreciation expense.

Using Goal Seek to Calculate Break-Even Points

As we've shown, the break-even point can be defined in numerous ways. We don't even need to define it in terms of EBIT. Suppose that we wanted to know how many units need to be sold to break even in terms of net income. We could easily derive a formula [just use equation (6-5) and set $EBIT_{Target}$ = Interest Expense], but that's not necessary.

Excel has a tool, called Goal Seek, to help with problems like this.[2] To use Goal Seek you must have a target cell with a formula and another cell that it depends on. For example, Net Income in B12 depends indirectly on the Unit Sales in B21. So, by changing B21, we change B12. When we use Goal Seek, we'll simply tell it to keep changing B21 until B12 equals zero.

Bring up the Goal Seek tool by choosing <u>T</u>ools <u>G</u>oal Seek from the menu. Fill in the dialog box as shown in Figure 6-2 and click the OK button. You should find that Unit Sales of 78,125 will cause Net Income to be equal to zero. You can experiment with this tool to verify the other break-even points that we've found.

---

2. For more complicated problems use the Solver add-in.

FIGURE 6-2
THE GOAL SEEK TOOL

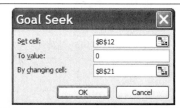

Leverage Analysis

In Chapter 4 (page 117) we defined leverage as a multiplication of changes in sales into even larger changes in profitability measures. Firms that use large amounts of operating leverage will find that their earnings before interest and taxes will be more variable than those who do not. We would say that such a firm has high *business risk*. Business risk is one of the major risks faced by a firm, and it can be defined as the variability of EBIT.[3] The more variable a firm's revenues, relative to its costs, the more variable its EBIT will be. Also, the likelihood that the firm won't be able to pay its expenses will be higher. As an example, consider a software company and a grocery chain. It should be apparent that the future revenues of the software company are much more uncertain than those for the grocery chain. This uncertainty in revenues causes the software company to have a much greater amount of business risk than the grocery chain. The software company's management can do little about this business risk; it is simply a function of the industry in which they operate. Software is not a necessity of life. People do, however, need to eat. For this reason, the grocery business has much lower business risk.

Business risk results from the environment in which the firm operates. Such factors as the competitive position of the firm in its industry, the state of its labor relations, and the state of the economy all affect the amount of business risk a firm faces. In addition, as we will see, the degree to which the firm's costs are fixed (as opposed

---

3. The use of EBIT for this analysis assumes that the firm has no extraordinary income or expenses. Extraordinary income and/or expenses are one-time events that are not a part of the firm's ordinary business operations. If the firm does have these items, one should use its net operating income (NOI) instead of EBIT.

to variable) will affect the amount of business risk. To a large degree, these components of business risk are beyond the control of the firm's managers.

In contrast, the amount of *financial risk* is determined directly by management. Financial risk refers to the probability that the firm will be unable to meet its fixed financing obligations (which includes both interest and preferred dividends). Obviously, all other things being equal, the more debt a firm uses to finance its assets, the higher its interest cost will be. Higher interest costs lead directly to a higher probability that the firm won't be able to pay. Since the amount of debt is determined by managerial choice, the financial risk that a firm faces is also determined by management.

Managers need to be aware that they face both business risk and financial risk. If they are in an industry with high business risk, they should control the overall amount of risk by limiting the amount of financial risk that they face. Alternatively, firms that face low levels of business risk can better afford more financial risk.

We will examine these concepts in more detail by continuing with our Spuds and Suds example.

The Degree of Operating Leverage

Earlier we mentioned that a firm's business risk can be measured by the variability of its earnings before interest and taxes. Obviously, if a firm's costs are all variable, then any variation in sales will be reflected by exactly the same variation in EBIT. However, if a firm has some fixed expenses, EBIT will be more variable than sales. We refer to this concept as *operating leverage*.

We can measure operating leverage by comparing the percentage change in EBIT to a given percentage change in sales. This measure is called the *degree of operating leverage* (DOL):

$$\text{DOL} = \frac{\%\Delta \text{ in EBIT}}{\%\Delta \text{ in Sales}} \qquad (6\text{-}7)$$

So, if a 10% change in sales results in a 20% change in EBIT, we would say that the degree of operating leverage is 2. As we will see, this is a symmetrical concept. As long as sales are increasing, a high DOL is desirable. However, if sales begin to decline, a high DOL will result in EBIT declining at an even faster pace than sales.

To make this concept more concrete, let's extend the Spuds and Suds example. Assume that management believes the unit sales will increase by 10% in 2008. Furthermore, they expect that variable costs will remain at 60% of sales and fixed costs will stay at $400,000. Copy B4:B27 to C4:C27. Now, insert a row above the Tax Rate in row 24. Enter the label: `Projected Sales Growth`, and in C24 enter: `10%`. We need to have the 2008 unit sales in C21, so enter: `=B21*(1+C24)` into C21. (Note that you have just created a percent of sales income statement forecast for 2008, just as we did in Chapter 5.) Change the label in C4 to `2008` and you have completed the changes.

Before continuing, notice that the operating break-even points (C27:C28) have not changed. This will always be the case if fixed costs are constant and variable costs are a constant percentage of sales. The break-even point is always driven by the level of fixed costs.

Since we wish to calculate the DOL for 2007, we first need to calculate the percentage changes in EBIT and Sales. In A32 enter the label: `% Change in Sales from Prior Year` and in A33 enter: `% Change in EBIT from Prior Year`. To calculate the percentage changes, enter: `=C5/B5-1` in cell C32and then: `=C8/B8-1` in C33. You should see that sales increased by 10% while EBIT increased by 16.67%. According to equation (6-7), the DOL for Spuds and Suds in 2007 is:

$$DOL = \frac{16.67\%}{10.00\%} = 1.667$$

So, any change in sales will be magnified by 1.667 times in EBIT. To see this, recall that the formula in C21 increased the 2007 unit sales by 10%. Temporarily, change the value in C24 to: `20%`. You should see that if sales increase by 20%, EBIT will increase by 33.33%. Recalculating the DOL, we see that it is unchanged:

$$DOL = \frac{33.33\%}{20.00\%} = 1.667$$

Furthermore, if we change the value in C24 to: `-10%`, so that sales decline by 10%, we find that EBIT declines by 16.67%. In this case, the DOL is:

$$DOL = \frac{-16.67\%}{-10.00\%} = 1.667$$

So leverage is indeed a double-edged sword. You can see that a high DOL would be desirable as long as sales are increasing, but very undesirable when sales are decreasing. Unfortunately, most businesses don't have the luxury of altering their DOL instantaneously.

Calculating the DOL with equation (6-7) is actually more cumbersome than is required. With this equation, we need to use two income statements. However, a more direct method of calculating the DOL is to use the following equation:

$$\text{DOL} = \frac{Q(P-V)}{Q(P-V)-F} = \frac{\text{Sales} - \text{Variable Costs}}{\text{EBIT}} \qquad \textbf{(6-8)}$$

For Spuds and Suds in 2007, we can calculate the DOL using equation (6-8):

$$\text{DOL} = \frac{2,500,000 - 1,500,000}{600,000} = 1.667$$

which is exactly as we found with equation (6-7).

Continuing with our example, enter the label: `Degree of Operating Leverage` in A36. In B36 we will calculate the DOL for 2007 with the formula: `=(B5-B6)/B8`. You should get the same result as before. If you copy the formula from B36 to C36, you will find that in 2008 the DOL will decline to 1.57. We will examine this decline in the DOL later.

Before continuing, it is worth discussing a refinement of the formula in B36. The formula that we entered could potentially cause a division by zero (#DIV/0!) error if EBIT is zero (that is, if the firm is operating exactly at its break-even point). We can use an **IF** statement to avoid this error. If EBIT = 0, then the function will return #N/A (Not Available) as the result. This is better than having a #DIV/0! error or simply returning zero or a blank as the result. Returning a zero can throw off the results of other formulas. For example, the **COUNT** function would count a zero, but not an #N/A. To return #N/A as a result, we can use the **NA** function. This function takes no arguments, but you must put a closed pair of parentheses after it:

NA( )

EXHIBIT 6-3
SPUDS AND SUDS BREAK-EVEN AND LEVERAGE WORKSHEET

	A	B	C
1	Spuds and Suds		
2	Income Statement		
3	For the Year Ended Dec. 31, 2007		
4		2007	2008*
5	Sales	$2,500,000	$2,750,000
6	Less: Variable Costs	1,500,000	1,650,000
7	Less: Fixed Costs	400,000	400,000
8	*Earnings Before Interest and Taxes*	*600,000*	*700,000*
9	Less: Interest Expense	100,000	100,000
10	*Earnings Before Taxes*	*500,000*	*600,000*
11	Taxes	200,000	240,000
12	*Net Income*	*300,000*	*360,000*
13			
14	Less: Preferred Dividends	100,000	100,000
15	*Net Income Available to Common*	*200,000*	*260,000*
16	Common Shares Outstanding	1,000,000	1,000,000
17	*Earnings per Share*	$ *0.20*	$ *0.26*
18			
19	Assumptions		
20	Price per Unit	$ 16.00	$ 16.00
21	Unit Sales	156,250	171,875
22	Target EBIT	$ 800,000	
23	Variable Costs as a Percent of Sales	60%	60%
24	Projected Sales Growth		10%
25	Tax Rate	40%	40%
26			
27	Operating Break-even Point (Units)	62,500	62,500
28	Operating Break-even Point (Dollars)	1,000,000	1,000,000
29			
30	Units to Meet EBIT Target	187,500	
31			
32	% Change in Sales from Prior Year		10.00%
33	% Change in EBIT from Prior Year		16.67%
34			
35			
36	Degree of Operating Leverage	1.67	1.57

We can modify the formula in B36 as follows: `=IF(ISERR((B5-B6)/B8),` `NA(),(B5-B6)/B8)`. Note that we have also used the **ISERR** function to check if the result will be an error. This function will return either TRUE or FALSE depending on whether the formula evaluates to an error condition. It is defined as:

$$\textsc{Iserr}(\textit{value})$$

where **VALUE** is any statement or formula that can be evaluated by Excel. This technique is useful anytime that a formula could result in an error that might render any dependent formulas incorrect. It is better to see a result of #N/A than to see an incorrect result.

Your worksheet should now appear similar to the one in Exhibit 6-3.

The Degree of Financial Leverage

Financial leverage is similar to operating leverage, but the fixed costs that we are interested in are the fixed financing costs. These are the interest expense and preferred dividends.[4] We can measure financial leverage by relating percentage changes in earnings per share (EPS) to percentage changes in EBIT. This measure is referred to as the *degree of financial leverage* (DFL):

$$\text{DFL} = \frac{\%\Delta \text{ in EPS}}{\%\Delta \text{ in EBIT}} \tag{6-9}$$

For Spuds and Suds we have already calculated the percentage change in EBIT, so all that remains is to calculate the percentage change in EPS. In A34 add the label: % Change in EPS from Prior Year and in C34 add the formula: =C17/ B17-1. Note that EPS is expected to increase by 30% in 2008 compared to only 16.67% for EBIT. Using equation (6-9) we find that the degree of financial leverage employed by Spuds and Suds in 2007 is:

$$\text{DFL} = \frac{30.00\%}{16.67\%} = 1.80$$

Therefore, any change in EBIT will be multiplied by 1.80 times in earnings per share. Like operating leverage, financial leverage works both ways. When EBIT is increasing, EPS will increase even more. And, when EBIT decreases, EPS will decline by a larger percentage.

As with the DOL, there is a more direct method of calculating the degree of financial leverage:

---

4. Preferred stock, as we'll see in Chapter 8, is a hybrid security that is similar to both debt and equity securities. How it is treated is determined by one's goals. When discussing financial leverage, we treat preferred stock as if it were a debt security.

$$DFL = \frac{EBIT}{EBT - \dfrac{PD}{(1-t)}} \tag{6-10}$$

In equation (6-10), PD is the preferred dividends paid by the firm, and t is the tax rate paid by the firm. The second term in the denominator, $PD/(1-t)$, requires some explanation. Since preferred dividends are paid out of after-tax dollars, we must determine how many *pre-tax* dollars are required to meet this expense. In this case, Spuds and Suds pays taxes at a rate of 40%, so they require \$166,666.67 in pre-tax dollars in order to pay \$100,000 in preferred dividends:

$$\frac{100,000}{(1-0.40)} = 166,666.67$$

We can use equation (6-10) in the worksheet to calculate the DFL for Spuds and Suds. In cell A37, enter the label: `Degree of Financial Leverage`. In B37, enter: `=B8/(B10-B14/(1-B23))`. You should find that the DFL is 1.80, which is the same as we found by using equation (6-9). Copying this formula to C37 reveals that in 2008 we expect the DFL to decline to 1.62.

The Degree of Combined Leverage

Most firms make use of both operating and financial leverage. Since they are using two kinds of leverage, it is useful to understand the combined effect. We can measure the total leverage employed by the firm by comparing the percentage change in sales to the percentage change in earnings per share. This measure is called the *degree of combined leverage* (DCL):

$$DCL = \frac{\%\Delta \text{ in EPS}}{\%\Delta \text{ in Sales}} \tag{6-11}$$

Since we have already calculated the relevant percentage changes, it is a simple matter to determine that the DCL for Spuds and Suds in 2007 was:

$$DCL = \frac{30.00\%}{10.00\%} = 3.00$$

Therefore, any change in sales will be multiplied threefold in EPS. Recall that we said earlier that the DCL was a combination of operating and financial leverage. You can see this if we rewrite equation (6-11) as follows:

$$\text{DCL} = \frac{\%\Delta \text{ in EPS}}{\%\Delta \text{ in Sales}} = \frac{\%\Delta \text{ in EBIT}}{\%\Delta \text{ in Sales}} \times \frac{\%\Delta \text{ in EPS}}{\%\Delta \text{ in EBIT}}$$

Therefore, the combined effect of using both operating and financial leverage is multiplicative rather than simply additive. Managers should take note of this and use caution in increasing one type of leverage while ignoring the other. They may end up with more total leverage than anticipated. As we have just seen, the DCL is the product of DOL and DFL, so we can rewrite equation (6-11) as:

$$\text{DCL} = \text{DOL} \times \text{DFL} \tag{6-12}$$

To calculate the DCL for Spuds and Suds in your worksheet, first enter the label: Degree of Combined Leverage into A38. In B38, enter the formula: =B36*B37, and copy this to C38 to find the expected DCL for 2008. At this point, your worksheet should look like the one in Exhibit 6-4.

Extending the Example

Comparing the three leverage measures for 2007 and 2008 shows that in all cases the firm will be using less leverage in 2008. Recall that the only change in 2008 was that sales were increased by 10% over their 2007 level. The reason for the decline in leverage is that fixed costs (both operating and financial) have become a smaller portion of the total costs of the firm. This will always be the case: *As sales increase above the break-even point, leverage will decline regardless of the measure that is used.*

We can see this by extending our Spuds and Suds example. Suppose management is forecasting that sales will increase by 10% each year for the foreseeable future. Furthermore, because of contractual agreements, the firm's fixed costs will remain constant through at least 2008. In order to see the changes in the leverage measures under these conditions, copy C4:C38 and paste into D4:F38. This will create pro forma income statements for three additional years. Change the labels in D4:F4 to: 2009, 2010, and 2011.

EXHIBIT 6-4
SPUDS AND SUDS WORKSHEET WITH THREE MEASURES OF LEVERAGE

	A	B	C
1	Spuds and Suds		
2	Income Statement		
3	For the Year Ended Dec. 31, 2007		
4		2007	2008*
5	Sales	$2,500,000	$2,750,000
6	Less: Variable Costs	1,500,000	1,650,000
7	Less: Fixed Costs	400,000	400,000
8	*Earnings Before Interest and Taxes*	*600,000*	*700,000*
9	Less: Interest Expense	100,000	100,000
10	*Earnings Before Taxes*	*500,000*	*600,000*
11	Taxes	200,000	240,000
12	*Net Income*	*300,000*	*360,000*
13			
14	Less: Preferred Dividends	100,000	100,000
15	*Net Income Available to Common*	*200,000*	*260,000*
16	Common Shares Outstanding	1,000,000	1,000,000
17	*Earnings per Share*	*$ 0.20*	*$ 0.26*
18			
19	Assumptions		
20	Price per Unit	$ 16.00	$ 16.00
21	Unit Sales	156,250	171,875
22	Target EBIT	$ 800,000	
23	Variable Costs as a Percent of Sales	60%	60%
24	Projected Sales Growth		10%
25	Tax Rate	40%	40%
26			
27	Operating Break-even Point (Units)	62,500	62,500
28	Operating Break-even Point (Dollars)	1,000,000	1,000,000
29			
30	Units to Meet EBIT Target	187,500	
31			
32	% Change in Sales from Prior Year		10.00%
33	% Change in EBIT from Prior Year		16.67%
34	% Change in EPS from Prior Year		30.00%
35			
36	Degree of Operating Leverage	1.67	1.57
37	Degree of Financial Leverage	1.80	1.62
38	Degree of Combined Leverage	3.00	2.54

You should see that the DOL, DFL, and DCL are all decreasing as sales increase. This is easier to see if we create a chart. Select A36:F38 and use the Chart Wizard to create a line chart of the data. Be sure to choose the Series tab and set B4:F4 as the Category (X) axis labels. You should end up with a chart that resembles the one in Figure 6-3.

FIGURE 6-3
CHART OF VARIOUS LEVERAGE MEASURES AS SALES INCREASE

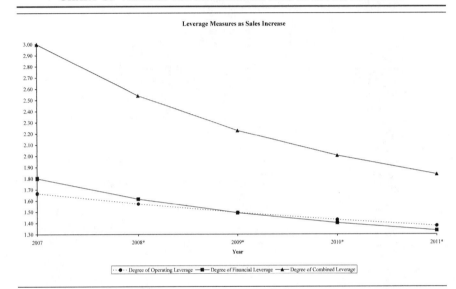

Obviously, as we stated earlier, the amount of leverage declines as the sales level increases. One caveat to this is that in the real world, fixed costs are not necessarily the same year after year. Furthermore, variable costs do not always maintain an exact percentage of sales. For these reasons, leverage may not decline as smoothly as depicted in our example. However, the general principal is sound and should be understood by all managers.

Summary

We started this chapter by discussing the firm's operating break-even point. The break-even point is determined by a product's price and by the amount of fixed and variable costs. The amount of fixed costs also played an important role in the determination of the amount of leverage a firm employs. We studied three measures of leverage:

1. The *degree of operating leverage* (DOL) measures the degree to which the presence of fixed costs multiplies changes in sales into even larger changes in EBIT.

2. The *degree of financial leverage* (DFL) measures the change in EPS relative to a change in EBIT. Financial leverage is a direct result of managerial decisions about how the firm should be financed.

3. The *degree of combined leverage* (DCL) provides a measure of the total leverage used by the firm. This is the product of the DOL and DFL.

We also introduced the Goal Seek tool, which is very useful whenever you know the result that you want, but not the input value required to get that result.

FUNCTIONS INTRODUCED IN THIS CHAPTER

Purpose	Function	Page
Return #N/A	NA( )	187
Determine if a formula returns an error value	ISERR(*VALUE*)	189

SUMMARY OF EQUATIONS

Name	Equation	Page
Operating Break-Even Level in Units	$Q^* = \dfrac{F}{P - V}$	179
Operating Break-Even Level in Dollars	$\$BE = P \times Q^*$ or $\$BE = \dfrac{F}{CM\%}$	179 179
Cash Break-Even Point in Units	$Q^*_{Cash} = \dfrac{F - \text{Depreciation}}{P - V}$	183

SUMMARY OF EQUATIONS (CONTINUED)

Name	Equation	Page
Degree of Operating Leverage (DOL)	$DOL = \dfrac{\%\Delta \text{ in EBIT}}{\%\Delta \text{ in Sales}}$ or $DOL = \dfrac{Q(P-V)}{Q(P-V)-F}$	185 187
Degree of Financial Leverage (DFL)	$DFL = \dfrac{\%\Delta \text{ in EPS}}{\%\Delta \text{ in EBIT}}$ or $DFL = \dfrac{EBIT}{EBT - \dfrac{PD}{(1-t)}}$	189 190
Degree of Combined Leverage (DCL)	$DCL = \dfrac{\%\Delta \text{ in EPS}}{\%\Delta \text{ in Sales}}$ or $DCL = DOL \times DFL$	190 191

Problems

1. Meyerson's Bakery is considering the addition of a new line of pies to its product offerings. It is expected that each pie will sell for $10, and the variable costs per pie will be $3. Total fixed operating costs are expected to be $20,000. Meyerson's faces a marginal tax rate of 35%, will have interest expense associated with this line of $3,000, and expects to sell about 2,500 pies in the first year.

    a. Put together an income statement for the pie line's first year. Is the line expected to be profitable?

    b. Calculate the operating break-even point in both units and dollars.

c. How many pies would Meyerson's need to sell in order to achieve earnings, before interest and taxes, of $15,000?

d. Use the Goal Seek tool to determine the selling price per pie that would allow Meyerson's to break even in terms of its net income.

2. Income Statements for Caterpillar, Inc., from 2001 to 2005 are shown below.

	A	B	C	D	E	F
1	Caterpillar Inc.					
2	Annual Income Statements					
3	For the Fiscal Years 2001 to 2005					
4		Dec-05	Dec-04	Dec-03	Dec-02	Dec-01
5	Sales	36,339	30,251	22,763	20,152	20,450
6	Cost of Sales	26,036	21,023	16,119	13,905	14,050
7	Gross Operating Profit	10,303	9,228	6,644	6,247	6,400
8	Selling, General & Admin. Expense	4,274	4,578	3,139	3,187	3,263
9	Depreciation & Amortization	1,477	1,397	1,347	1,220	1,169
10	EBIT	4,552	3,253	2,158	1,840	1,968
11	Other Income, Net	450	263	110	70	146
12	Interest Expense	1,028	750	716	800	942
13	Pre-tax Income	3,974	2,766	1,497	1,110	1,172
14	Income Taxes	1,120	731	398	312	367
15	Total Net Income	2,854	2,035	1,099	798	805
16						
17	Dividends Paid per Share	0.91	0.78	0.71	0.70	0.69
18	Preferred Dividends	0.00	0.00	0.00	0.00	0.00

a. Enter the data into your worksheet. Assume that 50% of SG&A expense is a variable cost, with the balance being a fixed cost.

b. Given that Caterpillar is a manufacturing company, would you expect that it would have more operating leverage or financial leverage?

c. Calculate the degree of operating leverage, degree of financial leverage, and the degree of combined leverage for each of the five years. Does it appear that Caterpillar's leverage measures have been increasing or decreasing over this period? Decreasing

d. Create a chart that shows how the various leverage measures have changed over this five-year period.

3. Information for three local auto dealers is given below:

	Bell's Domestics	Junior's Used	Europe's Best	Industry Average
Average Selling Price	$35,000	$27,000	$52,000	$30,000
Unit Sales	1,500	1,850	850	1,250
Interest Expense	750,000	1,000,000	3,000,000	1,500,000
Variable Costs (% of Sales)	60%	45%	40%	48%
Fixed Costs	10,000,000	7,000,000	20,000,000	11,000,000
Preferred Dividends	1,000,000	0	600,000	300,000
Common Shares	5,000,000	8,000,000	3,000,000	7,000,000

a. Using the information given in the above table, construct income statements for each company and the industry average. Assume that each company faces a tax rate of 35%.

b. Calculate the break-even points and the degrees of operating, financial, and combined leverage for each company and the industry average.

c. Compare the companies to each other and to the industry average. What conclusions can you draw about each operation?

Internet Exercise

1. Following the instructions from Internet Exercise 2 in Chapter 5, get the income statements for the company of your choice for the past five years from MSN Investor. Choose a company that is not in a manufacturing industry. Now repeat the analysis from Problem 2 above. What differences do you note between the leverage measures for your company and Caterpillar, Inc.?

CHAPTER 7

The Time Value of Money

After studying this chapter, you should be able to:

1. *Explain the concept of the time value of money.*
2. *Calculate the present value and future value of a stream of cash flows using Excel.*
3. *Explain the types of cash flows encountered in financial analysis, and know how to adjust for each type in making time value calculations in Excel.*
4. *Differentiate between the alternative compounding periods, and use Excel to compare present and future values under different compounding schemes.*

"A bird in the hand is worth two in the bush." That old aphorism, when translated into the language of finance, becomes "A dollar today is worth more than a dollar tomorrow." Intuitively, it probably makes sense, but why? Stated very simply, you can take that dollar today and invest it with the expectation of having more than a dollar tomorrow.

Because money can be invested to grow to a larger amount, we say that money has a "time value." This concept of a time value of money underlies much of the theory of financial decision making.

Future Value

Imagine that you have $1,000 available to invest. If you earn interest at the rate of 10% per year, then you will have $1,100 at the end of one year. The mathematics behind this example are quite simple:

$$1,000 + 1,000(0.10) = 1,100$$

In other words, after one year you will have your original $1,000 (the *principal* amount) plus the 10% interest earned on the principal. Since you won't have the $1,100 until one year in the future, we refer to this amount as the *future value*. The amount that you have today, $1,000, is referred to as the *present value*. If, at the end of the year, you choose to make the same investment again, then at the end of the second year you will have:

$$1,000 + 1,000(0.10) + 100(0.10) + 1,000(0.10) = 1,210$$

The $1,210 at the end of the second year can be broken down into its components: the original principal, the first year's interest, the interest earned in the second year on the first year's interest, and the second year's interest on the original principal. Note that we could restate the second year calculation to be:

$$1,100 + 1,100(0.10) = 1,210$$

or, by factoring out the 1,100 we get:

$$1,100(1 + 0.10) = 1,210$$

Notice that in the second year the interest is earned on both the original principal and the interest earned during the first year. The idea of earning interest on previously earned interest is known as *compounding*. This is why the total interest earned in the second year is $110 versus only $100 the first year.

Returning to our original one-year example, we can generalize the formula for any one-year investment as follows:

$$FV = PV + PV(i)$$

where FV is the future value, PV is the present value, and i is the one-year interest rate (compounding rate). The above equation is not in its simplest form. We can factor PV from both terms on the right-hand side, simplifying the future value equation to:

$$FV = PV(1 + i) \tag{7-1}$$

Recall that in our two-year example, we earned interest on both the principal and interest from the first year. In other words, the first-year FV became the second-year PV. Symbolically, the second-year FV is:

$$FV_2 = FV_1(1 + i)$$

Substituting $PV(1 + i)$ for FV_1 and simplifying, we have:

$$FV_2 = PV(1 + i)(1 + i) = PV(1 + i)^2$$

We can actually further generalize our future value equation. Realize that the exponent (on the right-hand side) is the same as the subscript (on the left-hand side) in the future value equation. When we were solving for the future value at the end of the first year, the exponent was 1. When we were solving for the future value at the end of the second year, the exponent was 2. In general, the exponent will be equal to the number of the year for which we wish to find the future value.

$$FV_N = PV(1 + i)^N \tag{7-2}$$

Equation (7-2) is the basis for all of the time value equations that we will look at in the sections ahead. Using this version of the equation, you can see that investing $1,000 for two years at 10% per year will leave you with $1,210 at the end of two years. In other words:

$$FV_2 = 1,000(1.10)^2 = 1,210$$

Using Excel to Find Future Values

It is easy enough to calculate future values with a hand calculator, especially a financial calculator. But, as we will see in the sections and chapters ahead, it is often necessary to use future values in worksheets. Excel makes these calculations easy with the use of the built-in **Fv** function:

$$\text{Fv}(\textit{Rate, NPer, Pmt, PV, Type})$$

There are five arguments to the **Fv** function. *RATE* is the interest rate per period (year, month, day, etc.), *NPER* is the total number of periods, and *PV* is the present value. *PMT* and *TYPE* are included to handle annuities (a series of equal payments, equally spaced over time), which we will deal with later. For problems of the type that we are currently solving, we will set both *PMT* and *TYPE* to 0.[1]

Let's set up a simple worksheet to calculate the future value of a single sum. Starting with a blank worksheet, enter the labels and numbers as shown in Exhibit 7-1.

EXHIBIT 7-1
FUTURE VALUE OF A SINGLE CASH FLOW

	A	B
1	**Future Value Calculations**	
2	Present Value	1,000.00
3	Years	1
4	Rate	10%
5	Future Value	

We want to use the **Fv** function to calculate the future value of $1,000 for one year at 10% per year. In B5 enter the formula: `=FV(B4,B3,0,-B2,0)`. The result, $1,100, is exactly the same as we found earlier. Note that we have entered –B2 for the *PV* argument. The negative sign is used because Excel realizes that either the *PV* or *FV* must be a cash outflow. If we had not used the negative sign, the result (*FV*) would have been negative. Users of financial calculators will recognize this as the *cash flow sign convention*.

You can now experiment with different values for the arguments. Try replacing the 1 in B3 with a 2. Excel immediately updates the result in B5 with $1,210, just as we found in the second part of our example. To see just how powerful compounding can be, insert 30 into B3. The result, $17,449.40, indicates that each $1,000 invested at 10% per year will grow to $17,449.40 after just 30 years. If we double the investment, to $2,000, then we should double the future value. Try it; you should get a result of $34,898.80, exactly twice what we got with a $1,000 investment. In general, any money invested for 30 years at 10% per year will grow to 17.449 times its initial value. To see even more powerful examples of compounding, try increasing the interest rate.

---

1. The *TYPE* argument tells Excel whether the cash flows occur at the end (0) or beginning (1) of the period.

Present Value

Our future value equation can be solved for any of its variables. We may wish to turn our example problem around to solve for the present value. Suppose that the problem is restated as, "What initial investment is required so that you will accumulate $1,210 after two years if you earn an interest rate of 10% per year?" In this case, we want to solve for the present value—we already know the future value.

Mathematically, all we need to do is to solve the future value equation (7-2) for the present value:

$$PV = \frac{FV_N}{(1 + i)^N} \qquad (7\text{-}3)$$

Of course, we already know that the answer must be $1,000:

$$PV = \frac{1,210}{(1.10)^2} = 1,000$$

In Excel, we can solve problems of this type by using the built-in **Pv** function:

PV(*RATE, NPER, PMT, FV, TYPE*)

The arguments to the **Pv** function are exactly the same as those for the **Fv** function, except that *PV* is replaced by *FV*. For this example, in cells D1:E5, set up the worksheet as shown in Exhibit 7-2.

EXHIBIT 7-2
PRESENT VALUE OF A SINGLE CASH FLOW

	A	B	C	D	E
1	**Future Value Calculations**			**Present Value Calculations**	
2	Present Value	1,000.00		Future Value	1,100.00
3	Years	1		Years	1
4	Rate	10%		Rate	10%
5	Future Value			Present Value	

In cell E5 place the formula: =PV(E4,E3,0,-E2,0). Again, we enter the future value reference as negative so that the present value result will be positive. The result will be $1,000, exactly as expected.

We have purposely constructed our future value and present value examples side by side in the worksheet to demonstrate that present value and future value are inverse functions. Let's change our worksheet to make this concept clear. We want to link the references in the present value function to the cells used in the future value function. This will allow changes in the future value arguments to change the present value arguments. First, select E2 and enter: =B5; in E3 type: =B3; and in E4 enter: =B4. Now, regardless of the changes made to the future value side of the worksheet, the present value should be equal to the value in B2. Try making some changes to the inputs in B2, B3, and B4. No matter what changes you make, the calculated present value (in E5) is always the same as the present value input in B2. This is because the present value and future value are inverse functions.

Annuities

Thus far we have examined the present and future values of single cash flows (also referred to as lump sums). These are powerful concepts that will allow us to deal with more complex cash flows. *Annuities* are a series of nominally equal cash flows, equally spaced in time. Examples of annuities abound. Your car payment is an annuity; so is your mortgage (or rent) payment. If you don't already, you may someday own annuities as part of a retirement program. The cash flow pictured in Figure 7-1 is another example.

FIGURE 7-1
A TIMELINE FOR AN ANNUITY CASH FLOW

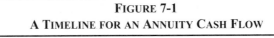
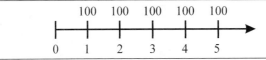

How do we find the value of a stream of cash flows such as that pictured in Figure 7-1? The answer involves the *principle of value additivity*. This principle says that "the value of a stream of cash flows is equal to the sum of the values of the components." As long as the cash flows occur at the same time, they can be added together. Therefore, if we can move each of the cash flows to the same time period (any time period), we can add them to find the value as of that time period. Cash flows can be moved around in time by compounding or discounting.

Present Value of an Annuity

One way to find the present value of an annuity is to find the present value of each of the cash flows separately and then add them together. Equation (7-4) summarizes this method:

$$PV_A = \sum_{t=1}^{N} \frac{Pmt_t}{(1+i)^t} \qquad (7\text{-}4)$$

where PV_A is the present value of the annuity, t is the time period, N is the total number of payments, Pmt_t is the payment in period t, and i is the discount rate.

Of course, this equation works fine for any annuity (or any stream of cash flows), but it can be very tedious for annuities with more than just a few payments. Imagine finding the current balance (i.e., present value) of a mortgage with more than 300 payments to go before it is paid off! We can find a closed-form solution (the above equation is an "open-form" solution because the number of additions is indefinite) by taking the summation:

$$PV_A = Pmt \left[\frac{1 - \dfrac{1}{(1+i)^N}}{i} \right] \qquad (7\text{-}5)$$

where all terms are as previously defined. Notice that we have dropped the subscript t, because this solution does not depend on our taking the present values separately. Instead, since each payment is the same, we can value the whole annuity in one step.

Let's find the present value of the cash flow pictured in Figure 7-1. Assuming that the discount rate for this cash flow is 8%, the equation is:

$$PV_A = 100 \left[\frac{1 - \dfrac{1}{(1.08)^5}}{0.08} \right] = 399.271$$

This means that if you were to deposit $399.27 into an account today that pays 8% interest per year, you could withdraw $100 at the end of each year and be left with a balance of $0.00 at the end of the five years.

Recall from our earlier discussion of single cash flows that we can use Excel's built-in **Pv** function to find present values. To recap, the **Pv** function is defined as:

Pv(*Rate*, *NPer*, *Pmt*, *Fv*, *Type*)

When dealing with single cash flows we set ***Pmt*** and *Type* to 0. Those arguments are used only in the case of annuities. ***Pmt*** will be set to the dollar amount of the periodic payment. *Type* is an optional binary (0 or 1) variable that controls whether Excel assumes the payment occurs at the end (0) or the beginning (1) of the period. For the time being, we will assume that all payments occur at the end of the period (that is, they are *regular* annuities).

EXHIBIT 7-3
PRESENT VALUE OF AN ANNUITY

	A	B
1	**Present Value of an Annuity**	
2	Payment	100
3	Interest Rate	8%
4	Number of Payments	5
5	Present Value	

Set up a worksheet with the data pictured in Exhibit 7-3 in cells A1:B5. In B5 we wish to find the present value of the annuity presented in Figure 7-1, so enter: =PV(B3,B4,B2,0,0). Note that we have entered the payment as a positive number, and the result is –$399.27. The interpretation is that if you were to make a deposit of (a cash outflow) $399.27 today, you could make a withdrawal of (a cash inflow) $100 each year for the next five years. Had we made the payment (B2) negative instead, the present value would have been a positive $399.27. The answer is the same, except for the sign, but the interpretation is different. In this case, the interpretation is that if you were to take out a loan of $399.27 (a cash inflow) today, you would need to repay $100 (a cash outflow) per year for each of the next five years to retire the loan.

We can, of course, experiment with various arguments. For example, suppose that instead of five withdrawals of $100 each, you wanted to make ten withdrawals of $50 each. How much would you need to deposit into this account in order to deplete the account after 10 withdrawals? Change the number of payments in B4 to: 10, and the payment in B2 to: 50. After these changes, you will see that an initial deposit of only $335.50 will allow you to achieve your goal.

Returning now to our original example, reset the payment amount to 100 and the number of payments to 5. How much would you have to deposit if you want to make your first withdrawal today, rather than one year from today? (An annuity that begins paying immediate is known as *annuity due*). To answer this question, realize that the only thing we have changed is the timing of the first withdrawal. We will still make a total of five withdrawals of $100 each, but they occur at the beginning of each period. In B5, change the *TYPE* argument to 1, from 0 originally, so that the formula is now: =PV(B3,B4,B2,0,1). The result is –$431.21 indicating that, because the first withdrawal occurs immediately, you will have to make a larger initial deposit. Note that the amount of the deposit must be larger because you will not earn the first year's interest before making the first withdrawal.

Another way to look at this is that we are effectively depositing $331.21 (= $431.21 deposit –$100 withdrawal) in order to be able to make four future withdrawals of $100 each. To see that this is the case, change the **Pv** formula back to its original form (*TYPE* = 0) and change the number of payments to 4. The present value is then shown to be $331.21, exactly as claimed.

Future Value of an Annuity

Imagine that you have recently begun planning for retirement. One of the attractive options available is to set up a traditional individual retirement account (IRA). What makes the IRA so attractive is that you can deposit up to $4,000 per year,[2] and the investment gains will accrue tax-free until you begin to make withdrawals after age $59\frac{1}{2}$. Furthermore, depending on your situation, the IRA deposits may reduce your taxable income.

To determine the amount that you will have accumulated in your IRA at retirement, you need to understand the future value of an annuity. Recalling the principle of value additivity, we could simply find the future value of each year's investment and add them together at retirement. Mathematically this is:

$$FV_A = \sum_{t=1}^{N} [Pmt_t(1+i)^{N-t}] \tag{7-6}$$

Alternatively, we could use the closed-form solution of equation (7-6):

---

2. As of this writing, current tax laws allow for contributions of $4,000 each year until 2008, when the limit will be $5,000. In 2009 and beyond, the limit will be adjusted for inflation.

$$FV_A = Pmt\left[\frac{(1+i)^N - 1}{i}\right] \qquad (7\text{-}7)$$

Assume that you are planning on retirement in 30 years. If you deposit $4,000 each year into an IRA account that will earn an average of 7.5% per year, how much will you have after 30 years? Because of the large number of deposits, equation (7-7) will be easier to use than equation (7-6), though we could use either one. The solution is:

$$FV_A = 4,000\left[\frac{(1.075)^{30} - 1}{0.075}\right] = 413,597.61$$

As usual, Excel provides a built-in function to handle problems such as this one. The **Fv** function, which we used to find the future value of a single sum earlier, will also find the future value of an annuity. Its use is nearly identical to the **Pv** function; the only difference is the substitution of **Pv** for **Fv**. Set up a new worksheet like the one in Exhibit 7-4.

EXHIBIT 7-4
FUTURE VALUE OF AN ANNUITY

	A	B
1	**Future Value of an Annuity**	
2	Payment	4,000.00
3	Interest Rate	7.50%
4	Number of Payments	30
5	Future Value	

In B5 place the formula: =FV(B3,B4,-B2,0,0). The result, $413,597.61, agrees exactly with the result from the formula. What if that amount is less than you had hoped for? One solution is to start making the investments this year, rather than next (i.e., the beginning of this period rather than the end of this period). To see the effect of this change, all that needs to be done is to change the *TYPE* argument to 1 so that the formula is now: =FV(B3,B4,-B2,0,1). That minor change in your investment strategy will net you a little over $31,000 extra at retirement. Perhaps a better alternative is to accept a little extra risk (we assume that you are young enough that this makes sense) by investing in stock mutual funds that will return an average of about 10% per year over the 30-year horizon. In this case, still assuming that you start investing right now, you will have $723,773.70 at retirement. Significantly better!

Solving for the Annuity Payment

Suppose that we want to know the amount that we have to deposit in order to accumulate a given sum after a number of years. For example, assume that you are planning to purchase a house five years from now. Since you are currently a student, you will begin saving for the $10,000 down payment one year from today. How much will you need to save each year, if your savings will earn a rate of 4% per year? Figure 7-2 diagrams the problem.

FIGURE 7-2
A TIMELINE FOR ANNUAL SAVINGS TO OBTAIN $10,000 IN FIVE YEARS

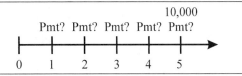

In this case, we wish to solve for the payment you would have to make each year. The future value of the annuity is already known, so the **FV** function would be inappropriate. What we need is Excel's **PMT** function:

$$\text{PMT}(\textit{RATE}, \textit{NPER}, \textit{PV}, \textit{FV}, \textit{TYPE})$$

The arguments for the **PMT** function are similar to those for the **PV** and **FV** functions, except that it has *PV* and *FV* arguments in place of the *PMT* argument. Enter the information from Exhibit 7-5 into cells A1:B6 of a new worksheet. In cell B6 enter the **PMT** function: =PMT(B5,B4,-B2,B3,0). The result indicates that

---

EXHIBIT 7-5
ANNUITY PAYMENT WHEN PV OR FV IS KNOWN

	A	B
1	**Solving for an Annuity Payment**	
2	Present Value	0.00
3	Future Value	10,000
4	Number of Payments	5
5	Interest Rate	4.00%
6	Annual Payment Amount	

you will have to save $1,846.27 per year (a cash outflow) in order to accumulate $10,000 for the down payment in five years.

The **PMT** function allows *both* Pv and Fv to be inputs. In the previous example, it was assumed that Pv was 0. However, let's suppose that you have recently inherited $3,000 from your uncle, and that you want to use this money to begin saving now for that down payment. Since the $3,000 will grow to only $3,649.96 after five years at 4% per year (this can be verified by using the worksheet created for Exhibit 7-1), you will still need to save some amount every year. How much will you need to save each year? To find out, simply set the present value, in B2, to 3000 and leave the other values unchanged. Because the initial investment *reduces* the total amount that you need to save to $6,350.04 (why?), your annual saving requirement is reduced to $1,172.39.

Solving for the Number of Periods in an Annuity

Solving for the present value, future value, and payment for annuities are fairly simple problems. That is, the formulas are straightforward and easy to apply. Solving for the number of periods, N, is not as obvious mathematically. To do so requires knowledge of logarithms. If you know the present value of the annuity, then solving equation (7-5) for N we get:

$$N = \frac{\ln\left(\frac{-iPV_A}{Pmt} + 1\right)}{-\ln(1 + i)} \qquad (7\text{-}8)$$

where $\ln(\cdot)$ is the natural logarithm operator. If you know the future value, then solving equation (7-7) for N results in:

$$N = \frac{\ln\left(\frac{iFV_A}{Pmt} + 1\right)}{\ln(1 + i)} \qquad (7\text{-}9)$$

Return now to our example of saving for the down payment for a house. Recall that it was determined that by saving $1,846.27 per year you could afford the down payment after five years, assuming no initial investment. Set up the worksheet in Exhibit 7-6.

EXHIBIT 7-6
NUMBER OF ANNUITY PAYMENTS WHEN PV OR FV IS KNOWN

	A	B
1	**Solving for N in an Annuity**	
2	Present Value	$0
3	Future Value	10,000.00
4	Annual Payment	1,846.27
5	Annual Rate	4.00%
6	Number of Years	

We can solve this problem using equation (7-9) and the built-in **LN** function:[3]

LN(*NUMBER*)

In B6 enter the formula: `=LN(B5*B3/B4+1)/LN(1+B5)`. The result is five years, as we would expect.

Excel also offers the built-in **NPER** function to solve problems of this type directly. This function is defined as:

NPER(*RATE*, *PMT*, *PV*, *FV*, *TYPE*)

where all of the arguments are as previously defined. To use this function, you must know the payment, per period interest rate, and either the present value or future value or both.

Since we want to solve for the number of periods, insert the **NPER** function into B6: `=NPER(B5,-B4,-B2,B3,0)`. Notice that both the *PV* and *PMT* arguments are made negative in this function. Again, this is because of the cash flow sign convention. In this case, we wish to be able to withdraw the future value (a cash inflow and therefore positive) and deposit the *PV* and *PMT*s (cash outflows, therefore negative). The result is five years, exactly as we would expect. If you enter the $3,000 inheritance into B2, you will have the down payment in only 3.39 years.

---

3. Logarithms are often useful tools, and Excel offers functions to handle them. In addition to **LN**, the other logarithm functions are **LOG10** and **LOG**. The former calculates the base 10 logarithm, and the latter can calculate a logarithm with any base.

Solving for the Interest Rate in an Annuity

Unlike the present value, future value, payment, and number of periods, there is no closed-form solution for the rate of interest of an annuity. The only way to solve this problem is to use a trial-and-error approach, perhaps an intelligent one such as the Newton-Raphson technique or the bisection method.[4]

Excel, however, offers a built-in function that will solve for the interest rate, though it requires a little more setup than the functions we've used so far. The function, **RATE**, is defined as:

$$\text{RATE}(\textit{NPER, PMT, PV, FV, TYPE, GUESS})$$

where the arguments are as defined earlier, and *GUESS* is your optional first guess at the correct answer. Ordinarily, the *GUESS* can be omitted.

> Suppose that you are approached with an offer to purchase an investment that will provide cash flows of $1,500 per year for 10 years. The cost of purchasing this investment is $10,500. If you have an alternative investment opportunity, of equal risk, that will yield 8% per year, which one should you accept?

There are actually several ways that a problem such as this could be solved. One method is to realize that 8% is your opportunity cost of funds, and should therefore be used as your discount rate. Using the worksheet created in Exhibit 7-3 we find that the present value (i.e., current worth to you) of the investment is only $10,065.12. Since the price ($10,500) is greater than the value, you should reject the investment and accept your alternative.[5]

---

4. These are powerful techniques for solving these types of problems. The bisection method, briefly, involves choosing two initial guesses at the answer that are sure to bracket the true answer. Each successive guess is halfway between the two previous guesses that bracket the solution. The Newton-Raphson technique requires calculus and is beyond the scope of this book. For more information, consult any numerical methods textbook.

5. Note that we are simply comparing the cost of the investment to its perceived benefit (present value). If the cost is greater than the benefit, the investment should be rejected. We will expand on this method in future chapters.

EXHIBIT 7-7
YIELD ON AN ANNUITY

	A	B
1	**Solving for *i* in an Annuity**	
2	Present Value	(10,500)
3	Future Value	0
4	Annual Payment	1,500
5	Number of Years	10.00
6	Annual Rate	

Another method of solving this dilemma is to compare the yields (i.e., compound annual return) offered by the investments. All other things being equal, the investment with the highest yield should be accepted. We already know that your alternative investment offers an 8% yield, but what is the yield of your new opportunity? We will use the worksheet in Exhibit 7-7 to find out.

Into B6 place the function: =RATE(B5,B4,B2,B3,0,0.1). The result is 7.07% per year, so you should reject the new investment in favor of the alternative that offers 8% per year. This is the same result we obtained with the present value methodology, as we would hope. Later, we will see that this will always be the case when comparing mutually exclusive investment opportunities.[6]

Deferred Annuities

Not all annuities begin their payments during the year following the analysis period. For example, if you are planning your retirement, you will probably start by determining the amount of income that you will need each year during retirement. However, if you are a student you will probably not retire for many years. Your retirement income, then, is an annuity that won't begin until you retire. In other words it is a *deferred annuity.* How do we determine the value of a deferred annuity?

Assume that you own a time machine (made of a superstrong, futuristic metal that can withstand the gravitational forces of a black hole in space). This machine can transport you to any time period that you choose. If we use this time machine to transport you to the year just prior to retirement, then valuing the

---

6. Mutually exclusive investment opportunities are those in which you may choose one investment or the other, but not both. That is, the choice of one precludes your also choosing the other.

stream of retirement income becomes a simple matter. Just use Excel's **Pv** function. The year before the first withdrawal is now considered to be year 0, the first year of retirement is year 1, and so on. Figure 7-3 demonstrates this time-shifting technique.

FIGURE 7-3
TIME-SHIFTING AS A FIRST STEP IN SOLVING DEFERRED ANNUITY PROBLEMS

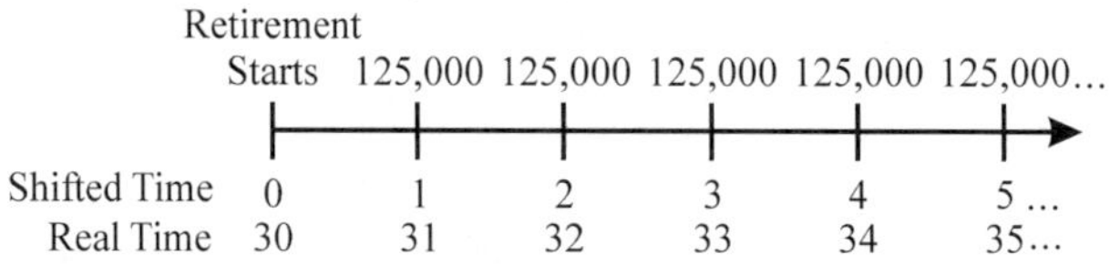

In constructing Figure 7-3, we have assumed that you will retire 30 years from now and will require income of $125,000 per year during retirement. If we further assume that you will need your retirement income for 35 years and expect to earn 6% per year, you will need to have accumulated $1,812,280.80 by year 30 to provide this income. In other words, $1,812,280.80 is the present value, at year 30, of $125,000 per year for 35 years at 6%. You can use the worksheet created for Exhibit 7-3 to verify these numbers.[7]

The problem in Figure 7-3 is that knowing the amount that we will need 30 years from now tells us nothing about how much we need to save today. The present value function in Excel, or the PV_A equation (7-5), must be thought of as a transformation function. That is, it transforms a series of payments into a lump sum. That lump sum ($1,812,280.80 in our example) is then placed *one period before the first payment occurs*. In our earlier examples, the annuities began payment at the end of period 1, so the present value was at time period 0 (one period earlier than period 1). In the current example, the present value is at time period 30, also one period before the first payment.

In order to determine the amount that we need to invest today, we must treat the required savings at retirement as a future value. This sum must then be discounted back to period 0. For example, if we assume that we can earn 8% per year before

---

7. While $125,000 per year may seem like a lot of money, we arrived at this figure by assuming that you would need $50,000 per year in today's dollars. We then adjusted that amount for an average inflation rate of 3% per year to arrive at $125,000. In fact, that won't be enough because inflation will continue during retirement. So, your retirement income will need to rise each year to keep pace with inflation.

retirement, we would need to invest $180,099.63 today in order to meet our retirement goals.

Exhibit 7-8 presents a simple worksheet to determine the investment required today in order to provide a particular income during retirement. Open a new worksheet and enter the data and labels from Exhibit 7-8.

EXHIBIT 7-8
PLANNING FOR RETIREMENT

	A	B
1	**Retirement Worksheet**	
2	Annual Retirement Income Need	125,000
3	Years until Retirement	30
4	Years in Retirement	35
5	Rate of Return before Retirement	8.00%
6	Rate of Return during Retirement	6.00%
7	Savings Required at Retirement	
8	Investment Required Today	
9	Annual Investment Required	

To complete our retirement worksheet, we need to enter functions into cells B7:B9. Recall that the first step in our retirement income problem was to determine the present value of your retirement income at period 30. To do this in our worksheet, enter the **Pv** function into B7: =PV(B6,B4,-B2,0,0). The result, $1,812,280.80, tells us that you will need to have saved this amount in order to provide the income indicated in B2 for the number of years indicated in B4. To determine the amount that you would need to invest today (a lump sum), you need to determine the present value, at time period 0, of the amount in B7. To do this, in B8 enter the formula: =PV(B5,B3,0,-B7,0). As before, the amount required today is $180,099.63.

Another feature of the retirement planning worksheet is that it will calculate the annual savings required to reach your goal. To make Excel do this calculation, we need to use the **PMT** function. In B9 enter: =PMT(B5,B3,0,-B7,0). The result is $15,997.79, which means that if you can save this amount each year for the next 30 years, and earn an average of 8% interest each year, you will reach your goal. As difficult as that may be, it is much easier than investing the lump sum today.

We have ignored the effect of inflation and taxes on your retirement planning for this worksheet. But if we assume that you save the amount in B9 in a tax-deferred account, the results are a bit more realistic. Experiment with this worksheet. You may be surprised at the difficulty of saving for a comfortable retirement!

Graduated Annuities

Previously, we defined an annuity as a series of nominally equal cash flows, equally spaced in time. However, not everything that is called an annuity has equal cash flows each period. For example, it is now common for people to invest a lump sum today in exchange for a series of payments that will escalate over time to maintain constant purchasing power. An insurance company may offer such an investment opportunity to retirees who are concerned about inflation in the future.

Return to our example in the previous section. Your stated goal was to receive $125,000 each year for the 35 years that you expect to spend in retirement. However, if your income doesn't rise each year, then your purchasing power will decline dramatically by the end of the 35 years. In fact, if inflation averages 3% per year, your income in the last year will have the same purchasing power as only about $44,423 would have had at the beginning of your retirement. Clearly, then, it would be beneficial if your retirement income would grow to keep up with the rate of inflation.

Present Value of a Graduated Annuity

Suppose that you expect inflation to be 3% per year during retirement, and you have revised your retirement income needs so that your income grows by 3% each year. Figure 7-4 shows the revised timeline.

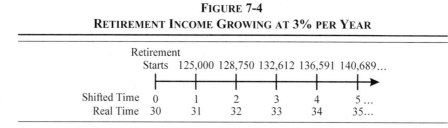

FIGURE 7-4
RETIREMENT INCOME GROWING AT 3% PER YEAR

How do we find the present value of such a cash flow stream? Obviously, we cannot use the **Pv** function because it assumes that all of the cash flows are the same in each period. That leaves us with the fallback position of using the principle of value additivity. In other words, calculate the present value of each cash flow separately, and then add them together to get the total present value. This method requires a table that lists all of the cash flows and the use of equation (7-4) on page 205.

Fortunately, if we can assume that the growth rate of the cash flows will be constant, as it is in this case, then there is a closed-form solution for the present value of a graduated annuity when the first payment occurs one period from now:

$$PV_{GA} = \frac{Pmt_1}{i-g}\left[1 - \left(\frac{1+g}{1+i}\right)^N\right] \tag{7-10}$$

where Pmt_1 is the first cash flow, i is the interest rate, g is the growth rate, and N is the number of cash flows.

$$PV_{GA} = \frac{125,000}{0.06-0.03}\left[1 - \left(\frac{1.03}{1.06}\right)^{35}\right] = 2,641,257.55$$

As before, if we assume that you will earn 6% per year during retirement and your withdrawals grow 3% per year to keep up with inflation, then you will need to accumulate $2,641,257.55 in order to meet your income goals.

We can easily modify the retirement worksheet that was present in Exhibit 7-8 to handle our new assumption regarding inflation. Make a copy of that worksheet, and then select row 5 and insert a new row. In A5 enter the label: `Expected Inflation Rate` and in B5 enter: `3%`. Now, we need to change the formula in B8 to: `=B2/(B7-B5)*(1-((1+B5)/(1+B7))^B4)`. You will see that the result is $2,641,257.55, exactly the same as before. Furthermore, the results in B9:B10 are automatically updated to include our new assumption. As you can see, you will now need to save $23,315.53 per year before retirement. That is about $7,318 more per year than the original projection, but this amount will allow you to maintain constant purchasing power during retirement. Exhibit 7-9 shows the new retirement planning worksheet.

EXHIBIT 7-9
PLANNING FOR RETIREMENT ADJUSTED FOR INFLATION

	A	B
1	**Retirement Worksheet with Growing Income**	
2	Annual Retirement Income Need	125,000
3	Years until Retirement	30
4	Years in Retirement	35
5	Expected Inflation Rate	3.00%
6	Rate of Return before Retirement	8.00%
7	Rate of Return during Retirement	6.00%
8	Savings Required at Retirement	$2,641,257.55
9	Investment Required Today	$262,481.13
10	Annual Investment Required	$23,315.53

In this example, the annuity payments begin at the end of the period. However, in many cases (such as lotteries), the first cash flow occurs immediately. This type of cash flow is called a *graduated annuity due*. We can easily modify equation (7-10) using the principle of value additivity to handle cash flows that start immediately.

Realize that we can treat a graduated annuity due as a regular graduated annuity with one less payment, plus an additional payment today:

$$PV_{GAD} = Pmt_0 + \frac{Pmt_0(1+g)}{i-g}\left[1 - \left(\frac{1+g}{1+i}\right)^{N-1}\right] \tag{7-11}$$

where Pmt_0 is the cash flow that occurs immediately. Because equations (7-10) and (7-11) are complex, we have written an add-in function to do the calculations. An add-in function is similar to a built-in function, but you must have the add-in installed and open to use the function.[8] The FAME_PVGA function is defined as:

FAME_PVGA(*PMT, NPER, GROWTHRATE, DISCRATE, BEGEND*)

where ***PMT*** is the first cash flow, ***NPER*** is the number of cash flows, ***GROWTHRATE*** is the rate at which the cash flows grow over time, and ***DISCRATE*** is the required

---

8. You can download the FAMEFNCS.xla add-in from the book Web site. This file can be opened just like a regular Excel file, and the functions accessed through the User Defined category of the Insert Function dialog box. Alternatively, you can "install" the add-in through the Tools Add-Ins dialog box. The latter method will allow the add-in to load every time you start Excel.

return. *BEGEND* is an optional argument that specifies if the cash flow occurs at the end (0) or beginning (1) of the period. (Note that *BEGEND* works just like the *TYPE* argument in the built-in **Pv** function.)

Using this add-in function, you can replace the formula in B8 with: =FAME_PVGA(B2,B4,B5,B7,0). You will get the same answer, but it is much easier to use the add-in function.

Uneven Cash Flow Streams

Annuities are very neat from a cash flow point of view, but most investments don't have cash flows that are the same in each period. When the cash flows are different in each period, we refer to them as *uneven cash flow streams*. Investments of this type are not as easy to deal with, though conceptually they are the same.

Recall our discussion of the principle of value additivity. This principle says that as long as cash flows occur in the same period, we can add them together to determine their combined value. The principle applies to any time period, not just to time period 0. So, to determine the present value of an uneven stream of cash flows, one option is to determine the present value of each cash flow separately and then add them together. The same technique applies to the future value of an uneven stream. Simply find the future value of each cash flow separately and then add them together.

Excel's **Pv** and **Fv** functions cannot be used for uneven cash flow streams because they assume equal (annuity) payments or a lump sum. Set up the worksheet in Exhibit 7-10 and we'll see what needs to be done.

EXHIBIT 7-10
PV AND FV FOR UNEVEN CASH FLOWS

	A	B
1	**Uneven Cash Flow Streams**	
2	Year	Cash Flow
3	1	1,000
4	2	2,000
5	3	3,000
6	4	4,000
7	5	5,000
8	Interest Rate	11.00%
9	Present Value	
10	Future Value	

First, we want to solve for the present value of the cash flows in B3:B7. To do this, we need to use the net present value, **NPV**, function. This function will be especially valuable in capital budgeting in Chapter 11. The **NPV** function is defined as:

$$\text{NPV}(\textbf{\textit{RATE}}, \textbf{\textit{VALUE1}}, \textit{VALUE2}, \ldots)$$

where **_RATE_** is the per period rate of return (i.e., the discount rate), **_VALUE1_** is the first cash flow (or range of cash flows), _VALUE2_ is the second cash flow, and so on. Excel will accept up to 29 cash flows in the list. To find the present value of the cash flows, enter: =NPV(B8,B3:B7) into B9.[9] Note that we have entered the cash flows as a range, rather than as individual values. Excel will accept the arguments either way, though a range is generally easier to enter. The result is $10,319.90. To verify this result, you can find the present value of each cash flow at 11% per year and add them together.

Finding the future value of an uneven stream is a bit more difficult because Excel has no built-in function to perform this calculation. Recall, however, the principle of value additivity. If we can get all of the cash flows into the same period, we can add them together and then move the result to the desired period. Figure 7-5 shows this solution.

---

9. If you are familiar with the definition of net present value (NPV), you should know that Excel's NPV function does not calculate the NPV as it is normally defined. Instead, it merely calculates the present value of the cash flows. This function is covered in more depth in Chapter 11.

FIGURE 7-5
FINDING THE FUTURE VALUE OF AN UNEVEN STREAM IN EXCEL

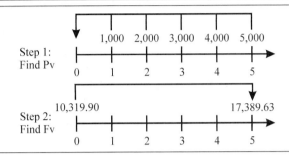

First we find the present value of the uneven stream of cash flows, perhaps using the **NPV** function, and then we find the future value of the present value of the cash flows. The easiest way to implement this method in Excel is to use the **NPV** function *nested* within the **FV** function. A nested function is one that is used as an input to another function. In cell B10, enter: `=FV(B8,A7,0,-NPV(B8,B3:B7),0)`. The future value is found to be $17,389.63. Notice that we have used the **NPV** function inside the **FV** function. As an alternative, we could have entered –B9 for the present value argument, but the result would be the same. Using nested functions can often simplify a worksheet by making use of fewer cells, though the formulas tend to be more complex.

Solving for the Yield in an Uneven Cash Flow Stream

Often in financial analysis, it is necessary to determine the yield of an investment given its price and cash flows. For example, we have already seen that one way to choose between alternative investments is to compare their yields, and we will see more examples in Chapter 11. This was easy when dealing with annuities and lump-sum investments. But, what about the case of uneven cash flow investments? We will use the worksheet in Exhibit 7-11 to find out.

EXHIBIT 7-11
YIELD ON AN UNEVEN CASH FLOW STREAM

	A	B
1	**Uneven Cash Flow Streams**	
2	Year	Cash Flow
3	0	(10,319.90)
4	1	1000
5	2	2000
6	3	3000
7	4	4000
8	5	5000
9	Yield	

To solve for the yield in problems such as this, we need to make use of the **IRR** (internal rate of return) function. The IRR is defined as the rate of return that equates the present value of future cash flows with the cost of the investment ($10,319.90 in this problem). In Excel, the **IRR** function is defined as:

IRR(*VALUES*, *GUESS*)

where ***VALUES*** is a range of cash flows (including the cost), and *GUESS* is the optional first guess at the correct interest rate. We will study this function in depth in Chapter 11, but for now we will just make use of it.

Before we find the solution, notice a couple of things about the worksheet. The cash flows are listed separately, so we cannot use the **IRR** function like we did the **FV**, **PV**, and **PMT** functions. Also, we must include the cost of the investment as one of the cash flows. To find the yield on this investment, insert into B9: =IRR(B3:B8,0.10). The result is 11%, which means that if you purchase this investment you will earn a compound annual rate of 11%.

We have used one form of the **IRR** function in B9. Another option is to omit the *GUESS* (0.10 in our example). In this case, either form will work. Sometimes, however, Excel will not be able to converge on a solution without a *GUESS* being specified. Remember that this is essentially a trial-and-error process, and sometimes Excel needs a little help to go in the right direction.

A few situations may cause an error when using the **IRR** function. One that we've already discussed is that Excel may not converge to a solution. In this case, you can usually find the answer by supplying Excel with a different *GUESS*. Another occurs if you have no negative cash flows. As an example, change the purchase price to a positive `10,319.90`. Excel will return the #NUM! error message indicating that there is a problem. In this case the problem is that your return is infinite (why?). A third problem can result from more than one negative cash flow in the stream. In general, there will be one solution to the problem for each sign change in the cash flow stream. In our original example, there is only one sign change (from negative to positive after the initial purchase).

Non-Annual Compounding Periods

There is no reason to restrict our analyses to investments that pay cash flows annually. Some investments make payments (e.g., interest) semiannually, monthly, daily, or even more frequently. Everything that we have learned to this point still applies, with only a minor change.

Recall our basic time value of money formula (7-2):

$$FV_N = PV(1 + i)^N$$

Originally, we defined i as the annual rate of interest and N as the number of years. Actually, i is the periodic rate of interest and N is the total number of periods. As an example, i might be the weekly interest rate and N the number of weeks for which we will hold the investment.[10] Since rates are usually quoted in terms of simple (i.e., not compounded) annual rates, we can restate our basic formula as:

$$FV_N = PV\left(1 + \frac{i}{m}\right)^{Nm} \tag{7-12}$$

where i is the annual rate, N is the number of years, and m is the number of periods per year.

Excel can handle non-annual compounding just as easily as annual compounding. Just enter the rate and number of periods adjusted for the length of the compounding period. Let's look at an example.

---

10. Since there are 52 weeks in a year, we would normally calculate the weekly rate as the annual rate divided by 52. Similarly, the number of weeks would be calculated by multiplying the number of years (perhaps a fractional number of years) by 52.

Assume that you are shopping for a new bank to set up a savings account. As you start shopping, you notice that all of the banks offer the same stated interest rate, but different compounding periods. To help make your decision, you set up the worksheet in Exhibit 7-12.

(Hint: The easiest way to set up this worksheet is to enter the data for the First National Bank and then make two copies. Next, edit the bank names and adjust the column widths to accommodate the labels.)

EXHIBIT 7-12
NON-ANNUAL COMPOUNDING PERIODS

	A	B
1	Non-Annual Compounding Worksheet	
2	First National Bank	
3	Investment	1,000.00
4	Simple Rate	10.00%
5	Periods per Year	1
6	Term of Investment (Years)	1
7	Future Value	
8	Second National Bank	
9	Investment	1,000.00
10	Simple Rate	10.00%
11	Periods per Year	2
12	Term of Investment (Years)	1
13	Future Value	
14	Third National Bank	
15	Investment	1,000.00
16	Simple Rate	10.00%
17	Periods per Year	12
18	Term of Investment (Years)	1
19	Future Value	

Notice that all of the banks are advertising a 10% annual rate. The only difference is how often they credit the interest to your account (i.e., the frequency of compounding). Being an economically rational thinker, you will choose the bank that will provide the highest balance at the end of the year. To determine the end-of-year balances, enter the **Fv** formula in B7: `=FV(B4/B5,B6*B5,0,-B3,1)`. Copy the formula from B7 to both B13 and B19. Note that we have again made use of nested functions. In this case, the rate is defined as the annual rate *divided* by the number of periods in a year, and the number of periods is the number of years *times* the number of periods in a year.

The choice is clear. You should choose the Third National Bank since it offers the highest end-of-year balance. All other things being equal, the more frequent the compounding, the higher your future value will be. To see this more clearly, set up the worksheet in Exhibit 7-13.

EXHIBIT 7-13
COMPARING VARIOUS NON-ANNUAL COMPOUNDING PERIODS

	A	B	C
1	Non-Annual Compounding Periods		
2	Present Value	1,000	
3	Annual Rate	10.00%	
4	**Frequency**	**Periods/Year**	**FV**
5	Annual	1	
6	Semiannual	2	
7	Quarterly	4	
8	Bimonthly	6	
9	Monthly	12	
10	Biweekly	26	
11	Weekly	52	
12	Daily	365	

To complete the worksheet, enter the **Fv** formula in C5: =FV(B$3/B5,B5,0,-B$2,1) and copy it down to the other cells. It is important that you insert the dollar signs as indicated so that the references to the present value and interest rate remain fixed when copying.

Notice that, as before, the more frequent the compounding, the higher the future value. Furthermore, the future value increases at a slower rate as the number of compounding periods increases. This can be seen more easily if we create a graph of the future values. To accomplish this, select the labels in A5:A13 and the numbers in C5:C13 (remember, you can select noncontiguous ranges by holding down the Ctrl key while dragging the mouse). Note that you are selecting one extra row because we will use this worksheet again later to add one more data point. Now, click on the Chart Wizard icon and follow the prompts. You should end up with a worksheet that resembles the one in Exhibit 7-14.

EXHIBIT 7-14
NON-ANNUAL COMPOUNDING RESULTS

	A	B	C	D	E	F	G	H
1	Non-Annual Compounding Periods							
2	Present Value	1,000						
3	Annual Rate	10.00%						
4	**Frequency**	**Periods/Year**	**FV**					
5	Annual	1	$1,100.00					
6	Semiannual	2	$1,102.50					
7	Quarterly	4	$1,103.81					
8	Bimonthly	6	$1,104.26					
9	Monthly	12	$1,104.71					
10	Biweekly	26	$1,104.96					
11	Weekly	52	$1,105.06					
12	Daily	365	$1,105.16					
13								

FV as Compounding Frequency Increases

Continuous Compounding

We have seen that more frequent compounding leads to higher future values. However, our examples extended this idea only as far as daily compounding. There is no reason that we can't also compound every half-day, every hour, or even every minute. In fact, this concept can be extended to the smallest imaginable time period: the instant. This type of compounding is referred to as *continuous compounding*.

Continuous compounding is an extension of what we have seen already. To recap, recall that we changed the basic future value function:

$$FV_N = PV\left(1 + \frac{i}{m}\right)^{Nm}$$

The more frequently we compound, the larger m is going to be. For example, with semiannual compounding $m = 2$, but with daily compounding $m = 365$. What if we set m equal to infinity? Actually, we can't do that because i/∞ is effectively equal to zero. What we can do is to take the limit as m approaches infinity. When we do this, we get:

$$\lim_{m \to \infty} FV_N = PVe^{iN} \tag{7-13}$$

where e is the base of the natural logarithm and is approximately equal to 2.718...

Excel does not offer functions to solve for the present or future value when compounding is continuous. However, we can easily create the formulas. To do so requires that you know about the **EXP** function, which raises e to a specified power.[11] This function is defined as:

EXP(*NUMBER*)

Using the worksheet in Exhibit 7-14, we can add, in cell C13: =B$2*exp(B$3). Since we have assumed a one-year period in this example, the power to which e is raised is simply the interest rate. Add the label: Continuous in A13 and the worksheet is complete. Note that continuous compounding doesn't offer much of an increase over daily compounding. The advantage does get larger as the amount invested grows, but it would take huge sums to make a significant difference. To see this, change the present value, B2, to 10,000,000.

We can also calculate the present value of a continuously compounded sum. All that needs to be done is to solve equation (7-13) for PV:[12]

$$\lim_{m \to \infty} PV = FV_N e^{-iN} \tag{7-14}$$

Summary

In this chapter we have discussed the concept of the time value of money. Present value represents the amount of money that needs to be invested today in order to purchase a future cash flow or stream of cash flows. Future value represents the amount of money that will be accumulated if we invest known cash flows at known interest rates. Further, we discussed various types of cash flows. Annuities are equal cash flows, equally spaced through time. Graduated annuities are similar to normal annuities, but the cash flows grow by a certain amount each period. Uneven cash flows are those in which the periodic cash flows are not equal.

---

11. e is the base of the natural logarithm, so $\exp(\cdot)$ is the inverse of $\ln(\cdot)$. In other words, $\exp(\ln(x)) = x$.

12. Many students find that the continuous compounding equations are easier to recall if we change the notation slightly. Specifically, let P be the present value, F be the future value, r is the annual rate of interest, and T is the number of years (which can be fractional). With this notation, equation (7-13) becomes $F = Pe^{rT}$, and equation (7-14) becomes $P = Fe^{-rT}$. This is easier because the formulas can be pronounced. For example, (7-13) is pronounced "Pert."

Before continuing with future chapters, you should be comfortable with these concepts. Practice by changing the worksheets presented in this chapter until you develop a sense for the type of results that you will obtain.

FINANCIAL FUNCTIONS USED IN THIS CHAPTER

Purpose	Function	Page
Find the future value	**FV**(*RATE*, *NPER*, *PMT*, *PV*, *TYPE*)	201
Find the present value	**PV**(*RATE*, *NPER*, *PMT*, *FV*, *TYPE*)	203
Payment of an annuity	**PMT**(*RATE*, *NPER*, *PV*, *FV*, *TYPE*)	209
Number of periods	**NPER**(*RATE*, *PMT*, *PV*, *FV*, *TYPE*)	211
Natural logarithm	**LN**(*NUMBER*)	211
Yield of an annuity	**RATE**(*NPER*, *PMT*, *PV*, *FV*, *TYPE*, *GUESS*)	212
Present value of a graduated annuity	**FAME_PVGA**(*PMT*, *NPER*, *GROWTHRATE*, *DISCRATE*, *BEGEND*)	218
Present value of unequal cash flows	**NPV**(*RATE*, *VALUE1*, *VALUE2*,...)	220
Find the yield of unequal cash flows	**IRR**(*VALUES*, *GUESS*)	222
Raise *e* to a power	**EXP**(*NUMBER*)	227

Problems

1. Upon starting your new job after college, you've been confronted with selecting the investments for your 401(k) retirement plan. You have four choices for investing your money:

   - A money market fund that has historically returned about 5% per year.
   - A long-term bond fund that has earned an average annual return of 8%.
   - A conservative common-stock fund that has earned 10% per year.
   - An aggressive common-stock fund that has earned 14% per year.

   a. If you were to contribute $5,000 per year for the next 35 years, how much would you accumulate in each of the above funds?

   b. Now, change your worksheet so that it allows for less than annual investments (monthly, biweekly, etc.). Your total annual investment will remain unchanged, but it may be made in smaller and more frequent amounts.

   c. Set up a scenario analysis that shows your accumulated value in each fund if you were to invest quarterly, monthly, biweekly, and weekly. Create a scenario summary of your results.

   d. What relationship do you notice between the frequency of investment and the future value? Create a column chart of the results that more clearly shows the outcome from more frequently investing.

2. Given the following set of cash flows:

Period	Cash Flow
1	25,000
2	20,000
3	15,000
4	10,000
5	5,000

a. If your required rate of return is 9% per year, what is the present value of the above cash flows? Future value?

b. Now, suppose that you are offered another investment that is identical, except that the cash flows are reversed (i.e., cash flow 1 is 5,000, cash flow 2 is 10,000, etc.). Is this worth more, or less, than the original investment? Why?

c. If you paid $50,000 for the original investment, what average annual rate of return would you earn? What return would you earn on the reversed cash flows?

d. Still assuming that your required return is 9%, would you be willing to purchase either of these investments?

3. Your five-year-old daughter has just announced that she would like to attend college. Your best guess is that it will cost approximately $35,000 per year (for four years) in tuition, books, rent, etc. for her to attend State College 13 years from now. You believe that you can earn a rate of 8% on investments to meet this goal.

a. If you were to invest a lump sum today in hopes of covering your daughter's college costs, how much would you have to invest?

b. If you now decided to invest annually instead, how much would you have to invest each year?

c. You just learned of a $10,000 inheritance and plan to invest it in your daughter's college fund. Given this new source of funds, how much will you now have to invest each year?

4. You have decided to invest in a small commercial office building that has one tenant. The tenant has a lease that calls for annual rent payments of $15,000 per year for the next three years. However, after that lease expires, you expect to be able to increase the rent by 5% per year for the next seven years. You plan to sell the building for $200,000 ten years from now.

a. Create a table showing the projected cash flows for this investment, assuming that the next lease payment will be made one year from today.

b. Assuming that you need to earn 11% per year on this investment, what is the maximum price that you would be willing to pay for the building today? Use the **NPV** function.

c. Notice that the cash flow stream starts out as a 3-year regular annuity, but it then changes into a 7-year graduated annuity plus a lump sum in year 10. Use the principle of value additivity to calculate the present value of the cash flows.

constant rate of change

d. Suppose that the current owner of the building is asking $175,000 for the building. If you paid this price, what annual rate of return would you earn? Should you buy the building at this price?

5. Congratulations! You have just won the State Lottery. The lottery prize was advertised as an annuitized $85 million, paid out in 30 equal annual payments beginning immediately. The annual payment is determined by dividing the advertised prize by the number of payments. You now have up to 60 days to determine whether to take the cash prize or the annuity.

a. If you were to choose the annuitized prize, how much would you receive each year?

b. The cash prize is the present value of the annuity payments. If interest rates are 7.5%, how much will you receive if you choose the cash option?

c. Now suppose that, as many lotteries do, the annuitized cash flows will grow by 3% per year to keep up with inflation, but they still add up to $85 million. In this case, the first payment will be $1,786,637.04 today. If you took the cash prize instead, how much would you receive?

CHAPTER 8   *Common Stock Valuation*

After studying this chapter, you should be able to:

1. *Differentiate among the definitions of "value" and explain the importance of intrinsic value in making financial decisions.*

2. *Explain how intrinsic value is calculated by considering the size, timing, and perceived riskiness of the cash flows.*

3. *Explain the concept of "required rate of return" and calculate this rate using the Capital Asset Pricing Model (CAPM).*

4. *Use several discounted cash flow models to value a common stock.*

5. *Use relative valuation models, especially for stocks that do not meet the assumptions of discounted cash flow (DCF) models.*

Determining the value of financial assets is important to both investors and corporate financial managers. The obvious reason is that nobody wants to pay more than an asset is worth, since such behavior would lead to lower returns. Less obvious, but equally important, is that we can draw some valuable conclusions from the observed prices of assets. We will examine one of these conclusions in detail in Chapter 10 when we use the value of corporate securities to determine the required rate of return on investments.

What Is Value?

The term "value" has many different meanings depending on the context in which it is used. For our purposes, there are four important types of value.

Generally, value can be defined as the amount that a willing and able buyer agrees to pay for an asset to a willing and able seller. In order to establish the value of an asset, it is important that both the buyer and seller be willing and able. Otherwise, no legitimate transaction can take place, and value cannot be determined without an exchange. Notice that we did not say that the value of an asset is always the same as its price. Price and value are distinct, though related, concepts. The price of an asset can be greater than its value (in which case we say that the asset is overvalued), less than its value (undervalued), or equal to its value (fairly valued).

Book value is the price of an asset minus its accumulated depreciation. Depreciation is a systematic method of accounting for the reduction in the value of an asset over its useful life. Because of the systematic nature of depreciation (i.e., it is determined in advance according to some well-defined formula), book value does not necessarily fairly represent the actual market value of the asset. Because of this, and other distortions of value, a school of investors (known as value investors) has arisen. These investors seek out the stocks of companies that they believe to be undervalued, in hopes that the market will eventually recognize the true value of the company.

Intrinsic value is the value of an asset to a particular investor. Intrinsic value can be determined by taking the present value of the future cash flows *at that investor's required rate of return*. Because we use the investor's required rate of return in the calculation, and because each investor has different preferences and perceptions, intrinsic value is unique to each individual. Without these differences in intrinsic values, markets could not function.

Market value is the price of an asset as determined in a competitive marketplace. The market price is the price that the marginal investor is willing to pay, and will fluctuate (sometimes wildly) throughout the trading day. Investors will purchase assets with market values below their intrinsic values (undervalued assets), and sell assets with market values above their intrinsic values (overvalued assets). It is easy to determine the market value of securities traded in the public markets, but not so easy for many other types of assets. Houses, for example, trade only rarely so it is difficult to determine their true market value. In these cases, we must rely on estimates of market value made by experts (e.g., appraisers).

Unless otherwise modified, or obvious from the context, all references to the term "value" from this point forward will refer to the individual's intrinsic value.

Fundamentals of Valuation

As noted above, the intrinsic value of an asset is the present value of the expected future cash flows provided by the asset. Mathematically, intrinsic value is given by:

$$V = \sum_{t=1}^{N} \frac{Cf_t}{(1+i)^t}$$

(8-1)

where Cf_t is the expected cash flow in period t, and i is the required rate of return for the investor performing the calculation.[1]

The most important components of value are likely to be the size and timing of the expected cash flows. The larger the expected cash flows, and the more quickly they are to be received, the higher the value will be. In other words, there is a positive relationship between the size of the cash flows and value, and a negative relationship between the time until the cash flows are received and value.

The other component of value is the investor's required rate of return. The required return is affected by the rates of return offered by competing investment vehicles and the riskiness of the investment. For example, if bonds are offering higher returns than stocks, we would expect that the prices of stocks would drop (and the prices of bonds would rise) as investors moved their money out of stocks and into bonds. This would occur because investors would recognize that bonds are less risky than are stocks, and they would raise their required returns for stocks. Since an increase in the required return will decrease value, investors would sell stocks, thereby driving down the prices. This process would continue until the prices of stocks had fallen enough, and bond prices risen enough, so that the expected returns reverted to the equilibrium relationship.

To determine the value of a security, then, we must first determine three things:

---

1. At this point we will assume that all future cash flows are known with certainty. In Chapter 12 we will examine what happens when future cash flows are uncertain.

1. What are the expected cash flows?
2. When will the cash flows occur?
3. What is the required rate of return for this particular stream of cash flows?

As we discuss the methods of valuing securities, keep these ideas in mind as they are the fundamentals of all security valuation.

Determining the Required Rate of Return

As mentioned above, one of the determinants of the required return for any stream of cash flows is the perceived riskiness of those cash flows. We will leave an in-depth discussion of risk for Chapter 12, but for now we will assume that the risk of a security is known.

In general, each investor can be classified by risk preference into one of three basic categories:

1. **Risk Averse** — The risk-averse investor prefers less risk for a given rate of return. The risk-averter can be encouraged to accept nearly any level of risk, but only if the rate of return is expected to compensate him fairly. In other words, he must be paid in order to accept risk.
2. **Risk Neutral** — The risk-neutral investor is indifferent to the level of risk. His required rate of return will not change, regardless of the risk involved.
3. **Risk Lover** — The risk-loving investor will actually lower his required rate of return as the risk increases. In other words, he is willing to pay to take on extra risk.

Under ordinary circumstances we assume that all investors are risk averse, and must receive a higher rate of return in order to accept a higher risk. Realize, however, that even investors in the same category can have different risk preferences, so two risk-averse investors will likely have different required returns for the same asset.

Figure 8-1 illustrates the *ex ante* (expected) risk-return trade-off for two risk-averse investors. We know they are risk averse because the lines have a positive slope. In this case security B is riskier than A and therefore has the higher expected return for both investors. Investor I_1 can be seen to be more risk averse than I_2 because the slope of the risk-return line is steeper. In other words, the risk premium grows at a faster rate for I_1 than it does for I_2.

FIGURE 8-1
THEORETICAL RISK-RETURN TRADE-OFF FOR TWO RISK-AVERSE INVESTORS

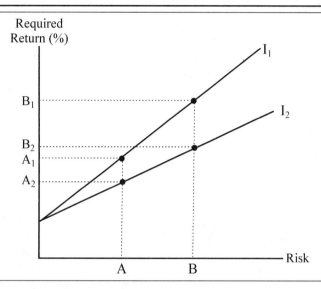

A Simple Risk Premium Model

An easy method of determining the rate of return for a security can be derived by assuming that the relationship pictured in Figure 8-1 is constant. If this is the case, then we can define the expected rate of return for an asset as a base rate (Y-axis intercept) plus a premium that is based on the riskiness of the security. In equation form:

$$E(R_i) = \text{Base Rate} + \text{Risk Premium}$$

where $E(R_i)$ is the expected rate of return for security i, the base rate is the rate of return on some benchmark security, and the risk premium is subjectively determined.

The problem with this model is that it is entirely subjective. Both the security chosen to provide the base rate and the risk premium are defined by the individual using the model. For example, one individual might choose as the base rate the rate of return on bonds issued by his company, while another might choose the average rate paid on AAA-rated corporate bonds. Furthermore, because of individual differences in risk preferences, each individual is likely to assign a different value to the risk premium. Obviously, what is needed is a more objective approach.

CAPM: A More Scientific Model

The Capital Asset Pricing Model (CAPM) provides us with a more objective version of the simple risk premium model for determining expected returns. For our purposes, we can consider the CAPM to be a version of the simple risk premium model with its inputs more rigorously defined. The CAPM is given by:

$$E(R_i) = R_f + \beta_i[E(R_m) - R_f] \qquad (8\text{-}2)$$

where R_f is the risk-free rate of interest, β_i is a measure of the riskiness of security i relative to the riskiness of the market portfolio, and $E(R_m)$ is the expected rate of return on the market portfolio.

In the CAPM, R_f serves as the base rate of interest. It is defined as the rate of return on a security with zero risk. Sometimes R_f is referred to as the "pure time value of money," or, in other words, the rate of return that is earned for delaying consumption but not accepting any risk. Because it is risk free, we know R_f with certainty in advance. Ordinarily, R_f is assumed to be the rate of return on a U.S. Treasury security with time to maturity equal to the expected holding period of the security in question. Treasury securities are chosen as a proxy for the theoretical risk-free rate because they are free of default risk, and are therefore the closest of all securities to being truly risk free.

The second term in the CAPM is the risk premium, and it is more difficult to understand. The market portfolio is a portfolio of all risky assets, usually proxied by a stock index such as the S&P 500, which serves as a sort of benchmark against which other portfolios are measured. Subtracting the risk-free rate of return from the expected market return gives the expected market risk premium. Beta (β) is an index of systematic risk.[2] It measures the risk of a

---

2. In the world of CAPM there are two types of risk: systematic and unsystematic. Systematic risk is the market-related risk that affects all assets. An example would be unexpected changes in interest rates. Unsystematic risk is the company-specific risk such as the risk of a strike or of losing a major contract. As we will see in Chapter 12, through proper diversification, unsystematic risk can often be eliminated from a portfolio.

particular security relative to the market portfolio. If a stock has a beta of 2, then we could say that the stock is twice as risky as the market portfolio. If it is twice as risky, then common sense (and the CAPM) tells us that the risk premium for this stock should be twice that of the market. Likewise, a stock with a beta of 0.5 should carry half of the risk premium of the market.

So the CAPM is no more than a sophisticated version of the simple risk premium model. With this in mind, we can redraw the risk-return trade-off graph (known as the security market line) in Figure 8-2.

FIGURE 8-2
THE SECURITY MARKET LINE

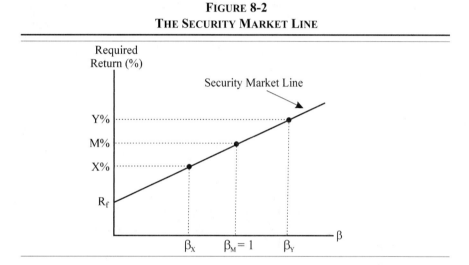

To see the CAPM in action, consider the following example:

> As a security analyst for Dewey, Cheatham, and Howe Securities you are preparing a report detailing your firm's expectations regarding two stocks for the year to come. Your report is to include the expected returns for these stocks and a graph illustrating the expected risk-return trade-off. Other analysts at DCH have informed you that the firm expects the S&P 500 to earn a return of 11% in the year ahead while the risk-free rate is 5%. According to *Value Line*, the betas for stocks X and Y are 0.5 and 1.5, respectively. What are the expected returns for X and Y?

To work this example, open a new workbook and enter the data so that it resembles the worksheet in Exhibit 8-1.

EXHIBIT 8-1
CALCULATING EXPECTED RETURNS WITH THE CAPM

	A	B	C	D	E
1		The Security Market Line			
2		Risk-free	X	Market	Y
3	Beta	0.00	0.50	1.00	1.50
4	Expected Return	5.00%		11.00%	

Before continuing, it is important to understand some of these inputs. The example problem did not mention the betas of the risk-free asset or of the market portfolio. How did we know that the beta of the risk-free asset is 0? Recall that beta measures the riskiness of the asset *relative to the market*. Since the risk-free asset has no risk, by definition, any measure of risk must be equal to zero. By definition the market has a beta of 1.00 because the risk is measured relative to the market itself.

To complete this example, we need to enter the formula for the CAPM, equation (8-2), into C4 and E4. In C4 enter: =$B$4+C3*($D$4-$B$4) and then copy this cell to E4. You should see that security X has an expected return of 8% and Y has an expected return of 14%. Notice that the expected return of X is not one-half that of the market, nor is the expected return of Y 50% greater than that of the market. Instead, it is the risk premium of these securities that is one-half (for X) or one and one-half (for Y) the risk premium of the market. The portion of the expected return that comes from delaying consumption (the risk-free rate) is the same for both securities.

Finally, we can create a graph of the security market line (SML) with these data points. Select B3:E4 and use the Chart Wizard to create an XY (Scatter) graph, being sure that you make the first row the category (X-axis) labels. You can experiment with the SML by changing the expected return for the market or the risk-free rate. You will notice that the slope of the SML changes as you change the market risk premium. At this point your worksheet should match the one in Exhibit 8-2.

EXHIBIT 8-2
EXPECTED RETURNS AND THE SECURITY MARKET LINE

	A	B	C	D	E
1	The Security Market Line				
2		Risk-free	X	Market	Y
3	Beta	0.00	0.50	1.00	1.50
4	Expected Return	5.00%	8.00%	11.00%	14.00%
5					
6					
7					
8					
9					
10					
11					
12					
13					
14					
15					

Valuing Common Stocks

The first question to ask when attempting to value any security is, "What are the expected cash flows?" In the case of common stocks there are two types of cash flows: dividends and the amount received at the time of the sale. Consider the following problem:

> Suppose that you are interested in purchasing shares of the common stock of the XYZ Corporation. XYZ recently paid a dividend of $2.40, and you expect that this dividend will continue to be paid into the foreseeable future. Furthermore, you believe (for reasons that will become clear) that you will be able to sell this stock in three years for $20 per share. If your required return is 12% per year, what is the maximum amount that you should be willing to pay for a share of XYZ common stock?

To clarify the problem, it helps to examine it in terms of a timeline. Figure 8-3 presents the timeline.

FIGURE 8-3
TIMELINE FOR XYZ COMMON STOCK

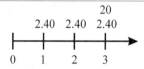

Calculating the value of this stock is a simple matter of calculating the present value of its cash flows (equation (8-1)). Given that your required return is 12%, the intrinsic value must be:

$$V = \frac{2.40}{1.12} + \frac{2.40}{(1.12)^2} + \frac{2.40 + 20}{(1.12)^3} = 20$$

If the stock is currently selling for $24 (the market value), would you purchase any shares? Obviously not, because the market value exceeds your intrinsic value by $4. If you did purchase the shares, and your cash flow expectations were realized, your average annual rate of return would be less than your required return.

Of course, the XYZ example problem is somewhat contrived because there is no way to know, for sure, what the dividends and selling price are going to be in the future. With dividends this is not so much of a problem, because firms tend to have a somewhat stable dividend policy. The advanced knowledge of the selling price is a different matter. It is impossible to know exactly what the market price will be tomorrow, and even more difficult to know the price three years hence.

The Constant-Growth Dividend Discount Model

To eliminate these problems, we can make a couple of assumptions. The first assumption is that dividends will grow at a constant rate.[3] With this assumption, knowing the most recent dividend is equivalent to knowing all future dividends. Also assume that we have an infinite holding period. In other words, we will never sell the stock, so we don't have to worry about forecasting the selling price. While this second assumption may sound ludicrous, we will see that it is little more than a mathematical trick that allows us to develop a model.

---

3. Note that this is not an assumption that the dividend stream will always get larger. The growth rate could be negative, in which case the dividends would be shrinking over time. Furthermore, the growth rate could be zero, which means that the dividends are constant.

These assumptions lead to a model for the valuation of common stock that is known as the constant-growth dividend discount model (DDM), or the *Gordon Model*. Recall that we have defined the value of a common stock as the present value of future dividends plus the present value of the selling price. Since the stock will never be sold, because of the infinite holding period, the model becomes:

$$V_{CS} = \frac{D_1}{(1 + k_{CS})} + \frac{D_2}{(1 + k_{CS})^2} + \frac{D_3}{(1 + k_{CS})^3} + \dots + \frac{D_\infty}{(1 + k_{CS})^\infty}$$

where V_{CS} is the value of the common stock, the D's are the dividends in a particular period, and k_{CS} is the required return.[4] Because the dividends are growing at a constant rate, they can be expressed as a function of the most recently paid dividend (D_0):

$$V_{CS} = \frac{D_0(1 + g)}{(1 + k_{CS})} + \frac{D_0(1 + g)^2}{(1 + k_{CS})^2} + \frac{D_0(1 + g)^3}{(1 + k_{CS})^3} + \dots + \frac{D_0(1 + g)^\infty}{(1 + k_{CS})^\infty}$$

This equation can be restated in closed form as:

$$V_{CS} = \frac{D_0(1 + g)}{k_{CS} - g} = \frac{D_1}{k_{CS} - g} \tag{8-3}$$

Returning to the example, realize that XYZ's dividend growth rate is 0% (i.e., the dividend stream is not growing). Therefore, the value of a share is:

$$V_{CS} = \frac{2.40(1 + 0)}{0.12 - 0} = 20$$

which is exactly the same value as was found when assuming that you knew the value of the stock three years hence.

To see how you knew that the value of the stock would be $20 in three years, we can again use the time-shifting technique from Chapter 7. Let's look at another example.

---

4. k_{CS} is the same as i, but is the more common notation for this model. As we will see later, this notation also helps to distinguish between the investor's required return for the different securities issued by the firm.

Suppose that you are interested in purchasing a share of the common stock of the ABC Corporation. ABC has not recently paid any dividends, nor is it expected to for the next three years. However, ABC is expected to begin paying a dividend of $1.50 per share four years from now. In the future, that dividend is expected to grow at a rate of 7% per year. If your required return is 15% per year, what is the maximum amount that you should be willing to pay for a share of ABC common stock?

FIGURE 8-4
VALUING ABC COMMON STOCK WITH TIME-SHIFTING

	0	0	0	1.50	1.61	1.72	1.84	1.97	2.10	2.25...
Shifted Time	0	1	2	3	4	5	6	7	8	9	10...
Real Time	-3	-2	-1	0	1	2	3	4	5	6	7 ...

In order to determine the value of ABC common stock as of today (period 0), we must first find the value as of some future time period. The constant growth dividend discount model can be used at any time period, and will always provide the value of the stock at the time period that is one period before the dividend which is used in the numerator:

$$V_N = \frac{D_{N+1}}{(K_{CS}-g)} \qquad (8\text{-}4)$$

For this particular problem, the future time period we choose is somewhat arbitrary as long as it is period 3 or later (but period 3 is the easiest). In this case, let's find the value as of period 3 (using the period 4 dividend):

$$V_3 = \frac{D_4}{k_{CS}-g} = \frac{1.50}{0.15-0.07} = 18.75$$

So we know that the stock will be worth $18.75 per share three years from today. Remembering that the value of a stock is the present value of its cash flows, and that the only relevant cash flow in this case is the value at year three (which encapsulates the value of all future dividends), the value as of today must be:

$$V_0 = \frac{18.75}{1.15^3} = 12.33$$

We could also begin the valuation process at period 5 (or any other period). In this case, the value at period 5 (using the period 6 dividend) is:

$$V_5 = \frac{1.72}{0.15 - 0.07} = 21.50$$

The next step is to find the present value of all future cash flows (in this case: D_4, D_5, and V_5):

$$V_0 = \frac{1.50}{1.15^4} + \frac{1.61 + 21.50}{1.15^5} = 12.35$$

The $0.02 difference in values is due to rounding. Incidentally, note that had we only discounted back to period 3, the value at that time would have been $18.75.

Earlier we said that the assumption of an infinite holding period was not as ludicrous as it sounds. Let's examine this assumption in more detail with a worksheet. Open a new worksheet and enter the labels as shown so that it matches the fragment of a worksheet in Exhibit 8-3.

EXHIBIT 8-3
WORKSHEET TO TEST THE INFINITE HOLDING PERIOD ASSUMPTION

	A	B	C	D	E
1	**Infinite Holding Period Assumption**				
2	Period	Dividends	Present Value	Growth Rate	7%
3	1	0.00		Req. Return	15%
4	2	0.00			
5	3	0.00			
6	4	1.50			
7	5	1.61			
8	6	1.72			
9	7	1.84			
10	8	1.97			
11	9	2.10			
12	10	2.25			

Note that the series of numbers representing the periods extends from 1 to 120 in cells A3:A122. To easily input these numbers, enter a 1 in A3 and use the **E**dit Fi**ll** **S**eries command to fill in the numbers. In the Series dialog box, set the **S**tep value to 1 and the St**o**p value to 120. Also be sure to set the series Type to **L**inear and Series in to **C**olumns. The dialog box should look like the one in Figure 8-5.

FIGURE 8-5
THE SERIES DIALOG BOX

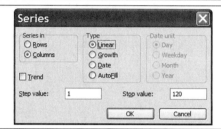

In this worksheet we want to calculate the value of the stock with various numbers of dividends included. From the example problem, we know that ABC will first pay a dividend of $1.50 in period 4 and that the dividend will grow at a 7% (cell E2) rate each year. Before continuing, enter the dividends into the worksheet as follows: First, enter a 0 for each of the first three dividends. For period 4, enter: 1.50 in B6. In B7 we want to calculate the period 5 dividend, so enter: =B6*(1+E$2). Now copy this formula to each cell in the range B8:B122. To make sure that the copy was successful, note that the value in B122 should be 3842.46 (the power of compounding!).

Now, we want to find the present values of dividends in cells C3:C122. We will use the NPV function to calculate the present values of the dividends. In C3 enter: =NPV(E$3,B$3:B3). The dollar sign will effectively freeze the first cell reference, so if we copy this formula down the range will expand. Copy the formula over the range C4:C122. Column C gives the value of the stock if we include only the dividends through the selected period. For example, the value in C20 ($8.15) is the value of the stock if we consider only the first 18 dividends. Similarly, the value in C50 ($11.85) is the value of the stock if we consider only the first 48 dividends.

Notice how the present value of the dividends converges to the value of the stock ($12.33) as we include more and more dividends in the calculation. It is not necessary to include more than about 120 dividends because the present value of all dividends beyond that point is effectively zero. This is easier to see if we create a graph of the values versus the number of dividends. Highlight the ranges A3:A122 and C3:C122. Now select the Chart Wizard icon and follow the prompts to create the XY (Scatter). Be sure to choose a graph without symbols. Your worksheet should now resemble the one in Exhibit 8-4, except that we have added a line to represent the known value of the stock ($12.33).

EXHIBIT 8-4
THE INFINITE HOLDING PERIOD IS JUST FOR SIMPLICITY

	A	B	C	D	E	F	G	H	I
1	Infinite Holding Period Assumption								
2	Period	Dividends	Present Value	Growth Rate	7%				
3	1	0.00	$0.00	Req. Return	15%				
4	2	0.00	$0.00						
5	3	0.00	$0.00						
6	4	1.50	$0.86						
7	5	1.61	$1.66						
8	6	1.72	$2.40						
9	7	1.84	$3.09						
10	8	1.97	$3.73						
11	9	2.10	$4.33						
12	10	2.25	$4.89						
13	11	2.41	$5.40						
14	12	2.58	$5.89						
15	13	2.76	$6.33						
16	14	2.95	$6.75						
17	15	3.16	$7.14						
18	16	3.38	$7.50						
19	17	3.61	$7.84						
20	18	3.87	$8.15						

The Value of ABC Common Stock

(chart: Dollars per Share vs. Number of Dividends Included)

The Two-Stage Growth Model

Assuming that the dividends will grow at a constant rate forever is convenient from a mathematical perspective, but it isn't very realistic. Other valuation models have been developed that are more realistic. For example, there is a two-stage growth model that allows for a period of supra-normal growth followed by constant growth. In addition, a three-stage model modifies the two-stage model to allow for a gradual decline into the constant-growth stage. Both of these models are more complex than the constant-growth model, but keep in mind that they are still present value calculations. The only thing that has changed is the pattern of the future cash flows.

The two-stage valuation model allows for the dividend to grow at one rate for several periods, and then to grow at a (usually, but not necessarily) slower rate from that point on. This is a much more realistic model because a firm's dividends may be growing at a fast rate now, but that rate of growth is unlikely to be continued forever. All companies will eventually mature and find that their earnings growth slows so their dividend growth rate must slow as well. The two-stage model assumes that the change in the dividend growth rate will happen instantaneously at some point.

Let g_1 represent the dividend growth rate from period 1 to n, and g_2 be the dividend growth rate for the remainder of time. Assuming that $D_0 \neq 0$, $g_1 \neq k_{CS}$ and $g_2 < k_{CS}$, the model is:

$$V_{CS} = \frac{D_0(1 + g_1)}{k_{CS} - g_1}\left[1 - \left(\frac{1 + g_1}{1 + k_{CS}}\right)^n\right] + \frac{\dfrac{D_0(1 + g_1)^n(1 + g_2)}{k_{CS} - g_2}}{(1 + k_{CS})^n} \tag{8-5}$$

Note that the first term in equation (8-5) is simply the present value of the first n dividends growing at a rate of g_1 (see equation (7-10) on page 217). The second term is the present value of all of the remaining dividends growing at a constant rate of g_2. This is exactly the same procedure we used earlier to value ABC's common stock, except that ABC not only had two growth rates (0% and 7%) but also was not originally paying a dividend.[5] Note that if $g_1 = g_2$ then equation (8-5) simplifies to equation (8-3).

To demonstrate the use of this model, let's consider an example.

> Oviedo Paper, Inc. is a major producer of paper products. Due to its immensely popular new stationery product, analysts expect that the firm's earnings and dividends will grow at a rate of 15% per year for the next five years. After that, analysts expect that the firm's growth rate will decline to its historical value of 8% per year as competitors launch similar products. If Oviedo Paper recently paid a dividend (D_0) of $0.35 and your required return is 12%, what is the value of the stock today?

To find the value, use equation (8-5):

$$V_{CS} = \frac{0.35(1.15)}{0.12 - 0.15}\left[1 - \left(\frac{1.15}{1.12}\right)^5\right] + \frac{\dfrac{0.35(1.15)^5(1.08)}{0.12 - 0.08}}{(1.12)^5} = 12.68$$

Since this equation is quite tedious, and Excel has no built-in function for this model, we have written a macro to do the calculations. Make sure that you have the

---

5. Note that we cannot use equation (8-5) in that case, because D_0 was equal to $0.00. Plugging in $0.00 for D_0 would give a value of $0.00 for the stock.

FAMEFNCS.xla add-in opened so that you have access to the macro. Now, return to your original workbook and open a new worksheet. The macro we will use is called **FAME_TwoStageValue** and is defined as:

FAME_TwoStageValue(*DIV1*, *REQRATE*, *GROWTHRATE1*, *GROWTHRATE2*, *G1PERIODS*)

where ***DIV1*** is the dividend to be paid at the end of period 1, ***REQRATE*** is the required return, ***GROWTHRATE1*** and ***GROWTHRATE2*** are the two growth rates, and ***G1PERIODS*** is the length of the first growth period.

Set up your new worksheet to look like the one in Exhibit 8-5. To get the value in B8, use the Insert Function dialog box. Choose the User Defined category, and then select **FAME_TwoStageValue** from the list. After you have entered the appropriate addresses in the dialog box, your function in B8 should be: =FAME_TwoStageValue(B2*(1+B3),B6,B3,B4,B5). Note that to get the dividend at period 1 (***DIV1***), we need to multiply the period 0 dividend by 1 + B3, which is the first growth rate. Your answer in B8 should confirm the calculations we made using equation (8-5).

EXHIBIT 8-5
THE TWO-STAGE GROWTH MODEL

	A	B
1	**Oviedo Paper Valuation**	
2	Dividend 0	0.35
3	Growth Rate 1	15%
4	Growth Rate 2	8%
5	Period 1 Length	5
6	Required Return	12%
7		
8	Two-Stage Value of Stock	$ 12.68

As noted earlier, if both growth rates are the same (that is, we have a single, constant growth rate) then this model will give the same value as equation (8-3). Let's assume that the long-run growth rate is 8%. Change the value in B3 to 8%, and you will see that the constant growth value of the stock is $9.45. Obviously, then, the higher initial growth rate in the early years adds a bit over $3 per share.

The Three-Stage Growth Model

The three-stage growth model is very similar in concept to the two-stage model. The difference is that the two-stage model assumes that the change in the growth rate occurs instantaneously, whereas the three-stage model assumes a linear decline in the growth rate over some period. In other words, the three-stage model allows the growth rate to decline more slowly to a constant rate. This is a more realistic assumption.

Mathematically, the three-stage model is given by:

$$V_{CS} = \frac{D_0}{k_{CS} - g_2}\left[(1 + g_2) + \frac{n_1 + n_2}{2}(g_1 - g_2)\right] \qquad (8\text{-}6)$$

Note that equation (8-6) looks quite similar to equation (8-3). The difference is that rather than using a single growth rate, the term in brackets in the three-stage model represents a factor by which the constant growth model must be multiplied to account for the higher initial growth rates. Also, note that all of the variables in (8-6) are as previously defined, except that n_2 is the number of years until the growth rate becomes constant.

It should be obvious that the average growth rate in the three-stage model will be higher than the average growth rate in the two-stage model. For this reason, the three-stage model will always give a somewhat higher valuation than the two-stage model. How much higher depends on the length of the transition period.

Let's return to our example using Oviedo Paper, Inc. In addition to the previous information, assume that the growth rate will transition from 15% to 8% over a three-year period. That makes the time in the first stage 5 years (n_1), and the time until constant growth of 8 years (n_2). Using equation (8-6), we find that the value of the stock has increased to:

$$V_{CS} = \frac{0.35}{0.12 - 0.08}\left[1.08 + \frac{5 + 8}{2}(0.15 - 0.08)\right] = 13.43$$

As with the two-stage model, we have written a function macro to make the calculations for the three-stage model. This function is defined as:

FAME_ThreeStageValue(*DIV1*, *REQRATE*, *GROWTHRATE1*, *GROWTHRATE2*, *G1PERIODS*, *TRANSPERIODS*).

All of the function's inputs are the same as before, except that ***TRANSPERIODS*** is the length of the transition period between growth rates.

To use this function, you will need to modify your worksheet from Exhibit 8-5 slightly. Select row 5 and insert a row. In cell A5 enter the label: Transition

Period Length, and in B5 enter 3. In A10 enter: 3-stage Value of Stock. In B10, use the Insert Function dialog box to enter the function. It is: =famefncs.xla!FAME_ThreeStageValue(B2*(1+B3),B7,B3,B4,B5 ,B6). As you can see in Exhibit 8-6, the three-year transition period adds $0.75 to the value of the stock as compared to the two-stage model.

EXHIBIT 8-6
THE THREE-STAGE GROWTH MODEL

	A	B
1	**Oviedo Paper Valuation**	
2	Dividend 0	0.35
3	Growth Rate 1	15%
4	Growth Rate 2	8%
5	Period 1 Length	5
6	Transition Period Length	3
7	Required Return	12%
8		
9	Two-Stage Value of Stock	$ 12.68
10	Three-Stage Value of Stock	$ 13.43

Ultimately, it's important to remember that all three of these common stock valuation models are nothing more than present value functions. Each uses a different assumption about the growth pattern of the dividends, but they are still present value calculations. When faced with a problem that doesn't fit the assumptions of any of these models, simply forecast the dividends in the future using whatever growth assumptions are appropriate. Then, calculate the present value of the future dividends. This is the method that was used to find the value of ABC common stock in the example problem on page 244.

Alternative Discounted Cash Flow Models

As noted previously, the value of a stock is given by the present value of its future cash flows—that is, the dividends that it will pay. However, we can restructure these models in a way that provides some additional insight into the valuation process. The two models presented in this section do just that.

The Earnings Model

Imagine a company that pays out 100% of its earnings as dividends. In this case, the dividend is equal to earnings per share (EPS), and the growth rate must be 0% because it is only investing enough (through the depreciation charge) to maintain the assets it currently owns. Using the constant-growth dividend discount model (with $g = 0\%$), equation (8-3), the value of the common stock would be:

$$V = \frac{EPS_1}{k}$$

This is the value of the stock if the firm doesn't reinvest, and therefore doesn't grow. However, most firms do reinvest at least some of their earnings, so the value of the stock must be equal to the value if it doesn't grow plus the present value of its future growth opportunities ($PVGO$):

$$V = \frac{EPS_1}{k} + PVGO \qquad \text{(8-7)}$$

The future earnings growth rate will be driven by the rate of return that is generated by the reinvested earnings (the return on equity, or ROE). If we let b = the retention ratio and r = the return on equity, then the growth rate (g) will be:[6]

$$g = br$$

The value of the stock will increase only if the firm's ROE (r) is greater than its required return (k). In other words, if the firm generates a positive net present value (NPV).[7] Therefore, the $PVGO$ is equal to the present value of the future NPVs generated by the reinvested earnings (RE). If we assume that the NPV is a perpetuity and will grow at a constant rate of g, then:

$$PVGO = \sum_{t=1}^{\infty} \frac{NPV_t}{(1+k)^t} = \frac{NPV_1}{k-g} \qquad \text{(8-8)}$$

---

6. Note that if $b = 0\%$ (100% payout ratio), then g must also be 0%.

7. Net present value is discussed in detail in Chapter 11 beginning on page 345.

The NPV in any given year is the present value of the earnings generated by the investment less the cost of the investment. Mathematically, the NPV is given by:

$$NPV_1 = \frac{RE_1 \times r}{k} - RE_1$$

By substituting that result into equation (8-8), it can be rewritten as:

$$PVGO = \frac{\frac{RE_1 \times r}{k} - RE_1}{k - g} = \frac{RE_1\left(\frac{r}{k} - 1\right)}{k - g} \tag{8-9}$$

Now substitute equation (8-9) into equation (8-7), and we have the earnings model for valuing common stock:

$$V = \frac{EPS_1}{k} + \frac{RE_1\left(\frac{r}{k} - 1\right)}{k - g} \tag{8-10}$$

This model is important because it directly links the company's ROE to the value of the stock. Specifically, note that the stock price can only rise if $r > k$. In fact, if $r < k$ (the company earns less than its required return) then the value of the stock will fall. Let's look at an example:

> Analysts expect that Aurora Foods will earn $1.40 per share in the coming year, and pay a dividend of $0.49 per share. Historically, the firm's ROE has been 15%, and its required return on investments is 12%. What is the value of the stock?

Note that RE_1 will be equal to $EPS_1 - D_1$, or $0.91 per share, and the retention ratio is 65%. The growth rate is $0.65 \times 0.15 = 0.0975$. So, using equation (8-10), we see that the value of the stock is:

$$V = \frac{1.40}{0.12} + \frac{0.91\left(\frac{0.15}{0.12} - 1\right)}{0.12 - 0.0975} = 11.67 + 10.11 = 21.78$$

We can create a worksheet that will make it easy to change the assumptions in the problem. Exhibit 8-7 shows the worksheet.

EXHIBIT 8-7
THE EARNINGS MODEL

	A	B
1	Aurora Foods Valuation	
2	Earnings per Share	1.40
3	Dividend	0.49
4	ROE	15.00%
5	Required Return	12.00%
6		
7	Retained Earnings	
8	Retention Ratio	
9	Growth Rate	
10		
11	Value without Growth	
12	Value of Growth Opportunities	
13	Value of Stock	

The values given in the example are in B2:B5. In B7:B9 are the intermediate calculations that need to be done before using the model. Retained earnings is calculated in B7 with the formula: =B2-B3. The retention ratio, in B8, is found with: =1-B3/B2, and the growth rate is: =B4*B8.

We have chosen to separate the components of the value into cells B11:B12 to highlight them separately. In B11 add the formula: =B2/B5. The value of the growth opportunities is given in B12 by the formula: =B7*(B4/B5-1)/(B5-B9). The total value of the stock is the sum of B11:B12. You should find that it is $21.78, exactly as we found above.

Using this worksheet, you can experiment with some of the assumptions. In particular, notice that if you change the ROE so that it is less than the required return, the value of the growth opportunities will be negative. For example, if you change the ROE to 10%, then the value of the growth opportunities is −$2.76, which reduces the total value of the stock to $8.91. This demonstrates that growth just for the sake of growth doesn't make economic sense. Only profitable growth opportunities are worth pursuing.

Finally, note that this model is equivalent to the constant-growth dividend discount model. In this case, the company will pay a dividend of $0.49 next year, and its growth rate is 9.75%. Therefore, the value of the stock must be $21.78:

$$V = \frac{0.49}{(0.12 - 0.0975)} = 21.78$$

The Free Cash Flow Model

Free cash flow is defined as total operating cash flow after taxes less the reinvestment in operating assets that is required to maintain the firm's growth rate. Recall from our discussion of economic profit in Chapter 4 (see page 138) that we defined net operating profit after tax (NOPAT) as:

$$NOPAT = EBIT(1 - \text{tax rate})$$

We can now define *operating cash flow* as:

$$\text{Operating Cash Flow} = NOPAT + \text{Non-cash Expenses}$$

Where "non-cash expenses" are depreciation, amortization, and sometimes other non-cash charges. Operating cash flow (after tax) is the cash flow that is available for the firm to reinvest in assets and/or pay out to investors (interest, principal, dividends, share repurchases). Therefore, the operating cash flow belongs to both the creditors and the shareholders of the firm.

As was noted earlier, all firms must reinvest in the business to maintain a positive growth rate. To calculate the required investment in operating assets, we first forecast the level of operating assets for the next period and then calculate the current level of those assets. The difference is the required investment:

$$\Delta \text{ Operating Assets} = \Delta \text{ NOWC} + \Delta \text{ Operating Fixed Assets}$$

where NOWC is net operating working capital (operating current assets less operating current liabilities). Note that we are referring to operating assets as defined on page 140. Therefore, we need to exclude any nonoperating assets and current liabilities (e.g., marketable securities and notes payable) from our calculations. We will account for these nonoperating items later.

If we subtract the required reinvestment in operating assets from the operating cash flow, then we have free cash flow (FCF):

$$\text{Free Cash Flow} = \text{Operating Cash Flow} - \Delta \text{ Operating Assets} \qquad \textbf{(8-11)}$$

This free cash flow belongs to all of the firm's capital providers. Therefore, the value of the firm's operating assets is the present value of the expected free cash flow, discounted at the firm's weighted average cost of capital. However, we have omitted any nonoperating assets from our calculations, and these assets have value too. For this reason, we must add the value of these nonoperating assets to the present value of the FCF in order to arrive at the value of the entire firm:[8]

$$V_F = \sum_{t=1}^{\infty} \frac{FCF_t}{(1+WACC)^t} + \text{Nonoperating Assets} \qquad (8\text{-}12)$$

Where WACC is the firm's weighted average cost of capital. Now, if we assume (as we did for dividends in earlier models) that the FCF will grow at a constant rate (g) forever, then the value of the entire firm (V_F) is:

$$V_F = \frac{FCF_1}{(WACC-g)} + \text{Nonoperating Assets} \qquad (8\text{-}13)$$

Note that we can make other assumptions about the growth pattern of FCF. For example, we might forecast FCF for each year over the next five years, and assume constant growth thereafter. In that case, we would use the general nonconstant growth model developed earlier. Or, we could assume that it will grow in two or three stages. In those cases, we could use the two-stage or three-stage models to find the present value, instead of the single-stage constant-growth model, for the first term in equation (8-13).

Ultimately, we are trying to get to the per share value of the common stock. The value of the entire firm is also given by:

$$V_F = V_D + V_P + V_C \qquad (8\text{-}14)$$

where V_D is the market value of the debt, V_P is the value of the preferred equity, and V_C is the value of the common equity. If we substitute equation (8-13) into equation (8-14) and solve for V_C, then we have the free cash flow model:

$$V_C = \frac{FCF_1}{(WACC-g)} + \text{Nonoperating Assets} - V_D - V_P \qquad (8\text{-}15)$$

---

8. Note that value of the nonoperating assets is the present value of their future cash flows. However, especially for short-term investments, the values reported on the balance sheet are very close to their market value.

Now, equation (8-15) gives the total market value of the common stock. Typically, however, we want to know the per share value. For this reason, we would divide V_C by the number of common shares outstanding.

To make this clear, let's look at an example:

> Analysts project that Front Range Mountaineering Supplies will generate pre-tax operating profits (EBIT) of $160,000 in the coming year. The firm will have $40,000 in depreciation expense and a tax rate of 30%. Management has told analysts that it expects to make net new investments of $30,000 in operating assets over the next year. It has $25,000 in marketable securities on the books, and the market value of its debt is $450,000. The analysts believe that the WACC is 12% and that free cash flow can grow at about 7% per year. If the company has 350,000 common shares outstanding, what is the intrinsic value per share?

First, note that NOPAT is equal to:

$$\text{NOPAT} = 160,000(1 - 0.30) = 112,000$$

and by adding the depreciation expense we get the operating cash flow after tax:

$$\text{Operating Cash Flow} = 112,000 + 40,000 = 152,000$$

Now, free cash flow is equal to the operating cash flow less the change in total operating assets:

$$\text{Free Cash Flow} = 152,000 - 30,000 = 122,000$$

Using equation (8-15) the total market value of the firm's equity, after adding the marketable securities and subtracting the market value of the debt, is:

$$V_C = \frac{122,000}{0.12 - 0.07} + 25,000 - 450,000 = 2,015,000$$

Finally, to find the per share value of the stock we divide by the number of common shares outstanding:

$$V_C = \frac{2,015,000}{350,000} = 5.76$$

EXHIBIT 8-8
FREE CASH FLOW VALUATION MODEL

	A	B
1	**Front Range Mountaineering Supplies**	
2	**Free Cash Flow Valuation Model**	
3	EBIT	160,000
4	Depreciation	40,000
5	Tax Rate	30%
6	Change in Op Cap	30,000
7	Non-Operating Assets	25,000
8	Market Value of Debt	450,000
9	WACC	12%
10	Growth in FCF	7%
11	Shares Outstanding	350,000
12		
13	NOPAT	112,000
14	Operating Cash Flow	152,000
15	Free Cash Flow	122,000
16		
17	Value of Firm	2,465,000
18	Value of Equity	2,015,000
19	Per Share Value	5.76

Exhibit 8-8 shows a worksheet for performing the valuation. The data in A3:B11 are taken directly from the example problem. Once the data and labels are entered, the formulas are quite simple. As we did above, the first step is to calculate NOPAT in B13 with the formula: `=B3*(1-B5)`. Operating cash flow, in B14, is: `=B13+B4` and free cash flow is: `=B14-B6`.

Again, the value of the entire firm, including debt, is the present value of the free cash flow plus the value of the nonoperating assets. We assume that free cash flow is growing at a constant rate forever, so the formula in B17 is: `=B15/(B9-B10)+B7`. To calculate the value of the firm's equity in B18, we subtract debt: `=B17-B8`. Finally, the per share value of the stock (in B19) is determined by dividing the total market value of the equity by the number of shares outstanding: `=B18/B11`. The result is $5.76 per share, exactly as we got from the formulas.

We have assumed that the company is in a constant growth phase, but this may not be correct for less mature companies. In that case, an analyst will typically create a model of the company over the next five years or so, and then assume constant growth after that. In this case, the nonconstant growth model should be used. The procedure is similar to that shown in Figure 8-4, except that we substitute free cash flow estimates for the dividends and get the value of the entire firm instead of the value of the stock. At that point, proceed as we did above by adding the current value of nonoperating assets and subtracting the current value of the debt to get the market value of the equity.

Relative Value Models

The models presented above are generally known as DCF (discounted cash flow) models. While these models are commonly used by analysts, they rely on forecasts of future cash flows that are often very uncertain. We can mitigate that problem somewhat by using scenario analysis with several alternative growth rates giving a range of values. However, we can also use a different kind of model altogether: *relative value models*.

Relative value models provide a way to value a stock relative to other, similar stocks using valuation ratios such as the price to earnings (P/E) ratio. These models have two major advantages: they are easy to use, and they can be used to value stocks for which the DCF models fail. For example, it is difficult to use the dividend discount models for stocks that don't currently pay a dividend and may not for the foreseeable future. However, as long as the company has positive earnings, you can use the P/E model. If the company is losing money, then you can use the price to sales (P/S) or price to book value (P/B) models instead.

The P/E ratio is defined as the current stock price divided by the expected earnings per share over the next year:

$$\text{Price to Earnings} = \frac{\text{Price per Share}}{\text{Earnings per Share}} \tag{8-16}$$

The essential idea is that the P/E ratio tells us how much investors are willing to pay for each dollar of expected earnings. Therefore, all we need is an estimate of earnings and a "justified" P/E ratio. For two identical companies, the P/E ratio should be the same. No two companies are ever identical, but if they are similar (in the same industry and share other characteristics), then their P/E ratios should be in the same general neighborhood. The justified P/E ratio is often calculated by averaging the P/E ratios of comparable firms. To value a stock using this model, we merely multiply the expected earnings by the justified P/E ratio:

$$V = EPS_1 \times PE \tag{8-17}$$

Any differences in P/E ratios should be able to be explained by differences in perceived risk or growth rates. If we substitute equation (8-3) into the numerator of equation (8-16), then we can see how the growth rate and required return (which is influenced by risk from a number of sources) affect the P/E ratio:

$$\text{P/E} = \frac{D_1/(k-g)}{EPS_1} \tag{8-18}$$

Note that a higher required return, as would be used for a riskier firm, will lead to a lower P/E ratio. Also, a company with a higher growth rate should have a higher P/E ratio. Now we can determine if a stock is undervalued or overvalued by comparing its P/E ratio to the average of its peers. If it has a higher-than-average P/E that doesn't seem to be justified by lower risk or higher growth, then the stock is overvalued relative to its peers. We can also compare the current P/E to the historical average for the firm to determine if it is undervalued or overvalued compared to the past.

Now suppose that the company doesn't have any earnings. A negative P/E ratio is meaningless, so we can't use that model. However, we can use the P/S ratio or the P/B ratio instead. In addition to the above ratios, several others can be used. For example, the Enterprise Value to EBIT ratio is commonly used by analysts, particularly to compute the takeover value of a company. *Enterprise value* is defined as the market value of the firm's equity plus the market value of debt less the amount of cash and equivalents on the balance sheet.

The relative value models are very commonly used by analysts these days, but they are not without their drawbacks. One of the problems is that there is no way to know what absolute value of a P/E ratio is appropriate. Instead, the models are relative. Therefore, if you are comparing one company to several other overvalued stocks, you will come up with a value that is too high. Another problem is that no two companies are the same, and it can be difficult to figure out whether valuation differences are due to expectations about risk, growth rates, or both. Finally, the relationship that should exist between earnings growth, risk, and P/E ratio is not clear and may change over time. Still, used with caution, relative value models can be used to validate the results of a DCF analysis.

Preferred Stock Valuation

Preferred stock is a kind of hybrid security. It represents an ownership claim on the assets of the firm, like common stock, but holders of preferred stock do not benefit from increases in the firm's earnings and they generally cannot vote in corporate elections, like bonds. Further, like a bond, preferred stock generally pays a fixed dividend payment each period. Also, like a common stock, there is no predefined maturity date, so the life of a share of preferred stock is effectively infinite.

With the complex nature of preferred stock, it would be natural to assume that it must be difficult to determine its value. As we will see, preferred stock is actually quite easy to value. To see how we can derive the valuation formula for preferred stock, consider the following example.

> The XYZ Corporation has issued preferred stock that pays a 10% annual dividend on its $50 par value. If your required return for investments of this type is 12%, what is the maximum amount that you should be willing to pay for a share of XYZ preferred?

As usual, the first step in valuing preferred stock is to determine the cash flows. In the case of XYZ preferred, we have an infinite stream of dividends that are 10% of the par value. That is, we have a perpetual annuity, or perpetuity, of $5 per year. Figure 8-6 illustrates the expected cash flows for XYZ preferred stock.

FIGURE 8-6
TIMELINE FOR XYZ PREFERRED STOCK

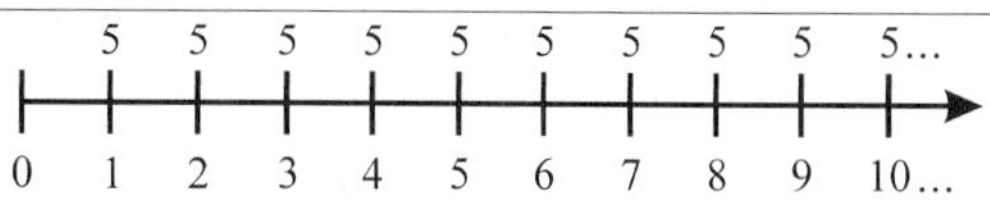

One way that we can arrive at a valuation formula for preferred stock is to realize that the cash flows resemble those of common stock. Preferred stock pays a dividend and never matures, just like common stock. The only difference, as far as the cash flows are concerned, is that the dividend never changes. In other words, the growth rate is zero. Therefore, we can say that the value of preferred stock is:

$$V_P = \frac{D_0(1+g)}{k_P - g}$$

but since the growth rate is 0 we can simplify this to:

$$V_P = \frac{D}{k_P} \tag{8-19}$$

Notice that the subscript has been dropped on the dividend because all dividends are equal.

As an alternative, we can value the preferred stock as an annuity with an infinite life using equation (7-5). In this case, we have:

$$V_P = D \left[\frac{1 - \dfrac{1}{(1 + k_P)^\infty}}{k_P} \right]$$

Realizing that any number greater than 1 raised to an infinite power is equal to infinity, we can rewrite this expression as:

$$V_P = D \left[\frac{1 - \dfrac{1}{\infty}}{k_P} \right]$$

But any number divided by infinity is effectively equal to 0, so this equation reduces to:[9]

$$V_P = \frac{D}{k_P}$$

which is exactly the same as equation (8-19). So, for valuation purposes, regardless of whether we treat preferred stock like common stock or perpetuity, we arrive at exactly the same valuation formula. To find the value of a share of preferred stock, we simply need to divide its dividend payment by our required rate of return. Therefore, the value of XYZ's preferred stock must be:

$$V_P = \frac{5}{0.12} = 41.66$$

---

9. Actually, we can't divide by infinity. Instead, we should take the limit as N approaches infinity.

You can prove this to yourself by recreating Exhibit 8-4 (page 247) with all of the dividends set to 5.

Summary

The valuation process is important to both financial managers and investors. As we will see in future chapters, understanding the valuation process is crucial to making sound financial decisions.

In this chapter we found that the value of a security depends on several factors:

- The size of the expected cash flows
- The timing of the expected cash flows
- And the perceived riskiness of the expected cash flows

Once the cash flows and required rate of return have been determined, we can value the security by finding the present value of its future cash flows.

The actual equations are different for different cash flow patterns, but they all reduce to the present value of future cash flows. The formulas are:

Valuation Model	Formula	Page
Constant-growth common stock	$V_{CS} = \dfrac{D_0(1 + g)}{k_{CS} - g} = \dfrac{D_1}{k_{CS} - g}$	243
Two-stage growth common stock	$V_{CS} = \dfrac{D_0(1 + g_1)}{k_{CS} - g_1}\left[1 - \left(\dfrac{1 + g_1}{1 + k_{CS}}\right)^n\right] + \dfrac{\dfrac{D_0(1 + g_1)^n(1 + g_2)}{k_{CS} - g_2}}{(1 + k_{CS})^n}$	248
Three-stage growth common stock	$V_{CS} = \dfrac{D_0}{K_{CS} - g_2}\left[(1 + g_2) + \dfrac{n_1 + n_2}{2}(g_1 - g_2)\right]$	250

Valuation Model	Formula	Page
Earnings model	$V = \dfrac{EPS_1}{k} + \dfrac{RE_1\left(\frac{r}{k} - 1\right)}{k - g}$	253
Free cash flow model	$V_C = \dfrac{FCF_1}{(WACC - g)} + \text{Nonoperating Assets} - V_D - V_P$	256
Preferred stock	$V_P = \dfrac{D}{k_P}$	262

FUNCTIONS INTRODUCED IN THIS CHAPTER

Purpose	Function	Page
Two-stage growth model	**FAME_TwoStageValue(*DIV1, REQRATE, GROWTHRATE1, GROWTHRATE2, G1PERIODS*)**	249
Three-stage growth model	**FAME_ThreeStageValue(*DIV1, REQRATE, GROWTHRATE1, GROWTHRATE2, G1PERIODS, TRANSPERIODS*)**	250

Problems

1. The Bobco Rawhide Company has a dividend payout ratio of 45%. Next year it will earn $2.15 per share and have a return on equity of 17%. The shareholders' required return is 13%.

    a. Calculate the company's growth rate of EPS.

    b. Using the earnings model, what is the value of the stock?

    c. Using the constant-growth dividend discount model, what is the value of the stock?

2. As an analyst at Churnem & Burnem Securities, you are responsible for making recommendations to your firm's clients regarding common stocks. After gathering data on Denver Semiconductors, you have found that its dividend has been

growing at a rate of 8% per year to the current (D_0) $1.25 per share. The stock is now selling for $24 per share, and you believe that an appropriate rate of return for this stock is 15% per year.

a. If you expect that the dividend will grow at a 8% rate into the foreseeable future, what is the highest price at which you would recommend purchasing this stock to your clients?

b. Suppose now that you believe that the company's new product line will cause much higher growth in the near future. Your new estimate is for a three-year period of 20% annual growth to be followed by a return to the historical 8% growth rate. Under these new assumptions, what is the value of the stock using the two-stage dividend growth model?

c. After considering your assumptions from part B, you realize that it is likely that the growth will gradually transition from 20% down to 8% rather than instantaneously. If you believe that this transition will take five years, what is the value of the stock today? Use the three-stage growth model.

3. The Miracle Clean Company has some new products that it expects to lead to high growth in the near future. It has given analysts the following forecasts for the next three years:

	2008	2009	2010
Depreciation	15,000	21,000	27,000
EBIT	125,000	145,000	165,000
Investment in Operating Assets	35,000	25,000	10,000

The firm's debt has a current market value of $250,000, and it has $64,000 in marketable securities. The expected tax rate is 35%, and the WACC is estimated to be 11%.

a. Calculate the company's free cash flow for each of the next three years.

b. After 2010, free cash flow growth is expected to slow to 8% per year permanently. What is the value of the stock today?

c. Without the new products, free cash flow in 2008 would be $55,000, and it would grow at 8% per year forever. What is the value of the stock if the new products aren't introduced?

Internet Exercises

1. Using the Yahoo! Finance Web site (http://finance.yahoo.com), get the current price and five-year dividend history for Eli Lilly & Co. To gather this data, enter the ticker symbol (LLY) in the Get Quotes box at the top of the page and then click the GO button. Record the current price from this page. Now, at the left side of the quote page, click on the Historical Prices link. To get a table of previous dividends, select Dividends Only at the top of the table, set the Start Date to five years before today's date, and click the Get Prices button. Click the Download to Spreadsheet link at the bottom of the table to download a file with this data. You should have the choice of either saving the file or opening it directly in Excel. It is easier to let it open in Excel. Otherwise, save the .csv (comma-separated variables) file and then open it with Excel. It shouldn't need any further processing other than some formatting. You now have the dividends in a worksheet.

   a. Since LLY pays dividends quarterly, calculate the quarterly percentage change in the dividends. Now, calculate the compound quarterly growth rate of the dividends using the **GEOMEAN** function.

   b. Now, annualize the quarterly dividend growth rate.

   c. Calculate the intrinsic value of the stock using a 10% required rate of return and the calculated annual growth rate. Use the sum of the most recent four dividends as D_0.

   d. How does the calculated intrinsic value compare to the actual market price of the stock? Use an **IF** statement to display whether the stock is undervalued, overvalued, or fairly valued. Would you buy the stock at its current price?

CHAPTER 9

Bond Valuation

After studying this chapter, you should be able to:

1. *Calculate the value of a bond using formulas and built-in functions.*

2. *Describe the factors that determine the price of a bond.*

3. *Calculate the various bond return measures in Excel.*

4. *Understand and demonstrate Malkiel's five bond-pricing theorems.*

5. *Calculate duration and convexity, and use them to make investment decisions.*

Fixed-income securities have long been an important source of capital for governments and corporations, and a relatively secure investment for both individual and institutional investors (pension funds, mutual funds, and insurance companies to name a few). Bonds are the focus of this chapter, but you should understand that the material in this chapter applies to any kind of cash flow.

Note that many of the functions used in this chapter are contained in an Excel add-in named the Analysis ToolPak. This add-in should have been installed when you originally installed Excel, but it is not enabled by default. Before continuing, make sure that you have enabled this add-in through the Tools Add-Ins dialog box.

Bond Valuation

A bond is an interest-bearing, or discounted, security that obligates the issuer to pay the bondholder periodic interest payments and to repay the principal at maturity. Bonds are valued in the same manner as most other securities. That is, the value of a bond is the present value of its future cash flows.

For a bond the cash flows consist of periodic (usually semiannual) interest payments and the return of the principal at maturity. The cash flow at maturity will therefore consist of both the last interest payment and the principal (often $1,000) repayment. For a four-year semiannual payment bond, the timeline is pictured in Figure 9-1.

FIGURE 9-1
TIMELINE FOR A FOUR-YEAR BOND WITH SEMIANNUAL INTEREST PAYMENTS

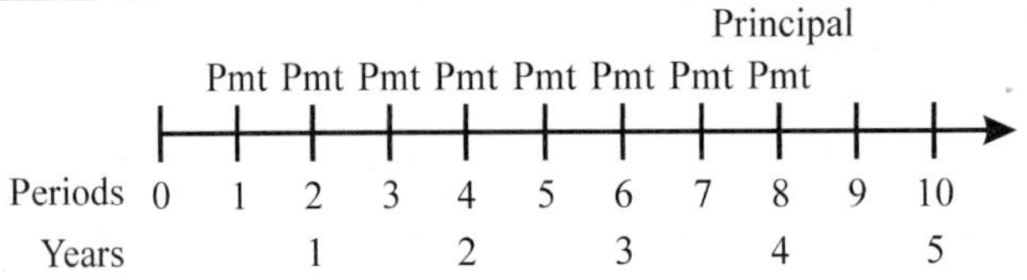

As Figure 9-1 makes clear, a bond consists of two types of cash flows: an annuity (the interest payments) and a lump sum (the principal). Recalling the principle of value additivity from Chapter 7, we know that this stream of cash flows can be valued by adding the present values of its components. For a bond, the value (V_B) is given by:

$$V_B = Pmt \left[\frac{1 - \dfrac{1}{(1 + k_B)^N}}{k_B} \right] + \frac{FV}{(1 + k_B)^N} \qquad (9\text{-}1)$$

where Pmt is the periodic interest payment, k_B is the periodic required rate of return for the bond, N is the number of periods, and FV is the face value. The first term of equation (9-1) is the present value of the stream of interest payments, and the second is the present value of the principal. A word of warning is in order: this formula is valid only on an interest payment date. We will soon discuss the adjustments necessary to fix this problem.

Consider an example problem:

> Nanoterials, Inc., has issued bonds with 20 years to maturity, an 8% coupon rate, and $1,000 face value. If your required rate of return is 9% and the bonds pay interest semiannually, what is the value of these bonds?

Before solving this problem, some definitions are required. Until fairly recently, bonds were printed on ornately decorated paper with small detachable coupons around the edges. These coupons were to be presented to the issuer in order to collect the periodic interest payments. Because of this practice, the interest payment has come to be known as the *coupon payment,* and the rate of interest that the issuer has promised to pay is referred to as the *coupon rate.* The annual interest payment is determined by multiplying the *face value* (principal) by the coupon rate. For bonds that pay interest more frequently than annually, the annual interest payment is divided by the number of payments per year. Most often, interest is paid twice per year, so the annual interest payment must be divided by two.

For the Nanoterials bonds, the annual interest payment is $80 (= $0.08 \times 1,000$), but the semiannual payment is $40 (= $80 \div 2$). Furthermore, because the interest is paid twice per year, we must also adjust the required return and number of periods to a semiannual basis. The required return is 9% per year, which is 4.5% (= $0.09 \div 2$) per six-month period. Since there are 20 years to maturity, there are 40 (= 20×2) six-month periods to maturity. Therefore, the value of the bonds is:

$$V_B = 40 \left[\frac{1 - \dfrac{1}{1.045^{40}}}{0.045} \right] + \frac{1,000}{1.045^{40}} = 907.99$$

As you may have guessed, we can use Excel's **Pv** function to find the value of this bond. Recall that this function allows for both annuity payments and a future value. Now, set up the worksheet pictured in Exhibit 9-1.

EXHIBIT 9-1
BOND VALUATION USING THE PV FUNCTION

	A	B
1	**Bond Valuation**	
2	Time to Maturity (Years)	20
3	Coupon Rate	8.00%
4	Required Return	9.00%
5	Frequency	2
6	Face Value	$ 1,000

Notice that we have added the payment frequency in row 5. This will allow us to change the bond to annual, quarterly, or monthly payments, if necessary. To complete the worksheet, enter Value into A8, and then in B8 add the formula: =PV(B4/B5,B2*B5,-B3*B6/B5,-B6). Take note of the fact that we have made adjustments for the semiannual nature of the payments. Specifically, the coupon rate and payment have been divided by the frequency, and the time to maturity was multiplied by the frequency. Also, the payment amount and the face value were made negative so that the resulting bond value will be a positive number. As expected, the result is a value of $907.99.

Valuing Bonds Between Coupon Dates

As noted above, equation (9-1) only works on coupon payment dates (it is correct twice a year!). The cause of the problem is accrued interest. Specifically, interest does not compound in between coupon dates. Instead, interest accrues equally on each day. For example, three months into a coupon period, the Nanoterials bond will have accrued (that is, earned but not yet paid) interest equal to one-half of the full-period interest, or $20.

Before continuing, let's calculate the value of the bond at the end of period 1. Realize that after one period has elapsed, the bond will now have 39 periods remaining to maturity. The bond will be worth:

$$V_B = 40 \left[\frac{1 - \frac{1}{1.045^{39}}}{0.045} \right] + \frac{1,000}{1.045^{39}} = 908.85$$

The price has increased by $0.86 (about 0.095%), but your required return is 4.5% per period. Where is the rest of your return? You have also earned $40 in interest, so your total return is \$40.86, or 4.5% (= 40.86/907.99). The equation above assumes that the bond is being valued instantaneously after the interest payment is made. So, the total value of your investment at the end of period 1 is \$948.85. Note that we can also arrive at this price by using the future value formula:

$$907.99(1.045)^1 = 948.85$$

This provides the necessary clue to valuing bonds between coupon dates: If we value the bond as of the previous coupon date, and then move it forward by the amount of time elapsed, we will find the total value of the bond. This is known as the invoice price (or, "dirty" price) of the bond. It is the amount that you would actually pay, including the accrued interest paid to the previous owner of the bond. However, bond dealers quote prices without the accrued interest (the "clean," or quoted, price). So, if we subtract the accrued interest from the invoice price (\$948.85), we get the quoted price (\$908.85) at the end of period 1.

So, what is the value of the Nanoterials bond if two months (1/3 of a period) have elapsed since the last coupon was paid? The invoice price ($V_{B,Invoice}$) would be:

$$V_{B,Invoice} = \left(40\left[\frac{1 - \frac{1}{1.045^{40}}}{0.045}\right] + \frac{1,000}{1.045^{40}}\right)(1.045)^{1/3} = 921.41$$

and, to get the quoted price ($V_{B,Quoted}$), we subtract the accrued interest:

$$V_{B,Quoted} = 921.41 - \frac{1}{3}(40) = 908.08$$

Note that if you change your worksheet to reflect the fact that there are 39 2/3 periods (19.83333 years) remaining, you will get the wrong answer (\$908.27, off by about \$0.19). We can fix this by modifying our worksheet. Make a copy of your bond valuation worksheet and change the label in A1 to: `Time to Maturity (Periods)`. In B1, enter: `39 2/3`. Switching to periods, rather than years, will make things a bit easier.

Before entering the formulas, we need to discuss the **ROUNDUP** function. This function rounds a number upwards, and is defined as:

ROUNDUP(*NUMBER, NUM_DIGITS*)

where *NUMBER* is the number to be rounded, and *NUM_DIGITS* is the number of digits to round to. If *NUM_DIGITS* is negative, the *NUMBER* will be rounded to that power of 10. For example, $10^0 = 1$, so if *NUM_DIGITS* is 0 the number will be rounded to the next highest integer. If *NUM_DIGITS* is −1, the number will be rounded to the next highest 10, and so on. You are encouraged to experiment with this function until you understand how it works.

Now, change the label in A8 to: `Invoice Price`. The formula, in B8, will be: `=PV(B4/B5, ROUNDUP(B2,0), -B3*B6/B5,-B6)*(1+B4/B5)^(ROUNDUP(B2,0)-B2)`. This looks complicated, but the **ROUNDUP** function is being used to handle adjustments for the fractional period. The result is $921.41. In A9 enter the label: `Accrued Interest`, and in B9 enter the formula: `=(ROUNDUP(B2,0)-B2)*B3*B6/B5`. Finally, to get the quoted price in B10, enter the formula: `=B8-B9`. The final answer is $908.08, exactly as we found earlier. Your new worksheet should look like the one in Exhibit 9-2.

EXHIBIT 9-2
VALUING A BOND BETWEEN COUPON DATES

	A	B
1	**Bond Valuation**	
2	Time to Maturity (Periods)	39 2/3
3	Coupon Rate	8.00%
4	Required Return	9.00%
5	Frequency	2
6	Face Value	$ 1,000
7		
8	Invoice Price	$ 921.41
9	Accrued Interest	13.33
10	Quoted Price	908.08

The worksheet that we have just created is complex, but it is actually too simple. In the real world, we need to worry about exact dates, not abstract periods. This leads to a couple of additional headaches that our worksheet can't handle. Fortunately, Excel has some add-in functions that can handle these situations without the need for complicated formulas.

Using Excel's Advanced Bond Functions

Excel has a number of built-in functions that can be used for bond valuation. Most of these functions are contained in the Analysis ToolPak add-in function library. Before continuing, go to **T**ools Add-**I**ns and make sure that this add-in is loaded.

To find the value of a coupon-bearing bond, Excel provides the **PRICE** function. Note that, unlike equation (9-1), the **PRICE** function works even on nonpayment dates. The **PRICE** function is defined as:

PRICE(*SETTLEMENT*, *MATURITY*, *RATE*, *YLD*, *REDEMPTION*, *FREQUENCY*, *BASIS*)

SETTLEMENT is the date on which money and securities actually change hands,[1] and *MATURITY* is the date on which the last coupon payment is made and the principal is returned. Excel uses the Windows date format to determine if what you have entered is a date. The Windows date format can be changed in the Control Panel if necessary, but most users will accept the default for their country. In the U.S. the default is the Month/Day/Year format so Excel will recognize, say, 2/4/2007 as February 4, 2007, and treat it as a date. You could also enter this date as Feb 4, 2007, and Excel will convert it to a date. Unrecognized date formats are treated as text strings. Dates are converted to a number that represents the number of days since January 1, 1900 (or January 1, 1904, on the Macintosh). In the 1900 date system the serial number 1 corresponds to January 1, 1900. In the 1904 date system the serial number 1 corresponds to January 2, 1904 (January 1, 1904, is 0). To see the actual serial number, you can use the General number format. The difference in date systems is important to those transferring files from PCs to Macs. Using serial numbers makes date math quite simple. For example, you can determine the number of days between two dates with simple subtraction.[2] Also, note that the date serial number is independent of the date format applied.

RATE is the annual coupon rate. **YLD** is the annual required rate of return. In Excel functions, rates are always entered in decimal form, which is different from the convention for financial calculators. If the coupon rate is 10%, you must enter it as 0.10, although Excel will convert a number followed by a percent sign (%) to this format. The effect of the percent sign is to cause Excel to divide the preceding number by 100.

---

1. Before June 1995, the settlement date was five days after the trade. Since that time it has been reduced by the SEC to three business days after the trade. This policy is known as T+3.

2. As an interesting, if pointless, demonstration of the power of serial date numbers and custom formatting, consider the following: To determine exactly how old you are, enter your birth date in a blank cell of a worksheet, say A1. In A2 enter the formula: =TODAY()-A1. The **TODAY()** function returns the serial number of the current date. Now, choose the Custom Category in the Number Format dialog box and type the following format in the **T**ype box: y" years "m" months and "d" days" and click on OK. We leave as an exercise for the reader the extension of this to display hours, minutes, and seconds.

REDEMPTION is the amount to be received per $100 of face value when the bond is redeemed. It is important to realize that the redemption price can be different than the face value of the bond. This would be the case, for example, if the bond was called by the issuer. Calling a bond issue is very similar to refinancing a mortgage in that the issuer usually wishes to reissue debt at a lower interest rate. There is often a premium that is paid to bondholders when bonds are called, and this premium plus the face value is the redemption price. If a bond issue has a 4% call premium, then **REDEMPTION** would be set to 104. For noncallable bonds, this will be set to 100.

FREQUENCY is the number of coupons paid each year. Most commonly this will be 2, though other values are possible. Excel will return the #NUM! error if **FREQUENCY** is any value other than 1, 2, or 4 (annual, semiannual, or quarterly). Note that bonds that pay interest on a monthly basis, while rare, do exist.[3] This function does not work with such bonds.

BASIS describes the assumption regarding the number of days in a month and year. Historically, different financial markets have made different assumptions regarding the number of days in a month and a year. Corporate, agency, and municipal bonds are priced assuming that there are 30 days in a month and 360 days in a year (a "bankers year"). Treasury securities are priced assuming a 365-day year (366 days in a leap year) and the actual number of days in a month.[4] Excel allows for four possibilities [days per month/days per year (code)]: 30/360 (0 or omitted); actual/actual (1); actual/360 (2); actual/365 (3). Any number greater than 3 will result in an error. For our purposes, the basis is unlikely to make a difference in the calculated price. However, if you are trading in large numbers of bonds, the basis can make a significant difference.

To see how the **PRICE** function works, open a new worksheet and enter the data displayed in Exhibit 9-3, which is taken from the example. The settlement date should be entered by simply typing the date as it appears. As noted above, Excel will automatically recognize it as a date. Recall that the Nanoterials bonds mature in 20 years. We have assumed that the settlement date is 2/15/2007, and that the

---

3. For example, Citigroup has a 5.25% bond that matures on 8/15/2020 and pays monthly coupons. The CUSIP number is 1730T3AF0.

4. For more information on day-count conventions, see *Standard Securities Calculation Methods*, by John J. Lynch, Jr., and Jan H. Mayle, Securities Industry Association, 1986.

maturity date is 2/15/2027. In actual practice, the maturity date of the bond could be found in the indenture,[5] by simply asking a broker, or by consulting a bond guide.

EXHIBIT 9-3
BOND VALUATION WORKSHEET USING THE PRICE FUNCTION

	A	B
1	**Bond Valuation**	
2	Settlement Date	2/15/2007
3	Maturity Date	2/15/2027
4	Coupon Rate	8.00%
5	Required Return	9.00%
6	Redemption Value	100
7	Frequency	2
8	Basis	0
9		
10	Value	$ 907.99

The current value of the bond can now be found by entering the function: =PRICE(B2,B3,B4,B5,B6,B7,B8)*10 in B10. The value is $907.99, exactly as we found by hand. Since bond prices are normally quoted as a percentage of par value, we have multiplied the **PRICE** function's return value by 10. This will convert the output to an actual price. If the face value is something other than $1,000, you will have to use a different multiplier. Also notice that we have not made any adjustment for the fact that the bond pays interest semiannually. Excel automatically makes this adjustment for you based on the frequency.

What is the value of the bond two months after the settlement date? Earlier, we found that the quoted price was $908.08, but that required a complicated formula using both the **PV** and **ROUNDUP** functions. The **PRICE** function will automatically calculate the quoted price between coupon dates, so all we need to do is set the settlement date to 4/15/2007 in B2. The answer is $908.08, as we found earlier.

Bond Return Measures

Most often, investors don't decide to buy a bond just because the price is below some calculated intrinsic value. Instead, they will examine available alternative investments and compare bonds on the basis of the returns that they offer. There are

---

5. The indenture is the formal agreement which specifies all of the conditions of the bond issue.

several ways to calculate the returns offered by bonds. In this section we will cover three return measures for bonds and two additional measures for discounted debt securities.

Current Yield

The current yield is defined as the annual coupon payment divided by the current price of the bond:

$$CY = \frac{\text{Annual Pmt}}{V_B} \qquad (9\text{-}2)$$

The current yield is considered to be a rough measure of the return earned over the next year. We say that it is rough because it ignores compounding and the change in price which may occur over the life of the bond.

Excel has no built-in function to calculate the current yield, but it is a simple matter to write the formula yourself. On your worksheet, move to A11 and type: Current Yield. Now, in B11 enter: =(B4*B6*10)/B10. We must multiply the redemption value (in B6) by 10 to convert to the annual interest payment. In our example the current yield is 8.81%, which is, in fact, the return that you would earn over the next year if you received $80 in interest on an investment of $907.99. However, if interest rates remain unchanged over the year, the value of the bond will increase to $909.75. The capital gain of $1.76 is ignored in the current yield calculation. Note that when a bond is selling at a discount to its face value, the current yield will understate the total return. If the bond is selling at a premium, then the current yield will overstate the total return.

Yield to Maturity

The *yield to maturity* is the compound annual rate of return that can be expected if the bond is held to maturity. The yield to maturity is not without its problems as a return measure, but it is superior to the current yield because it accounts for both interest payments and capital gains. Unfortunately, it is also much more complex to calculate.

Essentially, the yield to maturity is found by taking the bond price as given and solving the valuation equation for the required return (k_B).[6] No method exists, however, to solve directly for the yield to maturity. The yield can be found by using a trial-and-error approach, but it is a bit tedious. Excel makes the yield calculation simple with its built-in **YIELD** function, which is defined as:

YIELD(*SETTLEMENT, MATURITY, RATE, PR, REDEMPTION, FREQUENCY, BASIS*)

All of the variables are the same as previously defined with the exception of *PR*, which is the price of the bond as a percentage of the face value.

To make the calculation, first place the label: Yield to Maturity in A12 and then enter: =YIELD(B2,B3,B4,B10/10,B6,B7,B8) in B12. Note that the only difference from the **PRICE** function is that we replaced *YLD* with the current price of the bond as a percentage of par. In this case, we had to convert the bond price (in B10) back to a percentage of par by dividing it by 10. The result, as should be expected, is 9%.

Note that we could also use the **RATE** function (see page 212) to find the yield to maturity if we assume that the settlement date is also an interest payment date for the bond. This technique is especially useful if you don't know the exact settlement and maturity dates for the bond, and if you are calculating the yield on a payment date. Rather than replace our **YIELD** function, we'll simply insert the **RATE** function in C12 so that we can compare the results. In C12 enter the function: =RATE((B3-B2)/365*B7,B4*B6/2,-B10/10,B6)*2.

In order to use this function, we've had to embed several calculations. For the number of periods, we are taking the difference between the maturity and settlement dates to find the number of days. We next convert this to the number of periods by dividing by 365 and multiplying by the number of periods in a year. The payment amount is simply the coupon rate times the face (redemption) value divided by two. Finally, we need to adjust the price of the bond by dividing by 10 to convert it to a percentage of the face value. You'll note that after annualizing the result by doubling (because it pays semiannually), the answer is the same 9% as before.

---

6. It should be noted that for most purposes the terms "required return" and "yield to maturity" can be used interchangeably, and often are. However, there is a slight, but important difference between the terms. Specifically, the required return is specified by the investor, and can be different for different investors. The yield to maturity is not under the control of the investor; instead it is merely a function of the current bond price and cash flows promised from the bond. As such, the yield to maturity will be the same regardless of who calculates it.

As mentioned earlier, there are a few potential problems with the yield to maturity. Implicit in the calculation are some key assumptions: (1) That you hold the bond to maturity; and (2) That you reinvest the cash flows for the rest of the life of the bond at a rate equal to the yield to maturity. Note that if market returns change, and you have to sell the bond before it matures, you will receive a price that is different than you expected. This is known as *price risk*. Furthermore, if market rates change you will be reinvesting the cash flows at a different rate than expected. This is known as *reinvestment risk*. Either, or both, of these factors can cause your actual return to be different from the yield to maturity that was calculated when you purchased the bond. Thus, the combination of price and reinvestment risk is known as *interest rate risk* (see page 290 for more information).

Yield to Call

One other common measure of return is the *yield to call*. As noted earlier, many issuers reserve the right to buy back the bonds that they sell if it serves their interests. In most cases, bonds will be called if interest rates drop substantially so that the firm will save money by refinancing at a lower rate. If we calculate the yield to maturity assuming that the bond will be called at the first opportunity, we will have calculated the yield to call. Since it is common to have a contractual obligation to pay a premium over par value if the bonds are called, this must be taken into account in our calculation. Note that the call schedule specifies the exact call dates (typically, once per year on an anniversary date) and the premiums on those dates.

In order to make this calculation we must add a couple of lines to our worksheet. First, insert a row above row 4. To do this highlight row 4, and choose **I**nsert **R**ows. Now, in A4 type: `First Call Date` to indicate that this is the first date at which the firm has the option of calling the bonds. In B4 enter: `2/15/2012`. This date reflects the fact that the first call date is often a few years after the issue date (which we are assuming is the same as the settlement date in this case). Next, insert a row above row 8 and label it in A8: `Call Price`. Cell B8 will be the price at which the bonds can be called, in this case 5% over par value, so enter: `105`. In A15, enter the label: `Yield to Call`.

Finally, we will calculate the yield to call in B15 with the formula: `=YIELD(B2,B4,B5,B11/10,B8,B9,B10)`. This is exactly the same formula as the yield to maturity, except that we have changed the maturity date to the call date, and the redemption value to the call price. Note that the call premium plus the earlier receipt of the face value has caused the yield to call to be 11.23%. Of course, the issuer would never call the bond under these circumstances because interest rates have risen since the bond was originally issued.

Your worksheet should now resemble the one in Exhibit 9-4.

EXHIBIT 9-4
BOND VALUATION WORKSHEET WITH YIELD TO CALL ADDED

	A	B
1	**Bond Valuation**	
2	Settlement Date	2/15/2007
3	Maturity Date	2/15/2027
4	First Call Date	2/15/2012
5	Coupon Rate	8.00%
6	Required Return	9.00%
7	Redemption Value	100
8	Call Price	105
9	Frequency	2
10	Basis	0
11	Value	$ 907.99
12	**Return Measures**	
13	Current Yield	8.81%
14	Yield to Maturity	9.00%
15	Yield to Call	11.23%

Returns on Discounted Debt Securities

Not all debt instruments are bonds of the type that we have discussed above. Money market securities are short-term, high-quality debt instruments that are sold on a discounted basis. That is, they do not pay interest; instead, they are sold for less than their face value. Since the full face value is returned to the investor at maturity, the interest is the difference between the face value and the purchase price. Examples of this type of security would include U.S. Treasury Bills, commercial paper, banker's acceptances, and short-term municipals.

Returns on discount securities are usually quoted on a bank discount basis. The bank discount rate is calculated as follows:

$$BDR = \frac{FV - P_0}{FV} \times \frac{360}{M} \tag{9-3}$$

where FV is the face value of the security, P_0 is the purchase price, and M is the number of days until maturity. For example, if you purchase a six-month (181-day) T-Bill for $985, the bank discount rate is:

$$BDR = \frac{1,000 - 985}{1,000} \times \frac{360}{181} = 0.02983 = 2.983\%$$

We can calculate the bank discount rate in Excel using the **DISC** function:

$$\textbf{DISC}(\textit{Settlement, Maturity, Pr, Redemption, Basis})$$

All of the variables are as previously defined. To see how this function works, insert a new worksheet into your workbook and enter the data in Exhibit 9-5.

EXHIBIT 9-5
CALCULATING THE BANK DISCOUNT RATE

	A	B
1	**Discount Securities**	
2	Settlement Date	2/15/2007
3	Maturity Date	8/15/2007
4	Redemption Value	100
5	Purchase Price	98.50
6	Days to Maturity	181
7		
8	Bank Discount Rate	2.983%

Notice that both the redemption value and purchase price are entered as a percentage of par, though we could enter the actual values. In B8 enter the **DISC** function as: =DISC(B2,B3,B5,B4,2). Note that we have set the *BASIS* to 2 because we are using the actual/360 day-count convention. The answer is 2.983%, exactly as we calculated in equation (9-3).

The bank discount rate is the method that is used to quote discount securities in the market. However, it does have a couple of problems: (1) It uses the face value as the basis for calculating the return, but you have only paid the purchase price, not the face value. (2) It assumes that there are only 360 days in a year, instead of 365 (366 in a leap year). We can solve these problems by calculating the bond equivalent yield:

$$BEY = BDY \times \frac{FV}{P_0} \times \frac{365}{360} = \frac{FV - P_0}{P_0} \times \frac{365}{M} \tag{9-4}$$

Note that the bond equivalent yield is simply a "fixed" version of the bank discount rate: We are using the purchase price as the basis for calculating the return, and changing the day count convention to actual/actual. This allows us to compare the yield to yields on coupon-bearing bonds. In this example the bond equivalent yield is:

$$BEY = 0.02983 \times \frac{1,000}{985} \times \frac{365}{360} = \frac{1,000 - 985}{985} \times \frac{365}{181} = 0.03071 = 3.071\%$$

As you might expect, Excel has a built-in function to calculate the bond equivalent yield:

YIELDDISC(*SETTLEMENT, MATURITY, PR, REDEMPTION, BASIS*)

In A9 of your worksheet enter the label: `Bond Equivalent Yield`, and in B9 enter the formula: `=YIELDDISC(B2,B3,B5,B4,3)`. Note that the *BASIS* is set to 3 (actual/365) in this case. The answer is 3.071% as we found using the equation.

Bond Price Sensitivities

As should be clear, bond values are a function of several variables: coupon rate, face value, term to maturity, and the required return. It is useful to understand how changes in these variables lead to changes in bond prices.

Burton Malkiel set forth, and rigorously proved, five bond pricing theorems that will help us to understand how bond prices react to changing circumstances:[7]

1. Bond prices move inversely with interest rates.
2. For a given change in yield, long-term bond prices will change more than short-term bond prices.
3. The sensitivity of bond prices to yield changes increases at a decreasing rate as term to maturity increases.
4. For a given change in yields, bond prices will respond asymmetrically. That is, bond prices will rise more when rates fall than they will fall when rates rise.
5. High-coupon bonds are less sensitive to changes in yields than are low-coupon bonds.

In this section, we will examine these theorems in detail.

---

7. Malkiel, Burton G., "Expectations, Bond Prices, and the Term Structure of Interest Rates," *Quarterly Journal of Economics*, May 1962, pp. 197–218.

Changes in the Required Return

Because the value of a bond is the present value of its future cash flows, you probably expect that the value will increase as the interest rate declines, and vice versa. And you would be correct. Let's examine this idea to fix it in your mind, and to point out a factor which you may not have considered.

Return to the worksheet created for our bond valuation example (Exhibit 9-4). We want to create a new section on this worksheet that will show the value of the bond at various interest rates. Move to A19 and enter: YTM, and in B19 enter: Bond Value. Starting in A20, we want a column of interest rates ranging from 1% to 15% in steps of 1% (i.e., 0.01). Create this data series using the **E**dit F**i**ll **S**eries menu command. In B20 we need the value of the bond, using 1% as the required return. Using the **PRICE** function, this can be done with the formula: =PRICE($B$2,$B$3,$B$5,A20,$B$7,$B$9,$B$10)*10. This is the same formula as we used previously in B11, except that we have replaced the rate with the value in A20. Further, we have added dollar signs to fix most of the cell references so that they do not change as we copy this formula down. The interest rate is not fixed because we want it to change in each row.

If you now create an XY (Scatter) chart with the yield on the X-axis and the bond value on the Y-axis, your worksheet should look similar to the one in Exhibit 9-6. We have embellished our graph to show the current price and required rate of return.[8] Confirming Malkiel's first theorem, we can see that the price is inversely related to the required return. Furthermore, the relationship is not linear; instead it is convex to the origin. As we will see, this nonlinear relationship (known as *convexity*) demonstrates the fourth theorem.

---

8. Adding the lines is a simple matter of drawing them in. First, turn on the Drawing toolbar by choosing **V**iew **T**oolbars Drawing. Now, click on the line icon and click and drag the line onto the chart. To alter the style of the lines, click on one of them with the right mouse button and select Format Auto**S**hape from the menu that appears. Make the changes in the dialog box and click OK. To change the other line to the same style, click on it with the left button and choose **E**dit **R**epeat Format Shape.

EXHIBIT 9-6
BOND VALUE FOR VARIOUS REQUIRED RETURNS

	A	B	C	D	E	F	G	H	I
18	**Sensitivity to Yields**								
19	YTM	Bond Value							
20	1%	2266.03							
21	2%	1985.04							
22	3%	1747.90							
23	4%	1547.11							
24	5%	1376.54							
25	6%	1231.15							
26	7%	1106.78							
27	8%	1000.00							
28	9%	907.99							
29	10%	828.41							
30	11%	759.31							
31	12%	699.07							
32	13%	646.36							
33	14%	600.05							
34	15%	559.20							

Move the chart to the right so that column C is exposed. To do this, click once on the chart with the left mouse button and drag it to the right. In C19 enter the label: Change. In C20:C34 we want to enter the change in the bond price from the current price. In other words, the numbers in this range will be the gain or loss that would be experienced if you purchased the bond and then interest rates changed from the original 9% to the value in column A. In C20 enter the formula: =B20-B$28 which will fix the subtracted price at B28. Now copy the formula down the entire range.

In Figure 9-2 we have added some information to the chart that shows how the bond price will change. Examine cells C20:C34 in your worksheet carefully. In particular, notice that the price changes are not symmetric. For example, if the yield falls by 4% (to 5%), the price rises by $468.55. However, if the rate rises by 4% (to 13%), the price falls by only $261.63. In other words, as yields drop the price rises by more than it falls if yields rise a similar amount. This confirms Malkiel's fourth theorem.

FIGURE 9-2
BOND VALUE VS. REQUIRED RETURN

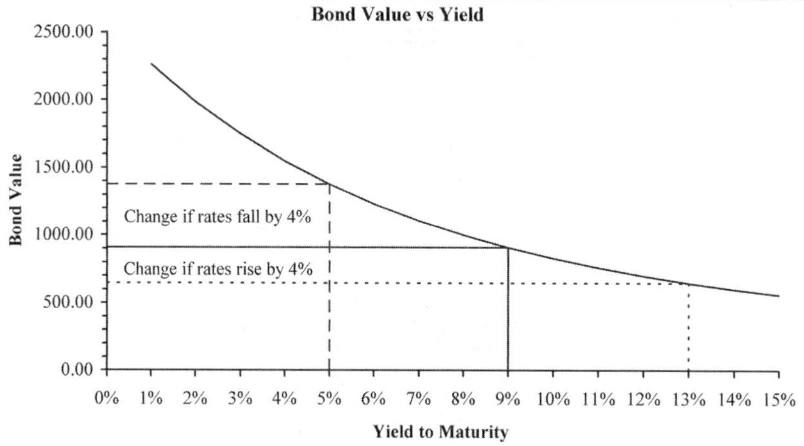

Changes in Term to Maturity

As a bond approaches its maturity date, the bond price must approach its face value (ignoring accrued interest). Since a bond can sell at a premium (above face value), at face value, or at a discount (below face value), the investor may realize a capital loss, no gain or loss, or a capital gain if they hold the bond to maturity.

To see how the price changes as maturity approaches, move to A37 and enter the labels so that your worksheet resembles the one in Exhibit 9-7. Create a series in A39:A59 from 20 down to 0. Use the **E**dit F**i**ll **S**eries command with a step value of –1. Notice that we have included a column for a second bond. Make a copy of the original bond data (in B2:B11) and place it in C2:C11. The only difference between the two bonds will be the required return. For the second bond set the required return to 7%, and notice that the price of this bond is $1106.72. We are doing this to compare bonds selling at a discount and premium as they move toward maturity.[9]

---

9. Note that this is a contrived situation. The "law of one price" guarantees that identical cash flows, with the same level of risk, will have identical prices, and thus identical yields. If this situation actually existed, arbitrageurs would buy bond 1 (driving its price up) and short sell bond 2 (driving its price down) until the prices were the same.

In B39, we want to enter the **PRICE** function for the first bond allowing only the time to maturity to change. The formula to do this is: =PRICE(B$2,EDATE (B$2 $A39*12),B$5,B$6,B$7,B$9,B$10)*10. Since the second argument is the maturity date, we must calculate it based on the number of years that is given in A39. To do this we used the **EDATE** function, which returns a date that is a number of months after the *START_DATE*:

$$\text{EDATE}(\textit{START\_DATE}, \textit{MONTHS})$$

In this case, we are using the settlement date for the *START_DATE*, and the number of months is the number of remaining years to maturity multiplied by 12 to convert it to months.

Copy this formula to C39 to find the price of the second bond, and then copy both of these down the entire range. Note that the **PRICE** function will return a #NUM! error when the term to maturity is 0. Therefore, in B59 enter the formula: =B$7*10 to get the face value. The numbers in your worksheet should be the same as those in Exhibit 9-7.

EXHIBIT 9-7
BOND PRICES VS. TIME TO MATURITY

	A	B	C
37	**Sensitivity to Time to Maturity**		
38	Years to Maturity	Bond 1	Bond 2
39	20	907.99	1,106.78
40	19	909.75	1,104.21
41	18	911.67	1,101.45
42	17	913.77	1,098.50
43	16	916.06	1,095.34
44	15	918.56	1,091.96
45	14	921.29	1,088.34
46	13	924.27	1,084.45
47	12	927.52	1,080.29
48	11	931.08	1,075.84
49	10	934.96	1,071.06
50	9	939.20	1,065.95
51	8	943.83	1,060.47
52	7	948.89	1,054.60
53	6	954.41	1,048.32
54	5	960.44	1,041.58
55	4	967.02	1,034.37
56	3	974.21	1,026.64
57	2	982.06	1,018.37
58	1	990.64	1,009.50
59	0	1,000.00	1,000.00

Notice that the first bond slowly increases in price as the time to maturity declines. The second bond's price, however, slowly decreases in price as time to maturity declines. This demonstration assumes that yields remain constant for the next 20 years. In actuality, required yields change on a daily basis, so the change in price will not be as smooth as the worksheet shows.

To see this more clearly, create an XY chart of this data with the Chart Wizard by selecting A38:C59. Once the chart is created, you may want to adjust the scale of the Y-axis. Right-click the Y-axis and choose Format Axis, then click on the Scale tab. Now set the Minimum edit box to: 850. This will change the scale so that the origin of the Y-axis is at 850, effectively magnifying the area of the chart that we are interested in. Note that we have also added a line to indicate the par value of the bond. In cell D39 enter: 1000 and copy it down to the rest of the range. Now, select D39:D59 and drag the series over the chart and drop it there. You should see that the data has been added to the chart as a new series. After adding labels to the chart, this part of your worksheet should look like Exhibit 9-8.

EXHIBIT 9-8
BOND PRICE VS. TIME TO MATURITY

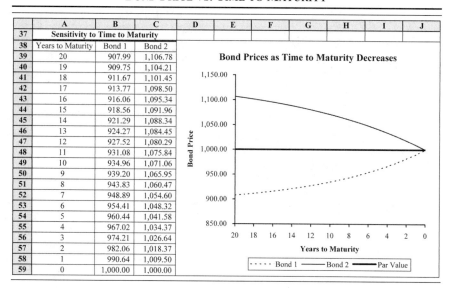

	A	B	C	D	E	F	G	H	I	J
37	Sensitivity to Time to Maturity									
38	Years to Maturity	Bond 1	Bond 2							
39	20	907.99	1,106.78							
40	19	909.75	1,104.21							
41	18	911.67	1,101.45							
42	17	913.77	1,098.50							
43	16	916.06	1,095.34							
44	15	918.56	1,091.96							
45	14	921.29	1,088.34							
46	13	924.27	1,084.45							
47	12	927.52	1,080.29							
48	11	931.08	1,075.84							
49	10	934.96	1,071.06							
50	9	939.20	1,065.95							
51	8	943.83	1,060.47							
52	7	948.89	1,054.60							
53	6	954.41	1,048.32							
54	5	960.44	1,041.58							
55	4	967.02	1,034.37							
56	3	974.21	1,026.64							
57	2	982.06	1,018.37							
58	1	990.64	1,009.50							
59	0	1,000.00	1,000.00							

Comparing Two Bonds with Different Maturities

When investors decide to purchase bonds, they have myriad choices including many combinations of term to maturity and coupon rates. Malkiel's second theorem says that long-term bond prices will change more than short-term bond prices when yields change. To see this, make a copy of A1:C11 from your worksheet and paste it into a new worksheet.

Our first goal is to set up the worksheet so that both bonds are identical, and then we will change the maturity date of the second bond. Previously, the only difference between the bonds was the required return. So, change that to: 9% for the second bond (cell C6). Now, change the maturity date for the second bond, in C3, to: 2/15/2017. It is now a 10-year bond, while the first bond is a 20-year bond. Set up the rest of the worksheet as shown in Exhibit 9-9.

EXHIBIT 9-9
PRICE CHANGES WITH DIFFERENT MATURITIES

	A	B	C
1	**Bond Valuation**		
2	Settlement Date	2/15/2007	2/15/2007
3	Maturity Date	2/15/2027	2/15/2017
4	First Call Date	2/15/2012	2/15/2012
5	Coupon Rate	8.00%	8.00%
6	Required Return	9.00%	9.00%
7	Redemption Value	100	100
8	Call Price	105	105
9	Frequency	2	2
10	Basis	0	0
11	Value	$907.99	$ 934.96
12			
13	Yield	Bond 1	Bond 2
14	9%		
15	12%		
16	Price Change		
17	Percentage Change		

In B14:C15 we will calculate the prices of the two bonds at the yields given in A14:A15. This will allow us to see how the prices change at different yields. In B14, enter the formula: =PRICE(B$2,B$3,B$5,$A14,B$7,B$9,B$10)*10, and then copy it to the other cells. In B16:C16 we want to calculate the price changes, so the formula in B16 is: =B15-B14. Copy that to C16. Finally, calculate the percentage change in B17 with: =B15/B14-1 and copy that formula to C17.

Notice that our starting yield is 9%, as before. If you purchased either bond and then rates instantaneously rose to 12%, the prices would fall by $208.92 (−23.01%) and $164.36 (−17.58%), respectively. Recall that the bonds are identical, except for their terms to maturity. The price of Bond 1 fell by more because it is a longer-term bond. Now, change the yield in A12 to 6%, so that the prices will now rise. Note that the price of Bond 1 rises by more than the price of Bond 2.

Now, change the maturity date on Bond 2 to: 2/15/2012, so that it has only five years to maturity. Note how the price of Bond 2 now changes by even less than it did as a 10-year bond. This is just as Malkiel's second theorem claims: Long-term bond prices will change by more (in percentage terms) than short-term bonds when yields change.

Malkiel's third theorem says that the sensitivity to yield changes increases at a decreasing rate as maturity lengthens. This means that, for example, when compared to a 20-year bond, a 30-year bond isn't that much more sensitive to yield changes. However, a 10-year bond will be considerably less sensitive to yield changes than the 20-year bond.

We can see this in our worksheet very easily. Bond 1 will serve as our point of comparison. First, change the maturity of Bond 2 to: 2/15/2017, and note that its price will rise by 22.87% when yields fall from 9% to 6%. That compares to a 35.59% for Bond 1, which has 10 additional years to maturity. That is a difference of about 12.72%.

Now, change the maturity date of Bond 2 (in C3) to: 2/15/2037. Note that the price change is 42.37%. That is a difference of only 6.78% compared to Bond 1. Finally, change the maturity date to: 2/15/2047. Table 9-1 shows the results.

TABLE 9-1
CHANGES IN PRICE WHEN YIELDS DROP FROM 9% TO 6%

Maturity Date (Term)	Change in Price	Difference from 20-Year Bond
2/15/2017	22.87%	12.72%
2/15/2027	35.59%	0.00%
2/15/2037	42.37%	6.78%
2/15/2047	45.94%	10.35%

This confirms Malkiel's third theorem. While longer-term bonds change more when yields change, the sensitivity decreases as the term increases. So, the difference in interest rate sensitivity between a 30-year bond and a 40-year bond is much less than the difference between a 10-year and 20-year bond.

Comparing Two Bonds with Different Coupon Rates

The fifth theorem says that high-coupon bonds are less sensitive to yield changes than low-coupon bonds are. We can use a slightly modified version of our worksheet to demonstrate this theorem. Make a copy of the previous worksheet, and reset the maturity date of Bond 2 to: 2/15/2027. Change the coupon rate of Bond 2 to: 4%, so that the bonds are identical, except that Bond 2 has a lower coupon rate.

Again, we will modify the yield in A15 to see how the changing yields affect the prices of bonds with different coupon rates. Enter 12% in A15, and notice that Bond 2 (with a lower coupon rate) has a larger percentage loss than Bond 1 (with a higher coupon rate). Now, change A15 to 6% and see that Bond 2 shows a greater percentage gain than Bond 1. Exhibit 9-10 shows this result.

EXHIBIT 9-10
PRICE CHANGES WITH DIFFERENT COUPON RATES

	A	B	C
1	**Bond Valuation**		
2	Settlement Date	2/15/2007	2/15/2007
3	Maturity Date	2/15/2027	2/15/2027
4	First Call Date	2/15/2012	2/15/2012
5	Coupon Rate	8.00%	4.00%
6	Required Return	9.00%	9.00%
7	Redemption Value	100	100
8	Call Price	105	105
9	Frequency	2	2
10	Basis	0	0
11	Value	$ 907.99	$ 539.96
12			
13	Yield	Bond 1	Bond 2
14	9%	907.99	539.96
15	6%	1,231.15	768.85
16	Price Change	323.16	228.89
17	Percentage Change	35.59%	42.39%

In both cases, Bond 1 actually had a larger change in dollar terms. However, that is misleading because the price of Bond 2 starts out at a much lower price (only

$539.96) due to its lower coupon rate. It is the percentage change that matters most, so this confirms theorem five.

Duration and Convexity

We have just demonstrated that long-term bonds and those with low coupon rates are much more sensitive to changes in yields than are short-term bonds and those with high coupon rates. That suggests a trading strategy for bond investors: *If you believe that interest rates will rise, you should move into short-term bonds with high coupon rates. On the other hand, if you believe that rates will fall, you should move into longer-term bonds with low coupon rates.*

Investors frequently make such directional trades based on interest rate forecasts. However, there are many combinations of coupon rates and maturities. Suppose that you have to choose between two bonds: a long-term bond with a high coupon rate, or a short-term bond with a low coupon rate. Which bond will lose less if interest rates rise? Which one will gain more if rates fall? In other words, which bond has the most *interest rate risk*?

Duration

It is difficult to answer those questions without doing the actual calculations. However, in 1938 Frederick Macaulay developed a measure of interest rate risk that can answer this question.[10] *Duration* is a weighted average of the time to receive the cash flows of the bond in present value terms.

Duration combines the effects of maturity, coupon rate, and yield into a single number that we can use to measure the interest rate sensitivity of a bond. The longer the duration, the greater the interest rate risk of the bond. As you might imagine, this allows investors to immediately determine which bond will better suit her portfolio, given her beliefs about future interest rate movements.

---

10. Macaulay, Frederick R., *Some Theoretical Problems Suggested by the Movements of Interest Rates, Bond Yields and Stock Prices in the United States Since 1856.* New York: National Bureau of Economic Research, 1938.

Mathematically, Macaulay's duration is calculated as:

$$D_{Mac} = \frac{\displaystyle\sum_{t=1}^{N} \frac{Pmt_t}{(1+YTM)^t}(t)}{V_B} \qquad\qquad (9\text{-}5)$$

where Pmt_t is the cash flow in period t, and YTM is the per period (usually semiannual) yield to maturity, and V_B is the current price. The fractional part is the present value of each cash flow as a percentage of the bond's price, which serves as the weighting in the average, and t is the number of periods until each cash flow is received. (As with equation (9-1), this formula is only accurate on a payment date.)

As an example, let's calculate the Macaulay duration (D_{Mac}) of Bond 1 from our previous example:

$$D_{Mac} = \frac{\dfrac{40}{1.045^1}(1) + \dfrac{40}{1.045^2}(2) + \dfrac{40}{1.045^3}(3)\ldots + \dfrac{1040}{1.045^{40}}(40)}{907.99} = 19.67 \text{ periods}$$

Note that the semiannual payment is $40, the semiannual yield is 4.5% (= 9%/2), and the current bond price is $907.99. This results in a duration of 19.67 semiannual periods. Duration is actually expressed in years, so we need to divide the result by the payment frequency. Therefore, the Macaulay duration of Bond 1 is 9.83 years.

Excel has a built-in function called, naturally, **DURATION**:

DURATION(*SETTLEMENT, MATURITY, COUPON, YLD, FREQUENCY, BASIS*)

Using the worksheet from Exhibit 9-10, let's calculate the duration of both bonds. In A19 type the label: Macaulay Duration, and in B19 enter the formula: =DURATION(B2,B3,B5,B6,B9,B10). Now copy the formula to C19 to find the duration of Bond 2.

Duration is accurate only for small changes in the yield, so change the yield in A15 to 10%. The duration of Bond 1 is 9.83 years, and for Bond 2 it is 11.45 years. Note that as we left things, the only difference between the two bonds is the coupon rate. In this case, Bond 2 has a longer duration so it should be more sensitive to interest rate changes than Bond 1. If you look at the percentage changes in row 17 (see Exhibit 9-11), you will see that Bond 2 does change more than Bond 1.

EXHIBIT 9-11
CALCULATING THE MACAULAY DURATION

	A	B	C
1	**Bond Valuation**		
2	Settlement Date	2/15/2007	2/15/2007
3	Maturity Date	2/15/2027	2/15/2027
4	First Call Date	2/15/2012	2/15/2012
5	Coupon Rate	8.00%	4.00%
6	Required Return	9.00%	9.00%
7	Redemption Value	100	100
8	Call Price	105	105
9	Frequency	2	2
10	Basis	0	0
11	Value	$ 907.99	$ 539.96
12			
13	Yield	Bond 1	Bond 2
14	9.0%	907.99	539.96
15	9.1%	899.51	534.09
16	Price Change	(8.48)	(5.87)
17	Percentage Change	-0.93%	-1.09%
18			
19	Macaulay Duration	9.83	11.45

If you make changes to the coupon rates and maturity dates, you will see how the duration changes. Pay particular attention to the fact that the bond with the longer duration always has the bigger-percentage price change. So, you can see that duration can be a useful tool for investors trying to gauge interest rate risk.

Modified Duration

If you paid careful attention to the previous exercise, you may have noticed that the Macaulay duration is close to the percentage change in the bond's price. In our original example, changing the yield in A15 to 10% from the original 9% caused a −8.76% change in the price of bond 1. That isn't too much different from the duration of 9.83 years. So, the duration can be used as an estimate of the percentage change in the value of the bond if interest rates change by 1%.

We can get a closer approximation to the percentage change in the bond price by using the *modified duration* (D_{Mod}):

$$D_{Mod} = \frac{D_{Mac}}{\left(1 + \dfrac{YTM}{m}\right)} \tag{9-6}$$

where *m* is the payment frequency. In this case, the modified duration of Bond 1 is:

$$D_{Mod} = \frac{9.83}{\left(1 + \dfrac{0.09}{2}\right)} = 9.41$$

Excel has the **MDURATION** function to calculate modified duration. It is defined as:

MDURATION(*SETTLEMENT, MATURITY, COUPON, YLD, FREQUENCY, BASIS*)

All of the arguments are identical to those in the **DURATION** function. Let's add this function to our worksheet (see Exhibit 9-12). In A20 the label is: `Modified Duration`, and in B20 the formula is: `=MDURATION(B2,B3,B5,B6,B9,B10)`. This gives the same result that we got from the equation above. Now copy this formula to C20.

This is closer to the percentage change in the bond's price, but it still isn't very accurate for a 1% change in the yield. The reason is that the approximation only holds for very small changes in yields. For small yield changes, we can get a very good approximation by using the following formula:

$$\% \text{ Change in Price} \approx -D_{Mod} \times \Delta YTM \tag{9-7}$$

If we change the yield by 0.10% (say, from 9% to 9.1%), then the price of Bond 1 will change by:

$$\% \text{ Change in Price} \approx -9.41 \times 0.001 = -0.0094 = -0.94\%$$

That is very close to the actual price change of −0.934%. We can easily see this in our worksheet. First, change the yield in A15 to: `9.10%`. Now, in A21 add the label: `% Change in Price`, and in B21 the formula is: `=-B20*($A15-$A14)`. Copy that formula to C21, and then notice how similar the values in B21:C21 are to the exact calculations in B17:C17.

EXHIBIT 9-12
CALCULATING THE % PRICE CHANGE USING MODIFIED DURATION

	A	B	C
1	Bond Valuation		
2	Settlement Date	2/15/2007	2/15/2007
3	Maturity Date	2/15/2027	2/15/2027
4	First Call Date	2/15/2012	2/15/2012
5	Coupon Rate	8.00%	4.00%
6	Required Return	9.00%	9.00%
7	Redemption Value	100	100
8	Call Price	105	105
9	Frequency	2	2
10	Basis	0	0
11	Value	$ 907.99	$ 539.96
12			
13	Yield	Bond 1	Bond 2
14	9.0%	907.99	539.96
15	9.1%	899.51	534.09
16	Price Change	(8.48)	(5.87)
17	Percentage Change	-0.93%	-1.09%
18			
19	Macaulay Duration	9.83	11.45
20	Modified Duration	9.41	10.96
21	% Change in Price	-0.94%	-1.10%

Convexity

As noted above, equation (9-7) only works well for small changes in the yield. The reason is that it is a linear approximation to a nonlinear function. Take another look at Figure 9-2 (page 284), and recall that the price/yield function is curved. More specifically, it is convex to the origin. A measure of the curvature is called *convexity*, and it can be used to improve our approximation of the change in price. Convexity (C) can be calculated (on a payment date) with:

$$C = \frac{\frac{1}{(1 + YTM)^2}\left[\sum_{t-1}^{N} \frac{Pmt_t}{(1 + YTM)^t}(t^2 + t)\right]}{V_B} \tag{9-8}$$

Note that, as usual, *YTM* is the per period yield to maturity. We can calculate the convexity of Bond 1 as follows:

$$C = \frac{\dfrac{1}{1.045^2}\left[\dfrac{40}{1.045^1}(1^2+1) + \dfrac{40}{1.045^2}(2^2+2)\dots\dfrac{1040}{1.045^{40}}(40^2+40)\right]}{907.99} = 545.92$$

As with the duration, we need to convert the convexity to an annual number. To do this we divide by the payment frequency squared. So, the annual convexity is:

$$C = \frac{545.92}{2^2} = 136.48$$

What does this number mean? Technically, convexity is the second derivative of the price function with respect to the yield, divided by the price of the bond. Therefore, it can be thought of as the rate of change in the bond's duration. In practice, it is just a measure of the degree of curvature in the price/yield function. The higher the convexity, the more curved is the function.

Unfortunately, Excel does not have a built-in function to calculate convexity. However, we have included the **FAME_CONVEXITY** function in the FameFncs.xla add-in. It will calculate convexity on a payment date, and is defined as:

FAME_CONVEXITY(*SETTLEMENT, MATURITY, FV, COUPON, YLD, FREQUENCY*)

where all of the arguments are as before, except that *FV* is the face value of the bond.

Select row 21 in your worksheet and insert a new row. In A21 enter: Convexity. Now, enter the formula: =FAME_Convexity(B2,B3,B7*10, B5,B6,B9) in B21. Note that we have to convert the redemption value (100) into the actual face value of the bond by multiplying it by 10. Copy this formula to C21. The convexity of Bond 1 is 136.48, and for Bond 2 it is 174.52.

We can use the convexity to improve our approximation of the percentage change in price because it accounts for the curvature of the price/yield function. To do this, we will modify equation (9-7) as follows:

$$\% \text{ Change in Price} \approx -D_{Mod} \times \Delta YTM + \frac{1}{2}C \times \Delta YTM^2 \qquad \text{(9-9)}$$

In your worksheet, change the formula in B22 to: `=-B20*($A15-$A14)+0.5*B21*($A15-$A14)^2`, and copy this formula to C22. Note that our approximation is now correct to two decimal places (see Exhibit 9-13). For bigger changes in the yield, the approximation improves dramatically over using only modified duration. For example, change the yield in A15 to `10%`, and notice how close the approximation is to the exact result.

EXHIBIT 9-13
USING CONVEXITY TO IMPROVE THE ESTIMATED PRICE CHANGE

	A	B	C
1	**Bond Valuation**		
2	Settlement Date	2/15/2007	2/15/2007
3	Maturity Date	2/15/2027	2/15/2027
4	First Call Date	2/15/2012	2/15/2012
5	Coupon Rate	8.00%	4.00%
6	Required Return	9.00%	9.00%
7	Redemption Value	100	100
8	Call Price	105	105
9	Frequency	2	2
10	Basis	0	0
11	Value	$ 907.99	$ 539.96
12			
13	Yield	Bond 1	Bond 2
14	9.0%	907.99	539.96
15	10.0%	828.41	485.23
16	Price Change	(79.58)	(54.73)
17	Percentage Change	-8.76%	-10.14%
18			
19	Macaulay Duration	9.83	11.45
20	Modified Duration	9.41	10.96
21	Convexity	136.48	174.52
22	% Change in Price	-8.73%	-10.09%

Convexity is not only useful for improving the estimate of the percentage change in bond prices. Frankly, with computers we can easily calculate the exact change. Instead, convexity is very useful when comparing bonds that have the same, or similar, durations. The more convex bond will gain more or lose less if yields change. Therefore, more convexity is preferred to less.

Summary

We have seen that the value of a bond is a function of its term to maturity, coupon rate, required return, and face value. In particular, the required return (yield) relative to the coupon rate determines whether the bond sells at par value, or at a discount or premium to par.

The rate of return that is expected for a bond may be computed in several ways. The current yield measures only the income portion of the return, while the yield to maturity takes both income and capital gains (or losses) into account. Therefore, the yield to maturity is superior to the current yield for most purposes. When a bond is callable by the issuer, the yield to call informs us about the return that would be earned if the bond is called at the next call date.

Interest rate risk is comprised of both price risk and reinvestment rate risk. If yields rise, then prices will fall. However, rising yields also mean that interest payments can be reinvested at higher returns. Duration can be used as a measure of the sensitivity of a bond's value to changes in interest rates. The longer the duration, the more the bond price will fluctuate in response to changing rates. Duration takes account of the term to maturity, the coupon rate, and the yield to determine interest rate sensitivity.

Convexity measures the curvature of the price/yield relationship. When comparing bonds with identical durations, more convexity equates to less risk. We can also use convexity to improve estimates of the change in a bond's price when yields change.

FORMULAS USED IN THIS CHAPTER

Purpose	Formula	Page
Value of a bond on a coupon date	$V_B = Pmt \left[\dfrac{1 - \dfrac{1}{(1+k_B)^N}}{k_B} \right] + \dfrac{FV}{(1+k_B)^N}$	268
Current yield	$CY = \dfrac{\text{Annual Pmt}}{V_B}$	276
Bank discount rate	$BDR = \dfrac{FV - P_0}{FV} \times \dfrac{360}{M}$	279

FORMULAS USED IN THIS CHAPTER (CONTINUED)

Purpose	Formula	Page
Bond equiv-alent yield	$BEY = BDY \times \dfrac{FV}{P_0} \times \dfrac{365}{360} = \dfrac{FV - P_0}{P_0} \times \dfrac{365}{M}$	280
Macaulay duration	$D_{Mac} = \dfrac{\displaystyle\sum_{t=1}^{N} \dfrac{Pmt_t}{(1 + YTM)^t}(t)}{V_B}$	291
Modified duration	$D_{Mod} = \dfrac{D_{Mac}}{\left(1 + \dfrac{YTM}{m}\right)}$	293
% Change in price using D_{Mod}	% Change in Price $\approx -D_{Mod} \times \Delta YTM$	293
Convexity	$C = \dfrac{\dfrac{1}{(1 + YTM)^2}\left[\displaystyle\sum_{t=1}^{N} \dfrac{Pmt_t}{(1 + YTM)^t}(t^2 + t)\right]}{V_B}$	294
% Change in price using con-vexity	% Change in Price $\approx -D_{Mod} \times \Delta YTM + \dfrac{1}{2}C \times \Delta YTM^2$	295

FUNCTIONS INTRODUCED IN THIS CHAPTER

Purpose	Function	Page
Round a number up, away from 0	**ROUNDUP(*NUMBER*, *NUM_DIGITS*)**	271
Value of a bond	**PRICE(*SETTLEMENT*, *MATURITY*, *YLD*, *REDEMPTION*, *FREQUENCY*, *BASIS*)**	273
Yield to maturity of a bond	**YIELD(*SETTLEMENT*, *MATURITY*, *RATE*, *PR*, *REDEMPTION*, *FREQUENCY*, *BASIS*)**	277
Bank discount rate	**DISC(*SETTLEMENT*, *MATURITY*, *PR*, *REDEMPTION*, *BASIS*)**	280

FUNCTIONS INTRODUCED IN THIS CHAPTER (CONTINUED)

Purpose	Function	Page
Bond equivalent yield	YIELDDISC(*SETTLEMENT, MATURITY, PR, REDEMPTION, BASIS*)	281
Find a date months after a specified date	EDATE(*START_DATE, MONTHS*)	285
Macaulay duration	DURATION(*SETTLEMENT, MATURITY, COUPON, YLD, FREQUENCY, BASIS*)	291
Modified duration	MDURATION(*SETTLEMENT, MATURITY, COUPON, YLD, FREQUENCY, BASIS*)	293
Convexity on a payment date	FAME_CONVEXITY(*SETTLEMENT, MATURITY, FV, COUPON, YLD, FREQUENCY*)	295

Problems

1. As an investor, you are considering an investment in the bonds of the Conifer Coal Company. The bonds, which pay interest semiannually, will mature in eight years, and have a coupon rate of 7.5% on a face value of $1,000. Currently, the bonds are selling for $900.

    a. If your required return is 9% for bonds in this risk class, what is the highest price you would be willing to pay? (Note: Use the **Pv** function.)

    b. What is the current yield of these bonds? If you hold the bonds for one year, what total rate of return will you earn? Why are these two numbers different?

    c. What is the yield to maturity on these bonds if you purchase them at the current price? (Note: Use the **RATE** function.)

    d. If the bonds can be called in three years with a call premium of 4% of the face value, what is the yield to call on these bonds? (Note: Use the **RATE** function.)

e. Now assume that the settlement date for your purchase would be 7/30/2007, the maturity date is 7/30/2015, and the first call date is 7/30/2010. Using the PRICE and YIELD functions, recalculate your answers to parts A, C, and D.

f. If market interest rates remain unchanged, do you think it is likely that the bond will be called in three years? Why or why not?

g. Create a chart that shows the relationship of the bond's price to your required return. Use a range of 0% to 15% in calculating the prices.

2. After recently receiving a bonus, you have decided to add some bonds to your investment portfolio. You have narrowed your choice down to the following bonds (assume semiannual payments):

	Bond A	Bond B
Settlement Date	12/15/2007	12/15/2007
Maturity Date	4/15/2014	6/15/2025
Coupon Rate	5.00%	9.50%
Price	$890	$1,040
Face Value	$1,000	$1,000
Required Return	7.25%	8.75%

a. Using the PRICE function, calculate the intrinsic value of each bond. Is either bond currently undervalued? How much accrued interest would you have to pay for each bond?

b. Using the YIELD function, calculate the yield to maturity of each bond using the current market prices.

c. Using the DURATION function, which bond would you rather own if you expect market rates to fall by 2% across the maturity spectrum? What if rates will rise by 2%? Why?

3. On May 18, 2006, the U.S. Treasury auctioned the three T-Bills:

	28-Day	**91-Day**	**182-Day**
Issue Date	5/18/2006	5/18/2006	5/18/2006
Maturity Date	6/15/2006	8/17/2006	11/16/2006
Face Value per $100	100	100	100
Price per $100	99.637556	98.801833	97.563222

a. Calculate the bank discount rate for each security using the formulas given in the chapter and using the **DISC** function.

b. Calculate the bond equivalent yield for each security using the formulas given in the chapter and using the **YIELDDISC** function.

c. Go to http://www.publicdebt.treas.gov and find the results of the most recent T-Bill auction. Repeat parts A and B.

Internet Exercises

1. Using the NASD bond search tool (http://www.nasdbondinfo.com/asp/bond_search.asp), find a AAA-rated corporate bond with at least 12 years to maturity. Click the link to get more detailed information on your chosen bond, and then set up a worksheet to answer the following questions. Note that since we are using corporate bonds, the basis should be set to 0 (30/360).

a. Using the information given, calculate the value of the bond using the **PRICE** function.

b. Using the information given, calculate the current yield.

c. Using the information given, calculate the yield to maturity using the **YIELD** function.

d. Calculate the duration of the bond using the **DURATION** function, and the modified duration using **MDURATION**. If interest rates rise by 1%, how much will the price change?

CHAPTER 10

The Cost of Capital

After studying this chapter, you should be able to:

1. Define "hurdle rate" and show how it relates to the firm's Weighted Average Cost of Capital (WACC).

2. Calculate the WACC using both book- and market-value weights.

3. Calculate component costs of capital with flotation costs and taxes.

4. Explain how and why a firm's WACC changes as total capital requirements change.

5. Use Excel to calculate the "breakpoints" in a firm's marginal WACC curve, and graph this curve in Excel.

Suppose that you are offered an investment opportunity that you believe will earn a return of 8%. If your required rate of return is 10%, would you make this investment? Clearly not. Even though you would earn a profit, in the accounting sense of the word, you wouldn't be making as much as required to make the investment attractive. Presumably, you have other investment alternatives, with similar risk, that will earn your required return. So, 10% is the opportunity cost of your funds, and you will reject investments that earn less than this rate. This rate is also known as your cost of capital, and corporations use the concept every day to make investment decisions.

Knowledge of a firm's cost of capital is vital if managers are to make appropriate decisions regarding the use of the firm's funds. Without this knowledge, poor investments may be made that actually reduce shareholder wealth. In this chapter you will learn what the cost of capital is, and how to calculate it.

The Appropriate "Hurdle" Rate

A firm's required rate of return on investments is often referred to as its *hurdle rate* because all projects must earn a rate of return high enough to clear this rate. Otherwise, a project will not cover its cost of financing, thereby reducing shareholder wealth. But what is the appropriate rate to use? Let's look at an example.

The managers of Rocky Mountain Motors (RMM) are considering the purchase of a new tract of land that will be held for one year. The purchase price of the land is $10,000. RMM's capital structure is currently made up of 40% debt, 10% preferred stock, and 50% common equity. Because this capital structure is considered to be optimal, any new financing will be raised in the same proportions. RMM must raise the new funds as indicated in Table 10-1.

TABLE 10-1
FUNDING FOR RMM'S LAND PURCHASE

Source of Funds	Amount	Dollar Cost	After-Tax Cost
Debt	$ 4,000	$ 280	7%
Preferred Stock	1,000	100	10%
Common Stock	5,000	600	12%
Total	10,000	980	9.8%

Before making the decision, RMM's managers must determine what required rate of return will simultaneously satisfy all of their capital providers. What is the minimum rate of return that will accomplish this goal?

Looking at the third column of Table 10-1, it is clear that the total financing cost is $980. So, the project must generate at least $980 in excess of its cost in order to cover the financing costs. This represents a minimum required return of 9.8% on the investment of $10,000. Table 10-2 shows what would happen under three alternative rate of return scenarios.

TABLE 10-2
ALTERNATIVE SCENARIOS FOR RMM

Rate of Return	8%	9.8%	11%
Total Funds Available	$ 10,800	$ 10,980	$ 11,100
Less: Debt Costs	4,280	4,280	4,280
Less: Preferred Costs	1,100	1,100	1,100
Available to Common Shareholders	5,420	5,600	5,720

Recall that the common shareholders' required rate of return is 12% on the $5,000 that they provided. This means that the shareholders expect to get back at least $5,600. If RMM earns only 8%, the common shareholders will receive only $5,420; $180 less than required. We assume that the common shareholders have alternative investment opportunities (with equal risk) that would return 12%. Therefore, if the project can return only 8%, the best decision that the managers could make would be to allow the common shareholders to hold on to their money. In other words, the project should be rejected.

On the other hand, if the project is expected to return 9.8% the common shareholders will receive exactly the amount that they require. If the project returns 11%, they will be more than satisfied. Under these latter two scenarios the project should be accepted because shareholder wealth will either be increased by the amount required ($600) or increased by more than required ($720).[1]

The Weighted Average Cost of Capital

It still remains to determine, in a general way, what required rate of return will simultaneously satisfy all of the firm's stakeholders. Recall that 40% of RMM's funds were provided by the debt holders. Therefore, 40% of this minimum required rate of return must go to satisfy the debt holders. For the same reason, 10% of this minimum required rate of return must go to satisfy the preferred stockholders, and 50% will be required for the common stockholders.

---

1. Note that the difference between the amount that is available to the common shareholders and the amount required is known as the net present value (*NPV*). This concept will be explored in Chapter 11.

In general, the minimum required rate of return must be a weighted average of the individual required rates of return on each form of capital provided. Therefore, we refer to this minimum required rate of return as the *weighted average cost of capital* (WACC). The weighted average cost of capital can be found as follows:

$$WACC = w_d k_d + w_p k_p + w_{cs} k_{cs} \qquad \text{(10-1)}$$

where the *w*'s are the weights of each source of capital, and the *k*'s are the costs (required returns) for each source of capital. In the case of RMM, the WACC is:

$$WACC = 0.40(0.07) + 0.10(0.10) + 0.50(0.12) = 0.098 = 9.80\%$$

which is exactly the required return that we found above.

Determining the Weights

The weights that one uses in the calculation of the WACC will obviously affect the result. Therefore, an important question is, "where do the weights come from?" Actually, there are two possible answers to this question. Perhaps the most obvious answer is to find the weights on the balance sheet.

The balance sheet weights (usually referred to as the *book-value* weights) can be obtained by the following procedure. Find the total long-term debt, total preferred equity, and the total common equity. Add together each of these to arrive at the grand total of the long-term sources of capital. Finally, divide each component by the grand total to determine the percentage that each source is of total capital. Table 10-3 summarizes these calculations for RMM.

TABLE 10-3
CALCULATION OF BOOK-VALUE WEIGHTS FOR RMM

Source of Capital	Total Book Value	Percentage of Total
Long-Term Debt	$400,000	40%
Preferred Equity	100,000	10%
Common Stock	500,000	50%
Grand Total	1,000,000	100%

The problem with book-value weights is that they represent the weights as they were when the securities were originally sold. That is, the book-value weights represent historical weights. The calculated WACC would better represent current reality if we used the present weights. Since the market constantly revalues the firm's securities, and we assume that the capital markets are efficient, we can find the weights by using the current market values of the securities.

The procedure for determining the market-value weights is similar to that used to find the book-value weights. First, determine the total market value of each type of security. Total the results and then divide the market value of each source of capital by the total to determine the weights.

TABLE 10-4
CALCULATION OF MARKET-VALUE WEIGHTS FOR RMM

Source	Price Per Unit	Units	Total Market Value	Percentage of Total
Debt	$ 904.53	400	$ 361,812	31.14%
Preferred	100.00	1,000	100,000	8.61%
Common	70.00	10,000	700,000	60.25%
Totals			1,161,812	100.00%

Table 10-4 shows RMM's current capital structure in market-value terms. Note that, in market value terms, the percentage of common equity has risen considerably, while the percentages of debt and preferred equity have fallen. Using these weights we can see that their WACC is:

$$WACC = 0.3114(0.07) + 0.0861(0.10) + 0.6025(0.12) = 0.1027 = 10.27\%$$

In this example, the book-value WACC and the market-value WACC are quite close together. This is not always the case. Whenever possible, use the market values of the firm's securities to determine the WACC.

WACC Calculations in Excel

We can easily set up a worksheet to do the calculations for the WACC as in Table 10-4. To do this, first copy the data from Table 10-4 into a new worksheet, starting with the headings in A1.

In column D we want to calculate the total market value of the securities, which is the price times the number of units outstanding. So, in D2 enter: =B2* C2 and copy the formula down to D3 and D4. Cell D5 should have the total market value of the securities, so enter: =Sum(D2:D4). In Column E we need the percentage that each security represents of the total market value. These are the weights that we will use to calculate the WACC. In E2 enter: =D2/D$5 and copy down to E3 and E4. As a check, calculate the total in E5.

Next, we want a column for the after-tax costs of each source of capital, and the weighted-average cost of capital. In F1 enter the label: After-tax Cost. Now, in F2:F4 enter the after-tax cost of each component from Table 10-1. We could calculate the WACC in F5 with the formula: =E2*F2+E3*F3+E4*F4. Even easier would be to use the array formula: =SUM(E2:E4*F2:F4); just remember to press Ctrl+Shift+Enter when entering this formula. The completed worksheet appears in Exhibit 10-1. Note that the WACC is exactly as we calculated earlier.[2] You are encouraged to experiment by changing the market prices of the securities to see how the weights, and the WACC, change.

EXHIBIT 10-1
WORKSHEET TO CALCULATE RMM'S *WACC*

	A	B	C	D	E	F
1	Source	Price	Units	Total Market Value	Percentage of Total	After-tax Cost
2	Debt	$ 904.53	400	$ 361,812	31.14%	7.00%
3	Preferred	$ 100.00	1,000	$ 100,000	8.61%	10.00%
4	Common	$ 70.00	10,000	$ 700,000	60.25%	12.00%
5	Totals			$ 1,161,812	100.00%	10.27%

Calculating the Component Costs

Up to this point, we have taken the component costs of capital as a given. In reality, these costs are anything but given, and, in fact, change continuously. How we calculate these costs is the subject of this section.

To begin, note that the obvious way of determining the required rates of return is to simply ask each capital provider what her required rate of return is for the particular

---

2. Note that this is a simplified example. In reality, most companies will have multiple debt issues outstanding, and many have more than one class of common and preferred stock outstanding as well. The calculations will work in exactly the same way, regardless of the number of issues outstanding. However, you will first have to calculate a weighted average cost for each source of capital (e.g., a weighted average after-tax cost of debt).

security that she owns. For all but the most closely held of firms, this would be exceedingly impractical and you would likely get some outlandish responses. However, there is a way by which we can accomplish the same end result.

Recall from Chapter 8 that the market value of a security is equal to the intrinsic value of the marginal investor. Further, if investors are rational, they will buy (sell) securities as the expected return rises above (falls below) their required return. Therefore, we can say that the investors in the firm "vote with their dollars" on the issue of the firm's cost of capital. This force operates in all markets.[3] So at any given moment, the price of a security will reflect the overall required rate of return for that security. All we need, then, is a method of converting the observed market prices of securities into required rates of return.

Since we have already discussed the valuation of securities (common stock, preferred stock, and bonds) you should recall that a major input was the investor's required rate of return. As we will see, we can simply invert the valuation equations to solve for the required rate of return.

The Cost of Common Equity

Because of complexities in the real world, finding a company's cost of common equity is not always straightforward. In this section we will look at two approaches to this problem, both of which we have seen previously in other guises.

Using the Dividend Discount Model

Recall that a share of common stock is a perpetual security, which we assume will periodically pay a cash flow that grows over time. We have previously demonstrated that the present value of such a stream of cash flows is given by equation (8-3):

$$V_{CS} = \frac{D_0(1+g)}{k_{CS} - g} = \frac{D_1}{k_{CS} - g}$$

assuming an infinite holding period and a constant rate of growth for the cash flows.

---

3. Anybody who isn't convinced should check the history of bond and stock prices for companies such as Enron and WorldCom. They were falling dramatically long before those firms filed for bankruptcy.

If we know the current market price of the stock, we can use this knowledge to solve for the common shareholder's required rate of return. Simple algebraic manipulation will reveal that this rate of return is given by:

$$k_{CS} = \frac{D_0(1+g)}{V_{CS}} + g = \frac{D_1}{V_{CS}} + g \qquad (10\text{-}2)$$

Note that this equation says that the required rate of return on common equity is equal to the sum of the dividend yield and the growth rate of the dividend stream. We could also use any of the other common stock valuation models, though solving for the required return is slightly more complicated.

Using the CAPM

Not all common stocks will meet the assumptions of the Dividend Discount Model. In particular, many companies do not pay dividends. An alternative approach to determining the cost of equity is to use the *Capital Asset Pricing Model* (CAPM).

The CAPM gives the expected rate of return for a security if we know the risk-free rate of interest, the market risk premium, and the riskiness of the security relative to the market portfolio (i.e., the security's beta). The CAPM, you will recall, is the equation for the security market line:

$$E(R_i) = R_f + \beta_i(E(R_m) - R_f)$$

Assuming that the stockholders are all price-takers, their expected return is the same as the firm's required rate of return.[4] Therefore, we can use the CAPM to determine the required rate of return on equity.

The Cost of Preferred Equity

Preferred stock, for valuation purposes, can be viewed as a special case of the common stock with the growth rate of dividends equal to zero. We can carry this idea to the process of solving for the preferred stockholders' required rate of

---

4. A price-taker cannot materially affect the price of an asset through individual buying or selling. This situation generally exists in the stock market because most investors are small when compared to the market value of the firm's common stock.

return. First, recall that the value of a share of preferred stock was given by equation (8-19):

$$V_P = \frac{D}{k_P}$$

As with common stock, we can algebraically manipulate this equation to solve for the required return if the market price is known:

$$k_P = \frac{D}{V_p} \tag{10-3}$$

The Cost of Debt

Finding the cost of debt is more difficult than finding the cost of either preferred or common equity. The process is similar: determine the market price of the security, and then find the discount rate which makes the present value of the expected future cash flows equal to this price. This rate is the same as the yield to maturity (see page 276). However, we cannot directly solve for this discount rate. Instead, we must use an iterative trial-and-error process.

Recall that the value of a bond is given by equation (9-1):

$$V_B = Pmt\left[\frac{1 - \frac{1}{(1 + k_d)^N}}{k_d}\right] + \frac{FV}{(1 + k_d)^N}$$

The problem is to find k_d such that the equality holds between the left and right sides of the equation. Suppose that, as in Exhibit 10-1, the current price of RMM's bonds is $904.53, the coupon rate is 10%, the face value of the bonds is $1,000, and the bonds will mature in 10 years. If the bonds pay interest annually, our equation looks as follows:

$$904.53 = 100\left[\frac{1 - \frac{1}{(1 + k_d)^{10}}}{k_d}\right] + \frac{1,000}{(1 + k_d)^{10}}$$

We must make an initial, but intelligent, guess as to the value of k_d. Since the bond is selling at a discount to its face value, we know that the yield to maturity (k_d) must be greater than the coupon rate. Therefore, our first guess should be something greater than 10%. If we choose 12% we will find that the price would be $886.99, which is lower than the actual price. Our first guess was incorrect, but we now know that the answer must lie between 10% and 12%. The next logical guess is 11%, which is the halfway point. Inserting this for k_d we get a price of $941.11, which is too high, but not by much. Further, we have narrowed the range of possible answers to those between 11% and 12%. Again, we choose the halfway point, 11.5%, as our next guess. This results in an answer of $913.48. Continuing this process, we will eventually find the correct answer to be 11.67%.[5]

Making an Adjustment for Taxes

Notice that the answer that we found for the cost of debt, 11.67%, is not the same as that listed in Exhibit 10-1. Because interest is a tax-deductible expense, interest payments actually cost less than the full amount of the payment. In this case, if RMM were to make an interest payment of $116.70, and the marginal tax rate is 40%, it would only cost them $70.02 $(= 116.70 \times (1 - 0.40))$. Notice that $70.02/1,000 \approx 0.07$, or 7%, which is the after-tax cost of debt listed in Exhibit 9-1.

In general, we need to adjust the cost of debt to account for the deductibility of the interest expense by multiplying the before-tax cost of debt (i.e., the yield to maturity) by $1 - t$, where t is the marginal tax rate. Note that we do not make the same adjustment for the cost of common or preferred equity, because dividends are not tax deductible.[6]

Using Excel to Calculate the Component Costs

A general principle that we have relied on in constructing our worksheet models is that we should make Excel do the calculations whenever possible. We will now make changes to our worksheet in Exhibit 10-1 to allow Excel to calculate the component costs of capital.

---

5. The method presented here is known as the bisection method. Briefly, the idea is to quickly bracket the solution and to then choose as the next approximation the answer that is exactly halfway between the previous possibilities. This method can lead to very rapid convergence on the solution if a good beginning guess is used.

6. This is just a close approximation, but close enough for most purposes since the cost of capital is just an estimate anyway. It would be more accurate to use the after-tax cash flows in the equation. This will result in the after-tax cost of debt with no additional adjustment required, and will differ slightly from that given above.

The After-Tax Cost of Debt

We cannot calculate any of the component costs on our worksheet without adding some additional information. We will first add information which will be used to calculate the after-tax cost of debt. Beginning in A7 with the label: `Additional Bond Data`, add the information from Table 10-5 into your worksheet. For simplicity, we assume that the bonds pay interest annually.

TABLE 10-5
ADDITIONAL DATA FOR CALCULATING THE COST OF DEBT FOR RMM

Additional Bond Data	
Tax Rate	40%
Coupon Rate	10%
Face Value	$1,000
Maturity	10

With this information entered, we now need a function to find the cost of debt. Excel provides two built-in functions that will do the job: **RATE** and **YIELD**. We have already seen both of these functions. Since **YIELD** (defined on page 277) requires more information than we have supplied, we will use **RATE**. Recall that **RATE**, which works only on a payment date, will solve for the yield for an annuity-type stream of cash flows and allows for a different present value and future value. Specifically, **RATE** is defined as:

$$\text{RATE}(\textit{NPER, PMT, PV, FV, TYPE, GUESS})$$

The only unusual aspect of our usage of this function is that we will be supplying both a *PV* and an *FV*. Specifically, *PV* will be the negative of the current bond price, and *FV* is the face value of the bond. In F2 enter the **RATE** function as: `=RATE(B11,B9*B10,-B2,B10)`. The result is 11.67%, which we found to be the pretax cost of debt. Remember that we must also make an adjustment for taxes, so we need to multiply by 1 − t. The final form of the formula in F2 then is: `=RATE(B11,B9*B10,-B2,B10)*(1-B8)`, and the result is 7.00%.

With the new bond information, your worksheet should resemble Exhibit 10-2.

EXHIBIT 10-2
RMM WORKSHEET WITH BOND DATA

	A	B	C	D	E	F
1	Source	Price	Units	Total Market Value	Percentage of Total	After-tax Cost
2	Debt	$ 904.53	400	$ 361,812	31.14%	7.00%
3	Preferred	$ 100.00	1,000	$ 100,000	8.61%	10.00%
4	Common	$ 70.00	10,000	$ 700,000	60.25%	12.00%
5	Totals			$ 1,161,812	100.00%	10.27%
6						
7	**Additional Bond Data**					
8	Tax Rate	40%				
9	Coupon Rate	10%				
10	Face Value	$ 1,000				
11	Maturity	10				

The Cost of Preferred Stock

Compared to calculating the after-tax cost of debt, finding the cost of preferred stock is easy. We need only add one piece of information: the preferred dividend. In C7 type: Additional Preferred Data. In C8 type: Dividend and in D8 enter: 10.

We know from equation (10-3) that we need to divide the preferred dividend by the current price of the stock. Therefore, the equation in F3 is: =D8/B3.

The Cost of Common Stock

To calculate the cost of common stock, we need to know the most recent dividend and the dividend growth rate in addition to the current market price of the stock. In E7 type: Additional Common Data. In E8 type: Dividend 0 and in F8 enter: 3.96. In E9 enter the label: Growth Rate and in F9 enter: 6%.

Finally, we will use equation (10-2) to calculate the cost of common stock in F4. Since we know the most recent dividend (D_0) we need to multiply that by $1 + g$. The formula in F4 is: =(F8*(1+F9))/B4+F9, and the result is 12% as we found earlier.

As you will see, we have not yet completed the calculation of the component costs for RMM. We have left out one crucial piece, which we will discuss in the next section. At this point, your worksheet should resemble that in Exhibit 10-3.

EXHIBIT 10-3
RMM COST OF CAPITAL WORKSHEET

	A	B	C	D	E	F
1	Source	Price	Units	Total Market Value	Percentage of Total	After-tax Cost
2	Debt	$ 904.53	400	$ 361,812	31.14%	7.00%
3	Preferred	$ 100.00	1,000	$ 100,000	8.61%	10.00%
4	Common	$ 70.00	10,000	$ 700,000	60.25%	12.00%
5	Totals			$ 1,161,812	100.00%	10.27%
6						
7	**Additional Bond Data**		**Additional Preferred Data**		**Additional Common Data**	
8	Tax Rate	40%	Dividend	$ 10.00	Dividend 0	$ 3.96
9	Coupon Rate	10%			Growth Rate	6%
10	Face Value	$ 1,000				
11	Maturity	10				

The Role of Flotation Costs

Any action that a corporation takes has costs associated with it. Up to this point we have implicitly assumed that securities can be issued without cost, but this is not the case. Selling securities directly to the public is a complicated procedure, generally requiring a lot of management time as well as the services of an *investment banker*. An investment bank is a firm that serves as an intermediary between the issuing firm and the public. In addition to forming the underwriting syndicate to sell the securities, the investment banker also functions as a consultant to the firm. As a consultant, the investment banker usually advises the firm on the pricing of the issue and is responsible for preparing the registration statement for the Securities and Exchange Commission (SEC).

The cost of the investment banker's services, and other costs of issuance, are referred to as *flotation costs*. (The term derives from the fact that the process of selling a new issue is generally referred to as floating a new issue.) These flotation costs add to the total cost of the new securities to the firm, and we must increase the component cost of capital to account for them.

There are two methods for accounting for flotation costs. The most popular method is the cost of capital adjustment. Under this method the market price of new securities is *decreased* by the per unit flotation costs. This results in the net amount that the company receives from the sale of the securities. The component costs are then calculated in the usual way except that the net amount received, not the market price, is used in the equation.

The second, less common, method is the investment cost adjustment. Under this methodology we increase the initial outlay for the project under consideration to account for the total flotation costs. Component costs are then calculated as we did above. The primary disadvantage of this technique is that, because it assigns all flotation costs to one project, it implicitly assumes that the securities used to finance a project will be retired when the project is completed.[7]

Because it is more common, and its assumptions are more realistic, we will use the cost of capital adjustment technique. When flotation costs are included in the analysis, the equations for the component costs are given in Table 10-6.

TABLE 10-6

COST OF CAPITAL EQUATIONS WITH FLOTATION COST ADJUSTMENT

Component	Equation*
Cost of new common equity	$k_{CS} = \dfrac{D_0(1+g)}{V_{CS}-f} + g = \dfrac{D_1}{V_{CS}-f} + g$
Cost of preferred equity	$k_P = \dfrac{D}{V_p-f}$
Pretax cost of debt (solve for k_d)	$V_B - f = Pmt\left[\dfrac{1 - \dfrac{1}{(1+k_d)^N}}{k_d}\right] + \dfrac{FV}{(1+k_d)^N}$

* In these equations the flotation costs (f) are a dollar amount per unit. It is also common for flotation costs to be stated as a percentage of the unit price.

---

7. For more information on both methods, see Brigham and Gapenski, "Flotation Cost Adjustments," *Financial Practice and Education* (Fall/Winter 1991): 29–34.

Adding Flotation Costs to Our Worksheet

We can easily incorporate the adjustment for flotation costs into our worksheet. All we need to do is change the references to the current price in each of our formulas to the current price minus the per unit flotation costs. These costs are given in Table 10-7.

TABLE 10-7
FLOTATION COSTS AS A PERCENTAGE OF SELLING PRICE FOR RMM

Security	Flotation Cost
Bonds	1%
Preferred Stock	2%
Common Stock	5%

Enter the information from Table 10-7 into your worksheet. For each security, we have added the information at the end of the "Additional information" section. For example, in A12 enter: Flotation and in B12 enter: 1%, which is the flotation cost for bonds. Add similar entries for preferred and common stock.

To account for flotation costs, change your formulas to the following:

F2	=RATE(B11,B9*B10,-B2*(1-B12),B10)*(1-B8)
F3	=D8/(B3*(1-D9))
F4	=(F8*(1+F9))/(B4*(1-F10))+F9

Once these changes have been made, you will notice that the cost of each component has risen. Your worksheet should now resemble the one pictured in Exhibit 10-4.

EXHIBIT 10-4
COST OF CAPITAL WORKSHEET WITH FLOTATION COSTS

	A	B	C	D	E	F
1	Source	Price	Units	Total Market Value	Percentage of Total	After-tax Cost
2	Debt	$ 904.53	400	$ 361,812	31.14%	7.10%
3	Preferred	$ 100.00	1,000	$ 100,000	8.61%	10.20%
4	Common	$ 70.00	10,000	$ 700,000	60.25%	12.31%
5	Totals			$ 1,161,812	100.00%	10.51%
6						
7	Additional Bond Data		Additional Preferred Data		Additional Common Data	
8	Tax Rate	40%	Dividend	$ 10.00	Dividend 0	$ 3.96
9	Coupon Rate	10%	Flotation	2%	Growth Rate	6%
10	Face Value	$ 1,000			Flotation	5%
11	Maturity	10				
12	Flotation	1%				

The Cost of Retained Earnings

We have shown how to calculate the required returns for purchasers of new common equity, preferred stock, and bonds, but firms also have another source of long-term capital: retained earnings. Is there a cost to such internally generated funding, or is it free? Consider that managers generally have two options as to what they do with the firm's internally generated funds. They can either reinvest them in profitable projects or return them to the shareholders in the form of dividends or a share repurchase. Since these funds belong to the common shareholders alone, the definition of a "profitable project" is one that earns at least the common shareholder's required rate of return. If these funds will not be invested to earn at least this return, they should be returned to the common shareholders. So there is a cost (an opportunity cost) to internally generated funds: the cost of common equity.

Note that the only difference between retained earnings (internally generated common equity) and new common equity is that the firm must pay flotation costs on the sale of new common equity. Because no flotation costs are paid for retained earnings, we can find the cost of retained earnings in the same way we did before learning about flotation costs. In other words,

$$k_{RE} = \frac{D_0(1+g)}{V_{CS}} + g = \frac{D_1}{V_{CS}} + g \qquad \text{(10-4)}$$

This notion of an opportunity cost for retained earnings is important for a couple of reasons. Most importantly, managers should be disabused of the notion that the funds on hand are "free." As you now know, there is a cost to these funds and it should be accounted for when making decisions. In addition, there may be times when a project that otherwise appears to be profitable is really unprofitable when the cost of retained earnings is correctly accounted for. Accepting such a project is contrary to the principle of shareholder wealth maximization and will result in the firm's stock price falling.

The Marginal WACC Curve

A firm's weighted average cost of capital is not constant. Changes can occur in the *WACC* for a number of reasons. As a firm raises more and more new capital, its *WACC* will likely increase due to an increase in supply relative to demand for the firm's securities. Furthermore, total flotation costs may increase as more capital is raised. Additionally, no firm has an unlimited supply of projects that will return more than the cost of capital, so the risk that new funds will be invested unprofitably increases.

We will see in the next chapter that these increases in the *WACC* play an important role in determining the firm's optimal capital budget. For the remainder of this chapter we will concentrate on determining the *WACC* at varying levels of total capital.

Finding the Breakpoints

We can model a firm's marginal *WACC* curve with a *step function*. This type of function resembles a staircase when plotted. They are commonly used as a linear (though discontinuous) approximation to nonlinear functions. The accuracy of the approximation improves as the number of steps increases.

Estimating the marginal *WACC* (MCC) curve is a two-step process:

1. Determine the levels of total capital at which the marginal *WACC* is expected to increase. These points are referred to as *breakpoints*.
2. Determine the marginal *WACC* at each breakpoint.

Figure 10-1 illustrates what a marginal *WACC* curve might look like for Rocky Mountain Motors. Notice that the breakpoints are measured in terms of dollars of total capital. In this section we will estimate where these breakpoints are likely to occur and determine the *WACC* at the breakpoints.

FIGURE 10-1
THE MARGINAL WACC (MCC) CURVE AS A STEP FUNCTION

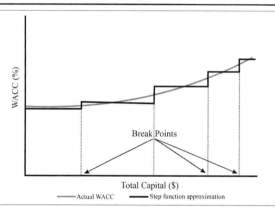

After consulting with their investment bankers, the managers of RMM have determined that they can raise new money at the costs indicated in Table 10-8. Open a new worksheet and enter the data from Table 10-8 beginning in cell A1. The percentages in the "% of Total" column should be referenced from the worksheet that was created for Exhibit 10-4.

TABLE 10-8
ROCKY MOUNTAIN MOTORS INFORMATION

Source	% of Total	Amounts Which Can Be Sold	Marginal After-Tax Cost
Common	60.25%	Up to 100,000	12.31%
		100,001 to 500,000	15.00%
		More than 500,000	17.00%
Preferred	8.61%	Up to 50,000	10.20%
		More than 50,000	13.00%
Debt	31.14%	Up to 250,000	7.10%
		More than 250,000	8.00%

Note that you should enter just the numbers from the "Amounts Which Can Be Sold" column. You can define custom formats, if desired, so the numbers are displayed with the text. This allows us to have the text, and still use the numbers for the calculations that follow. For example, you can format the first cell as: "Up to "#,##0 which will cause the number to be displayed as shown in the table. The second number (500,000) can be formatted with: "100,001 to "#,##0 so that it will display as shown.

RMM feels that its current capital structure is optimal, so any new money will be raised in the same percentages. For example, if the firm decides to raise $200,000 in total capital, then $120,500 (60.25% of $200,000) will come from common equity, $62,280 (31.14%) will be debt, and $17,220 (8.61%) will be preferred equity.

Using the information in Table 10-8, we can determine the breakpoints in RMM's marginal *WACC* curve. To do this, first realize that a break will occur wherever the cost of an individual source of capital changes (why?). There will be a breakpoint associated with the issuance of $100,000 in common stock, for example. But recall that breakpoints are measured in dollars of total capital. So the question is, "How do we convert this $100,000 in common stock into the amount of total capital?"

Since all of the capital will be raised in constant proportion, we can use the following equation:

$$\text{\$ Total Capital} = \frac{\text{\$ Common Stock}}{\text{\% Common Stock}} \qquad \text{(10-5)}$$

In this case, we can see that if RMM raised $100,000 in new common stock, then they must have raised $165,973 in total capital. Using equation (10-5):

$$\$165,973 \approx \frac{\$100,000}{0.6025}$$

We can use this information to see that if RMM issued $100,000 in new common stock, then they must also have raised $51,684 (= $165,973 \times 0.3114$) in new debt and $14,290 (= $165,973 \times 0.0861$) in new preferred stock.

To locate all of the breakpoints, all we need to do is find the points at which the cost of each source changes and then convert those into dollars of total capital. Table 10-9, using the information from Table 10-8, shows how to find these breakpoints.

TABLE 10-9
FINDING THE BREAKPOINTS IN RMM'S MARGINAL *WACC* CURVE

Source	Calculation	Breakpoint
Common Stock	100,000/0.6025	$ 165,973
Common Stock	500,000/0.6025	$ 829,866
Preferred Stock	50,000/0.0861	$ 580,906
Debt	250,000/0.3114	$ 802,773

In your worksheet enter: Breakpoints in cell E1. The first breakpoint is associated with the $100,000 level of new common stock. In E2, enter the formula: =C2/B$2. The result is $165,973, exactly as we found in Table 10-9. Copy this formula to E3. In E5 the formula is: =C5/B$5. In E7 your formula will be: =C7/$B$7.

The next step is to determine the WACC at each of the breakpoints. To find the WACC, we must convert each breakpoint into its components and then determine the cost of each component. There are a number of ways we might approach this problem in the worksheet. Because we would ultimately like to generate a chart of the marginal WACC, we will set up a table that shows the amount of total capital, the cost of each component, and the WACC at that level of total capital.

Begin by entering the labels in A10:E10. In A10 enter: Total Capital. In B10: Cost of Equity. In C10: Cost of Preferred. In D10: Cost of Debt. In E10: WACC. Now, in A11, enter 0. In A12, we want to enter the first breakpoint. We could just reference E2, which has the smallest breakpoint, but that may not be the smallest of the breakpoints if the weights change. To ensure that A12 always has the smallest breakpoint, we should use the **SMALL** function:

$$\text{SMALL}(\textit{ARRAY}, \textit{K})$$

where *ARRAY* is a range of numbers and *K* is the position that you want to return. In A12, enter: =SMALL(E2:E7,1) to get the smallest breakpoint. In A13, enter: =SMALL(E2:E7,2) to get the second smallest breakpoint, and so on. To finish this series with a round number, in A16 enter: `=ROUNDUP(MAX(E2:E7),-5)`. This will round the largest breakpoint up to the next $100,000.

Next, we will determine the cost of each source for each level of total capital. In B11, we need to find the cost of equity at $0 of total capital. To facilitate later copying, we will set up a nested **IF** statement. In this case, the formula is: `=IF(A11*$B$2<=$C$2,$D$2,IF(A11*$B$2<=$C$3,$D$3,$D$4))`. In words, this formula says: "If the amount of total capital (in A11) times the percentage of common stock (B2) is less than or equal to $100,000 (C2), then the cost is 12.31% (D2). Otherwise, if the amount is less than or equal to $500,000 then the cost is 15% (D3). Otherwise, the cost is 17% (D4)."

We use similar, but less complicated, formulas to determine the cost of preferred stock and debt at each level of total capital. For preferred stock, enter the formula: `=IF(A11*$B$5<=$C$5,$D$5,$D$6)` into C11. In D11 enter the formula: `=IF(A11*$B$7<=$C$7,$D$7,$D$8)` to determine the appropriate cost of debt.

Finally, we can calculate the marginal weighted average cost of capital (in E11), with the formula: `=$B$2*B11+$B$5*C11+$B$7*D11`. This formula calculates a weighted average of the costs which were calculated in B11:D11. Make sure that you have entered the formulas exactly as given, and then copy them down through each row to row 16. Your worksheet should now match the one in Exhibit 10-5.

EXHIBIT 10-5
THE WACC AT EACH BREAKPOINT

	A	B	C	D	E
1	**Source**	**% of Total**	**Max Level**	**After-tax Cost**	**Breakpoints**
2	Common	60.25%	Up to 100,000	12.31%	165,973
3			100,001 500,000	15.00%	829,866
4			More than 500,000	17.00%	
5	Preferred	8.61%	Up to 50,000	10.20%	580,906
6			More than 50,000	13.00%	
7	Debt	31.14%	Up to 250,000	7.10%	802,773
8			More than 250,000	8.00%	
9					
10	**Total Capital**	**Cost of Equity**	**Cost of Preferred**	**Cost of Debt**	**WACC**
11	0	12.31%	10.20%	7.10%	10.51%
12	165,973	12.31%	10.20%	7.10%	10.51%
13	580,906	15.00%	10.20%	7.10%	12.13%
14	802,773	15.00%	13.00%	7.10%	12.37%
15	829,866	15.00%	13.00%	8.00%	12.65%
16	900,000	17.00%	13.00%	8.00%	13.85%

Creating the Marginal WACC Chart

Recall that we want to create a chart of the marginal cost of capital, approximated by a step function. To create this chart we need the WACC's and the breakpoints that were created above. Select A10:A16 and then hold down the Ctrl key and select E10:E16. Now use the Chart Wizard to create an XY (Scatter) chart.[8]

EXHIBIT 10-6
THE MARGINAL WACC CURVE FOR RMM

	A	B	C	D	E
	Total Capital	Cost of Equity	Cost of Preferred	Cost of Debt	WACC
10					
11	0	12.31%	10.20%	7.10%	10.51%
12	165,973	12.31%	10.20%	7.10%	10.51%
13	580,906	15.00%	10.20%	7.10%	12.13%
14	802,773	15.00%	13.00%	7.10%	12.37%
15	829,866	15.00%	13.00%	8.00%	12.65%
16	900,000	17.00%	13.00%	8.00%	13.85%

Marginal WACC Curve for RMM

Note that the chart in Exhibit 10-6 does not depict a perfect step function, as shown in Figure 10-1. With a little trick, we can easily change this chart into a perfect step function.

---

8. The most common error in making this type of chart correctly is choosing the wrong type of XY (Scatter) chart. Choose the type illustrated in the lower-right corner of the samples on the Chart Wizard's Chart Type dialog box. If you choose an XY chart with smoothed lines, the result will be a little too smooth. Try it. Also note that you will not get a good step function using a line chart.

First, realize that we want the line to be perfectly vertical at each breakpoint. In order to do that, we must have two Y-values (WACC) corresponding to each particular X-value (amount of total capital). However, if we use the exact break point twice, then the WACC will be the same. To get the WACC to increase, we need to increase the breakpoint by a very tiny amount. To see this, select row 13 and insert a new row. Now, in A13 enter the formula: =A12+0.01, and then copy the other formulas in row 12 down to row 13. Note that the WACC (in E13) is now higher than in E12. Take a look at your chart and notice that you now have a nice step for the first breakpoint. If you zoomed far enough into the chart, you would see that the step is slightly sloped, but at normal size the slope isn't visible.

Repeat these steps with the other three breakpoints, and then your chart should look like the one in Exhibit 10-7.

EXHIBIT 10-7
RMM's MARGINAL WACC CURVE AS A STEP FUNCTION

	A	B	C	D	E
10	Total Capital	Cost of Equity	Cost of Preferred	Cost of Debt	WACC
11	0	12.31%	10.20%	7.10%	10.51%
12	165,973	12.31%	10.20%	7.10%	10.51%
13	165,973	15.00%	10.20%	7.10%	12.13%
14	580,906	15.00%	10.20%	7.10%	12.13%
15	580,906	15.00%	13.00%	7.10%	12.37%
16	802,773	15.00%	13.00%	7.10%	12.37%
17	802,773	15.00%	13.00%	8.00%	12.65%
18	829,866	15.00%	13.00%	8.00%	12.65%
19	829,866	17.00%	13.00%	8.00%	13.85%
20	900,000	17.00%	13.00%	8.00%	13.85%

Marginal WACC Curve for RMM

Summary

We began this chapter with a discussion of the appropriate required rate of return to use in the evaluation of a company's scarce capital resources. We demonstrated that a weighted average of the cost of each source of capital would be sufficient to simultaneously satisfy the providers of capital. In addition, we showed that the costs of the sources of capital can be found by simply inverting the valuation equations from Chapters 8 and 9 and including flotation costs. Finally, we saw that the firm's marginal weighted average cost of capital changes as the amount of total capital changes. We showed how to determine the location of the breakpoints and how to plot the marginal *WACC* curve.

FUNCTIONS INTRODUCED IN THIS CHAPTER

Purpose	Function	Page
Determine the yield to maturity for an annuity or bond	RATE(*NPER, PMT, PV, FV, TYPE, GUESS*)	313
Return the *K*th smallest number in a range	SMALL(*ARRAY, K*)	322

Problems

1. The Dempere Imports Company's earnings per share (EPS) in 2007 was $2.82, and in 2002 it was $1.65. The company's payout ratio is 30%, and the stock is currently valued at $41.50. Flotation costs for new equity will be 15%. Net income in 2008 is expected to be $15 million. The market-value weights of the firm's debt and equity are 40% and 60%, respectively.

   a. Based on the five-year track record, what is Dempere's EPS growth rate? What will the dividend be in 2008?

   b. Calculate the firm's cost of retained earnings, and the cost of new common equity.

   c. Calculate the breakpoint associated with retained earnings.

   d. If Dempere's after-tax cost of debt is 8%, what is the WACC with retained earnings? With new common equity?

2. TRM Consulting Services currently has the following capital structure:

Source	Book Value	Quantity
Common Stock	$6,500,000	350,000
Preferred Stock	$375,000	7,500
Debt	$4,000,000	4,000

Debt is represented by 15-year original maturity bonds, issued 5 years ago, with a coupon rate of 8% and currently selling for $965. The bonds pay interest semiannually. The preferred stock pays an $5 dividend annually and is currently valued at $60 per share. Flotation costs on debt and preferred equity are negligible and can be ignored, but they will be 8% of the selling price for common stock. The common stock, which can be bought for $32.00, has experienced a 5% annual growth rate in dividends and is expected to pay a $1.50 dividend next year. In addition, the firm expects to have $150,000 of retained earnings. Assume that TRM's marginal tax rate is 35%.

a.   Set up a worksheet with all of the data from the problem in a well-organized input area.

b.   Calculate the book-value weights for each source of capital.

c.   Calculate the market-value weights for each source of capital.

d.   Calculate the component costs of capital (i.e., debt, preferred equity, retained earnings, and new common equity).

e.   Calculate the weighted average costs of capital using both the market-value and book-value weights.

3.   Suppose that TRM Consulting Services has discussed its need for capital with its investment bankers. The bankers have estimated that TRM can raise new funds in the capital markets under the following conditions:

Source	Range	After-Tax Cost
Retained Earnings	Up to 150,000	9.69%
Common Equity	Up to 1,000,000	10.10%
	1,000,001 to 3,000,000	10.75%
	More than 3,000,000	11.25%
Preferred Equity	Up to 200,000	8.33%
	More than 200,000	8.75%
Debt	Up to 1,000,000	5.54%
	1,000,001 to 2,000,000	6.00%
	More than 2,000,000	6.50%

a.   Using the information developed in the previous problem, calculate each of the breakpoints. Don't forget to include the breakpoint due to retained earnings.

b.   Create a chart of TRM's marginal weighted average cost of capital curve using the market-value weights. Make sure that it is a perfect step function.

Internet Exercise

1. Using the Yahoo! Finance Web site (http://finance.yahoo.com) get the current price and five-year dividend history for PPG Industries, Inc. (NYSE: PPG). Use the same procedure as in the Internet Exercise of Chapter 8 to gather this data. In addition, get the beta for PPG from its key statistics page on Yahoo! Finance, and the five-year U.S. Treasury yield (ticker: ^FVX). Note that you will need to divide the index value by 10 to get the yield.

   a. Calculate the annualized dividend growth rate from the five year dividend history using the same procedure as in Chapter 8.

   b. Using the stock's current price, dividend, and growth rate, calculate the cost of retained earnings for PPG.

   c. Assuming that the average market return over the next five years will be 9%, calculate the cost of retained earnings using the CAPM. Use the actual beta and five-year Treasury yield (risk-free rate) in the model.

   d. To get your final estimate of the cost of retained earnings, simply average the results from parts B and C.

CHAPTER 11 — *Capital Budgeting*

After studying this chapter, you should be able to:

1. *Identify the relevant cash flows in capital budgeting.*

2. *Demonstrate the use of Excel in calculating the after-tax cash flows used as inputs to the various decision-making techniques.*

3. *Compare and contrast the six major capital budgeting decision techniques (payback period, discounted payback, NPV, PI, IRR, and MIRR).*

4. *Explain scenario analysis, and show how it can be done in Excel.*

5. *Use Excel's Solver to determine the firm's optimal capital budget under capital rationing.*

Capital budgeting is the term used to describe the process of determining how a firm should allocate scarce capital resources to available long-term investment opportunities. Some of these opportunities are expected to be profitable, while others are not. Inasmuch as the goal of the firm is to maximize shareholder's wealth, the financial manager is responsible for selecting only those investments that are expected to increase shareholder wealth.

The techniques that you will learn in this chapter have wide applicability beyond corporate asset management. Lease analysis, bond refunding decisions, mergers and acquisition analysis, corporate restructuring, and new product decisions are all examples of where these techniques are used. On a more personal level, decisions regarding mortgage refinancing, renting versus buying, and choosing a credit card are but a few examples of where these techniques are useful.

On the surface, capital budgeting decisions are simple. If the benefits exceed the costs the project should be accepted, otherwise it should be rejected. Unfortunately, quantifying costs and benefits is not always straightforward. We will examine this process in this chapter and extend it to decision making under conditions of uncertainty in the next.

Estimating the Cash Flows

Before we can determine whether an investment will increase shareholder wealth or not, we need to estimate the cash flows that it will generate. While this is usually easier said than done, there are some general guidelines to keep in mind. There are two important conditions that a cash flow must meet in order to be included in our analysis.

The cash flows must be:

1. *Incremental*—The cash flows must be in addition to those that the firm already has. For example, a firm may be considering an addition to an existing product line. But the new product may cause some current customers to switch from another of the firm's products. We must in this case consider both the cash flow increase from the new product and the cash flow decrease from the existing product. In other words, only the net new cash flows are considered.

2. *After-tax*—The cash flows must be considered on an after-tax basis. The shareholders are not concerned with before-tax cash flows because they can't be reinvested or paid out as dividends until the taxes have been paid.

But we should disregard cash flows that are:

1. *Sunk costs*—These are cash flows that have occurred in the past and cannot be recovered, regardless of the investment decision. Since value is defined as the present value of the expected *future* cash flows, we are only concerned with the future cash flows. Therefore, sunk costs are irrelevant for capital budgeting purposes.

2. *Financing costs*—The cost of financing is obviously important in the analysis, but it will be implicitly included in the discount rate used to evaluate the profitability of the project. Explicitly including the dollar amount of financing costs (e.g., extra interest expense) would amount to double counting. For example, suppose that you discovered an investment that promised a sure 15% return. If you could borrow money at 10% to finance the purchase of this investment, it obviously makes sense because you will earn 5% over your cost. Notice that the dollar interest cost is implicitly included, because you must earn at least 10% to cover your financing costs.

With these points in mind we can move on to discuss the estimation of the relevant cash flows. We will classify all cash flows as a part of one of the three groups illustrated in Figure 11-1.

FIGURE 11-1
TIMELINE ILLUSTRATING PROJECT CASH FLOWS

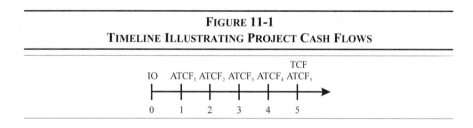

The Initial Outlay

The *initial outlay* (abbreviated IO in Figure 11-1) represents the net cost of the project. Though we will presume that the initial outlay occurs at time period 0 (today), there are many cases, perhaps most, in which the cost of a project is spread out over several periods. For example, the contractor in large construction projects is usually paid some percentage up front, with additional monies being paid as the project reaches various stages of completion. Furthermore, there is usually some delay between the analysis phase of a project and its implementation. So to be technically correct, the initial outlay actually occurs over some near-term future time period.

The initial outlay is comprised of several cash flows. It is impossible to enumerate all of the components for all possible projects, but we will provide some basic principles. The most obvious is the cash outlay required to purchase the project. The price of a piece of machinery or of a building are obvious examples. There are other components, however. Any shipping expenses, labor costs to install machinery, or employee training costs should be included. Together, the costs to get a project up and running are referred to as the *depreciable base* for the project because this is the amount that we will depreciate over the life of the project.

There may also be cash flows that serve to reduce the initial outlay. For example, in a replacement decision (e.g., replacing an existing machine with a newer model) there is often some salvage value for the old machine. This amount will be deducted from the initial outlay. However, there may be taxes associated with the sale of the old equipment. Whenever an asset is sold for an amount that differs from its book value, there are tax consequences. If an asset is sold for more than its book value, tax is owed on the difference. If it is sold for less than book value, the difference is used to offset the firm's taxable income, thus resulting in a tax savings. These extra taxes (tax savings) will increase (decrease) the initial outlay.

Finally, there may be costs that are not at all obvious. For example, suppose that a company is considering an investment in a new machine that is substantially faster than the older model currently being used. Because of the extra speed, the company may find that it needs to increase its investment in raw materials. The cost of these extra raw materials should be included as an increase in the initial outlay because they would not be purchased unless the project is undertaken. This cost is referred to as the increase in net working capital.

The calculation of the initial outlay can be summarized by the following equation:

IO = Price of Project + Shipping + Installation + Training − (Salvage Value − Additional Taxes) + Change in Net Working Capital

Again, every project is different. The formula given above is merely a summary of the possible components of the initial outlay. The key is to focus on any nonoperating cash flows that occur at the beginning of the project's life.

The Annual After-Tax Cash Flows

Calculating the initial outlay, as complicated as it may appear, is relatively easy compared with accurately calculating the annual after-tax cash flows (ATCF). The reason is that we really can't be sure of the cash flows in the future. For the time being, we will assume that we do know exactly what the future cash flows will be, and in the next chapter we will consider the complications of uncertainty.

Generally, the annual after-tax cash flows are made up of four components, but not necessarily all four:

1. *Additional Revenue*—New products, and sometimes production processes, can lead to net new revenue. Remember that we must consider only the incremental revenues.

2. *Cost savings*—There may be some savings that will accompany the acceptance of a project. For example, the firm may decide to replace a manually operated machine with a fully automated version. Part of the savings would be the salary and benefits of the operators of the old machine. Other savings might come from lower maintenance costs, lower power consumption, or fewer defects.

3. *Additional expenses*—Instead of purchasing a fully automated machine, the firm might opt for a process that is more labor intensive. This would allow the company more flexibility to adjust to changes in the market, but the extra labor costs must be considered when determining the cash flows.

4. *Additional depreciation benefits*—Whenever the asset mix of the firm changes, there is likely to be a change in the amount of depreciation expense. Since depreciation expense is a non-cash expense that serves to reduce taxes, we need to consider the tax savings, or extra taxes, due to depreciation.

We must be careful to remember that the only relevant cash flows are those that are after-tax and incremental. Keeping this in mind, we can summarize the calculation of the after-tax cash flows as follows:

$$\text{ATCF} = (\Delta \text{ Revenues} + \text{Savings} - \text{Expenses}) \times (1 - \text{marginal tax rate}) +$$
$$(\Delta \text{ Depreciation} \times \text{marginal tax rate})$$

The Terminal Cash Flow

The terminal cash flow consists of those nonoperating cash flows that occur only in the final time period of the project. Normally, there will also be operating cash flows that occur during this period, but we have categorized those as the final period after-tax cash flows. The terminal cash flow will consist of things such as the expected salvage value of the new machine, any tax effects associated with the sale of the machine, recovery of any investment in net working capital, and perhaps some shutdown costs.

$$\text{TCF} = \text{Recovery of NWC} - (\text{Shutdown Expenses} \times (1 - \text{marginal tax rate})) + \text{Salvage Value} - ((\text{Salvage Value} - \text{Book Value}) \times \text{marginal tax rate})$$

Estimating the Cash Flows: An Example

Throughout this chapter we will demonstrate the concepts with the following example.

> The Supreme Shoe Company is considering the purchase of a new, fully automated machine to replace a manually operated one. The machine being replaced, now five years old, originally had an expected life of 10 years, is being depreciated using the straight-line method from $40,000 down to $0, and can now be sold for $22,000. It takes one person to operate the machine, and he earns $29,000 per year in salary and benefits. The annual costs of maintenance and defects on the old machine are $6,000 and $4,000, respectively. The replacement machine being considered has a purchase price of $75,000 and an expected salvage value of $15,000 at the end of its five-year life. There will also be shipping and installation expenses of $6,000. Because the new machine would work faster, investment in raw materials would increase by a total of $3,000. The company expects that annual maintenance costs on the new machine will be $5,000 while defects will cost $2,000.
>
> Before considering this project, the company undertook an engineering analysis of current facilities to determine if other changes would be necessitated by the purchase of this machine. The study cost the company $5,000 and determined that existing facilities could support this new machine with no other changes. In order to purchase the new machine, the company would have

to take on new debt of $30,000 at 10% interest, resulting in increased interest expense of $3,000 per year. The required rate of return for this project is 15% and the company's marginal tax rate is 34%. Furthermore, management has determined that the maximum allowable time to recover its investment is three years. Is this project acceptable?

For this type of problem, it is generally easiest to separate the important data from the text. This is true regardless of whether you are doing problems by hand or with a spreadsheet program. Of course, a spreadsheet offers many advantages that we will examine later. For now, open a new worksheet and enter the data displayed in Exhibit 11-1.

Notice that in creating Exhibit 11-1 we have simply listed all of the relevant data from the Supreme Shoe problem. There are also some minor calculations entered. Remember, it is important that you set up your worksheets so that Excel does all of the possible calculations for you. This will allow us to more easily experiment with different values (i.e., perform a "what-if" analysis), or change assumptions later.

EXHIBIT 11-1
RELEVANT CASH FLOWS FOR SUPREME SHOE

	A	B	C	D
1	The Supreme Shoe Company			
2	Replacement Analysis			
3		*Old Machine*	*New Machine*	*Difference*
4	Price	40,000	75,000	
5	Shipping and Install	0	6,000	
6	Original Life	10	5	
7	Current Life	5	5	
8	Original Salvage Value	0	15,000	
9	Current Salvage Value	22,000	0	
10	Book Value	20,000	81,000	
11	Increase in Raw Materials	0	3,000	
12	Depreciation	4,000	13,200	(9,200)
13	Salaries	29,000		29,000
14	Maintenance	6,000	5,000	1,000
15	Defects	4,000	2,000	2,000
16	Marginal Tax Rate	34.00%		
17	Required Return	15.00%		

We have left the cost of the engineering study out of our model. Because the $5,000 was spent before our analysis, it is considered to be a sunk cost. That is, there is no way to recover that money, so it is irrelevant to any future decisions. Adding this to the cost of the project would unnecessarily penalize the project. Furthermore, we haven't considered the $3,000 in extra interest expense that will be incurred each year. The money spent to finance a project must be ignored because we will account for it in the required return. In addition, Supreme Shoe has decided to take on the debt for 10 years, which is longer than the expected life of the new machine. Therefore it wouldn't be correct to apply all of the interest expense to this one project.

With this in mind, the first calculation is depreciation. Supreme Shoe uses the straight-line method for analysis purposes. Straight-line depreciation applies depreciation equally throughout the expected useful life of the project, and is calculated as follows:[1]

$$\frac{\text{Depreciable Base} - \text{Salvage Value}}{\text{Useful Life}}$$

Excel has built-in functions for calculating depreciation in five different ways: straight-line (**S**LN), double-declining balance (**D**DB), fixed-declining balance (**D**B), sum of the years' digits (**S**YD), and variably-declining balance (**V**DB). The **V**DB function is interesting because it allows you to specify the rate at which the asset value declines, and whether to switch to straight-line when that method leads to higher depreciation. Since Supreme Shoe uses the straight-line method, we will use the **S**LN function that is defined as:

$$\textbf{SLN}(\textbf{\textit{COST}}, \textbf{\textit{SALVAGE}}, \textbf{\textit{LIFE}})$$

where **COST** is the depreciable base of the asset, **SALVAGE** is the estimated salvage value, and **LIFE** is the number of years over which the asset is to be depreciated.

Recall that the depreciable base includes the price of the asset plus the shipping and installation costs. For the old machine, then, in cell B12 insert: `=SLN(B4+B5, B8,B6)`. Because the annual depreciation will be calculated the same way for the new machine, simply copy the formula in B12 to C12.

We calculate the book value of the current machine in B10 because the book value and the salvage value together will determine the tax liability from the sale of this machine. Book value is calculated as the difference between the depreciable base and the accumulated depreciation. In this instance, the depreciable base is found by

---

1. Some finance textbooks use a form of straight-line depreciation referred to as "simplified straight-line" that assumes that the salvage value is always zero.

adding B4 and B5. The accumulated depreciation is the annual depreciation expense times the number of years of the original life that have passed. In our worksheet this is B12*(B6–B7). So the formula in B10 is: =B4+B5-B12* (B6-B7). Just for informational purposes, copy the formula to C10.

The difference column presents the savings that the new machine will provide. The formulas are simply the difference between the expenses of the current machine and those of the proposed machine. In D12 place the formula: =B12-C12 and then copy it to cells D13:D15. To avoid confusion, we only calculate differences for the relevant cells. Your worksheet should now resemble Exhibit 11-1 (page 337).

Now that the data are more clearly presented, we can calculate the relevant cash flows. The initial outlay consists of the price of the new machine, the shipping and installation costs, and the salvage value of the old machine and any taxes that might be due from that sale. We will calculate the initial outlay in B19 as: =- (C4+C5-B9+ (B9-B10) *B16+C11). The formula is less complex than it looks. The first three terms simply represent the total cost of the new machine minus the salvage value of the old machine. The next part of the formula calculates the tax that is due on the sale of the old machine. Notice that if the book value were less than the salvage value this formula will add a negative value, thus reducing the initial outlay. Again, it is important that you construct the worksheet formulas so that any changes are automatically reflected in the calculated values. Finally, we add the increased investment in raw materials because this investment would not be necessary unless the new machine were purchased.

Next we need to calculate the annual after-tax cash flows for this project. We will separate the calculation of the depreciation tax benefit from the other cash flows because it is informative to see the savings generated by the increased depreciation (also because, as we will see in the next chapter, the depreciation tax benefit is a less-risky cash flow than the others). In B20 we calculate the annual after-tax savings as: =SUM(D13:D15)* (1-B16). We have used the **SUM** function because it is more compact than simply adding the three cell addresses individually. Also, if we later discover any other savings (or extra costs), we can insert them into the range and the formula will automatically reflect the change. Note that this project will not have any impact on overall revenues.

The depreciation tax benefit represents the savings in taxes that we will have because of the extra depreciation expense. Remember that depreciation is a non-cash expense so that the only result of increasing depreciation is to reduce taxes and thereby increase cash flow. To calculate the depreciation tax benefit, in cell B21 enter the formula: =-D12* B16. We make the depreciation amount negative because the change in depreciation in D12 is negative (indicating extra expense). In B22 we total the annual after-tax savings and the depreciation tax benefit with the formula: =SUM(B20:B21).

Finally, the terminal cash flow consists of any nonoperating cash flows that occur only in the final period. For the Supreme Shoe project, the additional cash flows are the after-tax salvage value and the recovery of the investment in raw materials. In this case, there is no tax consequence of salvaging the machine for $15,000 because that is the same as the book value. The formula in B23 is: =C11+C8. Don't forget that the terminal cash flow is only a part of the total cash flow in year 5. We will have to add on the annual after-tax cash flow (operating cash flows) in year 5 before analyzing the profitability of the project.

At this point, your worksheet should resemble the one pictured in Exhibit 11-2.

EXHIBIT 11-2
CASH FLOWS FOR SUPREME SHOE

	A	B	C	D
1	The Supreme Shoe Company			
2	Replacement Analysis			
3		Old Machine	New Machine	Difference
4	Price	40,000	75,000	
5	Shipping and Install	0	6,000	
6	Original Life	10	5	
7	Current Life	5	5	
8	Original Salvage Value	0	15,000	
9	Current Salvage Value	22,000	0	
10	Book Value	20,000	81,000	
11	Increase in Raw Materials	0	3,000	
12	Depreciation	4,000	13,200	(9,200)
13	Salaries	29,000		29,000
14	Maintenance	6,000	5,000	1,000
15	Defects	4,000	2,000	2,000
16	Marginal Tax Rate	34.00%		
17	Required Return	15.00%		
18	Cash Flows			
19	Initial Outlay	(62,680)		
20	Annual After-Tax Savings	21,120		
21	Depreciation Tax Benefit	3,128		
22	Total ATCF	24,248		
23	Terminal Cash Flow	18,000		

Making the Decision

We are now ready to make a decision as to the profitability of this project. Financial managers have a number of tools at their disposal to evaluate profitability. We will examine six of these. Before beginning the analysis, examine the timeline presented in Figure 11-2, which summarizes the cash flows for the Supreme Shoe replacement decision.

FIGURE 11-2
TIMELINE FOR THE SUPREME SHOE REPLACEMENT DECISION

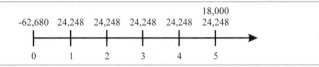

The Payback Method

The payback method answers the question, "How long will it take to recoup our initial investment?" If the answer is less than or equal to the maximum allowable period, the project is considered to be acceptable. If the payback period is longer than acceptable, then the project is rejected. Note that the payback period serves as a kind of break-even period, and thus provides some information regarding the liquidity of the project under analysis.

There are two ways to calculate the payback period. The easiest method, which we can use for the Supreme Shoe problem, is used when the cash flows are an annuity. To calculate the payback for these types of cash flows, simply divide the initial outlay by the annuity payment:

$$\text{Payback Period} = \frac{\text{Initial Outlay}}{\text{Annuity Payment}}$$

For Supreme Shoe, the cash flows are not strictly an annuity, except for the first four years. If the payback period is less than four years, then we can use this method. For this project the payback period is calculated as:

$$\text{Payback Period} = \frac{62,680}{24,248} = 2.58 \text{ years}$$

Because Supreme Shoe requires that projects have a maximum payback period of three years, the replacement machine is acceptable by this criteria. In A25, enter the label: `Payback Period` and in B25 enter the formula: `=-B19/B22`. Your result should be 2.58 years.

An alternative way to calculate the payback period, which must be used if the cash flows are not an annuity, subtracts the cash flows from the initial outlay until the outlay is recovered. This method is much easier to demonstrate than to describe. So let's look at the Supreme Shoe problem using this method. Table 11-1 illustrates this procedure.

TABLE 11-1
CALCULATING THE PAYBACK PERIOD

Calculation	Comments	Cumulative Payback
62,680	Initial outlay	
− 24,248	minus first cash flow	1 year
= 38,432	left to be recovered	
− 24,248	minus second cash flow	2 years
= 14,184	left to be recovered	2 years < payback < 3 years

At this point we know that the payback period must be between two and three years, and that the remainder will be recovered during the third year. Assuming that the cash flow in year 3 is evenly spread out through the year, we can simply divide the amount yet to be recovered by the cash flow in year 3 to arrive at the fraction of the year required to recover this amount. In this case, it will take 0.58 years ($= 14,184 \div 24,248$) to recover the remainder. Add this to the two years that we have already counted, and we arrive at 2.58 years, exactly as before. Note that when the project's cash flows are not an annuity, this is the method that must be used to calculate the payback period.

While the payback period makes a great deal of sense intuitively, it is not without its problems. Specifically, the principal problem is that the payback method ignores the time value of money. You know, from the discussion of time value in Chapter 7, that we cannot simply add cash flows that occur in different time periods. Furthermore, it should be obvious that most investments become increasingly attractive as the firm's required return (WACC) falls, and less attractive when the required return rises. However, the payback period doesn't change when the WACC changes. We will address this problem shortly.

A second difficulty with the payback period is that it does not take all of the cash flows into account. Because it ignores all cash flows beyond the payback period, it can lead to less-than-optimal decisions. Suppose, for example, that the year 5 cash flow for the Supreme Shoe project was –$100,000 instead of $42,248. The payback period is still 2.58 years, which suggests that it should be accepted, but anybody taking even a cursory look at the cash flows would reject the project immediately. This second problem will be remedied when we look at the NPV, PI, IRR, and MIRR techniques.

The Discounted Payback Period

We can remedy the time value of money problem by using the discounted payback period. This method is identical to the regular payback period, except that we use the present value of the cash flows instead of the nominal values. Because present values are always less than nominal values, the discounted payback period will always be longer than the regular payback period.

For Supreme Shoe, the discounted payback period is 3.53 years. Calculating this number is slightly more difficult than calculating the regular payback period because the present values of the cash flows are different in each period. For this reason we must use the second method to calculate the discounted payback period.[2] Since Excel does not have a payback function, we have included one in the workbook named FameFncs.xla. Writing function macros is covered in Chapter 13. Before continuing with this example, make sure that the FameFncs.xla add-in is installed.[3] This add-in contains a function macro called **FAME_PAYBACK** that can be used exactly like any other built-in function, as long as the workbook is open. The function is defined as:

$$\text{FAME\_PAYBACK}(\textit{CASHFLOWS, RATE})$$

where ***CASHFLOWS*** is a contiguous range of cash flows, and *RATE* is the optional discount rate to be used to calculate the present values of the cash flows. If *RATE* is left out, the default discount rate is 0% so this function will calculate the regular

---

2. In the case where all of the nominal cash flows are equal (an annuity) we could use the **NPER** function. This function calculates the number of periods that an annuity must pay to have the present value of the cash flows be equal to the price. We can also use this function to calculate the regular payback period for an annuity if we set the discount rate to zero.

3. Please see "Using Function Macros" on page 24 if you are unfamiliar with the FameFncs.xla add-in.

payback period. Be aware that the initial outlay (i.e., the first cash flow in the list) must be negative, or else you will get unpredictable results. All other cash flows may be either positive or negative.

Before using the **FAME_PAYBACK** macro, and the other functions that we will be using later, we need to set up a table of cash flows. In cells C18:D24 set up the following table:

EXHIBIT 11-3
CASH FLOWS FOR CALCULATING THE DISCOUNTED PAYBACK PERIOD

	C	D
18	Period	Cash Flows
19	0	(62,680)
20	1	24,248
21	2	24,248
22	3	24,248
23	4	24,248
24	5	42,248

In order to set up the table in Exhibit 11-3 very little data input is required since most of the data already exists or can be calculated. Start by typing the column labels in cells C18 and D18. To enter the period numbers, in cell C19 type a zero and then select the range C19:C24. From the Edit menu select Fill Series and click on OK when the dialog box appears (the default options should work fine). This command will enter a series of numbers starting with the first number in the selected range. It can be very helpful in situations where you need a list of consecutive numbers or dates.

The cash flows are most easily entered by using references to the cells where the original calculations exist. Entering the numbers in this way, rather than retyping them, will later allow us to experiment with various scenarios. In cell D19 enter: =B19 to capture the initial outlay. In cell D20 we need the first cash flow, so enter: =B$22. Note that the dollar sign will freeze the cell reference so that it will remain at row 22 when we copy it. Copy the formula from D20 to the range D21:D23, and note that the value is the same in each cell as it was in D20. Finally, to get the total cash flow for year 5 (in D24), enter: =B22+B23. Remember that the cash flow in the final year of the life of a project is the sum of its annual after-tax cash flow and the terminal cash flow. In the timeline pictured in Figure 11-2, we showed these cash flows separately, but we must add them together in Exhibit 11-3 for the following analysis.

Calculating the discounted payback period is a simple matter. In cell B26 enter the formula: =Fame_Payback(D19:D24,B17).[4] The discounted payback period is 3.53 years, which is longer than the maximum acceptable payback. You should verify this result by hand.

Using the three-year benchmark in this case would be incorrect, since it was presumably determined under the assumptions of the regular payback period. Some allowance must be made for the fact that the discounted payback period will always be greater than the regular payback period. Suppose then that management decides that the discounted payback must be 3.75 years or less to be acceptable. With the new criteria, the project is acceptable under both payback methods.

However, the benefit of the discounted payback period technique is that the acceptability of a project will change as required returns change. If the required return should rise to 18%, the discounted payback period will rise to 3.80 years and the project would be rejected. Since the regular payback period ignores the time value of money it would still suggest that the project is acceptable, regardless of the required return. Try changing the required return in B17 to verify this for yourself.

Note that the discounted payback period still ignores cash flows beyond the period where payback is achieved. All of the remaining techniques that we will introduce are considered to be superior because they recognize the time value of money, and all of the cash flows are considered in the analysis.

Net Present Value

Neither the regular payback period nor the discounted payback period are economically correct decision criteria. Even with the discounted payback method we are ignoring cash flows beyond the payback period. How then can the financial analyst make the correct decision? In this section we will cover the net present value decision criteria, which is the most theoretically correct method.

Most people would agree that purchasing an asset for less than its value is a good deal. Further, purchasing an asset for exactly its value isn't bad. What most people try to avoid is purchasing an asset for more than its value.[5] If we define value as the

---

4. You can also enter this function, just like any built-in function, using the Insert Function dialog box. Select the User Defined category and you'll see it in the list.

5. Theoretically, nobody would ever purchase an asset for more than it is worth to them at the time the decision is made. Purchasing an asset proves, ipso facto, that the cost is, at most, equal to the value to that individual at that moment.

present value of future cash flows (see Chapter 8), then net present value (NPV) represents the excess value (i.e., economic profit) captured by purchasing an asset. More specifically:

$$NPV = PVCF - IO = Value - Cost$$

or more mathematically:

$$NPV = \sum_{t=1}^{N} \frac{CF_t}{(1+i)^t} - IO \qquad \text{(11-1)}$$

There are a couple of important things to note about the NPV. Most importantly, since value can be greater than, equal to, or less than cost, the NPV can be greater than, equal to, or less than zero. If the value is less than the cost, the NPV will be less than zero, and the project will be rejected. Otherwise, the project will be accepted because the value is greater than (or equal to) the cost. In the latter case, the wealth of the shareholders will be increased (or at least unchanged) by the acceptance of the project. So NPV really represents the change in shareholder wealth that accompanies the acceptance of an investment. Since the goal of management is to maximize shareholder wealth, they must accept all projects where the NPV is greater than or equal to zero.

Why does NPV represent a change in shareholder wealth? To see this important point, remember that any cash flows in excess of expenses accrue to the common stockholders of the firm. Therefore, any project that generates cash flows sufficient to cover its costs will result in an increase in shareholder wealth.[6] Consider the following example:

> Huey and Louie are considering the purchase of a lemonade stand that will operate during the summer months. It will cost them $100 to build and operate the stand. Since they only have $50 of their own (common equity) they will need to raise the additional capital elsewhere. Huey's father agrees to loan the pair $30 (debt), with the understanding that they will repay him a total of $33 at the end of the summer. The other $20 can be raised in a

---

6. It is important to note that we are talking about the economic costs, not just the accounting costs. In particular, economists consider the cost of the equity and any other opportunity costs. Accounting costs ignore the cost of equity and other opportunity costs. Therefore, NPV is the same thing as the *economic profit* generated by the project.

preferred stock offering to several of the other kids in the neighborhood. The preferred stock is sold with the promise to pay a five-dollar dividend, if possible, at the end of the summer. Huey and Louie would have to earn at least $10 in order to compensate them for their time, effort, and money invested. Assuming that the stand will be demolished at the end of the summer, should they undertake this project?

The answer to this question depends on the cash flows that Huey and Louie expect the lemonade stand to generate. The three scenarios in Table 11-2 will demonstrate the possibilities:

TABLE 11-2
POSSIBLE SCENARIOS FOR THE LEMONADE STAND

	Scenario 1	Scenario 2	Scenario 3
Total cash inflow after operating expenses and taxes	$118	$130	$110
Less cost of debt	(33)	(33)	(33)
Less cost of preferred stock	(25)	(25)	(25)
Less cost of common equity	(60)	(60)	(60)
Remainder to common stockholders (NPV)	0	12	−8

Notice that the required returns of each of the stakeholders are unchanged in each scenario. The only variable is the cash inflow after operating expenses and taxes (NOPAT). In the first scenario all of the capital providers are exactly satisfied; even Huey and Louie get the $10 return that they have demanded. Therefore, the project is acceptable, and it has a net present value of zero (as indicated by the remainder). Under the second scenario, everybody is satisfied and there is an extra $12 that goes directly to Huey and Louie (the shareholders). This is an example of a positive NPV. Finally, under scenario 3, the debtholder and the preferred stockholders are satisfied, but there is a shortfall of $8 that will reduce Huey and Louie's return to only $2. Notice that in the last case, the return to the common stockholders is positive (i.e., they do make money), but less than required. This is an example of a negative NPV and will cause Huey and Louie to reject the project.

Returning now to our Supreme Shoe example, the NPV of this project can be determined by taking the present value of the after-tax cash flows and subtracting the initial outlay. In this case, performing the calculations by hand poses no great difficulty. However, Excel can calculate the NPV just as easily and allow us to experiment. You have already made use of the built-in **NPV** function in Chapter 7. At that point, we did not make clear the misleading nature of this function. It does not really calculate the NPV as we defined it. Instead, it simply calculates the sum of present values of the cash flows as of one period before the first cash flow. It is vitally important that you understand this point before using this function.

To use the **NPV** function for this problem, insert: =NPV(B17,D20:D24)+B19 into B27. Note that we do *not* include the initial outlay in the range used in the **NPV** function. Instead, we use the **NPV** function to determine the present value of the cash flows and then add the (negative) initial outlay to this result. The net present value is shown to be $27,552.24, so the project is acceptable. An alternative method is to include the initial outlay and then adjust the result. In this case, the present value would be as of time period –1, so multiplying by (1 + WACC) will bring it to time period 0. The alternative, then, is to place the formula: =NPV(B17, D19:D24)*(1+B17) into B27. This will give exactly the same result.

The Profitability Index

The beauty of the net present value is that it reports the dollar increase in shareholder wealth that would result from acceptance of a project. Most of the time this is desirable, but there is one problem. Comparing projects of differing size can be misleading when a firm is operating with a fixed amount of investment capital. Assuming that both projects are acceptable and mutually exclusive, the larger project will likely have a higher NPV. The profitability index (PI) provides a measure of the dollar benefit per dollar of cost ("bang for the buck"). PI is calculated by:

$$PI = \frac{\$ \text{ Benefit}}{\$ \text{ Cost}} = \frac{\sum_{t=1}^{N} \dfrac{CF_t}{(1+i)^t}}{IO} = \frac{PVCF}{IO} \qquad (11\text{-}2)$$

As indicated in the equation, the benefit is calculated as the present value of the after-tax cash flows and the cost is the initial outlay. Obviously, then, if the PI is greater than or equal to 1, the project is acceptable because the benefits exceed, or at least equal, the costs. Otherwise, the benefits are less than the costs and the project would be rejected. Note that the profitability index will always result in the same accept/reject answer as NPV.

There are two ways that we can calculate the PI in Excel. The most apparent is to use the **NPV** function and to divide that result by the initial outlay. In other words, in B28 type: =NPV(B17,D20:D24)/(-B19). This will give 1.4396 as the result, indicating that the project is acceptable. The alternative is to make use of the following relationship:

$$NPV = PVCF - IO$$

or, by rearranging we get:

$$PVCF = NPV + IO$$

Therefore, since we have already calculated the NPV in B27, we can calculate the PI with: =(B27-B19)/(-B19). This method will be slightly faster because Excel doesn't have to recalculate the present values. In all but the largest problems, the increase in speed probably won't be noticeable on a PC, but the technique is especially helpful when doing problems by hand.

The Internal Rate of Return

The internal rate of return (IRR) provides a measure of the compound average annual rate of return that a project will provide. If the IRR exceeds the required return for a project, the project will be accepted. Because it is a measure of the percentage return, many analysts prefer it to the other methods that we have discussed; but, as we will see, there are many problems with the IRR.

The IRR is the discount rate that makes the net present value equal to zero. An alternative, but equivalent, definition is that the IRR is the discount rate that equates the present value of the cash flows to the initial outlay. In other words, the IRR is the discount rate that makes the following equality hold:

$$IO = \sum_{t=1}^{N} \frac{CF_t}{(1 + IRR)^t} \tag{11-3}$$

Unfortunately, in most cases there is no closed-form method for solving for the IRR. The primary method of solving this equation is an iterative trial-and-error approach. While this may sound tedious, generally a solution can be found within three or four iterations if some intelligence is used. However, there is little need for this procedure since Excel has a built-in function that performs this operation.

The built-in **RATE** function in Excel will find the IRR for an annuity-type of cash flow stream, but it cannot accept a series of uneven cash flows. To deal with uneven cash flows, Excel provides the **IRR** function that is defined as:

$$\text{IRR}(\textit{VALUES}, \textit{GUESS})$$

where **VALUES** is the contiguous range of cash flows and **GUESS** is the (optional) initial guess at the true IRR. Note that your cash flow stream must include at least one negative cash flow (payment) or else the IRR would be infinite (why?). Since solving for the IRR is an iterative process, it is possible that Excel will not converge to a solution. Excel will indicate this situation by displaying #NUM! in the cell rather than an answer. If this error occurs, one possible solution is to change your **GUESS** until Excel can converge to a solution.

To calculate the IRR for the Supreme Shoe example, enter: =IRR(D19:D24) into cell B29. The result is 30.95%, which is greater than the required return of 15%. So the project is acceptable. At this point, let's try an experiment to prove our definition of the IRR. Recall that the IRR was defined as the discount rate that makes the NPV equal zero. To prove this, temporarily change the value in B17 to: =B29. Notice that the net present value in B27 changes to $0.00, which proves the point. Note also that the profitability index changes to 1.0000. Before continuing, change the required return back to its original value of 15%.

Problems with the IRR

The internal rate of return is a popular profitability measure because, as a percentage, it is easy to understand and easy to compare to the required return. However, the IRR suffers from several problems that could potentially lead to less-than-optimal decisions. In this section we will discuss these difficulties, and consider solutions where they exist.

Earlier, we mentioned that the NPV will almost always lead you to the economically correct decision. Unfortunately, the IRR and NPV will not always lead to the same decision when projects are mutually exclusive. *Mutually exclusive* projects are those for which the selection of one project precludes the acceptance of another. When projects that are being compared are mutually exclusive, a ranking conflict may arise between the NPV and IRR.[7] In other words, the NPV method may

---

7. This is not a problem with independent projects because all independent projects with a positive NPV (IRR > required rate) will be accepted. In other words, ranking is not required.

suggest that Project A be accepted while the IRR may suggest Project B. If you can't select both, which profitability measure do you believe?

There are two causes of this type of problem: (1) the projects are of greatly different sizes; or (2) the timing of the cash flows are different. To see the size problem more clearly, consider the following question. "Would you rather earn a 100% return on a $10 investment (Project A), or a 10% return on a $1,000 investment (Project B)?" Obviously, most of us would be more concerned with the dollar amounts and would choose the 10% return because that would provide $100 versus only $10 in the other case. The solution to this problem is actually quite simple. If you can raise $1,000 for the Project B, then the correct comparison is not between A and B, but between B and A plus whatever you could do with the other $990 (call it Project C) that is available if you choose Project A. If Project C would return 10%, then you could earn $109 by investing in both A and C, which is preferable to investing in B.

The timing problem is more difficult to deal with. Suppose that you are given the task of evaluating the two mutually exclusive projects in Table 11-3, with a 10% required return.

TABLE 11-3
THE TIMING OF CASH FLOWS CAN LEAD TO A CONFLICT

Period	Project A	Project B	Project C (= A – B)
0	(1000)	(1000)	0
1	0	400	(400)
2	200	400	(200)
3	300	300	0
4	500	300	200
5	900	200	700
NPV	$291.02	$248.70	$42.32
IRR	17.32%	20.49%	12.48%

Which would you choose? Obviously there is a conflict because Project A would be selected under the NPV criteria, but Project B would be selected by the IRR criteria. We can use logic similar to that used for the size problem to see that NPV is the correct criteria. If Project B is accepted, we must reject Project A and the differential cash flows (Project C). If the differential cash flows provide a positive NPV, then they should not be rejected. In effect, what we are arguing is that Project A is equivalent to Project B plus the differential cash flows. So choosing between these projects is effectively deciding whether the differential cash flows are profitable or not. Conveniently, all that we really need to do is to accept the project with the highest NPV.

Yet another problem with the IRR is that there may be more than one IRR. Specifically, because the general equation for the IRR is an Nth degree polynomial, it will have N solutions. In the usual case, where there is one cash outflow followed by several inflows, there will be only one real number solution; the others are imaginary numbers. However, when there are net cash outflows in the outlying periods, we may be able to find more than one real solution. In particular, there can be, at most, one real solution per sign change in the cash flow stream.[8]

FIGURE 11-3
CASH FLOWS FOR MULTIPLE IRRS

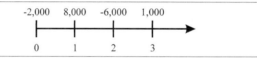

Consider, as an example, the cash flows depicted in Figure 11-3. Solving for the IRR in this example will lead to three solutions: 207.82%, –31.54%, and –76.27%. The answer that you get from Excel will depend on the initial *GUESS* that you supply. If you don't provide Excel with a *GUESS*, it will give –31.54% as the answer. Any *GUESS* of 21.7% or greater will get an answer of 207.82%, and a guess of –71.11% will get an answer of –76.27%. It is impossible to say which of these answers is correct since all will result in an NPV of zero if used as the discount rate (try it!).

The Modified Internal Rate of Return

An easy solution to the problems of the IRR as a profitability measure is to simply use the NPV instead. This is not likely to please everyone, however. Despite its problems, executives continue to prefer the IRR to the NPV because, as a percentage,

---

8. The interested reader is advised to study Descartes' Rule of Signs to understand this point in more depth.

it is easy to compare to the firm's cost of capital. To understand how we can use an IRR-type calculation and still arrive at correct answers requires that you understand the root cause of the problems with the IRR.

Implicit in the calculation of the IRR is the assumption that the cash flows are reinvested at the IRR. In other words, the IRR method assumes that as each cash flow is received, it is reinvested for the remaining life of the project at a rate that is the same as the IRR.[9] For projects with a very high, or very low, IRR this assumption is likely to be violated. If the cash flows are reinvested at some other rate, the actual average annual rate of return will be different than the IRR. To see this assumption at work, consider again our Supreme Shoe project. The timeline is pictured in Figure 11-4 with the explicit reinvestment of the cash flows at the IRR of 30.945%.

FIGURE 11-4
SUPREME SHOE CASH FLOWS WITH EXPLICIT REINVESTMENT AT THE IRR

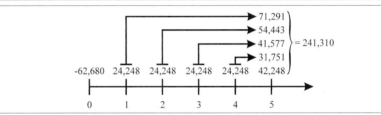

Assuming that the cash flows are reinvested at 30.945% per year, at the end of year 5 Supreme Shoe will have accumulated $241,310 from their original investment of $62,680. The compound average annual return, then, must be:

$$\sqrt[5]{\frac{241,310}{62,680}} - 1 \approx 30.945\%$$

which is exactly the same as the IRR. Note that we have used the geometric mean, equation (1-1) from Chapter 1, in this example.

---

9. This also explains why we cannot solve directly for the IRR: We must know the IRR to know the reinvestment rate, and without knowing the reinvestment rate we can't solve for the IRR.

It seems unlikely that Supreme Shoe can earn a rate this high over a five-year period. If we change the reinvestment rate to a more reasonable 15% (the WACC), then we have the timeline in Figure 11-5.

FIGURE 11-5
SUPREME SHOE CASH FLOWS WITH EXPLICIT REINVESTMENT AT 15%

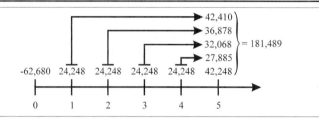

In this case, Supreme Shoe will have accumulated only $181,489 by the end of the fifth year. Their average annual rate of return with a 15% reinvestment rate will be:

$$\sqrt[5]{\frac{181,489}{62,680}} - 1 \approx 23.69\%$$

which is substantially lower than the 30.95% IRR. When we calculate the average annual return with a reinvestment rate that is different than the IRR we refer to it as the *modified internal rate of return*, or MIRR. For Supreme Shoe, the MIRR is 23.69%, which is greater than the required return of 15% so the project should be accepted.

Excel has a built-in function to calculate the MIRR. The function is defined as:

$$\text{MIRR}(\textit{VALUES}, \textit{FINANCE\_RATE}, \textit{REINVEST\_RATE})$$

where **VALUES** is the range of cash flows, **FINANCE_RATE** is the required rate of return, and **REINVEST_RATE** is the rate at which the cash flows are to be reinvested. To calculate the MIRR in your Supreme Shoe worksheet, enter: =MIRR(D19: D24,B17,B17) into B30. Exactly as we calculated above, the answer is 23.69%. In this example we have used the same rate for the required return and the reinvestment rate. This is normally the appropriate assumption to make (it is the same assumption that is implicit within the NPV calculation). But if you have other information that suggests a different reinvestment rate, then that different rate should be used.

Sensitivity Analysis

Probably the most important benefit of using a spreadsheet program is that it allows us to play "what-if" games with the data. That is, we can experiment with different values to determine how sensitive the results are to changes in the assumptions.

NPV Profile Charts

One useful technique that we can use is referred to as the *NPV profile*. This is simply a chart of the NPV at various discount rates. The analyst can determine, at a glance, how sensitive the NPV is to the assumed discount rate. To create an NPV profile chart, we merely set up a range of discount rates and NPV calculations and then create a chart.

To create an NPV profile chart for Supreme Shoe, let's create a range of discount rates from 0% to 35% in 5% increments. Move to cell A36 and enter: 0. To create the range of discount rates, select A36:A43 and then choose **E**dit F**i**ll **S**eries . . . from the menus. In the dialog box, change the **S**tep Value to: 0.05 and then click the OK button. You should now have a range of discount rates from 0% to 35%. We will use these rates in our NPV calculations.

In order to calculate the NPV at each discount rate, enter: =NPV(A36,D$20: D$24)+D$19 in B36. Notice that this is exactly the same formula as in B27, except that we have added a few dollar signs to freeze the references and we changed the discount rate to reference A36. Copying this formula to B37:B43 will calculate the NPV at each discount rate. Note that the NPV becomes negative at a discount rate just over 30% because the IRR was 30.95%.

Finally, to create the chart select the A35:B43 and press the Chart Wizard button on the toolbar. Follow the prompts, choosing an XY (Scatter) chart, until your chart appears. This section of your worksheet should resemble the one in Exhibit 11-4.

EXHIBIT 11-4
NPV PROFILE FOR SUPREME SHOE

	A	B	C	D	E	F	G
34	**NPV Profile Data**						
35	Required Return	NPV					
36	0%	$76,560.00					
37	5%	$56,404.62					
38	10%	$40,415.58					
39	15%	$27,552.24					
40	20%	$17,070.16					
41	25%	$8,427.90					
42	30%	$1,225.62					
43	35%	($4,836.13)					

NPV Profile chart: NPV (thousands) on the Y-axis ranging from -5 to 85, Required Return on the X-axis from 0% to 35%. IRR = 30.95%.

Notice that the chart clearly shows the IRR is just over 30%. This is the point where the NPV line crosses the X-axis of the NPV profile chart. Furthermore, it is obvious that for any discount rate below 30% the project has a positive NPV, thus it is acceptable. Typically, an NPV profile chart is used to compare two mutually exclusive projects. Whenever there is a ranking conflict, the NPV profiles will cross at a rate at which the firm would be indifferent between the two projects. This "crossover rate" can be found exactly by calculating the IRR of the difference in the cash flows of the two projects.

Scenario Analysis

Excel contains a very powerful tool called the *Scenario Manager* that helps in analyzing the effects of different assumptions. Scenario Manager can be used to toggle your worksheet between various alternative scenarios, or it can create a summary of the effects of changing the assumptions.

As an example we will create three scenarios in which the estimates of maintenance and defect costs are different than expected. The three scenarios are listed in Table 11-4.

TABLE 11-4
THREE POSSIBLE SCENARIOS FOR SUPREME SHOE

	Best Case	Expected Case	Worst Case
Maintenance	$2,000	$5,000	$8,000
Defects	$1,000	$2,000	$5,000

In the Best Case scenario both maintenance and defects are lower than in the Expected Case (which represents the original estimates). In the Worst Case, both are higher than expected. Since we are going to be changing our assumed values for maintenance and defects, it will be helpful to first define range names for these cells. Click on cell C14 and then choose Insert Name Define and assign the name Maintenance to this cell. Now define the name Defects for cell C15 (see page 9 for a discussion of named ranges).

Creating scenarios is quite simple. First select Tools Scenarios from the menus. Since no scenarios are defined at this point, the first dialog box will ask you to click the Add button to define your scenarios. In this case we want the maintenance and defect estimates to change, so press the Add button; then for the name enter: Best Case. Click in the Changing Cells edit box, highlight cells C14:C15, and then click the OK button.

The next dialog box will ask you to supply the new values for the changing cells. In the edit box labeled "Maintenance:" enter: 2000 and in the edit box labeled "Defects:" type: 1000. Note that this dialog box prompts you for the values using the names that we earlier defined for these cells. If you didn't define the names, then you will be prompted with the cell addresses instead of names.

FIGURE 11-6
THE SCENARIO VALUES DIALOG BOX

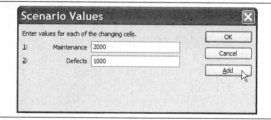

Click the Add button to enter the next scenario. Now, repeat these steps for the other two cases using the names "Expected Case" and "Worst Case" and the appropriate values from Table 11-4.

Figure 11-7 shows how the dialog box will look when you have entered all three scenarios.

FIGURE 11-7
THE SCENARIO MANAGER

At this point, you can change the worksheet to display the scenario of your choice by highlighting the name of the case and clicking the **S**how button. For example, if you highlight "Worst Case" and click the **S**how button, the maintenance and defect cells will change and the worksheet will update. You can now see the effects of these changes on the cash flows and profitability measures (for example, the NPV is $14,277.70 under the Worst Case scenario). Return to the original data by choosing "Expected Case" from the list and pressing the **S**how button. This type of flexibility is one of the promised results of proper worksheet design. Scenario analysis will not work properly unless you are diligent about using formulas, rather than retyping values, whenever possible.

It would be nice to see a summary of the different scenarios, and we can do just that. But first, exit from the Scenario Manager and define a name for each cell in B25:B30 so that the output will be easier to understand. Now, bring back the Scenario Manager and click the S**u**mmary button. When the Scenario Summary dialog box appears, select cells B25:B30 for the **R**esult cells and click OK. Excel will then automatically create a new worksheet that displays the changed values and the resulting profitability measures. Exhibit 11-5 shows the summary worksheet.

EXHIBIT 11-5
SCENARIO SUMMARY REPORT FOR SUPREME SHOE

Scenario Summary	Current Values	Best Case	Expected Case	Worst Case
Changing Cells:				
Maintenance	5,000	2,000	5,000	8,000
Defects	2,000	1,000	2,000	5,000
Result Cells:				
Payback_Period	2.58	2.33	2.58	3.09
Discounted_Payback	3.53	3.08	3.53	4.25
NPV	27,552.24	36,401.93	27,552.24	14,277.70
PI	1.44	1.58	1.44	1.23
IRR	30.95%	35.85%	30.95%	23.41%
MIRR	23.69%	26.03%	23.69%	19.82%
Notes: Current Values column represents values of changing cells at				
time Scenario Summary Report was created. Changing cells for each				
scenario are highlighted in gray.				

We have defined three simple scenarios, but other problems may require more scenarios or more changing variables. You can define as many scenarios as your PC's memory will hold, but only the first 251 will be displayed on the scenario summary worksheet. There is also a limit of 32 changing cells per scenario. Note that you can safely delete the "Current Values" column since it shows the same data as our "Expected Case." It is a good idea to always define a scenario that uses the default values so that you can easily return the spreadsheet to the original values.

The Optimal Capital Budget

How large a firm's capital budget should be is a serious problem that confronts financial managers. One solution that is often chosen is capital rationing. *Capital rationing* is the arbitrary limiting of the amount of capital available for investment purposes. This solution is, however, economically irrational and contrary to the goal of the firm. In order to maximize shareholder wealth, the firm must accept all positive NPV projects. Remember that a positive NPV project is one that will cover the cost of financing (i.e., the weighted average cost of capital). In effect, a positive NPV project is self-liquidating, so there should be no problem raising the required funds to make the investment. No matter how much must be raised, as long as positive NPV projects exist, a firm should continue to invest until the cost of investing exceeds the benefits to be gained.[10]

---

10. From your economics classes, recall that to maximize profits a firm should continue to produce until the marginal cost equals the marginal revenue. This is the same idea, but in a different context. Furthermore, we are evaluating costs and benefits in present value terms and, as we will see in the next chapter, we are taking risk into account.

Optimal Capital Budget Without Capital Rationing

We have seen in the previous chapter that a firm's weighted average cost of capital will increase as the amount of capital to be raised increases. We can make use of this fact to determine exactly what a firm's optimal capital budget should be in the absence of capital rationing. Briefly, we rank all projects by their IRR and compare this ranking to the marginal weighted average cost of capital schedule.

Recall the Rocky Mountain Motors (RMM) example from Chapter 10. Assume that RMM has found 10 potential new projects, each of which would be profitable at their current WACC of 10.51% (i.e., all have IRRs > 10.51%). The projects are listed in Table 11-5.

TABLE 11-5
ROCKY MOUNTAIN MOTORS PROJECTS

Cost	Cumulative Cost	IRR
$445,529	$445,529	15.02%
439,207	884,736	15.87%
407,769	1,292,505	16.51%
396,209	1,688,714	16.16%
271,477	1,960,191	15.38%
201,843	2,162,034	11.69%
189,921	2,351,955	13.82%
146,661	2,498,616	12.19%
138,298	2,636,914	11.48%
74,950	2,711,864	13.00%

Enter the data from Table 11-5 into your RMM worksheet beginning with the labels in A22:C22. The cumulative cost can be calculated by entering: =SUM(A$23: A23) into B23 and then copying the formula to the other cells. The first step in determining the optimal capital budget is to sort all independent projects by their IRR. Select the data in A22:C32. To sort the data choose **D**ata **S**ort . . . from the menus, and select IRR in the "**S**ort by" list. Since we want to select the projects with the highest IRRs first, choose to sort in **D**escending order. This sorted list of IRRs is known as the Investment Opportunity Schedule (IOS).

Next, we want to add the project IRRs to the marginal WACC chart that was created earlier (see Exhibit 10-7 on page 325). To add the new data, right-click in the chart area and choose **S**ource Data from the shortcut menu. Under the Series list, click on the **A**dd button to create a new data series. Now, for the **N**ame of the series type: IOS and then enter: B23:B32 for the **X** Values and C23:C32 for the **Y** Values. Finally, notice that the MCC schedule only goes out to $900,000, but the IOS extends out to over $2,700,000. To fix this, change the value in A20 to: 3,000,000. Your worksheet should look like the one in Exhibit 11-6.

EXHIBIT 11-6
MARGINAL WACC AND THE IOS FOR RMM

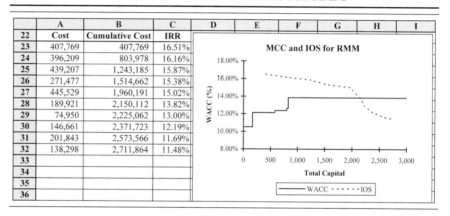

	A	B	C	D	E	F	G	H	I
22	Cost	Cumulative Cost	IRR						
23	407,769	407,769	16.51%						
24	396,209	803,978	16.16%						
25	439,207	1,243,185	15.87%						
26	271,477	1,514,662	15.38%						
27	445,529	1,960,191	15.02%						
28	189,921	2,150,112	13.82%						
29	74,950	2,225,062	13.00%						
30	146,661	2,371,723	12.19%						
31	201,843	2,573,566	11.69%						
32	138,298	2,711,864	11.48%						
33									
34									
35									
36									

As was shown on page 325, we can make the IOS line into a step function. The process is exactly the same as before: we must add additional data points for the cumulative cost and IRR so that we have two points at each change in the IRR. Once that is finished we can simply edit the data series by right-clicking the IOS and choosing **S**ource Data from the menu. Now, edit the X and Y data ranges to the new ones. Once complete, your chart should look like the one in Exhibit 11-7.

The optimal capital budget without capital rationing is the level of total capital at which the marginal WACC schedule and the Investment Opportunity Schedule cross. In this case that would be $1,960,191.

EXHIBIT 11-7
COMPLETED MCC AND IOS CHART

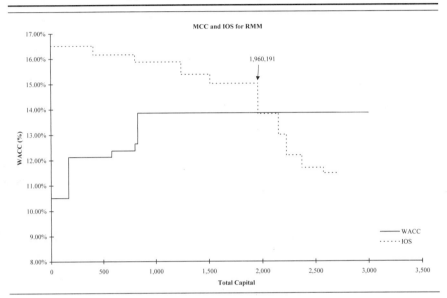

Optimal Capital Budget Under Capital Rationing

Though technically irrational, capital rationing is common. How then can we determine the optimal capital budget in the presence of restricted capital? In this situation we need to find that combination of projects that maximizes the total net present value, subject to the capital constraint.

This can be a tedious exercise when there are a large number of positive NPV projects from which to choose. For example, assume that we have four positive NPV projects. At a minimum we must select one project, but we can select up to four. If we must look at every possible combination of these four projects, then we must examine 16 possible combinations. As the number of projects grows, the number of combinations grows even faster. In general there are 2^N possible combinations, where N is the number of positive NPV projects. Note that negative NPV projects are excluded from this calculation and further consideration because we cannot increase the total NPV by adding a negative NPV project.[11]

---

11. Strictly speaking, this is not always true. Under a multi-period capital budgeting scenario with multi-period cash flow constraints, it is possible that adding negative NPV projects could increase the total NPV if they provide needed cash flows at the right time.

Excel provides a tool called the *Solver* that can be used in any type of constrained maximization or minimization problem. The Solver provides a dialog box in which you describe the problem, the cells that may be changed, and the constraints under which the Solver must operate. It then finds the optimal solution. Let's look at an example.

Because of declining demand for high-pressure frammis valves, the Frammis Valve Corporation of America (FVCA) is considering expanding into a number of other businesses. After discussions with its consultants, FVCA has determined that it has 13 potential new investments (see Table 11-6). The total cost of these investments would be $7,611,990, but they are limited to a maximum total investment of only $3,000,000. You have been asked to determine which combination of the projects the company should choose.

TABLE 11-6
FVCA'S AVAILABLE PROJECTS UNDER CAPITAL RATIONING

Project	Cost	NPV
A	$237,005	$84,334
B	766,496	26,881
C	304,049	23,162
D	565,178	82,598
E	108,990	20,590
F	89,135	90,404
G	795,664	18,163
H	814,493	97,682
I	480,321	52,063
J	826,610	53,911
K	734,830	56,323
L	910,598	88,349
M	978,621	69,352

Since there are 13 acceptable projects, you will have to examine each of the 8,192 ($= 2^{13}$) possible combinations and determine which provides the highest total NPV. This problem is obviously going to be time-consuming unless you have access to a computer. Enter the data from Table 11-6 into a new worksheet beginning in cell A4.

To solve this problem, we need some way to determine the sum of the costs and NPVs for only those projects that are to be selected. Since each project will either be selected or not, this is a perfect use for a *binary variable*. A binary variable can take on one of two values, most commonly 0 or 1. In this case, we will set up a column with 0s and 1s where 1 indicates that a project is selected, and 0 indicates rejection. Your worksheet should resemble that in Exhibit 11-8.

Note that we have initially set each cell in D4:D16 to: 1. Also, due to the nature of the problem, we cannot use an ordinary SUM function to total columns B and C. Recall that we only want the sum of the costs and NPVs of the projects that are to be selected. This requires an array formula.

EXHIBIT 11-8
FVCA's CAPITAL BUDGETING PROBLEM

	A	B	C	D
1	The Optimal Capital Budget			
2	Under Capital Rationing			
3	Project	Cost	NPV	Include
4	A	237,005	84,334	1
5	B	766,496	26,881	1
6	C	304,049	23,162	1
7	D	565,178	82,598	1
8	E	108,990	20,590	1
9	F	89,135	90,404	1
10	G	795,664	18,163	1
11	H	814,493	97,682	1
12	I	480,321	52,063	1
13	J	826,610	53,911	1
14	K	734,830	56,323	1
15	L	910,598	88,349	1
16	M	978,621	69,352	1
17	Total	7,611,990	763,812	13
18	Constraint	3,000,000		

An *array formula* is one that operates on each element in a range, but without specifying each element separately. Array formulas are therefore easier to write and save space. To calculate the total cost of the accepted projects in B17, we want to write a formula that multiplies the costs in column B by the corresponding 0 or 1 in column D and keeps a running total of the results. One way to do this is to write a formula such as: =B4*D4 + B5*D5 + B6*D6.... However, this would be a long formula to enter. The equivalent array formula would be: =Sum(B4:B16*$D4:$D16). This is much shorter and easier to understand.

Excel will not understand this formula unless you enter it in a specific way. You must enter array formulas with the Shift+Ctrl+Enter key combination. After you have correctly entered an array formula, it will appear in the formula bar surrounded by a pair of curly braces ({}). The formula in B17 will be displayed as: { =Sum(B4:B16*$D4:$D16)}. Note that you do not type the braces. They are only displayed as an indicator that the formula is an array formula. If you see a #VALUE! error in B17, you probably did not hold down Shift+Ctrl when pressing the Enter key. Copy the formula from B17 to C17, and your totals should be the same as those in Exhibit 11-8.

To restate the problem, we want to maximize the total NPV in C17 by changing the cells in D4:D16 subject to two constraints. The first constraint is that the total cost, in B17, must be less than or equal to 3,000,000. Next we must constrain the values in D4:D16 to be either 0 or 1, but they cannot take on any non-integer values (i.e., they must be binary values).

Bring up the Solver by selecting **T**ools Sol**v**er... from the menus. In the S**e**t Target Cell edit box enter: C17 and then click on the **M**ax radio button. This tells the Solver that we want to maximize the function in C17. Note that, under different circumstances, we could also minimize this formula or force it to a specific value. Next we need to tell Solver which cells it may change to find a solution. In the **B**y Changing Cells edit box enter: D4:D16.

The hardest part of solving many optimization problems is setting up the appropriate constraints. In this problem we have two constraints, and it will take only two statements to fully specify them. In other cases it may take more than one statement to fully specify a single constraint. To add a constraint, click on the **A**dd button. This will bring up a second dialog box in which we can enter a cell reference and the constraint. Note that the dialog box contains a drop-down list in the center that describes the possible relationships. These are <=, =, >=, int, and bin. The term "int" tells the Solver that the values in the cells must be an integer, and "bin" says that they must be either 0 or 1.

FIGURE 11-8
THE SOLVER DIALOG BOX

Add the first constraint by entering: B17 in the Cell Reference edit box, select <=, and enter: B18 in the constraint exit box. This will make sure that the total cost is less than the $3,000,000 constraint. For the second constraint, we must constrain the cells in D4:D16 to be binary. Add this constraint and the problem is almost ready to solve.

Because of the large number of possible solutions, the default configuration of the Solver may not find the solution. In the main Solver dialog box click on the **O**ptions . . . button. This will bring up another dialog box containing the options that you can set. Most of these are beyond the scope of this text. Set the Max **T**ime to at least 500 seconds (higher if you have a very slow PC) and **I**terations to at least 500. These two options control how long the Solver will try to solve the problem (they are maximums and Solver will stop as soon as it finds the solution). Finally make sure that Assume Linear **M**odel is checked. Click on the OK button.

Finally, to start the Solver working on the problem, click the **S**olve button. When Solver finds the solution it will present you with a dialog box that asks if you would like to save the solution or return to the original values. If you choose to save the optimal solution, your worksheet will resemble the one in Exhibit 11-9. Note that projects A, C, D, F, H, and L are selected.

EXHIBIT 11-9
THE OPTIMAL SOLUTION FOR THE FVCA CAPITAL BUDGET

	A	B	C	D
1	The Optimal Capital Budget			
2	Under Capital Rationing			
3	Project	Cost	NPV	Include
4	A	237,005	84,334	1
5	B	766,496	26,881	0
6	C	304,049	23,162	1
7	D	565,178	82,598	1
8	E	108,990	20,590	0
9	F	89,135	90,404	1
10	G	795,664	18,163	0
11	H	814,493	97,682	1
12	I	480,321	52,063	0
13	J	826,610	53,911	0
14	K	734,830	56,323	0
15	L	910,598	88,349	1
16	M	978,621	69,352	0
17	Total	2,920,458	466,529	6
18	Constraint	3,000,000		

As a final point about the Solver, you can easily change the constraint of $3,000,000 to any other value and then run the Solver again. Since the Solver settings are saved, you do not need to reenter the data every time. Further, once the optimal solution is found, you can save it as a named scenario and then use the Scenario Analysis tool to view all of the different scenarios. For example, we could create scenarios with total investment constraints of $3 million, $5 million, and $7 million. Once you've run the Solver with each of those constraints, choose Tools Scenarios and view the scenarios. You can also create a scenario summary as shown in Exhibit 11-10. In this case, we have edited the worksheet a bit to label the result cells (B17:D17) and hidden the changing cells to improve readability.

EXHIBIT 11-10
SCENARIO SUMMARY FOR OPTIMAL CAPITAL BUDGETING PROBLEM

Scenario Summary	$3 million constraint	$5 million constraint	$7 million constraint
Changing Cells:			
Result Cells:			
Total Investment	2,920,458	4,919,171	6,816,326
Total NPV	466,529	641,695	745,649
Number of Projects	6	9	12
Notes: Current Values column represents values of changing cells at			
time Scenario Summary Report was created. Changing cells for each			
scenario are highlighted in gray.			

Other Techniques

Because of the time required to maximize the total NPV, other techniques can be used to approximate the optimal capital budget. The first is to select the projects with the highest profitability indices. You may have to discard some high-PI projects, and you will likely not achieve the maximum NPV, but the solution can often be found with less work than maximizing NPV. As an alternative, we could choose the projects with the highest IRRs. However, this could be misleading if the projects are of greatly different sizes (as in the RMM example).

Summary

Capital budgeting is one of the most important functions of the corporate financial manager. In this chapter we have seen how to calculate the relevant cash flows and how to evaluate those cash flows to determine the profitability of accepting the project.

We demonstrated six profitability measures that are summarized in the following.

SUMMARY OF PROFITABILITY MEASURES

Profitability Measure	Acceptance Criteria
Payback period	<= Maximum allowable period
Discounted payback	<= Maximum allowable period
Net present value	>= 0
Profitability index	>= 1
Internal rate of return	>= WACC
Modified IRR	>= WACC

In addition, we introduced the Scenario Analysis and Solver tools provided by Excel. The Scenario Analysis tool allows us to easily compare the outcomes based on various inputs. The Solver allows us to find optimal values for a cell in a model.

FUNCTIONS INTRODUCED IN THIS CHAPTER

Purpose	Function	Page
Calculate straight-line depreciation	SLN(*COST, SALVAGE, LIFE*)	338
Calculate the payback period	FAME_PAYBACK(*CASHFLOWS, RATE*)	343
Calculate the IRR	IRR(*VALUES, GUESS*)	350
Calculate the MIRR	MIRR(*VALUES, FINANCE_RATE, REINVEST_RATE*)	354

Problems

1. The Auraria Pet Foods Company is considering the purchase of more flexible equipment that will allow them to create new products and will also be less expensive to operate than the current machinery. The existing equipment could be sold for $50,000 after taxes. As of today, management forecasts call for after-tax cash flows of $15,000 next year if the current machinery is retained. The cash flows are expected to increase at a rate of 6% per year for the next five years. The new machinery under consideration has a price of $70,000. It would be expected to produce cash flows of $20,000 next year, and the cash flows would grow by 8% per year for the next five years.

   a. Calculate the net present value, IRR, and MIRR of the existing equipment. If the new equipment was not available, would it make more sense to keep the existing equipment or to sell it?

   b. Calculate the net present value, IRR, and MIRR of the new equipment. If the new equipment is treated as a stand-alone investment, would it make sense to make the investment?

   c. If you had to choose between keeping the existing equipment, or investing in the new equipment, which would you choose? Make the comparison by looking at both the NPVs and IRRs.

   d. Now, calculate the incremental cost and annual after-tax cash flows if the new equipment is purchased. Evaluate the investment in the new equipment as a replacement project. Would you make the investment? Use the NPV, IRR, and MIRR to explain your decision.

   e. At what discount rate would you be indifferent between keeping the existing equipment or purchasing the new equipment?

2. You are considering an investment in two projects, A and B. Project A will cost $60,000, Project B will cost $50,000, and the projected cash flows are as follows:

Year	Project A	Project B
1	20,000	35,000
2	25,000	30,000
3	30,000	25,000
4	35,000	20,000
5	40,000	15,000

   a. Assuming that the WACC is 12%, calculate the payback period, discounted payback period, NPV, PI, IRR, and MIRR. If the projects are mutually exclusive, which project should be selected?

   b. Create an NPV profile chart for projects A and B. What is the exact crossover rate for these two projects?

3. Chicago Turkey is considering building a new turkey farm to service their western region stores. The stores currently require 500,000 turkeys per year, and they are purchased from various local turkey farms for an average price of $7 per bird. The managers of Chicago Turkey believe that their new farm would lower the cost per bird to $6, while maintaining their average selling price of $10 per bird. However, due to the centralized structure of this operation, shipping expenses will increase to $1.50 per bird from the current average of $1.00. In addition, the firm will need to increase its inventory of live turkeys by $15,000. It is estimated that it will cost $150,000 to purchase the land, and $300,000 to construct the buildings and purchase equipment. In addition, labor expenses will rise by $130,000 per year. The buildings and equipment will be depreciated using the straight-line method over five years to a salvage value of $100,000. At the end of five years the company will sell the farm for $300,000 ($100,000 for the buildings and equipment and $200,000 for the land). Assume that the firm's marginal tax rate is 35%, and note that land is not depreciable.

a. Calculate the initial outlay, annual after-tax cash flows, and terminal cash flow for this project.

b. If the WACC is 11%, calculate the payback period, discounted payback period, NPV, PI, IRR, and MIRR.

c. The managers of Chicago Turkey are uncertain about several of the variables in your analysis and have asked you to provide three different scenarios. Create a scenario analysis showing the profitability measures for this investment using the information in the table below. (Note: The salvage value of the buildings is the actual forecasted salvage value, not the salvage value used for depreciation.)

Scenario	Labor Expense	Salvage Value of Buildings	Salvage Value of Land
Best Case	$100,000	$150,000	$300,000
Expected Case	130,000	100,000	200,000
Worst Case	140,000	50,000	100,000

4. The Chief Financial Officer of Eaton Medical Devices has determined that the firm's capital investment budget will be $5,000,000 for the upcoming year. Unfortunately, this amount is not sufficient to cover all of the positive NPV projects that are available to the firm.

Project	Cost	NPV
A	$628,200	$72,658
B	352,100	36,418
C	1,245,600	212,150
D	814,300	70,925
E	124,500	11,400
F	985,000	56,842
G	2,356,400	93,600
H	226,900	65,350
I	1,650,000	48,842
J	714,650	39,815

You have been asked to choose which investments, of those listed in the table below, should be made.

a. Using the Solver, determine which of the above projects should be included in the budget if the firm's goal is to maximize shareholder wealth. (Note: Make sure to set the Solver options to Assume Linear Model.)

b. Now assume that the CFO has informed you that projects A and B are mutually exclusive, but one of them must be selected. Change your Solver constraints to account for this new information and find the new solution.

c. Ignore the constraints from part B. The CFO has now informed you that Project I is of great strategic importance to the survival of the firm. For this reason it must be accepted. Change your Solver constraints to account for this new information and find the new solution.

CHAPTER 12

Risk, Capital Budgeting, and Diversification

After studying this chapter, you should be able to:

1. *Define the five major statistical measures used in finance and calculate these both manually and in Excel.*

2. *Explain how risk can be incorporated into capital budgeting decisions, and show how to calculate the "risk-adjusted discount rate" (RADR) in Excel.*

3. *Explain five alternative techniques for incorporating risk into the capital budgeting decision process.*

4. *Explain diversification and give an example using Excel.*

5. *Calculate portfolio risk and return measures with Excel.*

Risk is a difficult concept to define, but most people recognize such obvious risks as swimming in shark-infested waters. If you consider risky situations for a moment, you will realize that the thing that they all have in common is the possibility of a loss. Many times we face the loss of life or money. In this chapter we are concerned with the possibility of a financial loss. Specifically, we will say that the larger the possibility of loss, the larger the risk.

We will begin by attempting to measure the riskiness of an investment, and then we will consider how we can adjust our decision-making process to account for the risk that we have measured. Finally, we will consider how we can reduce risk through diversification.

Review of Some Useful Statistical Concepts

Any situation that has an uncertain outcome can be said to have a probability distribution associated with the possible outcomes. A *probability distribution* is simply a listing of the probabilities associated with potential outcomes. A probability distribution is said to be *discrete* if there are a limited number of potential outcomes, and *continuous* if an infinite number of possible outcomes can occur. Figure 12-1 illustrates both continuous and discrete probability distributions. Continuous probability distributions can be approximated by discrete distributions if we have enough possible outcomes. To keep things simple, in this chapter we will use only discrete distributions in our examples.

FIGURE 12-1
CONTINUOUS VS. DISCRETE PROBABILITY DISTRIBUTIONS

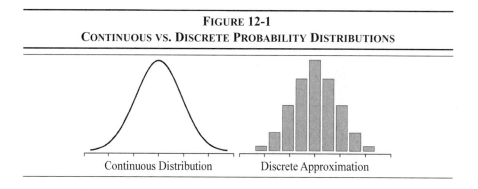

Continuous Distribution   Discrete Approximation

One type of probability distribution has numerous properties that make it attractive for our use: the *normal distribution*. In particular, the normal distribution can be completely described by its mean and variance, which will prove useful in our efforts to understand risk.

The Expected Value

The *expected value* of a distribution is a weighted average of all possible outcomes where the weights are the probabilities of occurrence. The expected value can be thought of as the most likely outcome, or the average outcome if we could run an experiment thousands of times. For any discrete probability distribution, the expected value is given by:

$$E(X) = \sum_{t=1}^{N} \rho_t X_t \qquad (12\text{-}1)$$

where $E(X)$ is the expected or most likely X, X_t is the tth possible outcome, and ρ_t is the probability that X_t will occur. For the normal distribution, the expected value is the same as the more familiar arithmetic mean.

To illustrate the calculation of the expected value, suppose that you have been offered an opportunity to participate in a game of chance. The rules of this particular game are such that you must pay $200 to play, and Table 12-1 describes the possible payoffs.

TABLE 12-1
PROBABILITY DISTRIBUTION FOR A GAME OF CHANCE

Probability	Cash Flow
0.25	100
0.50	200
0.25	300

To determine whether or not you should play this game, we must compare the expected payoff to the cost of playing. If the expected cash flow is equal to or exceeds your cost it makes sense to play. The expected cash flow, $E(Cf)$, of this game is:

$$E(Cf) = 0.25(100) + 0.50(200) + 0.25(300) = 200$$

so that you expect to break even after subtracting your cost to play. Note that in actuality, if the game is played only once you could lose as much as $100 or win as much as $100 net of your cost of entry. However, the most likely outcome is a net gain of $0.00. The arithmetic mean of cash flows $(\overline{Cf})$ is:

$$\overline{Cf} = \frac{100 + 200 + 300}{3} = 200$$

and subtracting your cost, you can see that they are the same. Again, in this case, the expected value and the arithmetic mean are the same because the outcomes of this game are symmetrically distributed.

It is important to understand that many times the assumption of a symmetrical distribution is not accurate, and in this case the arithmetic mean and the expected value will not be the same.[1] Whenever possible, it is better to use the expected value as an estimate instead of the arithmetic mean.

Measures of Dispersion

Whenever we use an expected value, it is useful to know how much, on average, the actual outcome might deviate from the expected outcome. The larger these potential deviations are, the less confidence we will have that the expected outcome will actually occur. Another way of saying this is that the larger the potential deviations from the expected value, the higher the probability of an outcome far away from the expected outcome.

Recall that we earlier said that high probabilities of loss indicate a high-risk situation. Therefore, when comparing distributions we can say that the distribution with the larger potential deviations has a higher probability of greater loss, and therefore has higher risk.

The Variance and Standard Deviation

To measure risk, what we need is a way to measure the size of the potential deviations from the mean. One measure we could use is the average deviation from the mean. The average deviation is calculated as:

$$\overline{D} = \sum_{t=1}^{N} \rho_t (X_t - E(X)) \tag{12-2}$$

But, in the case of the normal distribution (or any symmetrical distribution), the average deviation will always be zero. So we need another measure of dispersion

---

1. This is particularly true in many financial situations where your maximum loss is limited to 100% of the investment, but your potential gain is unlimited. This results in a distribution that is skewed to the right.

that doesn't suffer from this flaw. One possibility is the *variance*. The variance is the average of the squared deviations from the mean and is calculated as:[2]

$$\sigma_X^2 = \sum_{t=1}^{N} \rho_t (X_t - E(X))^2 \tag{12-3}$$

Because we are squaring the deviations from the mean, and the result of squaring a number is always positive, the variance must be positive.[3] The larger the variance, the less likely it is that the actual outcome will be near the expected outcome, and the riskier it is considered to be. Figure 12-2 illustrates this by comparing two distributions.

FIGURE 12-2
COMPARISON OF THE RISKINESS OF TWO DISTRIBUTIONS

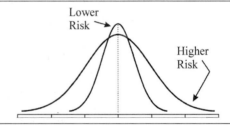

Returning to the example in Table 12-1, we can calculate the variance of possible outcomes as follows:

$$\sigma^2 = 0.25(100 - 200)^2 + 0.50(200 - 200)^2 + 0.25(300 - 200)^2 = 5,000$$

So the variance of possible outcomes is 5,000. But 5,000 in what units? In this case the units are squared dollars, an unusual unit of measurement to be sure. In order to

---

2. Note that in your beginning statistics class you probably defined the population variance as:

$$\sigma_X^2 = \frac{1}{N} \sum_{t=1}^{N} (X_t - \bar{X})^2$$

Our definition is equivalent if we assume that all outcomes are equally likely.

3. It is possible that the variance could be zero, but only if just one possible outcome exists.

make this measurement more understandable we commonly take the square root of the variance, which gives us the *standard deviation* in the original units:

$$\sigma_X = \sqrt{\sigma_X^2} = \sqrt{\sum_{t=1}^{N} \rho_t (X_t - E(X))^2} \qquad (12\text{-}4)$$

The standard deviation of potential outcomes in our game example is:

$$\sigma = \sqrt{5{,}000} = 70.71$$

which means that about 68% of all outcomes will be within one standard deviation of the mean (200 ± 70.71), and about 95.5% will be within two standard deviations (200 ± 141.42). Furthermore, it is exceedingly unlikely (< 0.30%), but not impossible, that the actual outcome will fall beyond three standard deviations from the mean.[4]

The Coefficient of Variation

Suppose that after playing our original game, you are offered a chance to play the game again, but this time the game is 10 times larger and so is your cost to play. The possible outcomes are presented in Table 12-2.

TABLE 12-2
SAME GAME, BUT TEN TIMES LARGER

Probability	Cash Flow
0.25	1000
0.50	2000
0.25	3000

Is this game riskier than the old game? Let's look at the standard deviation to see:

$$\sigma = \sqrt{0.25(1000 - 2000)^2 + 0.50(2{,}000 - 2{,}000)^2 + 0.25(3{,}000 - 2{,}000)^2}$$
$$\sigma = 707.106$$

Since the standard deviation is 10 times larger, it appears that the new game is much riskier. Recall, however, that we said that high risk was associated with a high

---

4. This is known as the empirical rule. For non-normal distributions, Chebyshev's Theorem gives similar (though not as precise) results.

probability of loss. In the new game your probability of loss is unchanged (25%). Since the probability of loss is unchanged, the risk should be the same.

Apparently the standard deviation has a scale problem. That is, larger numbers cause larger standard deviations, even if the relative dispersion is unchanged. The coefficient of variation handles the scale problem by dividing the standard deviation by the mean, so it is a measure of risk per unit of return:

$$\gamma_X = \frac{\sigma_X}{E(X)} \tag{12-5}$$

If the new game is truly riskier than the old game, it will have a higher coefficient of variation. Let's compare the coefficients of variation for both games:

$$\gamma_1 = \frac{70.7106}{200} = 0.3535$$
$$\gamma_2 = \frac{707.106}{2,000} = 0.3535$$

Since $\gamma_1 = \gamma_2$, both games must be equally risky.

Using Excel to Measure Risk

Now that we understand how risk can be evaluated, let's look at how Excel might be used to simplify the calculations. In this section we will introduce several of Excel's built-in functions and several macro functions that are contained in the file FameFncs.xla. Before continuing, open that add-in and also a new workbook, into which we will enter data from an example of a capital budgeting project.

The Freshly Frozen Fish Company Example

The Freshly Frozen Fish Company currently markets frozen fish fillets and other related products. While seeking expansion ideas, management of the company decided to look into the possibility of a line of frozen catfish fillets. Entry into this business would require the purchase of an existing 80-acre catfish farm in western Alabama at a cost of $250,000 for the land, and $400,000 for the buildings and equipment. The buildings and equipment will be depreciated at a rate of $40,000 per year for the five-year life of the project. At the end of the five years, management anticipates that the farm can be sold for $550,000 ($350,000 for the land and $200,000 for the buildings and equipment).

The marketing department estimates that the firm will be able to sell 200,000 pounds of fillets at an average wholesale price of $2.50 per pound during the first year. Unit demand is expected to grow at a rate of 8% annually thereafter. Variable operating expenses are expected to average 60% of gross sales, and fixed costs (not including depreciation) will be $80,000 per year. The company's marginal tax rate is 35% and its weighted average cost of capital is 10%.

Before we can determine the riskiness of this project, we must determine its cost and annual cash flows. Let's begin by entering all of the data from the problem into the worksheet starting in cell A1. The easiest way to extract data from a problem such as this is to take it as it comes and enter it into the worksheet in that order, being careful to label every row. This way, you are less likely to overlook an important piece of data. That is exactly what we've done in Exhibit 12-1. If necessary, we can rearrange this table later.

EXHIBIT 12-1
FRESHLY FROZEN FISH COMPANY INPUTS

	A	B
1	**Frozen Catfish Fillet Project Inputs**	
2	Cost of Land	250,000
3	Cost of Buildings & Equipment	400,000
4	Annual Depreciation	40,000
5	Life of Project (Years)	5
6	Terminal Value of Land	350,000
7	Terminal Value of Buildings & Equipment	200,000
8	First Year Catfish Sales (lbs)	200,000
9	Price per Pound	2.50
10	Unit Sales Growth Rate	8%
11	Variable Costs as % of Sales	60%
12	Fixed Costs	80,000
13	Tax Rate	35%
14	WACC	10%

Recall from Chapter 11 (page 333) that our first task is to determine the initial outlay. The example problem in that chapter was a little different than this one because it was a replacement problem. However, exactly the same techniques can be used to determine the cash flows. Just realize that in the case of this entirely new project we aren't replacing anything, so cash flows associated with selling off old equipment are set to zero.

Before continuing, let's take a little time to set up our calculation area on the worksheet. Realize that the annual after-tax cash flows are going to be different in each of the five years. To keep things as simple as possible, we will set up the calculations in a modified income statement format. In A16 enter: Annual Cash Flows for Frozen Catfish Fillet Project, and center this title over A16:G16. Next, in B17 enter: Year 0 and use AutoFill to extend that to Year 5 in G17.

We have purposely simplified this example, so we have no shipping, installation, training, or construction costs. The initial outlay is simply the cost of the land and buildings. In A18 enter: Initial Outlay, and in B18 enter: =-(B2+B3). This will give us the initial outlay as a negative number. The result is –$650,000.

Our next step is to calculate the annual after-tax cash flows (ATCF) for each year. As noted above, the cash flows will be different each year because sales and variable operating expenses are expected to increase every year by 8%. We will calculate the ATCF for each year as:

$$\text{ATCF}_N = (S_N - V_N - F_N)(1 - t) + tD_N$$

where S_N is the total revenue in year N, V_N is the total variable costs, F_N is the fixed costs, t is the marginal tax rate, and D_N is the annual depreciation expense. Note that tD_N is the annual tax savings from the additional depreciation expense. This is exactly the same equation as shown on page 335, except it has been modified slightly to suit this problem.

In A19 enter: Sales as the label. We will calculate the first-year sales in C19 by multiplying unit sales (200,000 pounds) by the selling price ($2.50), so the equation is: =B8*B9. This gives us $500,000 in sales revenue for the first year. Each additional year's sales will be 8% greater than previous sales, so in D19 enter: =C19*(1+$B$10). Now copy this formula over the range E19:G19. As a check, note that under these assumptions, sales will grow to $680,244.48 by year 5.

Next, to calculate the annual variable costs enter: `=C19*$B$11` into C20, and copy it across over D20:G20. In A20 enter: `Variable Costs` as the label for the row. In A21 enter: `Fixed Costs` for the label, and then in C21 enter: `=$B$12`. Copy this over D21:G21.

We can now calculate the taxable cash flows before depreciation in row 22. In A22 add the label: `Taxable Cash Flows`. Subtract the fixed and variable costs from sales in C22 with the formula: `=C19-SUM(C20:C21)` and copy this across the other columns. In A23 enter the label: `Taxes`, and in C23 enter: `=C22*$B$13` and copy it to D23:G23.

At this point, to get the ATCF we need to add the depreciation tax benefit. In A24 enter: `Depreciation Tax Benefit` as the label, and then in C24: `=$B$4*$B$13`. Copy this to the remaining cells, and then in A25 enter: `Annual After-tax Cash Flows`. Finally, in C25 we can enter: `=C22-C23+C24`. Copy this to the other cells in D25:G25.

The last cash flow that we must calculate is the terminal cash flow. Recall that this is the sum of the nonoperating cash flows that occur at the end of the life of the project. In this problem, those would be the sale of the land and buildings as well as any taxes required on the gains. The land is not depreciable, so any gain on the sale of land is taxable. To calculate the tax on the buildings and equipment, we must first determine their book value at year 5. Since the firm will pay $400,000 and receive $40,000 per year in depreciation, the book value will be $200,000. In this case, the expected selling price is exactly equal to the book value, so no tax is due. However, our formula must account for the possibility of taxes in case we change the expected selling price. In A26 enter: `Terminal Cash Flow`, and the formula in G26 is: `=B6-(B6-B2)*B13+B7-(B7-(B3-B4*B5))*B13`.

In order to summarize our calculations, we will add one more row. In A27 enter: `Total Annual Cash Flows`. In B27 enter: `=B18`. In C27 enter: `=C25+C26`, and copy it across. Check your worksheet against that shown in Exhibit 12-2 to be sure that your calculations are correct.

EXHIBIT 12-2
CALCULATION OF THE ANNUAL AFTER-TAX CASH FLOWS

	A	B	C	D	E	F	G
16	Annual Cash Flows for Frozen Catfish Fillet Project						
17		Year 0	Year 1	Year 2	Year 3	Year 4	Year 5
18	Initial Outlay	(650,000)					
19	Sales		500,000	540,000	583,200	629,856	680,244
20	Variable Costs		300,000	324,000	349,920	377,914	408,147
21	Fixed Costs		80,000	80,000	80,000	80,000	80,000
22	Taxable Cash Flows		120,000	136,000	153,280	171,942	192,098
23	Taxes		42,000	47,600	53,648	60,180	67,234
24	Depreciation Tax Benefit		14,000	14,000	14,000	14,000	14,000
25	Annual After-Tax Cash Flow		92,000	102,400	113,632	125,763	138,864
26	Terminal Cash Flow						515,000
27	Total Annual Cash Flows	(650,000)	92,000	102,400	113,632	125,763	653,864

At this point we are ready to calculate the net present value to give a preliminary assessment of the merits of this project. In A29 enter: Net Present Value, and in B29 enter: =NPV(B14,C27:G27)+B27. The NPV is $95,533.22, which would seem to indicate that the project is acceptable.

Introducing Uncertainty

If we lived in a world of perfect certainty, the catfish fillet project would be accepted without question. After all, it appears that it will increase shareholder wealth by $95,533.22. Unfortunately, the world is not certain. Even in this simplified example, it should be clear that many sources of uncertainty may arise. For example, the marketing department doesn't really *know* that the firm will sell 200,000 pounds of catfish fillets in the first year. Likewise, it doesn't know that it will be able to get the assumed $2.50 per pound, or that demand will grow at an annual rate of 8% per year. Consumer demand may be far less than expected. This could lead to a double whammy: Not only would unit demand be less than expected, but the wholesale price would likely be less than $2.50 per pound. Poor first-year acceptance could also mean lower subsequent growth rates. These and many other uncertainties naturally result in uncertainty surrounding our expected annual cash flows that, in turn, results in uncertainty surrounding the estimated NPV.

In such an uncertain world, it is helpful to develop models that allow us to determine how much uncertainty surrounds our estimate of the NPV. For example, we might like to make an educated guess as to the probability that the NPV will actually turn out to be less than zero. The following sections will lead us to an answer to this question.

Sensitivity Analysis

As noted above, many uncertain variables exist in our catfish fillet example. In fact, we could say that virtually all of the variables are uncertain, as are many others that we have not explicitly considered. However, some of these variables have more of an impact on the NPV than others. Since it would take a lot of time and effort to generate precise forecasts of every variable, it is helpful to concentrate on only the most important variables. Sensitivity analysis is the tool that helps us to identify the variables that deserve the most attention.

The idea is to make small changes in variables, one at a time, and observe the effect on the NPV (or any other decision criteria). For example, we might change the selling price from $2.50 per pound to $2.25 (a change of −10%) and then calculate that the NPV would decline to $38,552.35. Record this fact and reset the selling price to its original value. Now, reduce the terminal value of the land to $225,000 (a change of −10%) and note that the NPV declines to $81,407.26. Reducing the selling price by 10% leads to a much bigger decline in the NPV than does a similar reduction in the terminal value of the land. Therefore, we should devote more resources to determining the selling price.

There are two problems with the procedure outlined above. First, by making only a single small change to each variable, we may miss nonlinear relationships. Second, to carry out this procedure for each uncertain variable would be cumbersome. We would have to change a variable, write down the resulting NPV, reset the variable to its original value, change another variable, write down the resulting NPV, and so on. To solve the first problem we can simply make several changes in each variable, both up and down. For example, we could change the selling price per pound by −30% to +30% in, say, 10% increments. This, however, exacerbates the second problem by making the analysis even more onerous. Fortunately, Excel provides a solution.

Using Data Tables

A data table is an Excel tool that automatically performs the process described previously. To see how they work, let's set up a simple example. Suppose that we wish to see what happens to the expected NPV as the selling price varies from $1.50 to $3.50 per pound. To start, enter: $1.50 in G5 and $2.00 in

H5.[5] Now use AutoFill to create the rest of the price series. The next step is to enter a formula into F6. In this case, we are interested in the NPV so we need to enter: `=NPV(B14,C27:G27)+B27`.

FIGURE 12-3
THE DATA TABLE DIALOG BOX

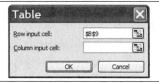

When we execute the data table command, Excel will automatically substitute the values from G5:K5 into our model (in cell B9) one at a time, and record the resulting NPVs in the table. Select F5:K6 (this is the entire area of the table we are creating, including the NPV formula) and then choose **D**ata **T**able from the menu. In the resulting dialog box, type: `B9` into the Row input cell edit box as shown in Figure 12-3. After clicking the OK button, this section of your worksheet should look like the one in Exhibit 12-3.

EXHIBIT 12-3
THE DATA TABLE FOR DIFFERENT PRICES

	F	G	H	I	J	K
5	Unit Price	$1.50	$2.00	$2.50	$3.00	$3.50
6	95,533.22	(132,390.24)	(18,428.51)	95,533.22	209,494.94	323,456.67

The values in G6:K6 are the NPVs. For example, if the price per pound was $1.50 the NPV would be −$132,390.24. Similarly, if the price was $3.50 the NPV would be $323,456.67. If necessary, you can change any or all of the prices in row 5 and the table will automatically update.

Note that the original NPV in F6 is not a part of the table per se, and it might confuse some people. It is only there so that Excel knows what formula to use when calculating the table. We can easily hide this value by simply selecting F6 and changing the font color to white. This will make the table easier to read.

---

5. The data table can be created anywhere on this worksheet, but it cannot be in another worksheet. You can get around this limitation by carefully constructing your formulas.

Excel allows for other types of data tables than we have demonstrated here. The data table in Exhibit 12-3 is called a row-oriented one-variable table because our prices are in a row. If the prices were in a column instead, we could create a column-oriented one-variable table. To create a column-oriented table, the only difference is that you would enter the changing cell (B9) into the Column input cell edit box (see Figure 12-3). The result would be exactly the same, except for the orientation table. We can also create two-variable data tables that allow for two changing variables. The procedure is similar, but you should check the online help for the details.

Since we have more than one uncertain variable in our catfish fillet problem, we will need several data tables. It will also be helpful, for comparison purposes, to deviate a bit from the methodology described above. Specifically, we can set up several data tables based on percentage changes in our uncertain variables. This will make it easier to compare the result from a change in unit sales to the result from a change in the growth rate.

EXHIBIT 12-4
THE INPUT AREA SET UP FOR SENSITIVITY ANALYSIS

	A	B	C	D
1	**Frozen Catfish Fillet Project Inputs**			
2	Cost of Land	250,000		
3	Cost of Buildings & Equipment	400,000		
4	Annual Depreciation	40,000		
5	Life of Project (Years)	5		Sensitivity %
6	Terminal Value of Land	350,000		0%
7	Terminal Value of Buildings & Equipment	200,000		0%
8	First Year Catfish Sales (lbs)	200,000		0%
9	Price per Pound	2.50		0%
10	Unit Sales Growth Rate	8%		0%
11	Variable Costs as % of Sales	60%		0%
12	Fixed Costs	80,000		
13	Tax Rate	35%		
14	WACC	10%		

Let's start by changing the input area of the worksheet so that it can accommodate this type of sensitivity analysis more easily. In D5 enter: Sensitivity %, and then in D6:D11 enter: 0% in each cell. Change B6 so that it has a formula rather than a number: =350000*(1+D6). Now if we put 10% into D6, for example, the terminal value of the land will change from $350,000 to $385,000. Make similar changes in cells B7:B11 so that those values change as we change the corresponding percentages. Your input area should now look like the one in Exhibit 12-4. Note that we will be doing the sensitivity analysis on only six of the variables.

At this point we can proceed in a similar manner as we did above. Let's first create a percentage-based data table for the terminal value of the land. Go to A38 and enter: Terminal Value of Land. In B38:H38 enter a series from –30% to +30% in 10% increments (–30%, –20%, –10%, etc.). In A39, enter the **NPV** function: =NPV(B14,C27:G27)+B27. We have now set up the table, and all that remains is to select it and execute the **D**ata **T**able command. In this case the row input cell is D6, which is the percentage that corresponds to the terminal value of the land. The data table will plug –30% into D6, which will change the terminal land value in B6 resulting in a different NPV. Next, it will plug in –20% and so on.

Using the same procedure, create data tables for each of the uncertain variables, each time changing the row input cell (D7, D8, etc.). You should end up with six data tables as shown in Exhibit 12-5. Note that, as mentioned above, we have hidden the original NPV formula so that the table is easier to read.

EXHIBIT 12-5
DATA TABLES FOR THE UNCERTAIN VARIABLES

	A	B	C	D	E	F	G	H
37	Sensitivity Tables							
38	Terminal Value of Land	-30%	-20%	-10%	0%	10%	20%	30%
39		53,155	67,281	81,407	95,533	109,659	123,785	137,911
40								
41	Value of Buildings & Equipment	-30%	-20%	-10%	0%	10%	20%	30%
42		71,317	79,389	87,461	95,533	103,605	111,677	119,749
43								
44	First Year Catfish Sales (lbs)	-30%	-20%	-10%	0%	10%	20%	30%
45		(75,409)	(18,429)	38,552	95,533	152,514	209,495	266,476
46								
47	Price per Pound	-30%	-20%	-10%	0%	10%	20%	30%
48		(75,409)	(18,429)	38,552	95,533	152,514	209,495	266,476
49								
50	Unit Sales Growth Rate	-30%	-20%	-10%	0%	10%	20%	30%
51		71,214	79,201	87,307	95,533	103,881	112,352	120,947
52								
53	Variable Costs as % of Sales	-30%	-20%	-10%	0%	10%	20%	30%
54		351,947	266,476	181,005	95,533	10,062	(75,409)	(160,881)

Sensitivity Diagrams

Many people can look at the data tables and see at a glance that the most important variables are the unit sales, price per pound, and the variable cost as a percentage of sales. Others, however, find it helpful to create charts of the data. The most appropriate type of chart for this analysis is an XY (Scatter) chart. We can either create a separate chart for each variable, or put all of the variables in one chart.

To create one chart that shows all of the variables,we must first start with a chart of one of the variables. Select B38:H39 and create an XY (Scatter) chart and place it somewhere convenient on the screen. Now, select B42:H42 and drag the range over the chart and drop it there. You have now added a second data series. Continue adding each of the other data series in the same way. For this example problem, it turns out that some of the lines overlap, so it is impossible to tell them apart on the chart. This is not generally the case. However, even when we don't have this problem, it can be much easier to see which variables are most important if they are all in separate charts. This is particularly true when we have a lot of variables.

FIGURE 12-4
SENSITIVITY DIAGRAMS FOR EACH VARIABLE

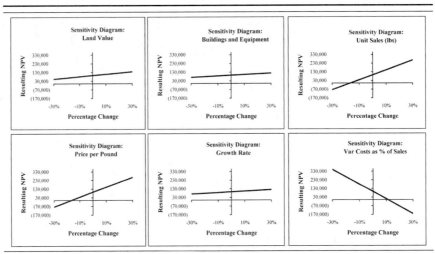

Creating a separate chart for each variable is more time-consuming, and you need to make sure that the scaling of the axis is the same in each chart. The advantage to this approach is that it is much easier to identify the individual data series. As can be seen in Figure 12-4, the lines with the steepest slopes are the same as those previously identified as the most important variables. In order to make this comparison, it is vital that the axis scaling is identical in each chart. To make creating all of these charts easier, you can copy and paste the first one and then simply change the data ranges. Clearly, the most important variables are the unit sales, price per pound, and the variable cost as a percentage of sales. These are the variables that we will use in our scenario analysis in the next section.

Scenario Analysis

The sensitivity analysis has identified the three most important variables, but we've only seen their impact on the NPV in isolation. A *scenario analysis* will allow us to see the combined effects of changing all of these variables simultaneously. Suppose that after seeing the sensitivity analysis report, a meeting was held to determine three possible scenarios. The best and worst cases are shown in Table 12-3 along with the base case, which represents the original expectations. It also shows the probability that each scenario will actually occur.

TABLE 12-3
THREE SCENARIOS

Variable	Worst Case 20%	Base Case 60%	Best Case 20%
Unit Sales	125,000	200,000	275,000
Price per Pound	$2.25	$2.50	$2.65
Variable Cost %	65%	60%	55%

Note that the worst-case scenario is one in which all of the variables are at their worst possible values. Similarly, the best case assumes that all of the variables take on their best possible values simultaneously. While such outcomes are unlikely, they are useful for determining the extreme boundaries around the expected NPV.

Excel provides the Scenario Manager to help us to analyze such scenarios. In Chapter 3 (page 86) we used the Scenario Manager to perform a sensitivity analysis to see the effect of the timing of a large capital expenditure on total borrowing. In Chapter 11 (page 356) we performed a scenario analysis to determine the combined effect of changing maintenance and defect costs on the profitability measures of a replacement project.[6]

---

6. We could have used the Scenario Manager to do the sensitivity analysis, but that would have required 42 different scenarios. It is much easier to use data tables for sensitivity analysis, but they are not adequate for scenario analysis because data tables only allow (at most) two variables to change at the same time.

In this section, we will again use the Scenario Manager, but our goal is to get a better understanding of the riskiness of the frozen catfish product. Specifically, we want to get an idea of the probability distribution around the expected NPV, especially the range of possible outcomes. Before using the Scenario Manager, it is helpful to define names for the changing cells. Set up the scenarios given in Table 12-3, and create a scenario summary report with the NPV as the result cell.

EXHIBIT 12-6
SCENARIO SUMMARY REPORT

Scenario Summary			
	Worst Case	Base Case	Best Case
Changing Cells:			
Catfish_Sales_Pounds	125,000	200,000	275,000
Price_Per_Pound	2.25	2.50	2.65
Var_Costs_Percent	65%	60%	55%
Result Cells:			
Net_Present_Value	$(193,822.73)	$ 95,533.22	$ 460,032.68

Exhibit 12-6 shows the scenario summary report. Note that in the worst case, where the price and unit sales are low and variable costs are high, the NPV is significantly negative. On the other hand, the NPV is very high in the best case. So far, the scenario analysis has shown a risk of a negative NPV. However, we haven't yet quantified that risk.

Assume that the experts who defined the three scenarios were also asked to assign the probabilities of occurrence to each scenario. Feeling that the extreme scenarios are relatively unlikely, they assigned a probability of 20% to the best and worst cases. This leaves 60% for the base case. On your Scenario Summary worksheet, enter: `Probabilities` in D12, `20%` in E12, `60%` in F12, and `20%` in G12. Figure 12-5 shows a histogram of the probability distribution.

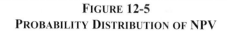

FIGURE 12-5
PROBABILITY DISTRIBUTION OF NPV

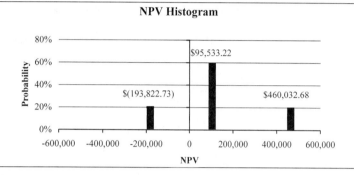

Calculating Expected Values in Excel

With this information we can now calculate the expected NPV for the project. We might try to calculate the expected value in several ways. For example, we might try using the **AVERAGE** function. Recall from Chapter 1 that the **AVERAGE** function calculates the arithmetic (unweighted) average of the observations. However, a glance at Figure 12-5 shows that the distribution is somewhat skewed to the right, and the possible outcomes are not all equally likely, so the average will overstate the expected value (as we discussed on page 380).

It would be more appropriate to calculate the expected value (see equation (12-1) on page 379). Recall that the expected value is found by multiplying each possible outcome by its associated probability and summing the results. In C13 enter: `Expected NPV`. We might make this calculation in any one of several ways. For example, in D13 we could enter: `=D10*D12+E10*E12+F10*F12`, but that's not the best way. A better way would be to use an array formula: `=SUM(D10:F10*D12:F12)`; just remember to hold down the Shift and Ctrl keys when pressing the Enter key. Finally, we have supplied a macro called **FAME_EXPVALUE** that will calculate the expected value of a probability distribution. It is defined as:

FAME_EXPVALUE(*VALUES*, *PROBABILITIES*)

where ***VALUES*** is the range of possible outcomes, and ***PROBABILITIES*** is the range of probabilities. To use this function, make sure that the file FameFncs.xla is open, and then enter: `=Fame_ExpValue(D10:F10,D12:F12)` into D13. As an alternative, you can use the Insert Function tool that will list this function in the "User Defined" category.

Whichever way you choose to calculate it, the expected NPV for this project is $110,561.92. This means that, if our assumptions are correct, it is likely that this project is a good investment. If we could repeat this investment thousands of times under the same conditions, the average NPV would be $110,561.92. Unfortunately, we only get one chance so it would be nice to know a little more about the distribution around the expected value, that is, a measure of dispersion.

Calculating the Variance and Standard Deviation

The scenario summary report makes it obvious that a negative NPV is possible. The question to ask is, "How risky is this project, and what is the likelihood that the NPV will be negative?" The first step toward answering this question is to calculate one or more of the measures of dispersion (variance, standard deviation, and coefficient of variation) that were mentioned earlier in this chapter.

Excel provides two functions for calculating the variance of a range of numbers: **VAR** calculates a sample variance while **VARP** calculates a population variance.[7] These functions are defined as:

$$\text{VAR}(\textit{Number1}, \textit{Number2}, \dots)$$

and

$$\text{VARP}(\textit{Number1}, \textit{Number2},\dots)$$

Again, we can substitute a range of numbers for the individual numbers in the definition. For our purposes we should use **VARP** because we know the entire set of possible outcomes. In C14 enter: `Variance`, and in D14 enter: `=VARP(D10:F10)`. The result is 71,568,179,048.23, which is a huge number!

One problem with this is that it ignores the probabilities that we assigned to the scenarios. To calculate the variance correctly, using all of the available information, we can use equation (12-3). Again, we have some choices about how to implement

---

7. The difference between a sample *statistic* and a population *parameter* is that the sample statistic includes an adjustment to account for the bias introduced because we aren't dealing with the full population. In this case the adjustment is to divide by $N-1$ instead of N.

the equation. One way is to use an array formula: =SUM(D12:F12*(D10:F10-D13)^2). This will give the correct answer of 43,091,482,025.75.

We can make this calculation much easier by using a function macro from FameFncs.xla called **FAME_VAR**. This function, which will make use of the probabilities, is defined as:

FAME_VAR(VALUES, PROBABILITIES)

and the inputs are the same as with the **FAME_EXPVALUE** function. To use this macro enter: =FAME_Var(D10:F10,D12:F12) into D14. Whether you use the array formula or the macro, you will get the correct answer of 43,091,482,025.75.

Of course, the problem with the variance is that it is difficult to interpret because the basic units (dollars) are squared. The standard deviation will correct this problem. As with the variance, Excel provides two functions: **STDEVP** and **STDEV**. These functions are defined as:

STDEVP(NUMBER1, NUMBER2,...)

and

STDEV(NUMBER1, NUMBER2,...)

However, these functions do not take into account the probabilities that have been provided.[8] Since we have already calculated the variance in D14, the easiest way to calculate the standard deviation is to enter: =SQRT(D14) into D15. Alternatively, we could use an array function or the macro **FAME_StdDev**:

FAME_StdDev(VALUES, PROBABILITIES)

The inputs are the same as with **FAME_VAR**. To use this function, enter: =Fame_StdDev(D10:F10,D12:F12) in D15. The result is 207,584.88.

Now we know quite a bit more about the distribution around the expected NPV. For example, we know that the 95.5% confidence interval for the NPV is from

---

8. That's not to say that **VAR**, **VARP**, **STDEV**, and **STDEVP** are useless functions. Anytime you don't have information regarding probabilities, or anytime you can safely assume that your data are normally distributed, they are very useful.

−$305,091 to $526,215 (plus or minus two standard deviations). Implied by that wide confidence interval is the fact that the probability of a negative NPV is quite high.

Calculating the Probability of a Negative NPV

Given the expected NPV and its standard deviation, we can calculate the probability of a negative NPV using a test statistic. Specifically, we would like to know the probability of the NPV being less than zero, so the test statistic is:

$$z = \frac{0 - E(NPV)}{\sigma_{NPV}} \qquad \text{(12-6)}$$

Equation (12-6) tells us how many standard deviations 0 is away from the mean. Using the expected NPV and the standard deviation from the scenario analysis, we find:

$$z = \frac{0 - 110,561.92}{207,584.88} = -0.5326$$

This means that zero is 0.5326 standard deviations below the expected value. We can look up this value in a statistical table showing the area under a standard normal curve to determine the probability that the NPV is less than or equal to zero. Go ahead, pull out your dusty old statistics textbook and you'll see that the probability is about 29.81% (−0.5326 isn't in the table, so look up −0.53 as an approximation).

Of course, we can automate this calculation. Excel provides the **NORMSDIST** function that calculates the area under a standard normal curve. This function is defined as:

NORMSDIST(Z)

where Z is calculated as above, and measures the number of standard deviations above or below the expected value. In C16 enter: `Prob(NPV <= 0)` as the label, and in D16 enter: `=NORMSDIST((0-D13)/D15)`. The result is that we have a 29.72% chance of the NPV being less than zero.

Obviously, we have learned a lot more about the nature of this project than we knew before. But, what are we to make of this almost 30% chance of a negative NPV? Should we accept the project because it has a positive expected NPV, or reject it because there is a relatively high probability of a negative NPV? The answer is that there is no answer. The individual decision maker must decide.

However, this result certainly suggests that it would be prudent to go back and expend more effort to firm up the estimates of the uncertain variables, which would reduce the uncertainty surrounding the estimated NPV.

Monte Carlo Simulation

Still another method for dealing with risk is *Monte Carlo simulation*. A simulation is similar to a scenario analysis, but a computer generates thousands of scenarios automatically. Each of the uncertain variables in the model is assumed to be a random variable with a known probability distribution. So, we can create a scenario by randomly drawing a value for each of the uncertain variables from their probability distributions and plugging those numbers into the model. The model is then recalculated, and the model outputs (e.g., NPV) are collected and stored. This process is then repeated thousands of times, resulting in thousands of potential NPVs.

From this long list of NPVs, we can get a much better understanding of the expected NPV of the project and the amount of uncertainty surrounding it. As we saw in the scenario analysis, we can learn about the range of potential NPVs, the standard deviation of the NPVs, and the probability that the NPV will actually turn out to be negative (or positive, depending on how you choose to look at it). Furthermore, rather than seeing just an unlikely best- and worst-case scenario, we can see all of the potential in-between scenarios. The result is that we have a much better understanding of the risks of the project than the scenario analysis can provide. An additional benefit of simulation over scenario analysis is that it should result in less uncertainty (standard deviation around the expected NPV) because we have many more, and more realistic, possible outcomes.

The key to getting good results from a simulation is to choose the correct probability distributions and correlation structure for the variables.[9] This can be difficult and may require a good deal of judgement on the part of the analyst, especially when historical data is not available. On occasion, the analyst can use general principles or theoretical knowledge to determine the correct distribution of a variable. For example, any variable that is the product of two normally distributed variables will be lognormally distributed. Suppose that we need to make a guess at the distribution of total revenue. Since total revenue is the product of unit sales and

---

9. For an excellent discussion of several commonly used probability distributions see "Uncertainty & Risk Analysis," by Chris Rodger and Jason Petch, PricewaterhouseCoopers, United Kingdom, April 1999.

the price per unit, and since it could be very large but never fall below zero, a lognormal distribution would seem to be appropriate.

Excel does not have any built-in simulation tools, though it does have a random number generator. However, we have included an add-in to do simulations on the book's Web site at http://thomsonedu.com/finance/mayes. We will use this add-in to perform a Monte Carlo simulation on the catfish fillet problem. Make sure that your workbook is on the catfish fillet worksheet that you used to do the scenario analysis and then open the ExcelSim.xla file.[10] Note that a new menu item will be added to the menu bar. Choosing Excel<u>S</u>im Sim<u>u</u>late will launch the program.

Before beginning the simulation, let's define the problem. We have identified three important uncertain variables in the model: Unit sales in the first year, price per unit, and the variable costs as a percentage of sales. Further, let's assume that management has specified the probability distributions for each of these variables as shown in Table 12-4.

TABLE 12-4
PROBABILITY DISTRIBUTIONS FOR SIMULATION

Variable	Probability Distribution
Unit sales in pounds	Normal with mean 200,000 and standard deviation of 25,000
Price per pound	Triangular with minimum of 2.25, most likely of 2.50, and maximum of 2.65
Variable cost as % of sales	Uniform with minimum of 55% and maximum of 65%

These distributions were chosen primarily to demonstrate three of the most commonly used distributions, but also with some logic. We assume that unit sales will tend to cluster around 200,000 pounds in the first year. Even though the distribution of unit sales will be skewed to the right (it can be very high, but not below 0), it was felt that the skewness will be so minor as to be safely ignored. Therefore, a normal distribution seems appropriate. A triangular distribution was chosen for the unit price because management feels confident that it can identify the minimum, maximum, and most likely prices but is not confident in choosing any particular distribution. Finally, a uniform distribution was chosen for variable

---

10. Please see the "ExcelSim 2007 Documentation" file on the Web site for this book at http://thomsonedu.com/finance/mayes for more information on installing and using this add-in.

costs because management feels that it could be anywhere between 55% and 65%, but isn't comfortable in saying that any one value is more likely than another. Figure 12-6 shows the distributions graphically.

FIGURE 12-6
GRAPHS OF PROBABILITY DISTRIBUTIONS

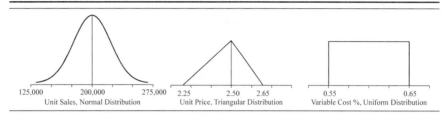

Again, make sure that your catfish fillet worksheet is open and then choose Excel**S**im Sim**u**late from the menus. The main ExcelSim dialog box will appear. The first edit box is for the "Changing Cells." These are the cells that contain the uncertain variables (unit sales, etc.). Type: B8,B9,B11 into this edit box, or you may select the cells with the mouse (hold down the Ctrl key as you click on each cell). Next we need to select the "Watch Cells," which are the cells that will be stored after each trial. In this case, we would like to keep track of the NPV for each trial, so enter: B29 into the edit box. The "Watch Names" edit box is optional. You can use it to specify a cell that contains a descriptive label for each of the watch cells. Type: A29 into this edit box.

FIGURE 12-7
EXCELSIM MAIN DIALOG BOX

At this point, all that remains is to tell ExcelSim how many trials to run and what to name the worksheet that will be created for the output (this is optional). Keep in mind that the more trials you run, the more accurate the simulation will be. The maximum number of iterations is 30,000 but we will only run 500 to keep the output more manageable. Type 500 into the "Iterations" edit box. Finally, enter Frozen Catfish Simulation into the "Sheet Name" edit box. If you choose not to enter a sheet name for the output, it will be named "Simulation Report" by default. Figure 12-7 shows the main dialog box with the data entered.

After clicking the OK button, you will be presented with the first of the distribution dialog boxes. These dialog boxes are where you will describe the probability distribution for the uncertain variables. There will be one for each changing cell. Note that if you have used defined names for the changing cells (as we have already done before running the scenario analysis), the names will be shown in the title bar. The first variable is the unit sales. Table 12-4 tells us that the distribution is normal with a mean of 200,000 and standard deviation of 25,000. So, select "Normal" from the distribution list. At this point, the dialog box will change to prompt you for a mean and standard deviation for the distribution. Enter 200,000 for the mean, and 25,000 for the standard deviation. Figure 12-8 shows the completed dialog box.

FIGURE 12-8
DISTRIBUTION DIALOG BOX FOR UNIT SALES

Click the OK button, and we will repeat this process for the other two changing cells. The next dialog box is for the unit price. Note that the dialog box is, at first, showing the exact settings as were previously entered. That is helpful if the distribution is the same, but we need to choose a different distribution. Choose a triangular distribution from the drop-down list. You will now be prompted for the left side, mode (or most likely), and right side of this distribution. Enter: 2.25 for the left side, 2.50 for the mode, and 2.65 for the right side as shown in Figure 12-9, and then click the OK button.

FIGURE 12-9
DISTRIBUTION DIALOG BOX FOR PRICE PER POUND

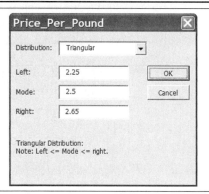

Finally, choose a uniform distribution for the variable costs. In this case, you will be asked to supply the lower and upper limits of the distribution. Since variable costs are expected to be somewhere between 55% and 65% of sales, enter: 0.55 for the lower limit and 0.65 for the upper limit.

FIGURE 12-10
DISTRIBUTION DIALOG BOX FOR VARIABLE COSTS

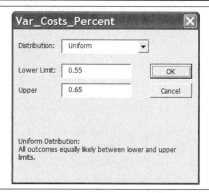

When you click the OK button, the simulation will begin to run. You can follow the progress by watching the status bar at the lower left corner of the Excel window. (If you rerun the simulation, uncheck the Screen Updating Off box and you can watch the spreadsheet change.) After a few seconds, a new worksheet containing the

401

output will be displayed. The output consists of the 500 NPVs that were generated during the simulation, and some descriptive statistics at the bottom. Exhibit 12-7 shows the results of the first five and last five trials (the rest are hidden to save space), as well as the summary statistics. Since these results are based on random draws from the probability distributions, your results will be somewhat different. However, the mean and standard deviation of the NPVs should be similar.

EXHIBIT 12-7
THE SIMULATION OUTPUT

	A	B
1	*Simulation Report by ExcelSim*	
2	Trial Results	
3	Trial	Net Present Value
4	1	$204,665.95
5	2	$58,482.36
6	3	$159,176.81
7	4	$21,327.41
8	5	$198,178.68
499	496	$36,975.52
500	497	$90,791.74
501	498	$103,596.78
502	499	$187,176.41
503	500	$44,633.45
504	Min	($155,668.00)
505	Max	$332,745.75
506	Mean	$94,202.27
507	Median	$87,827.03
508	Mode	#N/A
509	Avg Dev	65,319.05
510	Std Dev	80,883.83
511	Coef. Var.	0.8586
512	Skewness	0.0423
513	Kurtosis	(0.2083)

Just as we did with the output from the scenario analysis, we can draw some important conclusions from this data. It will also be useful to compare the results of the simulation to the scenario analysis. First, note that the mean NPV was $94,202 while the minimum and maximum NPVs were –$155,668 and $332,746 respectively. Note that the minimum and maximum NPVs are not as extreme as the worst-case and best-case NPVs from the scenario analysis. This suggests that the extra information provided by the simulation has reduced the uncertainty.

The standard deviation of the NPVs is $80,884, which is considerably less than the standard deviation from the scenario analysis. The reason for the reduction in uncertainty is that we have run many more scenarios, and most of them are not nearly as extreme as the best- and worst-case scenarios. The reduction in uncertainty is also reflected in the probability that the NPV is less than or equal to zero. Recall that we can use the **NORMSDIST** function to calculate this probability as we did for the scenario analysis. In D506 enter the label: `Prob(NPV <= 0)`, and in E506 enter the formula: `=NORMSDIST((0-B506)/B510)`. The result shows a 12.21% chance of a negative NPV (again, your results may vary slightly depending on the mean and standard deviation from your simulation). We can also verify this by doing an actual count of the NPVs that are less than 0. Copy the label from D506 and paste it into D507. Excel has a useful function called **COUNTIF** that is defined as:

$$\text{COUNTIF}(\textit{RANGE}, \textit{CRITERIA})$$

where **RANGE** is the range of numbers, and **CRITERIA** is the particular counting rule that you wish to apply. In this case, we wish to count the number of NPVs that are less than or equal to 0, so in E507 enter the formula: `=COUNTIF(B4:B503, "<=0")/500`. From our simulation there were 64 negative NPVs out of 500 total, or 12.80%, which conforms closely to the previous result.[11] So, the project appears to be far less risky than was suggested by the scenario analysis.

Finally, we can use Excel's built-in Histogram tool to get a visual look at the probability distribution. Choose Tools Data Analysis Histogram from the menus. This will display the dialog box pictured in Figure 12-11.

---

11. The array formula `=SUM((B4:B503<=0)*1)/500` will give the same result.

FIGURE 12-11
THE HISTOGRAM DIALOG BOX

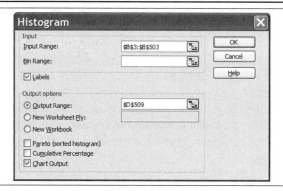

All you need to do is to specify the **I**nput Range (B3:B503), check the **L**abels box, specify the **O**utput Range (D509), and that you want to create **C**hart Output. Excel will automatically decide how to group the data and will create the histogram as shown in Figure 12-12.

FIGURE 12-12
HISTOGRAM OF NPVS FROM THE SIMULATION

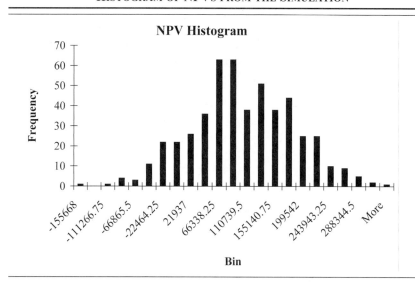

The Risk-Adjusted Discount Rate Method

Yet another method of incorporating risk into our capital budgeting decision process is to use a risk-adjusted discount rate. When we discussed how to determine the required rate of return in Chapter 8, we mentioned a model referred to as a "simple risk premium model." The risk-adjusted discount rate (RADR) is an example of this model. Recall that the simple risk premium model was defined as:

$$\text{Required Return} = \text{Base Rate} + \text{Risk Premium}$$

and that the base rate and risk premium are subjectively determined. The idea behind this model is that the investor (or firm) has some minimum required return for tying up her funds to which a premium is added in order to compensate for risk. Projects with greater risk require larger risk premiums. In using the RADR technique, we will modify this model so that it becomes:

$$\text{RADR} = \text{WACC} + \text{Risk Premium}$$

Note that the risk premium is still subjectively determined, but the base rate is the firm's WACC. The correct discount rate for average-risk projects is the WACC, but for riskier-than-average projects a positive risk premium is added. This higher discount rate is meant to penalize the riskier project and will result in a lower, and possibly negative, NPV. If the project still has a positive NPV then the project is expected to more than compensate the shareholders for the extra risk and it should be accepted. For projects with less risk than average, the risk premium would be negative.

Normally, the risk premium will be determined according to a schedule that has been approved by the firm's upper management. This schedule will typically assign risk premiums according to the type of project. For example, if the firm is analyzing the possibility of replacing an existing machine, it would probably be considered a very low-risk project and the risk premium might be –2%. On the other hand, a new product line, such as we are examining in this chapter, would be considered quite risky and might require a 3% risk premium. Expansion of an existing and successful project would probably be considered an average risk and the WACC with no risk premium would be used as the discount rate. Ultimately, the risk premium will be determined by managerial judgement. This judgement may be based on experience, some statistical measure of risk, or the outcome of a scenario analysis or a Monte Carlo simulation.

In our Freshly Frozen Fish problem, suppose that management has determined that a 3% risk premium is required. Since the WACC for the firm is 10%, the required return for this project would be 13%. Plugging this rate into your frozen catfish fillet worksheet reveals that the risk-adjusted NPV is $22,386.31. The fact that the NPV is still positive suggests that this is a good investment. It will likely more than compensate shareholders for the extra risk.

We can also look at the IRR of the project and turn the question around. Instead of asking what risk premium is required, we can ask if the expected risk premium is sufficient. Under the original assumptions the IRR was calculated to be 14.01%. Recall that the IRR is the discount rate that would result in the NPV being equal to zero. Since the IRR is 4.01% greater than the WACC, this is the expected risk premium. The project will obviously have a positive NPV for any risk premium up to 4.01% (RADR up to 14.01%). Therefore, the question is, "Is an extra 4.01% per year enough of a risk premium to compensate for the extra risk of this project?"

The Certainty-Equivalent Approach

The problem with the RADR approach to adjusting for risk is that it combines two adjustments: one for risk and another for time. This approach implicitly assumes that risk is an increasing function of time. In many cases this may be true. Cash flow forecasts for a period five years from now are generally less certain than are forecasts for next year. However, such is not necessarily the case. For example, suppose that a firm has a maintenance contract that calls for a major overhaul of a machine in three years. If the cost of this overhaul is specified in the contract, this is a very low-risk cost, even though it occurs in three years.

The *certainty-equivalent* (CE) approach separates the adjustments for time and risk. Where the RADR technique increases the discount rate to adjust for risk, the CE approach decreases the cash flow. To adjust for risk with the CE approach, we multiply the cash flow by the certainty-equivalent coefficient. The net result is the same: The cash flow is penalized for risk. To adjust for time, we discount the cash flows at the risk-free rate of interest. This is the basis for the theoretical superiority of the certainty-equivalent approach: It makes separate adjustments for risk and time, rather than the intermingled adjustments of the RADR.

Certainty-equivalent coefficients are determined as follows: The decision maker is asked what *certain* cash flow she would be willing to accept in exchange for the risky cash flow at some point in the future. The ratio of these cash flows determines the CE coefficient (α).

$$\alpha = \frac{\text{Riskless cash flow}}{\text{Risky cash flow}} \tag{12-7}$$

As an example, assume that you are willing to accept $95 dollars for sure in place of a risky $100 one year from now. Your CE coefficient for this cash flow would be:

$$\alpha = \frac{95}{100} = 0.95$$

Cash flows that are riskier would be deflated with lower CE coefficients. In effect, this risky cash flow times $(1 - \alpha)$ is the amount that you would be willing to pay for an insurance policy to guarantee that you receive the risky cash flow (we are ignoring the time value of money for the moment). Note that the CE coefficient will always be between 0 and 1, and will generally decrease with time because of increased risk. To use the certainty-equivalent approach, each cash flow is multiplied by the appropriate coefficient, α_n, and then the net present value is found using the risk-free rate of interest as the discount rate. The risk-free rate is used to discount the cash flows because all of the risk has been removed by the CE adjustment. Effectively, the CE technique converts a risky stream of cash flows into a risk-free stream of cash flows.

Let's remake our Freshly Frozen Fish worksheet to see how the CE approach works. First, make a copy of your worksheet. To do this, right-click the sheet tab and choose **M**ove or Copy from the menu. Now, in the new worksheet, change A14 to: Risk-free Rate, and B14 to: 4%. Assume that management has given you the following information regarding the appropriate certainty-equivalent coefficients:

TABLE 12-5
FRESHLY FROZEN FISH CE COEFFICIENTS

Year	CE Coefficient (α)
0	1.00
1	0.95
2	0.90
3	0.85
4	0.80
5	0.75

Select rows 28 and 29 and then choose **I**nsert **R**ows to add two new rows just below the annual cash flows. In A28 enter Certainty Equivalent Coefficients and then enter the certainty-equivalent coefficients from the table in B28:G28. In A29 enter: Risk-adjusted Cash Flows. In B29 enter the formula =B27*B28 and copy it across. To calculate the risk-adjusted NPV, in B31 enter the formula: =NPV(B14,C29:G29)+B29. Note that the risk-adjusted NPV is $94,184.26, which is very close to our previous result. We don't need to calculate the risk-adjusted cash flows in separate cells (B29:G29). Instead, we could calculate the NPV with the array formula: =NPV(B14,C27:G27*C28:G28)+B27.

We can also calculate the IRR and MIRR of the risk-adjusted cash flows. The formula for the IRR in B33 is: =IRR(B29:G29). Similarly, the formula for the MIRR is: =MIRR(B29:G29,B14,B14). Just remember that these measures must now be compared to the risk-free rate of interest, not to the firm's WACC. Since both are greater than the 4% risk-free rate, the project is acceptable. Exhibit 12-8 shows the completed worksheet.

EXHIBIT 12-8
THE CATFISH FILLET WORKSHEET USING THE CE METHOD

	A	B	C	D	E	F	G
16	Annual Cash Flows for Frozen Catfish Fillet Project						
17		Year 0	Year 1	Year 2	Year 3	Year 4	Year 5
18	Initial Outlay	(650,000)					
19	Sales		500,000	540,000	583,200	629,856	680,244
20	Variable Costs		300,000	324,000	349,920	377,914	408,147
21	Fixed Costs		80,000	80,000	80,000	80,000	80,000
22	Taxable Cash Flows		120,000	136,000	153,280	171,942	192,098
23	Taxes		42,000	47,600	53,648	60,180	67,234
24	Depreciation Tax Benefit		14,000	14,000	14,000	14,000	14,000
25	Annual After-Tax Cash Flow		92,000	102,400	113,632	125,763	138,864
26	Terminal Cash Flow						515,000
27	Total Annual Cash Flows	(650,000)	92,000	102,400	113,632	125,763	653,864
28	Certainty Equivalent Coefficients	1.00	0.95	0.90	0.85	0.80	0.75
29	Risk-adjusted Cash Flows	(650,000)	87,400	92,160	96,587	100,610	490,398
30							
31	Net Present Value	$94,184.26					
32	Profitability Index	1.14					
33	Internal Rate of Return	7.75%					
34	Modified Internal Rate of Return	6.85%					

If the certainty equivalents and the RADR are correctly determined, the decision that results from both methods will usually be the same. However, the CE technique suffers from the need to understand the utility function of the decision maker, and thus is very difficult to correctly implement in practice. At best, the CE coefficients could be found by interviewing the relevant decision maker as described earlier. Unfortunately, most modern corporations are owned by many shareholders and it is their risk preferences that we need to be concerned about, not those of some individual corporate officer. For this reason, the certainty-equivalent method is not generally used in practice.

Portfolio Diversification Effects

So far, we have examined investment risk in isolation. However, from the stockholder's point of view, a corporation is nothing more than a collection of investments managed by a professional management team. Therefore, it will be helpful to examine the effect that the addition of risky projects has on the overall risk of the firm. Let's look at an example, using stock selection rather than a capital investment project.

Suppose that you have $10,000 available for investment purposes. Your stockbroker has suggested that you invest in either Stock A or Stock B, but you are concerned about the riskiness of these stocks. During your investigation, you have gathered the historical returns for these stocks, which are presented in Table 12-6.

TABLE 12-6
HISTORICAL ANNUAL RETURNS FOR A AND B

Year	Stock A Returns	Stock B Returns
2003	10.30%	10.71%
2004	−0.10%	25.00%
2005	23.30%	0.38%
2006	2.20%	26.20%
2007	14.00%	11.52%

To quantify your concerns about the riskiness of these stocks, you open a new worksheet and enter the data from Table 12-6.

Since both firms have had their ups and downs, you want to calculate the average annual return for the last five years. Further, to get a feeling for their riskiness, you want to calculate the standard deviation of these returns. Assuming that you have entered the data from Table 12-6 starting in A1, you can calculate the average return for Stock A in B7 with: =AVERAGE (B2:B6). Copying this to C7 will calculate the

409

average return for Stock B. The results show that Stock A has earned an average of 9.94% per year over the last five years, while Stock B has earned 14.76% per year.[12]

Obviously, if the average historical return reflects the expected future average return, Stock B is to be preferred. Recall, however, that higher returns are generally accompanied by higher risk. We can measure the riskiness of these returns with the standard deviation. To calculate the standard deviation of Stock A's returns enter: =Stdev(B2:B6) in B8 and copy it to C8. We can use Excel's built-in formula in this case because we do not have information regarding the probability distribution of returns, so we assume that each one is equally likely. The results show that the standard deviation of returns is 9.43% for Stock A and 10.83% for Stock B.

Now we have a problem. If the risk of Stock B was less than Stock A, we would obviously prefer B with a higher return for less risk. In this case, though, we do not have enough information to know if the extra 4.82% return per year from Stock B is enough to offset the extra risk. Suppose that we decided to purchase both stocks instead of just one of them. We will put 50% of your funds in Stock A and 50% in Stock B. We can determine the returns that you would have earned in each year, by calculating a weighted average of each stock's return. In D2 enter the formula: =0.5*B2+0.5*C2. This shows that our portfolio would have earned 10.51% in the year 2003. Copy this formula to each cell in the range D3:D6, and then copy the expected return formula from C7 to D7.

Notice that the expected portfolio return is 12.35%, exactly halfway between the returns on the individual stocks (remember that we put 50% into each stock). Now, let's see what happens to the standard deviation. Copy the formula from C8 to D8. Notice that the standard deviation of the portfolio is only 1.35%—significantly less than the standard deviation of either stock alone! This is a demonstration of the benefits of diversification. Exhibit 12-9 shows these results.

Because the portfolio consisting of both A and B provides a higher return and less risk than Stock A, you would certainly prefer the portfolio to Stock A alone. We cannot, however, definitively say that you would prefer the portfolio to Stock B. To determine which you would pick, we would need information regarding your risk-return preferences.[13] In this case, most people would prefer the portfolio because the difference in returns is slight, but the difference in risk is relatively large.

---

12. We are ignoring compounding for simplicity. To find the compound average annual rate of return, use the **GEOMEAN** function (see page 22).

13. More specifically, we would require knowledge of your utility function.

EXHIBIT 12-9
PORTFOLIO OF STOCKS A AND B

	A	B	C	D
1	**Year**	**Stock A Returns**	**Stock B Returns**	**Portfolio**
2	2003	10.30%	10.71%	10.51%
3	2004	-0.10%	25.00%	12.45%
4	2005	23.30%	0.38%	11.84%
5	2006	2.20%	26.20%	14.20%
6	2007	14.00%	11.52%	12.76%
7	Exp. Ret.	9.94%	14.76%	12.35%
8	Std. Dev.	9.43%	10.83%	1.35%

Determining Portfolio Risk and Return

As you have seen in the previous example, combining assets into a portfolio (whether that portfolio consists of stocks or equipment or product lines) may result in the reduction of risk below that of any individual asset. You have also seen that the expected return for a portfolio will be between that of the lowest return asset and the highest return asset. In general, we can say that the expected return for a portfolio is a weighted average of the expected returns for the individual assets. The weights are given by the proportion of total portfolio value that each asset represents. In mathematical terms:

$$E(R_P) = \sum_{t=1}^{N} w_t E(R_t) \tag{12-8}$$

where w_t is the weight and $E(R_t)$ is the expected return of the tth asset. Equation (12-8) is applicable regardless of the number of assets in the portfolio. From the previous example, the expected return for the portfolio is:

$$E(R_P) = 0.5(0.0994) + 0.5(0.1476) = 0.1235 = 12.35\%$$

which is exactly the result we got when we calculated it in D7 using a different methodology. The difference with equation (12-8) is that we can use the expected future returns, which may differ from the average of historical returns.

Portfolio Standard Deviation

While the expected return of the portfolio is a weighted average of the expected returns for the assets, the portfolio standard deviation is not so simple. If we calculated a weighted average of the standard deviations of Stocks A and B, we would get:

Weighted average $\sigma = 0.5(0.0943) + 0.5(0.1083) = 0.1013 = 10.13\%$

But we know that the portfolio standard deviation is 1.35%. Obviously, there is something else going on here.

What is going on is that we have ignored the *correlation* between these two stocks. Correlation describes how the returns of two assets move relative to each other through time. The easiest way to measure correlation is with the correlation coefficient (r). The correlation coefficient can range from −1 to +1. Figure 12-13 illustrates the extremes that the correlation coefficient can have.

FIGURE 12-13
PERFECT POSITIVE AND PERFECT NEGATIVE CORRELATION

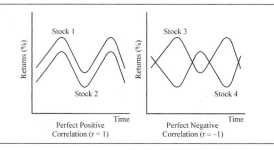

Another way to measure the co-movement of returns is with the *covariance*. The covariance is calculated in the same way as the variance, except that we have two return series rather than one. The covariance is calculated as:

$$\sigma_{X,Y} = \sum_{t=1}^{N} \rho_t (X_t - \bar{X})(Y_t - \bar{Y}) \qquad \text{(12-9)}$$

The covariance is a very useful statistic, but it is difficult to interpret. The correlation coefficient is related to the covariance by the following relation:

$$r_{X,Y} = \frac{\sigma_{X,Y}}{\sigma_X \sigma_Y} \qquad \text{(12-10)}$$

So the correlation coefficient is the same as the covariance, but it has been transformed so that it will always be between -1 and $+1$, which makes it much easier to interpret. The closer the correlation coefficient is to 1, the more the returns tend to move in the same direction. The closer it is to -1, the more the returns tend to move in opposite directions. A correlation coefficient of 0 means that there is no identifiable linear relationship between the returns (i.e., they are independent).

Assume that you wish to form a portfolio consisting of 50% in Stock 1 and 50% in Stock 2 (from Figure 12-13). Because these stocks are perfectly positively correlated, a plot of the portfolio returns would be exactly halfway between the plots of the returns for Stocks 1 and 2. Your portfolio returns would be just as volatile as if you owned either stock alone. On the other hand, a similar portfolio of Stocks 3 and 4 would result in a substantial reduction in volatility. Notice that the volatility of the returns of Stock 3 is canceled out by the volatility of the returns of Stock 4. This risk reduction is due to diversification.

The correlation is obviously important in the calculation of the portfolio risk. For a portfolio of two securities, the portfolio variance is given by:

$$\sigma_P^2 = w_1^2 \sigma_1^2 + w_2^2 \sigma_2^2 + 2 w_1 w_2 r_{1,2} \sigma_1 \sigma_2 \qquad \text{(12-11)}$$

where the w's are the weights of each security, and $r_{1,2}$ is the correlation coefficient for the two securities. The standard deviation of a two-security portfolio is:

$$\sigma_P = \sqrt{w_1^2 \sigma_1^2 + w_2^2 \sigma_2^2 + 2 w_1 w_2 r_{1,2} \sigma_1 \sigma_2} = \sqrt{\sigma_P^2} \qquad \text{(12-12)}$$

From the above equation, it is clear the lower the correlation ($r_{1,2}$) between the securities, the lower the risk of the portfolio will be. In other words, the lower the correlation, the greater the benefits of diversification.

Returning to our example with Stocks A and B, we can calculate the correlation coefficient with Excel's built-in function CORREL. This function is defined as:

CORREL(*ARRAY1*, *ARRAY2*)

where *ARRAY1* and *ARRAY2* are the two ranges containing the stocks' returns. Before using **CORREL**, let's create a graph of the returns to see if you can guess what the correlation coefficient is. Select B2:C6 and then use the Chart Wizard to create a line chart of the returns.

Examining the chart, it is clear that when Stock A's returns are high, Stock B's returns are low, and vice versa. The correlation coefficient is obviously negative, and probably near -1. We can confirm this by using the **CORREL** function. In B9 enter the formula: =CORREL(B2:B6,C2:C6). Note that the answer is -0.974, so our suspicions are confirmed. This low correlation is the reason that the standard deviation of the portfolio is so low. Your worksheet should now resemble that in Exhibit 12-10.

EXHIBIT 12-10
WORKSHEET DEMONSTRATING LOW CORRELATION BETWEEN A AND B

	A	B	C	D	E	F	G	H	I
1	Year	Stock A Returns	Stock B Returns	Portfolio					
2	2003	10.30%	10.71%	10.51%					
3	2004	-0.10%	25.00%	12.45%					
4	2005	23.30%	0.38%	11.84%					
5	2006	2.20%	26.20%	14.20%					
6	2007	14.00%	11.52%	12.76%					
7	Exp. Ret.	9.94%	14.76%	12.35%					
8	Std. Dev.	9.43%	10.83%	1.35%					
9	Correlation	-0.9741							

As one final exercise, we can examine the portfolio standard deviation as we change the weights of A and B. Place the following labels in your worksheet. In A11: Stock A, in B11: Stock B, and in C11: Port Std Dev. Enter a series in A12:A22 ranging from 1 down to 0 in increments of 0.1. These will represent the weights allocated to Stock A. In B12 we want the weight of Stock B, which is equal to 1 – weight of Stock A,[14] so enter: =1-A12. The portfolio standard deviation, in cell C12, can be found with the following formula: =SQRT(A12^2*B$8^2 + B12^2*C$8^2+2*A12*B12*B$8*C$8*B$9). Now simply copy the formulas in B12:C12 down to the rest of the range. If you create an XY chart of the data (use the ranges: A12:A22, C12:C22) your worksheet should resemble that in Exhibit 12-11.

---

14. The weights must sum to 100%.

EXHIBIT 12-11
PORTFOLIO STANDARD DEVIATION AS WEIGHTS CHANGE

	A	B	C	D	E	F	G	H	I
10	Weights								
11	Stock A	Stock B	Port. Std. Dev.						
12	100%	0%	9.43%						
13	90%	10%	7.44%						
14	80%	20%	5.46%						
15	70%	30%	3.51%						
16	60%	40%	1.74%						
17	50%	50%	1.35%						
18	40%	60%	2.95%						
19	30%	70%	4.87%						
20	20%	80%	6.84%						
21	10%	90%	8.83%						
22	0%	100%	10.83%						

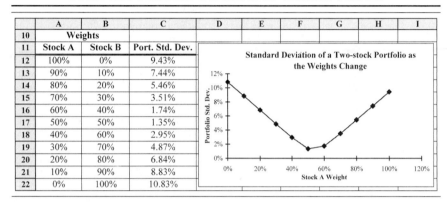

It is instructive to examine the extremes in the chart in Exhibit 12-11. First, note that when 100% of your funds are allocated to Stock A, the portfolio standard deviation is equal to that of Stock A. Similarly, if 100% is allocated to Stock B, the portfolio standard deviation is equal to that of Stock B. Also notice that the minimum standard deviation is achieved with about one-half of your funds allocated to each stock.[15]

The benefits of diversification in an individual's investment portfolio should be clear. By selecting securities that are less than perfectly positively correlated (e.g., in different industries, different countries, etc.) you can reduce risk significantly while reducing return slightly. Diversification works exactly the same way within corporations. A firm that invests in projects that are not perfectly correlated will reduce the volatility of its earnings. However, while diversification is undoubtedly a good idea for individuals, many believe that corporations should not seek out diversification. The reason is that the shareholders are perfectly capable of diversifying away company-specific risks on their own, and they can do it in a way that suits their unique purposes. On the other hand, a firm's managers, employees, customers, and suppliers will benefit if the company diversifies because of a lower possibility of financial distress. Whether or not a firm should diversify is, however, an open question.

---

15. The actual weights are 53.50% in Stock A and 46.50% in Stock B. We leave it as an exercise for you to find these weights using the Solver.

Portfolios with More Than Two Securities

Of course we can create portfolios of more than two securities. Most individuals who own stocks, own more than two. Corporations have many ongoing projects and multiple brands. And, many mutual funds own hundreds of stocks and/or other securities.

Regardless of the number of securities in a portfolio, the expected return is always a weighted average of the individual expected returns. The standard deviation is, however, more complicated. Recall that when we were evaluating the standard deviation of the two-stock portfolio, we had to account for the correlation between the two stocks. Similarly, when we have a three-stock portfolio, we must account for the correlation between each pair of stocks. The standard deviation of a three-stock portfolio is thus given by (using the covariance form):

$$\sigma_P = \sqrt{w_1^2\sigma_1^2 + w_2^2\sigma_2^2 + w_3^2\sigma_3^2 + 2w_1w_2\sigma_{1,2} + 2w_1w_3\sigma_{1,3} + 2w_2w_3\sigma_{2,3}} \qquad \text{(12-13)}$$

Obviously, the expression for the portfolio standard deviation gets to be cumbersome for more than two securities. Therefore, when more than two securities are included, the expression is usually simplified to:

$$\sigma_P = \sqrt{\sum_{i=1}^{N}\sum_{j=1}^{N} w_i w_j r_{i,j}\sigma_i\sigma_j} \qquad \text{(12-14)}$$

or, in the equivalent covariance form:

$$\sigma_P = \sqrt{\sum_{i=1}^{N}\sum_{j=1}^{N} w_i w_j \sigma_{i,j}} \qquad \text{(12-15)}$$

Equations (12-14) and (12-15), while not exactly simple, will calculate the standard deviation of a portfolio of any number of securities.

To avoid entering long formulas for the standard deviation of a portfolio, we have included several macros. Each macro (described in the summary to this chapter) requires the weight of each security and a variance/covariance matrix, or a correlation matrix and the individual standard deviations.

Summary

We began this chapter with a discussion of risk, and determined that risk is roughly equivalent to the probability of a loss. The higher the probability of a loss, the higher the risk. We also found that we could measure risk in any of several ways, but that the standard deviation or coefficient of variation are the generally preferred methods.

Risk can be incorporated into the analysis of capital investments in many ways. We've demonstrated that sensitivity analysis is an important first step in order to identify the variables that most impact the NPV. Once identified, we can focus our efforts on getting good estimates of these variables. Next, we can perform a scenario analysis or a Monte Carlo simulation to better understand the uncertainty surrounding the expected NPV.

While Monte Carlo simulation is beginning to be more widely used, the primary method of incorporating risk into capital budgeting is the risk-adjusted discount rate technique. This technique involves the addition of a premium to the WACC in order to account for the riskiness of the investment. We also discussed the certainty-equivalent (CE) method whereby the risky cash flows are deflated according to a decision maker's utility function. This method is superior to the RADR in theory, but is difficult to use in practice.

Finally, we introduced the concept of diversification. Diversification involves forming portfolios of risky investments so that some of the risk of the individual investments will be canceled by other investments whose returns are less than perfectly correlated. Diversification works just as well with corporate projects as it does with securities.

FUNCTIONS INTRODUCED IN THIS CHAPTER

Purpose	Function	Page
Calculate the expected value	FAME_EXPVALUE(*VALUES, PROBABILITIES*)	393
Calculate a population variance	VARP(*NUMBER1, NUMBER2,…*)	394
Calculate a sample variance	VAR(*NUMBER1, NUMBER2,…*)	394

FUNCTIONS INTRODUCED IN THIS CHAPTER (CONTINUED)

Purpose	Function	Page
Calculate variance when the probability distribution is known	**FAME_VAR**(*VALUES, PROBABILITIES*)	395
Calculate a population standard deviation	**STDEVP**(*NUMBER1, NUMBER2,...*)	395
Calculate a sample standard deviation	**STDEV**(*NUMBER1, NUMBER2,...*)	395
Calculate standard deviation when the probability distribution is known	**FAME_StdDEV**(*VALUES, PROBABILITIES*)	395
Calculate coefficient of variation when the probability distribution is known	**FAME_CV**(*VALUES, PROBABILITIES*)	N/A
Calculate the area under a standard normal curve	**NORMSDIST**(*Z*)	396
Count the numbers in a range that meet a specified criteria	**COUNTIF**(*RANGE,CRITERIA*)	403
Calculate the correlation coefficient	**CORREL**(*ARRAY1, ARRAY2*)	413
Calculate the portfolio variance	**FAME_PORTVAR1**(*VARCOVMAT,WEIGHTS*)	N/A
Calculate the portfolio variance	**FAME_PORTVAR2**(*CORRMAT,WEIGHTS*)	N/A

*   All functions with names beginning in **FAME_** are macros supplied on the FameFncs.xla add-in, which is available from the official Web site.

Problems

1. Trail Guides, Inc., is currently evaluating two mutually exclusive investments. After doing a scenario analysis and applying probabilities to each scenario, they have determined that the investments have the following distributions around the expected NPVs.

Probability	NPV_A	NPV_B
15%	−$40,000	−$15,000
20%	−10,000	2,500
30%	20,000	20,000
20%	50,000	37,500
15%	80,000	55,000

Several members of the management team have suggested that Project A should be selected because it has a higher potential NPV. Other members have suggested that Project B appears to be more conservative and should be selected. They have asked you to resolve this question.

a. Calculate the expected NPV for both projects. Can the question be resolved with this information alone?

b. Calculate the variance and standard deviation of the NPVs for both projects. Which project appears to be riskier?

c. Calculate the coefficient of variation for both projects. Does this change your opinion from part B?

d. Which project should be accepted?

2. The Salida Salt Company is considering making a bid to supply the highway department with rock salt to drop on roads in the county during the winter. The contract will guarantee a minimum of 17,000 tons in each year, but the actual quantity may be above that amount if conditions warrant. Management believes that the actual quantity will average 25,000 tons per year. The firm will need an initial $1,500,000 investment in processing equipment to get the project started. The project will last for five years. The

accounting department has estimated that annual fixed costs will be $300,000 and that variable costs should be about $90 per ton of the final product. The new equipment will be depreciated using the straight-line method to $100,000 over the five-year life of the project based on an estimate of the salvage value by the engineering department. The marketing department estimates that the state will grant the contract at a selling price of $130 per ton, though it may get some lower bids if the contract is opened for competitive bidding. The engineering department estimates that the project will need an initial net working capital investment of $90,000. The firm's weighted average cost of capital is estimated to be 12%, and the marginal tax rate is 35%.

a. Set up a worksheet containing all of the relevant information in this problem, and calculate the initial outlay, annual after-tax cash flows, and the terminal cash flow.

b. Calculate the payback period, discounted payback period, NPV, IRR, and MIRR of this project. Is the project acceptable?

c. If the state decides to open the project for competitive bidding, what is the lowest bid price that you can enter without reducing shareholder wealth? Explain why your answer is correct.

d. Perform a Monte Carlo simulation to determine the expected NPV and the standard deviation of the expected NPV. The uncertain variables and their probability distributions are given below. Note that each year's unit sales is a separate variable in the simulation.

Variable	Distribution
Tons of Rock Salt in Each Year	Triangular with a minimum of 17,000, most likely 25,000, and maximum of 35,000.
Variable Cost per Ton	Normal with a mean of $90, and a standard deviation of $3.
Actual Salvage Value of Equipment	Uniform with a minimum of $70,000 and a maximum of $120,000.

e.   Create a histogram showing the probability distribution of NPV.

f.   Using the output of the simulation, what is the probability that the NPV will be less than or equal to zero? Would you suggest that the project be accepted?

3.   Ormsbee Aviation, Inc., is considering two potential investments. Each project will cost $60,000 and have an expected life of five years. The CFO has estimated the probability distributions for each project's cash flows as shown in the following table.

	Potential Cash Flows	
Probability	**Project 1**	**Project 2**
30%	$15,000	$14,000
40%	25,000	30,000
35%	35,000	46,000

The expected cash flow will be used for each of the five years of the projects' lives. Ormsbee Aviation uses the risk-adjusted discount rate technique to determine the worthiness of potential investments. As a guide for assigning the risk premiums, the CFO has put together the following table based on the coefficient of variation.

Coefficient of Variation	**Risk Premium**
0.0	–2.00%
0.2	0.00%
0.3	2.00%
0.4	3.00%
0.5	4.00%

a.   Calculate the expected cash flows, standard deviation, and coefficient of variation for each project.

b.   If the firm's weighted average cost of capital for average-risk projects is 12%, what is the appropriate risk-adjusted discount rate for each project?

    c. Using the appropriate discount rates, calculate the payback period, discounted payback period, NPV, PI, IRR, and MIRR for each project.

    d. If the projects are mutually exclusive, which should be accepted? What if they are independent?

4. You are considering an investment in the stock market and have identified two potential stocks (XYZ and ABC) to purchase. The historical returns for the past five years are shown in the table below.

Year	XYZ Returns	ABC Returns
2003	11%	25%
2004	15%	12%
2005	21%	19%
2006	9%	13%
2007	13%	8%

    a. Calculate the average return and standard deviation of returns for each stock over the past five years. Which stock would you prefer to own? Would everyone make the same choice?

    b. Calculate the correlation coefficient between the two stocks. Does it appear that a portfolio consisting of XYZ and ABC would provide good diversification?

    c. Calculate the annual returns that would have been achieved had you owned a portfolio consisting of 50% in XYZ and 50% in ABC over the past five years.

    d. Calculate the average return and standard deviation of returns for the portfolio. How does the portfolio compare with the individual stocks? Would you prefer the portfolio to owning either of the stocks alone?

    e. Create a chart that shows how the standard deviation of the portfolio's returns changes as the weight of XYZ changes.

f.   Using the Solver, what is the minimum standard deviation that could be achieved by combining these stocks into a portfolio? What are the exact weights of the stocks that result in this minimum standard deviation?

Internet Exercise

1.   Choose two stocks from different industries that you think would have a low correlation. Get the closing prices for each month over the past five years for both stocks. To get the prices from Yahoo! Finance (http://finance.yahoo.com), follow the same procedure as was used in Chapter 8 to get the dividends, but this time select "Monthly" rather than "Dividends." Download the data to your disk drive and then load the files into Excel.

   a.   Calculate the returns for both stocks in each month during the five-year period.

   b.   Calculate the average monthly return and standard deviation of monthly returns for each stock. Using only this information, which of the two stocks would you have preferred to own over this period?

   c.   Calculate the correlation coefficient for the two sets of returns. Is it as low as you expected?

   d.   Assuming that the historical returns, standard deviations, and correlation fairly represent the future, calculate the expected return and standard deviation of a portfolio consisting of 50% invested in each stock. How does the portfolio compare on a risk-return basis with the individual stocks?

   e.   Using the Solver, find the weights for each stock that would result in the minimum portfolio standard deviation.

CHAPTER 13

Writing User-Defined Functions with VBA

After studying this chapter, you should be able to:

1. *Identify and explain the parts of the VBA editor.*

2. *Describe the two types of "macros" and explain the difference between them.*

3. *Write your own VBA user-defined function for any given formula.*

4. *Use the debugging tools that are available in the VBA editor.*

5. *Create an Excel add-in program.*

Despite its hundreds of built-in functions, Excel doesn't always have the one you need. Fortunately, it does provide a method by which you can add your own functions to the program and use them in your worksheets.

In previous chapters we have used several custom functions that extend Excel in ways that are useful. Those custom functions, known as *user-defined functions* (UDFs), are written in the Visual Basic for Applications (VBA) programming language. VBA is available in all of the Microsoft Office applications, and in some third-party applications.

425

In this chapter we will provide a brief demonstration of how to use VBA to create functions to meet your needs. If you have ever done any computer programming, you will find it easy to learn. If not, don't worry. If you can understand a mathematical formula, it is likely that you will be able to convert it into a user-defined function without much trouble after reading this chapter.

VBA is quite powerful, and can be used for everything from simply changing the formatting of a cell in a worksheet to writing complete applications that don't appear to be Excel worksheets to doing everything in between.

What Is a Macro?

In computer science, a *macro* is a word or keystroke that serves as a substitute for a long series of commands. Excel has many macros of this type built in. For example, you can press Ctrl-B to make the font in a cell, or range, bold. This is a shortcut for the series of steps that would otherwise be required. When you press Ctrl-B, Excel will automatically perform all of those steps behind the scenes. This type of macro is known as a *keystroke macro*.

While we can create VBA programs that replicate the functionality of keystroke macros, VBA is not, strictly speaking, a macro language. Instead, it is a fully functional object-oriented programming language. Still, in common usage, VBA programs are often called macros.

Two Types of Macros

In Excel, there are two types of macros. Closest to the traditional definition of keystroke macros are *procedure macros*. Procedure macros can do things like changing to another worksheet, opening a file, formatting a range of cells, etc. As an example, I have written a procedure macro called "Add_Shaded_Headings" that I use to create the pictures of spreadsheets that appear in the exhibits throughout this book. It does several things, very quickly and consistently, that would be very time-consuming to do manually:

1. Inserts a row at the top and a column to the left of the current worksheet.
2. Sets the background color to light gray, makes the font bold, adds borders around the cells, and adds the row numbers and column headers.

This macro recreates the column and row headings within the worksheet itself, which makes it possible to copy a range of cells and paste it into a word processor so that it looks much like a screen shot of Excel.

Macros such as this one are more easily recorded than written from scratch. Excel has a macro recorder (**T**ools **M**acro **R**ecord New Macro) that will record everything that you do while recording and convert it into the VBA language. The recorded macro will be saved into a code module within the VB Editor. Once it is recorded, you can easily assign a key combination to run the macro, and you can edit it to make it better suit your purposes.

Procedure macros can be incredibly useful, but they are not the focus of this chapter. Instead, we are more concerned with writing *function macros*. Function macros (more correctly called *user-defined functions*) cannot modify Excel worksheets like procedure macros. Instead, all they can do is to take some inputs (arguments), process them through an algorithm, and then return a result to the spreadsheet. Function macros are identical to the built-in functions like SUM, PV, GEOMEAN, etc. The difference is that you can create your own user-defined functions (UDFs) that calculate results for which there are no built-in functions.

UDFs are useful for frequently used formulas that would require an excessive amount of time to type into a cell. A good example of this would be the **FAME_TwoStageValue** function that is included in the FameFncs.xla add-in. If you look back to equation (8-5) on page 248, you will see that this equation would be time-consuming to accurately type into a cell. The macro function saves time and effort and assures accuracy.

In other cases, UDFs can calculate results that would be difficult, or impossible, to perform in a single cell formula. For example, try to write a worksheet formula to calculate the payback period for any set of cash flows. While it is easy to write such a formula for a given set of cash flows, making it generic enough to work for any stream of cash flows is much more difficult. In this case, it is far easier to write a UDF to do the job. That is exactly what the **FAME_PAYBACK** function does.

In the next section we will introduce you to the Visual Basic Editor that is used to create both types of macros. Later, we will focus on how to write your own UDFs.

The Visual Basic Editor

Visual Basic macros are not written in worksheets. Instead, they are created in the Visual Basic editor, which provides many useful tools for writing code, keeping track of it, and debugging it. The editor can be thought of as a word processor that was specifically designed for writing macros. You can open the editor with the **T**ools **M**acro **V**isual Basic Editor menu choice, or by using Alt-F11. Note also that the Alt-F11 keystroke will allow you to easily move back and forth between Excel and the VBA editor.

FIGURE 13-1
THE VISUAL BASIC EDITOR

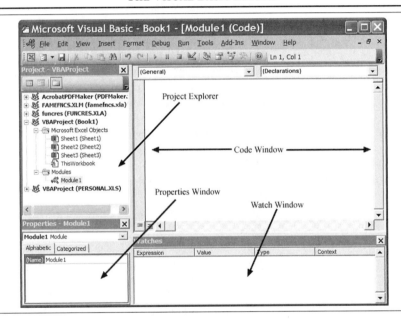

Figure 13-1 shows the VBA editor with several useful windows open. Most of your work will be done in the code window, as that is where the macros are written. The Project Explorer allows you to choose the project and particular code module to work on. The Properties Window allows you to set properties (names, visibility, behavior) of code modules and worksheets. The Watch Window allows you to monitor the values of variables as you are debugging your code.

If any of these windows are not visible on the screen, you can make them visible by selecting them in the **V**iew menu of the VBA editor.

The Project Explorer

The Project Explorer shows a list of all of the open VBA projects. A VBA project is an ordinary Excel workbook, but it may also have VBA code modules attached. Note that any VBA code that you write for a project is saved with the workbook, not in a separate file. However, you can easily export the code to a text file for backup purposes or so that you can import it into another workbook.

FIGURE 13-2
THE VBA PROJECT EXPLORER

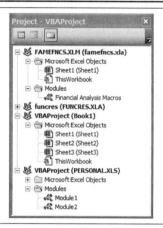

In Figure 13-2, you can see that there are four open projects. Each one has a name and a collapsible outline to show or hide its components. The first project is FameFncs.xla, which contains one worksheet, the ThisWorkbook code module, and another code module named "Financial Analysis Macros." All of this is hidden from the casual user. Since FameFncs.xla is an add-in, even its worksheet is invisible outside of the VBA editor, though it is available for macros to use for various purposes. ThisWorkbook is a special code module that is used for procedure macros that respond to workbook-level events such as when there is a right-click, the workbook is deactivated, the workbook is about to be closed, etc.

The real work in FameFncs.xla is done in the "Financial Analysis Macros" code module. This is where the user-defined functions reside. To see what the functions look like, make sure that FameFncs.xla is opened (either through <u>F</u>ile <u>O</u>pen, or by using <u>T</u>ools Add-<u>I</u>ns). Now, open the VBA editor and double-click on "Financial Analysis Macros." You can now browse through the code for all of the user-defined functions in the code window.

The Code Window

As mentioned above, the code window is a sort of specialized word processor. It has many features that are specially designed to make writing macros easier. For example, some of the text will be color-coded to make it easier to understand: reserved keywords are shown in blue, and comments are shown in green. Of course, this can be customized to your preferences.

FIGURE 13-3
THE CODE WINDOW

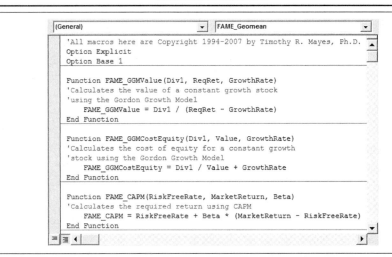

Figure 13-3 shows the code window with the first three user-defined functions visible. These are three of the least complex UDFs in the add-in, but they contain all of the required elements to calculate and return a result to your worksheet. Even without any programming experience, you can probably understand what each function does.

Take note of the procedure drop-down list in the upper-right corner of the editor. This list contains the names of all of the procedure and function macros in the current code module. By selecting a particular function from the list, you can immediately jump to the code for that function. This is especially useful if you prefer to use the code window in its Procedure View, which shows only one function at a time in the editor. Figure 13-3 shows the editor in its Full Module View, which shows the entire contents of the module. In this view, you can either jump directly to a function, or scroll through the code module until you find the one that you want to work on. The icons in the lower-left corner are used to switch between the different views.

The Parts of a Function

Every user-defined function must have at least five elements in order to work:

1. The keyword "Function" at the beginning of the first line. This tells VBA that you are beginning a new function, as opposed to a procedure macro, which would begin with the keyword "Sub."

2. The name of the function. You can choose nearly any name for your functions, except that they must be unique within a code module. Also, the name cannot contain spaces and must not be a reserved keyword. The name will be used when calling the function from your worksheets.

3. A list of the function arguments, surrounded by parentheses. These arguments are the variables that must be passed to the function from your worksheet. Even if your function doesn't require any arguments, it still needs to have a set of closed parentheses after the function name.

4. An assignment of the result of the calculations to the name of the function. This tells VBA the value to return to the cell on your worksheet from which the function was called.

5. The last part is the "End Function" statement. This informs VBA that it has reached the ending point of the function.

This is nearly everything that you need to know in order to write simple functions. However, just as we suggested in Chapter 1 (page 37) that you should document the complex formulas in your spreadsheets, you should do the same with your user-defined functions. In VBA, you can use comments to provide explanations of how your functions work. Comments begin with an apostrophe, and can contain any text that you require. Comments are ignored by VBA, but they are invaluable to the humans who may read your code. You cannot use too many comments, so make liberal use of them. This simple step will avoid many difficulties when you revisit your code in the future.

Writing Your First User-Defined Function

Let's begin by writing a very simple function to calculate a firm's net profit margin, which was the first worksheet formula that was discussed back in Chapter 1. There is really no need for a function like this since it is so easy to create a worksheet formula to do the job, but it will serve as an easy starting point.

Start by opening a new workbook, and then open the VBA editor. In the Project Explorer window, you should see a list of open VBA projects, including one named "VBAProject (Book1)," or something similar. The part of the name in parentheses will match the name of the workbook, so it may be Book2, or Book3 depending on how many other workbooks you have opened previously in this session. Now, right-click on the project name and select Insert Module from the shortcut menu. This will insert a new code module named Module1 into your project. The code window will now be available to enter new code into this module, and the VBA editor should look very much like the picture in Figure 13-1. Note that you can easily tell which code module you are working on by checking the text in the title bar of the editor.

Recall that the net profit margin is calculated by dividing sales by net income. We will call our user-defined function "NetProfitMargin," and it will require two arguments: net income and sales. The easiest way to begin a new function is to let the VBA editor insert a function template for you, though you are free to do the typing for yourself. Choose Insert Procedure from the menu. This will launch the Add Procedure dialog box, where you can specify some basic information about the function as shown in Figure 13-4.

FIGURE 13-4
THE ADD PROCEDURE DIALOG BOX

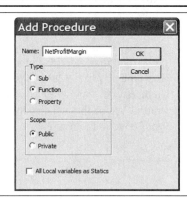

Make sure that you type a name and specify that the type of procedure is "Function." When you press the OK button, the following text will appear in the code window:

Public Function NetProfitMargin()

End Function

All that remains is to type in the arguments after the function name, and add the code to calculate the result. In this case, we need two arguments (inputs): net income and sales. We can name these arguments nearly anything, but it is best to use descriptive names. So, inside the parentheses type: `NetIncome, Sales`. Note that just like function names, the names of the arguments cannot contain spaces, though you could use an underscore character if you feel that it would improve readability (e.g., Net_Income). At this point, your function looks like this:

Public Function NetProfitMargin(NetIncome, Sales)

End Function

So far, the function doesn't actually do anything, but we can now call it from a worksheet. Set up the worksheet pictured in Exhibit 13-1 (this is the same as Exhibit 1-4, on page 19) and save it as "Chapter 13 Worksheets.xls."

EXHIBIT 13-1
MICROSOFT PROFITABILITY ANALYSIS WORKSHEET

	A	B	C	D	E	F	G
1		Microsoft Corporation Profitability Analysis					
2		(Millions of Dollars)					
3		2000 to 2005					
4		2005	2004	2003	2002	2001	2000
5	Sales	39,788.00	36,835.00	32,187.00	28,365.00	25,296.00	22,956.00
6	Net Income	12,254.00	8,168.00	7,531.00	5,355.00	7,346.40	9,421.00
7	Net Profit Margin						

Now select B7 and bring up the Insert Function dialog box. Choose the User Defined category, and scroll down the list to NetProfitMargin and select it. This will launch the Function Arguments dialog box just as it would for any built-in Excel function. Notice how you are prompted for the arguments with the names that you supplied in the function definition. This is why it is important to give meaningful names to the arguments.

FIGURE 13-5
THE FUNCTION ARGUMENTS DIALOG BOX FOR NETPROFITMARGIN

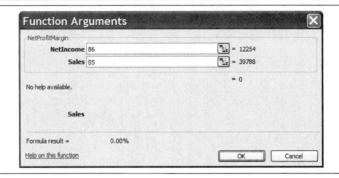

Enter: B6 for NetIncome and B5 for Sales. When you press the OK button, the function will be inserted into cell B7 as =NetProfitMargin(B6,B5). However, the answer will be 0.00 because the function doesn't yet do any calculations.

Recall that every function must assign a value to the function name in order to return a value to the worksheet. Let's now add the calculation to our function:

> **Public Function NetProfitMargin(NetIncome, Sales)**
> **NetProfitMargin = NetIncome / Sales**
> **End Function**

In VBA the "=" is the assignment operator.[1] That is, it assigns the value of the right-hand side to the variable on the left-hand side. In this case, we are assigning the result of dividing net income by sales to the name of the function. This is how we pass the result back to the worksheet.

Finally, let's add a comment that describes the purpose of the function so that anybody who reads the code can easily figure out what it does. Remember that comments are denoted by an apostrophe at the beginning of the comment:

---

1. It can also be used as a comparison operator, to compare the values of two variables. For example, we can use a statement such as If X = Y Then Z = 2*Y Else Z = 2*X.

```
Public Function NetProfitMargin(NetIncome, Sales)
'Calculates Net Profit Margin given Net Income and Sales
    NetProfitMargin = NetIncome / Sales
End Function
```

Return to your worksheet, and notice that the result is still 0.00. Whenever you change a function, you must force the worksheet to recalculate in order to see the new result. To do this, simply select B7 and then click in the Formula Bar at the end of the formula and press the Enter key. You should now see that the result is 30.80%, exactly as we had originally calculated using a worksheet formula. You can now copy the formula to C7:G7.

The NetProfitMargin function is available for use in any workbook, as long as the workbook that contains the code is open. As an example, create a copy of this worksheet in a new workbook. Right-click on the sheet tab and choose **M**ove or Copy from the shortcut menu. In the "To Book:" drop-down list, choose (New Book), and make sure to check the "Create a copy" box.

The first thing you should notice in the new workbook is that the NetProfitMargin function returns the #NAME! error. This is because Excel doesn't recognize the name of the function, since it isn't contained in this workbook. We need to change the reference to the function name so that it contains the name of the file that contains the function. We can do this either by reentering the function using the Insert Function dialog box, or by typing the full path and file name. It is easiest to reenter the function through the Insert Function dialog box. After you have done that, you should see that the formula now contains the file name as well as the name of the function: ='Chapter 13 Worksheets.xls'!NetProfitMargin(B6,B5).

Whenever you link to an external worksheet, or a function in an external worksheet, Excel needs to know the name and location of the file to which you are linking. This is so that it can find the function or data. If it cannot find the file, it will give the #NAME! error in every cell that contains a broken link, and others that are dependent on those cells.

Typically, this problem arises because the source file has been moved or deleted. Save this new workbook, and then close both workbooks. Now, move "Chapter 13 Worksheets.xls" into a different directory. When you reopen the workbooks, you should see the #NAME! error in the new workbook. If you look at the formula, you will see a reference to "Chapter 13 Worksheets.xls," but the path to the file will be incorrect.

FIGURE 13-6
THE EDIT LINKS DIALOG BOX

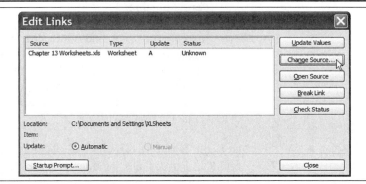

To fix this problem, choose Edit Links from the menus and tell Excel where to find "Chapter 13 Worksheets.xls." Figure 13-6 shows the Edit Links dialog box. Click on the Cha**n**ge Source button and then navigate to the file location. Be aware that the file that contains the function must also be opened in order for the function to recalculate.

As we will see later, one easy way around this problem is to create an Excel add-in from the workbook that contains your functions. As you know, add-ins can be "installed" through the **T**ools Add-**I**ns dialog box so that they are always opened automatically when you start Excel. That way, the functions that are contained within the add-in are also always available.

Writing More Complicated Functions

Normally, you won't write user-defined functions to do calculations that are easily done by writing worksheet formulas. Instead, you will probably write UDFs for functions that you need to use repeatedly, perhaps in several different workbooks. In this section we will discuss several additional features of VBA that make more complex functions easy to write.

Variables and Data Types

A *variable* is a temporary storage location that can be used to hold values until you need them again in your function. Variables can hold many different types of data, and can be declared so as to hold only a specific data type (say, an integer value or a text string), or any of the data types that are supported by VBA (variant).

Since you will most likely be writing functions to do mathematical calculations, we have summarized the numerical data types in Table 13-1. VBA also supports many other types that may be useful. For example, the variables that are declared to be the Boolean data type can be either True or False. We can manipulate dates with variables that are declared to be the Date data type. Finally, we can declare variables to be a String if they will hold text values.

TABLE 13-1
SOME OF VBA'S NUMERIC DATA TYPES

Type Name	Numeric Range
Byte	0 to 255
Integer	$-32,768$ to $32,767$
Long Integer	$-2,147,483,648$ to $2,147,483,647$
Single	-3.40×10^{38} to -1.40×10^{-45} for negative values; 1.40×10^{-45} to 3.40×10^{38} for positive values
Double	-1.79×10^{308} to -4.94×10^{-324} for negative values; 4.94×10^{-324} to 1.79×10^{308} for positive values
Variant (default type)	Variants can hold any data type, including numbers up to the range of a double. This is the most flexible data type, and is the default type that is used if a variable is not declared.

It is good programming practice to announce the names and data types of variables before you use them so that memory can be set aside to hold them. This is known as *declaring* your variables, and it is done with the Dim statement. Consider the following examples:

```
Dim SmallNumber As Byte
Dim X As Integer, Y As Integer, Z As Integer
Dim BigNumber As Double
Dim UnknownType as Variant
```

There are several things to note about the declarations above. First, note that the Byte and Integer data types can only hold whole numbers. That is, we can assign them a value such as 1 or 19, but we cannot assign a value of 1.618 (a real number). We can assign either whole or real numbers to variables that are declared to be Single, Double, or Variant. If you don't know whether a variable will hold whole numbers or real numbers, it is generally best to declare them as Single. Secondly, notice that we can declare multiple variables with a single Dim statement. This saves space in your code and makes it easier to read. Finally, you don't have to declare variables before using them. If you use an undeclared variable, VBA will implicitly declare it to be a Variant so that it can hold any type of data that you may want to store. However, this is discouraged as it can lead to errors if your code implicitly expects a certain data type.

Declaring your variables has a couple of advantages: It makes your code less susceptible to errors, and it makes your functions run faster. Because of these advantages, it is a good idea to make VBA force you to declare all of your variables before using them with the Option Explicit statement at the beginning of the file. If you look back at Figure 13-3, you will see that this statement is used at the beginning of the FameFncs.xla code.

It is important to understand the lifetime and scope of a variable. The *lifetime* of a variable defines whether or not the variable retains its value after the function exits. Most of the time, variables have a lifetime that is limited to the running time of the function in which they are used. Unless you use the keyword Static when declaring the variable, it will lose its value when the function completes its work. The *scope* of a variable determines whether its value can be read outside of a function or not. Variables that are declared within a function can only be read within the function itself. You can also use global variables outside of functions that will be visible to, and can be modified by, all functions within a module. It is usually best to use variables that have a local scope rather than global.

The If-Then-Else Statement

In Chapter 3 (page 83) we introduced Excel's **IF** statement, which returns one value or another depending on the result of a logical test. VBA has a similar, though more powerful, construct. As with the worksheet function, this is useful when a function needs to return different results depending on whether a particular condition is true or false. The If-Then-Else statement has two possible forms: the single-line form or the block form. A single-line statement looks like this:

If *condition is true* Then *do this* Else *do this instead*

For simple tests the single-line format works well. The drawback is that you can only take one action if the condition is true, or one action if it is false. In other words, it works exactly like a single **IF** statement in a worksheet. The block form can take multiple actions, and serially evaluate multiple conditions. The block form looks like this:

If *condition is true* **Then**
    do this first
    do this second
Else
    do this instead
End If

Notice that the block form must be terminated with the End If statement so that VBA knows that you are done with the If-Then-Else statement.

Let's create a function that calculates the present value of a lump sum (it will not handle annuities). Recall that the formula to calculate the present value of a lump sum is:

$$PV = \frac{FV}{(1 + i)^N}$$

where FV is the future value, i is the per period interest rate, and N is the number of periods. Let's call our function MyPV, and it will require three arguments to represent the variables in the formula.

Return to the "Chapter 13 Worksheets.xls" file that we created earlier for the NetProfitMargin function. Open the VBA editor and go to Module1. Now, click in the code window below the NetProfitMargin function, and type the following:

```
Public Function MyPV(FV, Rate, NPer)
'Calculates the present value of a lump sum
    MyPV = FV / (1 + Rate) ^ NPer
End Function
```

Can you think of any potential problems with this function? One very important thing to always keep in mind is that users are unpredictable. Therefore, it is helpful to try to anticipate everything and anything. Switch back to your Excel workbook and create the worksheet pictured in Exhibit 13-2.

EXHIBIT 13-2
PRESENT VALUE WORKSHEET

	A	B
1	**Present Value Function Test**	
2	Future Value	1,000
3	Interest Rate	0.10
4	Number of Periods	5.00
5		
6	Present Value	

Select B6 and enter the formula: =MyPV(B2,B3,B4). You should find that the present value of $1,000 to be received five years from now at 10% is $620.92. You can easily verify that this is correct by using Excel's **Pv** function or your financial calculator.

So, what is wrong with the MyPV function? Notice that we entered the interest rate (in B3) in decimal form. That is, 10% is entered as 0.10. We have built our function on the implicit assumption that users will understand that they must enter percentages in this way. Suppose, though, that some hapless user doesn't understand this and enters 10 into B3 instead of 0.10. They probably don't realize it, but they are telling the function that the interest rate is 1000% per period! Try it yourself, and you will see that the answer is $0.0062. Not quite what the user expected.

We can anticipate this kind of error and handle it automatically with the function by using the If-Then-Else statement. Edit your function so that it looks like the one below:

```
Public Function MyPV(FV, Rate, NPer)
'Calculates the present value of a lump sum
'If Rate is greater than or equal to 1, it will be divided by 100
    If Rate >= 1 Then Rate = Rate / 100
    MyPV = FV / (1 + Rate) ^ NPer
End Function
```

Now, if the user puts any number greater than or equal to 1 into B3, the function will automatically assume that they meant it to be a percentage and automatically adjust. Return to your worksheet and force the function to recalculate. You will now get $620.92, exactly as you expected.

Note that we may have done something unexpected in the Then clause. We have assigned a different value to the Rate argument by modifying the Rate argument itself. This is a common programming technique to avoid declaring a variable that isn't really needed. Instead, we could have declared a new variable to stand in for the rate. In this case, our function might look like this:

```
Public Function MyPV(FV, Rate, NPer)
'Calculates the present value of a lump sum
'If Rate is greater than or equal to 1, it will be divided by 100
Dim IntRate as Single
    If Rate >= 1 Then IntRate = Rate / 100 Else IntRate = Rate
    MyPV = FV / (1 + IntRate) ^ NPer
End Function
```

Note that we declared the variable IntRate to be the Single data type because it is a real number. There is no need to declare it as a Double because we would never need an interest rate as large as that data type can handle. Using the Single data type saves a small amount of memory. It is good practice to always use the smallest data type that will get the job done. Don't forget to replace Rate with IntRate in the last line of the function. If you do, you will get the wrong answer if a user types in 10 instead of 0.10. This is exactly the type of bug that can be difficult to spot in your code.

To make the function less subject to errors, we should take the further step of declaring the data types of our function arguments. This will make sure that the user doesn't call the function with, say, a text string instead of a number for the FV argument. It will also make sure that the user can only supply single cells as arguments, rather than ranges of cells. Change the function declaration to:

Public Function MyPV(FV As Single, Rate As Single, NPer As Single)

Now, return to your worksheet and force a recalculation of the function. It should still produce the correct answer. However, if you now change B4 to `Five` (a String value), you will get a #VALUE! error. In fact, you would get that error whether the arguments were declared or not. Still, with the arguments' data types specified, if the user passes the wrong data type the function will immediately return an error value. The function will not be executed at all, which may avoid other types of errors.

Looping Statements

Some kinds of formulas can be calculated only by cycling through the same calculation multiple times. An example would be any formula that has a summation sign, such as the expected value formula. The formula for calculating the expected value of a set of possible outcomes is:

$$E(X) = \sum_{t=1}^{N} \rho_t X_t$$

where $E(X)$ is the expected or most likely X, X_t is the tth possible outcome, and ρ_t is the probability that X_t will occur. You will no doubt recognize this as equation (12-1) on page 377. In order to do this calculation, we must cycle through each possible outcome and multiply it by its probability. We also need to keep a running total as we work through the calculation.

VBA has several statements that can loop through calculations such as this one. In functions such as this one, the most relevant is the For…Next loop. This looping statement requires a variable to serve as a counter so that it can keep track of how many times it goes through the loop. After each pass through the loop, the counter variable is incremented and then it returns to the beginning of the loop. If the counter still hasn't reached its ending value, then the calculation continues. As an example, consider the following code snippet:

```
X = 0
For t = 1 to 10
    X = X + t
Next t
```

In this case, the variable X is initially assigned a value of 0, then it is increased with each of the 10 passes through the loop by the value of t. On the first pass, X will be set equal to 1. On the next pass, t = 2 so that will be added to the existing value of X, which will now be equal to 3. This process will continue until t gets incremented to 11, at which point the loop will end. Clearly, this kind of calculation is difficult to do with a normal worksheet formula, though we can sometimes achieve the result with an array formula or the **SUMPRODUCT** worksheet function.

Let's create a function to calculate the expected value of a variable. But first, create the worksheet shown in Exhibit 13-3.

EXHIBIT 13-3
A WORKSHEET FOR THE EXPECTED VALUE FUNCTION

	A	B
1	Probability	Value
2	0.25	100
3	0.50	150
4	0.25	220
5	Expected Value	

Return to Module1 in the VBA editor and type in the following function:

```
Public Function ExpValue(Values As Range, Weights As Range)
'Calculates the expected value of a probability distribution
Dim t as Integer, VarCount As Integer
Dim EV As Single
VarCount = Values.Count 'Number of values in the range
EV = 0                          'Initialize variable
For t = 1 To VarCount
    EV = EV + Values(t) * Weights(t)
Next t
    ExpValue = EV
End Function
```

Aside from the For…Next loop, there are a couple of new things in this function. First, notice that we have declared our arguments to be of the Range data type. The Range data type represents a collection of worksheet cells, not a specific numeric type. It is a type of array, and it may contain one or more worksheet cells. Even though we expect that each of the values and weights will be of the Single data type, we cannot declare the arguments to be Single. Doing so would limit the function to only one value and one weight. Secondly, notice that we have added to comments at the end of some of the lines of code. This can be useful to save space and improve the readability of the code.

Now, take another look at the following line of code:

```
VarCount = Values.Count
```

Recall that we said that VBA is an object-oriented programming language. An object is a combination of VBA code and data that can be operated on as a single unit. In VBA an Excel workbook is an object (as are worksheets, ranges, cells, and many other things), and it has certain properties that we can access (read or write to) programmatically. We can read the name of the workbook object as follows:

WbName = MyWorkbook.Name

Assuming that WbName is a String variable, and MyWorkbook refers to a specific workbook object, this line of code will assign the name of the workbook to the string variable. We access object properties by using "dot notation." The .Name that appears after MyWorkbook tells VBA that we want to know the Name property of the workbook object. Most objects have at least several properties that we can access in this way.

In our ExpValue function, we have defined both of our arguments to be of the Range data type. Ranges are objects in VBA, so we can learn about their properties by using the dot notation. In this case, Values.Count tells VBA to look at the Values range and tell us how many cells are contained in the range.

We can also find out about the properties of the individual cells in a Range object. Each cell is also an object, so we can use dot notation to find the value that a cell holds. If we want to know the value of the second cell in the Values range, we could use the following code:

X = Values(2).Value

Assuming that the variable X is of the correct data type, this will assign the value of the second cell in the range to X. Note that the Value property is the default property of a cell object, so we could accomplish the same thing with this code:

X = Values(2)

In other words, to read the default property we don't need to use the Value syntax. Now take another look at the line of code in our For…Next loop:

EV = EV + Values(t) * Weights(t)

Notice that we are referencing Values(t) and Weights(t). Depending on the value of t (our counter variable), this will read the values of the cells that are in the Values and Weights ranges. In our example problem, Values(2) is equal to 150 and Weights(2) is equal to 0.50. As the code cycles through the loop, the appropriate values and weights are read, multiplied together, and then added to EV so as to create a running sum of the results.

Debugging VBA Code

It would be nice if we could write functions that always work perfectly under all conditions. Unfortunately, nobody is perfect, and errors (bugs) in software are a regular occurrence. Therefore, it is important that you have some idea of the tools that are available to help you find the errors in your code.

The VBA editor provides many tools for debugging code: breakpoints, the Watch Window, the Immediate Window, and several others. We will cover these tools in this section.

Breakpoints and Code Stepping

Typically, when a user-defined function is called from a worksheet, the code runs from beginning to end without interruption. However, if the function is returning incorrect answers, it would be nice to be able to interrupt the code execution so that you can examine its current state. This is exactly what *breakpoints* allow us to do. Before a function runs, we can enter the VBA editor and set a breakpoint on a particular line of code by using the F9 function key, or the **D**ebug **T**oggle Breakpoint menu choice. When the code is executed and reaches that line, the code will stop running and the VBA editor will appear. Figure 13-7 shows the code window with the code stopped at a breakpoint.

FIGURE 13-7
THE CODE WINDOW WITH A BREAKPOINT

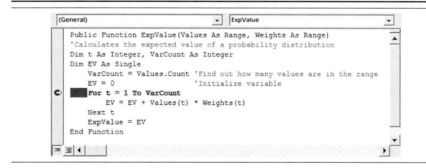

```
(General)                                    ExpValue

     Public Function ExpValue(Values As Range, Weights As Range)
     'Calculates the expected value of a probability distribution
     Dim t As Integer, VarCount As Integer
     Dim EV As Single
         VarCount = Values.Count 'Find out how many values are in the range
         EV = 0                  'Initialize variable
     For t = 1 To VarCount
             EV = EV + Values(t) * Weights(t)
         Next t
         ExpValue = EV
     End Function
```

Go into the VBA editor and click on the line shown in Figure 13-7. Now press F9 to set the breakpoint. You will notice that the background of that line is now red to indicate that a breakpoint has been set. Return to your worksheet and force a recalculation of the ExpValue function. At this point, you should see the code window as it appears in Figure 13-7.

We can now easily examine the value of the variables. Simply move the mouse pointer over any variable and let it hover there for a few seconds. You should see a tag pop up that shows the current value of the variable at this point. Note that if a variable hasn't yet been initialized, it may show up as "Empty" or it may simply give the wrong value. Move the mouse pointer of the VarCount variable, and it should say VarCount = 3. However, if you let the mouse hover over Values(t), it will show Values(t) = "Value" because right now the variable t is set to 0.

In Chapter 3 on page 97 we discussed the Evaluate Formula tool that allowed us to debug worksheet formulas by stepping through the calculations one at a time. The VBA editor offers a similar stepping function that lets us go through the code line by line. In order to use this feature, you must first set a breakpoint so that the code stops executing on some line. We have already set and activated a breakpoint in the ExpValue function, so all we need to do is press the F8 function key. This will cause the current line of code to execute. Each time you press F8, the next line will be executed, and you can examine the values of the variables to verify that they are correct. If not, then you may be able to spot the source of the error. Being able to step line by line through the code is an invaluable tool when it comes to debugging functions.

The Watch Window

The Watch Window, pictured at the bottom of Figure 13-1, allows us to more easily watch the values of variables and expressions as we step through the code. To add a variable or expression to the Watch Window, right-click on it to bring up the Add Watch dialog box. Right-click on VarCount and choose Add Watch.

FIGURE 13-8
THE ADD WATCH DIALOG BOX

Figure 13-8 shows the Add Watch dialog box. Note that we can actually set three different types of watches. Typically, you will select Watch Expression, which will add the variable to the Watch Window where its value will be updated as you step through the code. The other two types set an automatic breakpoint either when the value is true or when it changes. Click the OK button to add VarCount to the Watch Window. Now, add a couple of other watches and step through the code.

FIGURE 13-9
THE WATCH WINDOW

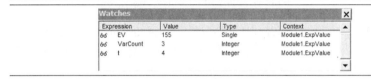

Figure 13-9 shows the Watch Window with the values of three variables immediately before the function exits. That is, the function has finished running, except that it hasn't yet returned the value to the worksheet. Notice that EV has a value of 155, which we know is the correct value to return.

The Immediate Window

The Immediate Window allows us to query for the current value of a variable, reset a variable to a different value, or execute VBA commands. If the Immediate Window is not visible, select <u>V</u>iew <u>I</u>mmediate Window from the menu or press Ctrl-G on your keyboard.

As with the other tools, the Immediate Window is only useful if we have triggered a breakpoint so that code execution has been paused. Return to your worksheet and force a recalculation of the ExpValue function. Step through the For…Next loop exactly one time. Now click in the Immediate Window and type ? EV and then press the Enter key. This will generate a query for the value of the EV variable at this point in the code. You should see that it is equal to 25. This same value is displayed in the Watch Window because we previously set a watch for this variable.

FIGURE 13-10
THE IMMEDIATE WINDOW

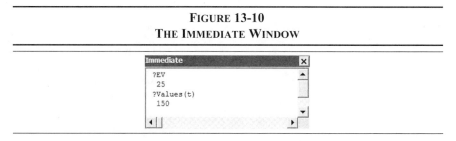

Figure 13-10 shows the Immediate Window with two queries. The second one asks for the current value of Values(t). Note that we can put Values(t) into the Watch Window as well, but it won't display the current value because Values is a range variable.[2] The Immediate Window doesn't have this problem.

As mentioned above, we can also execute VBA commands. For example, we could change the value of EV by typing: EV = 200 into the Immediate Window. Notice that we don't use the leading question mark if we want to execute a statement. Depending on where the code is when you execute this command, you will end up with a different result from the function. For example, if you enter that command when t = 2, the function will ultimately return 255 as the result.

There are more debugging tools, but these should be enough to get you started. You may consult the online help to learn more about debugging your VBA code.

---

2. Actually, we can force the Watch Window to display the value by entering Values(t).Value or by drilling down into the outline.

Creating Excel Add-Ins

Oftentimes you will create user-defined functions (or procedure macros) that are primarily of use in a single workbook. If you aren't likely to use a function outside of that workbook, then it makes sense to write it in a code module that is attached to the workbook. This is what we have done above. However, if you want to use your functions in multiple workbooks, or make them available for others to use, then it is best to create an Excel add-in. This is exactly what has been done with the FameFncs.xla add-in that is distributed with this book. Add-ins can be distinguished from regular Excel workbooks by the .xla file extension, as opposed to .xls.

Add-ins are created from normal Excel workbooks, but they have several advantages:

1. If you distribute your functions in an add-in, users can install the add-in once through the **T**ools Add-**I**ns menu command, and then never have to worry about opening the file again. As long as there is a check mark next to the add-in's name in the Add-Ins dialog box, it will automatically be opened every time Excel is started. This means that your functions are always available to be used.

2. Referencing functions is less complicated if they are contained in an add-in. To access one of the above functions from another workbook, we must specify the name and full path to the workbook. For example, to call the MyPV function, we would have to use ='Chapter 13 Worksheets.xls'!MyPV(A1,A2,A3). However, if the function was in an add-in, we could call the same function from any workbook with =MyPV(A1,A2,A3).

3. The worksheets in an add-in are hidden from the users. This means less confusion on their part, since they won't feel like they have to use your worksheets to use the functions.

4. It is easier to protect your code from prying eyes, and restrict access to it. Since the workbook is hidden from the user, and you can protect the code with a password, users can't view or modify the code without your permission.

Fortunately, creating an add-in is very easy. First, you will open a new workbook and write your code, just as we have done above. Then, choose **F**ile Save **A**s from Excel's main menu (not the VBA editor's menus). From the Save As Type drop-down list, scroll to the very last item, which says "Microsoft Office Excel Add-In (*.xla)." Make sure that you save the add-in in a location that you can remember.

You have now created an add-in. To use it, close your "Chapter 13 Worksheets.xls" file, and then go to Tools Add-Ins. Click on the Browse button and navigate to the directory where you saved the add-in. Finally, select the add-in file, click the OK button, and then make sure there is a check mark next to the name in the Add-Ins dialog box. You can now use your functions in any workbooks that you create.

Summary

In this chapter we have attempted to provide a few short lessons in how to use the VBA editor to write and debug user-defined formulas. We have discussed the components of the VBA editor, the five requirements for a user-defined function (UDF) that returns a value to the worksheet, several programming concepts, and the tools that are available for debugging your code. Finally, we covered the steps that are necessary to convert your code into an Excel add-in so that your functions can be used in any workbook, or even distributed to others who may find the functions useful.

Clearly, one short chapter in a textbook is not enough instruction for you to be completely comfortable working in VBA. Also, due to space constraints we didn't have time to discuss procedure macros or more advanced concepts. Hopefully, though, this chapter has taught you something useful, and you will try your hand at writing some user-defined functions. If you want to learn more about VBA programming, here are several very useful resources:

1. I am a big fan of John Walkenbach, and can highly recommend any of his books. In particular, *Excel 2003 Power Programming with VBA* (Wiley, 2004) should be excellent. I have a previous edition of this book that has helped me immensely.

2. Chip Pearson, of Pearson Software Consulting, LLC has an excellent Web site devoted to Excel and VBA programming located at: http://www.cpearson.com/excel.htm.

3. There are several excellent Excel newsgroups on Usenet, the Internet's bulletin boards. These groups are hosted on Microsoft's server at msnews.microsoft.com. They can be accessed through any newsreader software, and most e-mail programs offer newsreader

functionality. Probably the easiest way to access these groups is through http://groups.google.com. First go to that Web site, and then do a search for microsoft.public.excel.

If those sources fail to answer your questions, there is always the World Wide Web. Do a search and you are almost guaranteed to find your answer, or something else that's interesting.

Excel 2003 Menu Descriptions

The *F*ile Menu

New—Opens a new (blank) workbook or template.

Open—Opens an existing workbook. Can also be used to import text files.

Close—Closes an open workbook. If changes have been made, Excel will prompt you to save the workbook before it is closed.

Save—Saves changes to an open workbook using its current name.

Save **A**s—Saves an open document. Excel will prompt you for a new name, with the current name as the default. You can also use this choice to change the file format (e.g., to Lotus 1-2-3, CSV, etc.).

Save as Web Page—Saves the file as an HTML file. The resulting file may be viewed and manipulated in a Web browser from a Web site.

Save **W**orkspace—Saves any unsaved files and creates a workspace file. The workspace file stores the names of all open files so that they can be reopened with one command at a later time.

File Search—Launches a search pane to help find files that meet the specified criteria.

We**b** Page Preview—Opens a Web browser and displays file as it will appear if saved as a Web page.

Page Set**u**p—Shows the details of the page format (e.g., margin settings, headers and footers, etc.) and allows you to change them.

Prin**t** Area—Allows you to set or clear the area to be printed.

Print Pre**v**iew—Shows a page-by-page preview of how the page will look when printed.

Print—Sends the file to the printer.

Sen**d** To—Allows you to e-mail the workbook.

Propert**i**es—Allows you to enter information regarding the author of the workbook, the subject, comments, etc. This information can then be used with the Find command on the Open File dialog box to help locate the file.

1...**9**—Lists the last several files that have been opened. Clicking on one of these choices will open that file.

E**x**it—Quits Excel.

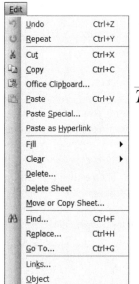

The **E**dit Menu

Undo—Allows you to Undo the last action if possible, or indicates that the last option cannot be undone.

Repeat—Repeats the last action if possible, or indicates that the last action cannot be redone.

Cu**t**—Copies the current selection to the clipboard, and deletes it when it is pasted elsewhere.

Copy—Copies the current selection to the clipboard without deleting it.

Office Clip**b**oard—Opens the Office Clipboard application.

Paste—Pastes the contents of the clipboard into the worksheet at the current location.

Paste **S**pecial—Same as **P**aste, but allows you to change the pasted data in certain ways (e.g., paste values only, formats only, transpose the selection, etc.).

Paste as **H**yperlink—Pastes the contents of the clipboard as a hyperlink to a Web page or e-mail address.

F**i**ll—Fills a range with selected data, or a series based on the selected data.

Cle**a**r—Deletes the contents of the selected area. Can also be used to delete only the formats, only the data, or notes attached to the cells.

Delete—Removes the current selection, rows, or columns from the worksheet.

Del**e**te Sheet—Removes the selected sheet(s) from the workbook.

Move or Copy Sheet—Moves or copies the selected sheet(s) to another location in the workbook or to another workbook.

Find—Locates the specified text string in the selected worksheet(s).

Replace—Finds the specified text string in the selected worksheet(s) and replaces it with other specified text.

Go To—Makes the specified cell active.

Lin**k**s—Opens linked workbooks, or allows you to edit links.

Object—Edits an object (e.g., a Microsoft Word file, lines, circles, etc.).

The View Menu

Normal—Displays the worksheet in its normal view.

Page Break Preview—Displays the worsheet in a preview window, and displays and allows you to change the print area.

Task Pane—Opens the Task Pane so that you can open a new workbook, view the clipboard, launch a search, or insert clip art.

Toolbars— Turns on or off the display of the specified toolbar and allows you to customize a Toolbar.

Formula Bar—Turns the formula bar on or off.

Status Bar—Turns the status bar on or off.

Header and Footer—Allows you to change the header and footer for printing. This may also be accessed via File Page Setup.

Comments—Displays all of the cell comments in a worksheet and opens the Reviewing toolbar.

Custom Views—Activates the Custom Views dialog box, which allows you to define and display custom views of the worksheet.

Full Screen—Enlarges the current worksheet to full screen, and turns off Toolbars.

Zoom—Controls the magnification level of the worksheet.

The Insert Menu

Cells—Inserts a new row, column, or cells at the current selection.

Rows—Inserts new rows above the current selection.

Columns—Inserts new columns to the left of the current selection.

Worksheet—Adds a new worksheet to the active workbook.

Chart—Adds a new chart to the worksheet or workbook and activates the Chart Wizard.

Symbol—Inserts special characters into the current cell or formula bar.

Page Break—Inserts or removes a page break above and to the left of the selection.

Function—Activate the Paste Function dialog box and inserts a function into the cell.

Name—Defines, deletes, or applies a name to the selection.

Comment—Adds or edits a comment in the selected cell.

Picture—Inserts a picture from a graphic file, clip art, organization chart, or autoshape into the worksheet.

Diagram—Inserts an organization chart, Venn diagram, etc.

Object—Inserts an object (e.g., Microsoft Word file) into the worksheet.

Hyperlink —Allows you to add a hyperlink to a Web page or e-mail address in a cell.

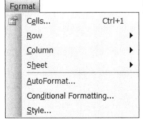

The Format Menu

Cells—Allows you to change the font, border, alignment, and number format of the selected cells.

Row—Allows you to change the row height, or hide and unhide rows.

Column—Allows you to change the column width, or hide and unhide columns.

Sheet—Allows you to hide, unhide, rename, or set the background picture on selected worksheets.

Autoformat—Applies a predefined format to the selected cells.

Conditional Formatting—Allows you to set a format that will change depending on the value in the cell.

Style—Applies or defines a formatting style.

The Tools Menu

Spelling—Activates the spelling checker.

Research—Launches a search for a term in various online services.

Error Checking—Runs the error-checking tools. This is usually running automatically in the background at all times.

Speech—Shows the Text to Speech toolbar, which allows you to listen as Excel reads the worksheet.

Shared Workspace—Creates a workspace to allow the document to be shared among multiple people. Requires Microsoft Windows SharePoint Services.

Share Workbook—Allows more than one user to edit a single spreadsheet at the same time on a network.

Track Changes—Highlights suggested changes by other users to a worksheet.

Compare and Merge Workbooks—Merges changes from one copy of a shared workbook into another.

Protection—Allows protection, or removes protection, for worksheets or workbooks.

Online Collaboration—Allows you to set up an online meeting and to share a workbook over the Internet.

Goal Seek—Changes the value of one cell to force another to a target value.

Scenarios—Activates the Scenario Manager.

Formula Auditing—Helps to locate cell dependencies, locate errors, step through formulas, and display the Watch Window.

Solver—Activates the Solver.

Macro—Runs a selected procedure macro, or allows you to record a new procedure macro. Also controls the security levels for macros and opens the VBA editor.

Add-Ins—Installs or removes add-in programs.

AutoCorrect Options—Allows you to change or set AutoCorrect options.

Customize—Allows you to customize toolbars and set menu options.

Options—Allows changes to various categories of options for the worksheet (e.g., turn gridlines on or off).

Data Analysis—Runs various data analysis tools (e.g., regression analysis). Requires that the Analysis ToolPak add-in is activated.

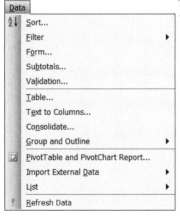

The Data Menu

Sort—Sorts the selected data by up to three keys.

Filter—Applies an automatic, or a user-defined, filter to the selected data.

Form—Creates a form for editing database records.

Subtotals—Creates subtotals with specified functions (e.g., **SUM**, **PRODUCT**).

Validation—Allows you to set up messages regarding acceptable data values in a cell.

Table—Creates a data table for what-if analysis.

Text to Columns—Activates the Text Wizard to parse text files into columns.

Consolidate—Creates summaries of multiple worksheets.

Group and Outline—Creates or clears outlines for selected areas.

PivotTable and PivotChart Report—Creates or changes a pivot table.

Import External **D**ata—Runs a query on a database file or Web page to bring the data into Excel.

L**i**st—Converts a range into an Excel list, which is an area that can be worked on without affecting other ranges.

Refresh Data—Updates the data retrieved from a database or Web query.

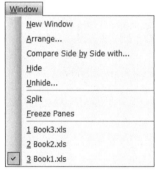

The **W***indow Menu*

New Window—Opens a new window on the workbook (i.e., a second copy).

Arrange—Arranges open workbooks.

Compare Side **b**y Side with— Arranges any two open workbooks so that they are easy to compare.

Hide—Hides the active workbook.

Unhide—Unhides workbooks selected from list.

Split—Splits or removes a split in the worksheet at the active cell.

Freeze Panes—Freezes or unfreezes panes at the active cell.

1 . . . **9**—Activates the selected open workbook.

The **H***elp Menu*

Microsoft Excel **H**elp—Displays a table of contents for the help files.

Show the **O**ffice Assistant—Brings up an animated assistant to help you search for help.

Microsoft Office Online—Opens a connection to the Internet and takes you to the Office Update Web site.

Contact Us—Opens a help window with contact information.

Chec**k** for Updates—Opens a Web browser on the Microsoft Office Web site where you can download files and check for critical Office updates.

Detect and **R**epair—Searches through the various Excel program files looking for errors. If any are found it fixes them. You will probably need the original disks or CD if errors are found.

Acti**v**ate Product—Performs the product activation function, which is required to use Office XP components for more than 30 days.

Customer **F**eedback Options—Allows you to opt into a program that allows Microsoft to collect information about your computer and the Microsoft software installed on it. No personally identifiable information is collected.

About Microsoft Excel—Displays a dialog box that provides information about the version of Excel.

Index